CIMA

PRACTICE & REVISION KIT

Stage 4 Paper 13

Strategic Financial Management

BPP Publishing
January 2000

First edition 1995
Sixth edition January 2000

ISBN 0 7517 3857 3 (previous edition 0 7517 3876 X)

British Library Cataloguing-in-Publication Data
A catalogue record for this book
is available from the British Library

Published by

BPP Publishing Limited
Aldine House, Aldine Place
London W12 8AW

www.bpp.com

Printed in Great Britain by
WM Print Ltd
Frederick Street
Walsall
West Midlands WS2 9NE

We are grateful to the Chartered Institute of Management Accountants for permission to reproduce past examination questions. The answers to past examination questions have been prepared by BPP Publishing Limited.

CONTENTS *Page number*

Question and answer checklist/index	**(iv)**
Revision	**(vi)**
Question practice	**(vii)**
Exam technique	**(viii)**
The exam paper	**(x)**
Current issues	**(xviii)**
Examiners' instructions	**(xix)**
Syllabus	**(xx)**
Guidance notes	**(xxiii)**
Mathematical tables	**(xxviii)**
Formulae and symbols	**(xxx)**
Question bank	**3**
Answer bank	**87**
Mock exam (November 1999 paper): questions	**263**
Mock exam (November 1999 paper): answers	**271**
Review form & free prize draw	
Order form	

Question and answer checklist/index

The headings indicate the main topics of questions, but questions often cover several different topics.

Tutorial questions, listed in italics, are followed by advice on how to **approach the question,** thus easing the transition from study to examination practice.

A date alone (11/98, say) or 'specimen paper' after the question title refers to a current syllabus paper.

Questions preceded by * are **key questions** which we think you must attempt in order to pass the exam. Tick them off on this list as you complete them.

			Time allocation	*Page number*	
		Marks	*Mins*	*Question*	*Answer*
PART A: FINANCIAL STRATEGY FORMULATION					
	1 Various goals (11/94)	25	45	5	87
	2 Main principles (11/95)	20	36	5	90
*	3 Public sector objectives (11/97)	20	36	6	92
*	4 Costs and benefits (11/96)	20	36	6	94
	5 *Tutorial question: AIM companies*	-	-	7	96
	6 Indicators (5/96)	20	36	8	97
*	7 PDQ plc (5/94)	30	54	9	99
*	8 Balanced scorecard (5/99)	20	36	10	103
*	9 Difficulties (5/98)	20	36	11	105
	10 Forecasting failure (5/95)	20	36	11	107
*	11 Strategic review (5/96)	20	36	11	108
	12 Financial model (5/94)	20	36	12	111
PART B: TREASURERSHIP					
The treasury function. Sources of finance. Dividend policy					
	13 Policy decisions (11/98)	20	36	15	113
*	14 Treasury department (11/95)	20	36	15	115
	15 S plc (5/92)	20	36	15	117
	16 Debt instruments (5/92)	25	45	16	118
	17 *Tutorial question: Efficient market hypothesis*	-	-	16	119
*	18 MRF (11/96)	20	36	16	120
	19 ABC plc (Specimen paper)	25	45	17	123
*	20 Policy change (5/95)	20	36	18	125
	21 XYZ plc (Specimen paper)	25	45	19	126
	22 RG plc (5/93)	25	45	20	128
*	23 DIVS plc (5/97)	20	36	21	130
	24 Expansion (11/98)	20	36	21	132
Investment and portfolio management. Working capital management					
*	25 Risk and market efficiency (5/95)	20	36	25	135
	26 Capital market line (5/92)	20	36	25	137
*	27 Company's portfolio (11/97)	20	36	26	139
	28 PMS (5/93)	25	45	27	141
	29 Leisure International plc (11/92)	25	45	27	145
*	30 4D plc (5/96)	20	36	28	148
*	31 CW Limited (11/98)	20	36	29	150
	32 RT plc (Specimen paper)	25	45	29	152
	33 Recent research (11/97)	20	36	30	154
	34 Discount (5/93)	25	45	31	156
*	35 V plc (11/96)	20	36	31	159
	36 MP Limited (11/98)	20	36	32	161

			Marks	Time allocation Mins	Page number Question	Answer
	37	Overdraft (11/94)	25	45	32	163
*	38	KL Ltd (11/95)	20	36	33	165
*	39	Miller-Orr model (5/97)	20	36	35	168
		PART C: INVESTMENT DECISIONS				
	40	RP plc (5/98)	20	36	39	170
	41	Alternative sites	20	36	39	172
	42	CBA Ltd (5/97)	20	36	41	173
*	43	Three opportunities (5/96)	20	36	41	176
	44	CP Limited (5/99)	20	36	42	177
*	45	Adjusted present value (5/98)	20	36	43	179
*	46	Megapower plc (11/92)	35	63	43	181
	47	*Tutorial question: Bases of valuation*	-	-	45	184
*	48	Mr Jones (5/95)	20	36	46	186
	49	Provincial plc (11/92)	25	45	47	188
	50	WT plc and SZ plc (11/93)	30	54	48	190
*	51	Financial analyst (5/99)	20	36	50	192
		PART D: INTERNATIONAL FINANCIAL MANAGEMENT				
	52	Expo plc (11/97)	20	36	53	194
*	53	Eastasia (11/95)	20	36	53	197
	54	Overseas investment (Specimen paper)	25	45	54	198
*	55	Canada (5/99)	20	36	55	200
*	56	Swiss multinational (5/98)	20	36	55	201
*	57	Swaps (11/96)	20	36	56	203
*	58	Freimarks (5/90)	25	45	57	205
	59	X and Y (5/91)	25	45	58	206
*	60	OJ Ltd (5/97)	20	36	58	207
		CASE STUDY QUESTIONS				
*	61	Dobson Ltd (5/99)	60	108	59	209
*	62	Spearhead plc (11/98)	60	108	62	214
*	63	Ibsen plc (5/98)	60	108	64	221
*	64	Premoco plc (11/97)	60	108	67	225
*	65	Lavinia Products plc (5/97)	60	108	69	232
*	66	DP plc (11/96)	60	108	71	239
	67	Tutwiler plc (5/96)	60	108	74	243
	68	TS Products plc (11/95)	60	108	77	247
	69	Global Telecommunications Inc (5/95)	60	108	79	253
	70	Garden World plc (Specimen paper)	50	90	82	258

REVISION

This is a very important time as you approach the exam. You must remember three things.

Use time sensibly
Set realistic goals
Believe in yourself

Use time sensibly

1 **How much study time do you have?** Remember that you must EAT, SLEEP, and of course, RELAX.

2 **How will you split that available time between each subject?** What are your weaker subjects? They need more time.

3 **What is your learning style?** AM/PM? Little and often/long sessions? Evenings/ weekends?

4 **Are you taking regular breaks?** Most people absorb more if they do not attempt to study for long uninterrupted periods of time. A five minute break every hour (to make coffee, watch the news headlines) can make all the difference.

5 **Do you have quality study time?** Unplug the phone. Let everybody know that you're studying and shouldn't be disturbed.

Set realistic goals

1 Have you set a **clearly defined objective** for each study period?

2 Is the objective **achievable**?

3 Will you **stick to your plan**? Will you make up for any **lost time**?

4 Are you **rewarding yourself** for your hard work?

5 Are you leading a **healthy lifestyle**?

Believe in yourself

Are you cultivating the right attitude of mind? There is absolutely no reason why you should not pass this exam if you adopt the correct approach.

- **Be confident** - you've passed exams before, you can pass them again
- **Be calm** - plenty of adrenaline but no panicking
- **Be focused** - commit yourself to passing the exam

QUESTION PRACTICE

There is little point in simply opening this Kit and, beginning with question 1, attempting all of the questions. You need to ask yourself three questions.

Am I ready to answer questions?
Do I know which questions to do first?
How should I use this Kit?

Am I ready to answer questions?

1 Try to fill in the blanks on the **Do you know? checklist** for a particular syllabus area. Compare your answers with the corresponding **Did you know? checklist**.

2 If you are happy with what you have written, you can go ahead and start answering questions. **Do not attempt questions if you could not fill in any of the blanks**. Go back to your BPP Study Text and revise first.

Do I know which questions to do first?

1 **Start with tutorial questions**. They warm you up for key and difficult areas of the syllabus. Try to produce at least a plan for these questions, using the guidance notes following the question to ensure your answer is structured so as to gain a good pass mark.

2 Don't worry about the time it takes to answer these questions. Concentrate on producing good answers. There are a number of tutorial questions in this Kit.

How should I use this Kit?

1 Once you are confident with the Do you know? checklists and the tutorial questions, you should try as many as possible of the exam-standard questions; at the very least you should attempt the **key questions,** which are highlighted in the **question and answer checklist/index** at the front of the Kit.

2 Try to **produce full answers under timed conditions**; you are practising exam technique as much as knowledge recall here. Don't look at the answer, your BPP Study Text or your notes for any help at all.

3 **Mark your answers to the non-tutorial questions as if you were the examiner**. Only give yourself marks for what you have written, not for what you meant to put down, or would have put down if you had had more time. If you did badly, try another question.

4 Read the **Pass marks** in the answers very carefully and take note of the advice given and any **comments by the examiner**. Don't worry unduly if you found something difficult; there are some parts of questions that only a prizewinner might get right in an exam.

5 When you have practised the whole syllabus, go back to the areas you had problems with and **practise further questions.**

6 Finally, when you think you really understand the entire subject, **attempt the mock exam** at the end of the Kit. Sit the paper under strict exam conditions, so that you gain experience of selecting and sequencing your questions, and managing your time, as well as of writing answers.

EXAM TECHNIQUE

Passing professional examinations is half about having the knowledge, and half about doing yourself full justice in the examination. You must have the right approach to two things.

The day of the exam
Your time in the exam hall

The day of the exam

1 Set at least one **alarm** (or get an alarm call) for a morning exam.

2 Have **something to eat** but beware of eating too much; you may feel sleepy if your system is digesting a large meal.

3 Allow plenty of **time to get to the exam hall**; have your route worked out in advance and listen to news bulletins to check for potential travel problems.

4 **Don't forget** pens, pencils, rulers, erasers.

5 Put **new batteries** into your calculator and take a spare set (or a spare calculator).

6 **Avoid discussion** about the exam with other candidates outside the exam hall.

Your time in the exam hall

1 ***Read the instructions (the 'rubric') on the front of the exam paper carefully***

Check that the exam format hasn't changed. It is surprising how often examiners' reports remark on the number of students who attempt too few - or too many - questions, or who attempt the wrong number of questions from different parts of the paper. Make sure that you are planning to answer the **right number of questions**.

2 ***Select questions carefully***

Read through the paper once, then quickly jot down key points against each question in a second read through. Select those questions where you could latch on to 'what the question is about' - but remember to check carefully that you have got the right end of the stick before putting pen to paper.

3 ***Plan your attack carefully***

Consider the **order** in which you are going to tackle questions. It is a good idea to start with your best question to boost your morale and get some easy marks 'in the bag'.

4 ***Check the time allocation for each question***

Each mark carries with it a **time allocation** of 1.8 minutes (including time for selecting and reading questions). A 20 mark question therefore should be completed in 36 minutes. When time is up, you *must* go on to the next question or part. Going even one minute over the time allowed brings you a lot closer to failure.

5 ***Read the question carefully and plan your answer***

Read through the question again very carefully when you come to answer it. Plan your answer to ensure that you **keep to the point**. Two minutes of planning plus eight minutes of writing is virtually certain to earn you more marks than ten minutes of writing.

6 ***Produce relevant answers***

Particularly with written answers, make sure you **answer the question set**, and not the question you would have preferred to have been set.

7 *Gain the easy marks*

Include the obvious if it answers the question and don't try to produce the perfect answer.

Don't get bogged down in small parts of questions. If you find a part of a question difficult, get on with the rest of the question. If you are having problems with something, the chances are that everyone else is too.

8 *Produce an answer in the correct format*

The examiner will **state in the requirements** the format in which the question should be answered, for example in a report or memorandum.

9 *Follow the examiner's instructions*

You will annoy the examiner if you ignore him or her. The **examiner will state** whether he or she wishes you to 'discuss', 'comment', 'evaluate' or 'recommend' (see the section on examiners' instructions on page (xix)).

10 *Lay out your numerical computations and use workings correctly*

Make sure the layout fits the **type of question** and is in a style the examiner likes.

Show all your **workings** clearly and explain what they mean. Cross reference them to your solution. This will help the examiner to follow your method (this is of particular importance where there may be several possible answers).

11 *Present a tidy paper*

You are a professional, and it should show in the **presentation of your work**. Students are penalised for poor presentation and so you should make sure that you write legibly, label diagrams clearly and lay out your work neatly. Markers of scripts each have hundreds of papers to mark; a badly written scrawl is unlikely to receive the same attention as a neat and well laid out paper.

12 *Stay until the end of the exam*

Use any spare time **checking and rechecking** your script.

13 *Don't worry if you feel you have performed badly in the exam*

It is more than likely that the other candidates will have found the exam difficult too. Don't forget that there is a competitive element in these exams. As soon as you get up to leave the exam hall, ***forget* that exam** and think about the next - or, if it is the last one, celebrate!

14 *Don't discuss an exam with other candidates*

This is particularly the case if you **still have other exams to sit**. Even if you have finished, you should put it out of your mind until the day of the results. Forget about exams and relax!

THE EXAM PAPER

Format of the Year 2000 exams

The examination paper will be divided into two sections.

Section A will contain a compulsory case study-type question, normally for 60 marks. This compulsory question will cover a number of syllabus topics from more than one syllabus section. There will typically be four or five parts to the question. It will contain a substantial calculation element worth between 30% and 50% of the marks (ie between 18 and 30 marks) and a report section which requires candidates to provide detailed analysis and commentary on their calculations and on the implications for the organisation which is the subject of the case study.

Section B will offer a choice of two from four questions, each normally carrying 20 marks. Usually at least one of the questions will require discussion only and will involve *no* calculations.

Time allowed: 3 hours

Mathematical Tables will be provided.

Recent pass rates

The UK pass rate for the May 1999 exam was 40.0% and for November 1998 was 37.3%. These pass rates were below average for the Stage 4 papers.

Analysis of past papers 1995-1999

The analysis below shows the topics which have been examined in the eight sittings of the syllabus and the CIMA Specimen paper for *Strategic Financial Management.*

November 1999

Section A (60 marks)

1 Corporate restructuring

Section B (40 marks)

2 Currency risk and hedging
3 Asset replacement; leasing
4 Public and private sector
5 Sources of finance; interest rate risk

This paper forms the mock exam at the end of the Kit, and so only an outline of its contents is given here.

Question number in this Kit

May 1999

Section A (60 marks)

1	Working capital policy and calculations; managing exchange risk; currency of invoice	61

Section B (40 marks)

2	Share valuation methods; takeover bid evaluation	51
3	Evaluation of two alternative investments including non-financial factors, converting real cash flows to nominal terms	44
4	Balanced scorecard approach; stakeholder theory	8
5	NPV and sources of finance for an overseas project	55

Examiner's comments

The overall performance in this examination was very poor, especially on the compulsory question. Candidates continue to demonstrate astonishing weaknesses in understanding some very basic aspects of finance and accounting. The structure and presentation of answers, especially calculations, also continue to disappoint.

Performance on the optional questions was very mixed although, on average, rather better than on Question 1. Questions 3 and 4 were the most popular and question 2 the least.

November 1998

Section A (60 marks)

1	High technology company: contract evaluation; exchange risk; technical and political risk; foreign investment decisions	62

Section B (40 marks)

2	Interest rate risk	31
3	Management of working capital: creditors	36
4	Financial objectives; role of treasurer and financial controller	13
5	Cost of capital; capital structure	24

Examiner's comments

Time management appeared to pose a particular problem with this paper. In many cases the candidate's inability to finish the paper was due to spending far too long on sub-sections of questions writing about something that they knew a lot about. Usually the time spent was quite disproportionate to the marks available. For example, Question 1(a), although requesting some comment on the use of CAPM in international investment decisions, did not require a lengthy discourse on everything the candidate knew about it: systematic risk, unsystematic risk, single period model, etc. Question 4(a) asked for comments on three types of policy (investment, financing and dividend) and their interrelationship, for ten marks. It would be reasonable to assume that discussion of each policy carried around three marks. A three page essay on Modigliani and Miller's theory of dividend irrelevancy (which is what some candidates provided) was clearly not sensible. If these candidates felt time-pressured, they have only themselves to blame.

May 1998

		Question number in this Kit
Section A (60 marks)		
1	Company flotation: pricing of new issue and effect on shareholders. Raising finance by equity or convertible debt	63
Section B (40 marks)		
2	Hedging and foreign exchange risk. Foreign currency arithmetic: interest rate parity and purchasing power parity	56
3	Capital investment decision, including inflation, working capital and selection of appropriate discount rate	40
4	Adjusted present value of an investment; evaluation of leasing; comparison of leasing and long-term debt	45
5	Costs incurred in periods of financial difficulty; business failure prediction models	9

Examiner's comments

Better performance on the case study was maintained, perhaps reflecting better time management. Many candidates chose to answer Question 1 last. This is quite acceptable and, if answering a shorter question first gives the candidate confidence, might be a good exam technique. However, it is a strategy requiring careful time management.

November 1997

Section A (60 marks)		
1	Plc diversifying by acquisition: evaluation of different options. Methods of valuation; assessment of the offer price; method of financing. Services of a merchant bank and stockbroker	64
Section B (40 marks)		
2	Credit management problems in a small company. Credit control policy in a medium-sized manufacturing company	33
3	Corporate objectives in the public and private sectors compared; performance measures for the public sector	3
4	Hedging of foreign exchange risk for an importer/exporter; management of risks in trading with developing countries	52
5	Review of a portfolio of investments; convertible loan stock: explanations and calculations	27

Examiner's comments

Candidates appear to be allocating their time more efficiently and are beginning to realise what is required for the report part of the case study question. Candidates seem to assume that once the obvious numerical part of the question is out of the way, no more calculations are required. This is not true and as many, if not more and certainly more complicated, calculations could have been provided in part (d) of Question 1 as were required for part (b).

Some candidates do not understand some fundamental aspects of accounting and finance. For example:

- a company cannot sensibly make a bid for a listed company at a price lower than the target's market price
- reserves are not cash
- P/E ratios are *earnings* multiples not *dividend* multiples

May 1997

		Question number in this Kit
Section A (60 marks)		
1	Case study of a growing small business, covering: problems in raising finance; cash flow and p&l forecasts; report on the company's prospects, its objectives and its methods of financial forecasting	65
Section B (40 marks)		
2	NPV evaluation of a joint venture abroad; exchange rate relationships; currency swaps	60
3	Dividend policy; share repurchase	23
4	IRR and NPV methods compared; role of regulators of monopolistic industries	42
5	Electronic funds transfer; cash management models; application of the Miller-Orr model	39

Examiner's comments

Many candidates continue to misunderstand some basic accounting and finance issues; for example how to calculate return on shareholders' funds, the meaning of IRR and NPV and even the difference between profit and cash. Candidates continue to misunderstand the term 'plc': this means public limited company, not public listed company.

Some candidates show great ingenuity in worming CAPM and Modigliani and Miller (MM) into every paper (and sometimes every question!). In this paper it was possible to refer, correctly, to MM's theories of dividend irrelevancy and capital structure (Question 3) and comment on the CAPM could be justified (just about) in answering Question 4(a). Miller of course featured in Question 5. However, financial management is not entirely dependent on these theories.

November 1996

Section A (60 marks)		
1	Case study of a family-owned company in financial difficulties, covering: the role of merchant banks; business valuation; financial controls; profit improvement	66
Section B (40 marks)		
2	Decision to grant credit: evaluation using probabilities	35
3	Goals of companies; incorporation of environmental costs into investment appraisal	4
4	Discussion of interest rate swaps, currency swaps and hedging strategies	57
5	Leasing decision, from lessee's and lessor's viewpoints	18

Examiner's comments

There were fewer calculations in this paper than in previous diets and the compulsory question contained little corporate finance theory. This may have contributed to the improved performance at this sitting. The November 1996 paper should not however be taken as an indication of a change in direction. The case study addressed topics on the syllabus which have not been specifically examined previously (for example, capital reconstruction) and the number of calculations needed for this paper were the minimum the examiner would consider acceptable for SFM. Many candidates continue to have difficulties in handling the case study question.

May 1996		*Question number in this Kit*
Section A (60 marks)		
1	Case study of an AIM-quoted company, covering: CAPM and alternative methods; appraisal of alternative projects; risk and uncertainty; venture capital compared with other sources of finance	67
Section B (40 marks)		
2	Use of performance indicators; financial and non-financial factors in success	6
3	Investments in marketable securities by a company	30
4	Capital rationing with indivisible projects	43
5	The interest yield curve; statistical information sources; Monte Carlo simulation; sensitivity analysis	11

Examiner's comments

The main problem is lack of preparation and an inability to bring forward knowledge which should have been acquired at earlier stages. The majority of candidates did not understand much about the core topic of investment appraisal.

More careful reading of the syllabus guidance notes is recommended to students studying for future examinations.

Some candidates are evidently unable to calculate the time required per question based on the marks available. On a strict *pro rata* basis, the 60 mark question should take approximately 1 hour 50 minutes.

As long as a case study is required for Stage 4 examinations and it is considered appropriate to include calculations in the SFM case (which I think is essential), the length of the paper in terms of word count is unlikely to fall much below the May 1996 level, which was slightly below that for either May or November 1995.

The use of the Capital Asset Pricing Model (CAPM) in the paper was significantly less than some post-exam commentators seemed to think. It was needed to Question 1(a), although this question was more about the use of Modigliani and Miller's theories of capital structure and cost of capital. CAPM also featured in Question 1(d) in respect of its shortcomings as a method of calculating risk adjusted discount rate. The basic form of the model was required for Question 3 as a tool in risk analysis.

November 1995		
Section A (60 marks)		
1	Case study of a listed manufacturing company, covering: earnings per share; share and company valuations; alternative capital structures; P/E ratios; effects of directors' share options on decision making	68
Section B (40 marks)		
2	Cash budget; cashflow improvements	38
3	Role of the financial manager in different types of organisation	2
4	Responsibilities of and separation of the treasury function	14
5	Calculation of NPV of a project overseas; methods of financing overseas operations	53

Examiner's comments

The following weaknesses were evident.

- Failing to read the question
- Failing to answer the question as set
- Providing answers which ignore the case or question details
- Poor preparation

Poor preparation was demonstrated by ignorance of some issues that are basic to financial management. These issues should have been covered in earlier stages, for example the return on shareholders' funds and EPS calculations required for Question 1(a). Other examples were the inability of many candidates to understand the relationship/difference between profit and cash, as demonstrated in answers to Question 2, or the relationship/difference between the roles of treasurers and financial controllers as evidenced in answers to Question 4.

May 1995

		Question number in this Kit
Section A (60 marks)		
1	**Case study of a high technology company planning to invest in a developing country; the activities of a regulatory authority**	69
Section B (40 marks)		
2	**Explanations on systematic, unsystematic and total risk, and market efficiency**	25
3	**Computations using share valuation methods; dividend policies**	20
4	**Valuation of shares in a proposed takeover, taking account of synergy effects**	48
5	**Discussions on the use of financial analysis to predict corporate collapse and the valuation of a company as a going concern versus its liquidation value**	10

Examiner's comments

The poor performance which was demonstrated in this examination may be partially explained by the fact that this was the first paper under the new syllabus. However, many topics are common to the old and new syllabuses and the change should not have presented too many problems to candidates. Questions 2 and 3 were by far the most popular of the optional questions. The Question 2 topic was on the old syllabus as well as the new, and dividend policy and the dividend valuation model (the topic of Question 3) featured in the Specimen Paper.

Specimen paper

Section A (50 marks)		
1	**Case study of a business supplying horticultural products and planning to create a new retail subsidiary**	70
Section B (50 marks)		
2	**Dividend policy of a company; scrip dividends**	21
3	**Lease or buy decision of a company**	19
4	**Calculations using forward exchange rates; discussions on exchange rate risks**	54
5	**Company's selection of marketable securities; comments on: interest rate influences; cash management**	32

Tables and formulae

The CIMA *Mathematical Tables* include tables and formulae for use in the exam (see pages (xxviii) to (xxxiv) of this Kit).

Case study questions

An article giving guidance on Stage 4 case studies is summarised below.

Analysing information: How to approach Stage 4 case studies, CIMA Student, August 1994

To answer a case study style examination question, data needs to be assimilated, problems need to be understood, the data needs to be analysed and typically a report has to be prepared in a limited time. The problem of selecting techniques to analyse unfamiliar data can cause considerable difficulty for students, and this article gives guidance on the approach which should be adopted.

Analysing a case study is a matter of determining which facts and issues are critical, using these as the basis for exploring possible alternative actions and then making recommendations.

The usual areas of difficulty are:

(a) spending insufficient time reading and assimilating the data before writing an answer (the result being that key data are ignored);

(b) lack of a structured approach in working through the data (see below);

(c) lack of question practice before the exam;

(d) failure to use a wide enough range of techniques for the analysis and presentation of data (see below).

A structured approach to data can involve making preliminary notes (probably including comparisons of periods or forecasts, ratios and growth rates) and answer plans.

Use of appropriate data analysis and presentation techniques demands a good knowledge of the techniques available and the situations in which they can be of use. Different approaches to a single case study may be acceptable, but some may lead to greater problems of presentation than others. A balance needs to be struck between simplicity and accuracy.

How the syllabus has been examined - an overview

The analysis below shows the topics that have been examined since the revised Paper 13 syllabus was introduced in May 1998.

	11/99	*5/99*	*11/98*	*5/98*
(a) Financial strategy formulation				
Financial objectives	✓	✓	✓	✓
'Not for profit' objectives				
Internal constraints: funding and gearing				✓
External constraints: legislation, other stakeholders etc				
Published information, eg balanced scorecard				
Risk analysis			✓	
Illiquidity; corporate collapse	✓			✓
Profit improvement schemes		✓		
(b) Treasurership				
Efficient market hypothesis				
Securities markets; merchant banks etc				✓
Treasury function			✓	
Sources of capital	✓	✓		✓
Cost of capital	✓	✓	✓	✓
Capital structure	✓		✓	✓
Dividend policy	✓			
Working capital management	✓	✓	✓	
Cash management		✓	✓	
Debtors management		✓		
Interest rate risk management	✓		✓	
(c) Investment decisions				
Evaluating investment decisions	✓	✓	✓	✓
Impact of different finance sources, APV				✓
Investments as options				
Capital rationing		✓		
Discount rate for projects			✓	✓
Portfolio theory, CAPM			✓	
Business valuation		✓		
Corporate restructuring	✓			
(d) International financial management				
Foreign exchange relationships	✓		✓	✓
Risk in foreign operations	✓	✓	✓	✓
Hedging techniques	✓	✓	✓	✓
International capital budgeting			✓	

(The full syllabus is on pages (xx) to (xxii).)

CURRENT ISSUES

The Competition Commission

The UK's Monopolies and Mergers Commission has changed its name to the **Competition Commission.**

Summary of recent articles

Details of recent technical articles relevant to *Strategic Financial Management* are set out below.

Double your money, David Allen, Management Accounting, October 1999

Risk and return, Merrill Cassell, Management Accounting, October 1999

Beyond DCF, Roger Peskett, CIMA Student, November 1999

EXAMINERS' INSTRUCTIONS

The examinations department of the CIMA has asked the Institute's examiners to be precise when drafting questions. In particular, examiners have been asked to use precise instruction words. It will probably help you to know what instruction words may be used, and what they mean. With the Institute's permission, their list of recommended requirement words, and their meaning, is shown below.

Recommended requirement words

Advise/recommend	Present information, opinions or recommendations to someone to enable that recipient to take action
Amplify	Expand or enlarge upon the meaning of (a statement or quotation)
Analyse	Determine and explain the constituent parts of
Appraise/assess/evaluate	Judge the importance or value of
Assess	See 'appraise'
Clarify	Explain more clearly the meaning of
Comment (critically)	Explain
Compare (with)	Explain similarities and differences between
Contrast	Place in opposition to bring out difference(s)
Criticise	Present the faults in a theory or policy or opinion
Demonstrate	Show by reasoning the truth of
Describe	Present the details and characteristics of
Discuss	Explain the opposing arguments
Distinguish	Specify the differences between
Evaluate	See 'appraise'
Explain/interpret	Set out in detail the meaning of
Illustrate	Use an example - chart, diagram, graph or figure as appropriate - to explain something
Interpret	See 'explain'
Justify	State adequate grounds for
List (and explain)	Itemise (and detail meaning of)
Prove	Show by testing the accuracy of
Recommend	See 'advise'
Reconcile	Make compatible apparently conflicting statements or theories
Relate	Show connections between separate matters
State	Express
Summarise	State briefly the essential points (dispensing with examples and details)
Tabulate	Set out facts or figures in a table

Requirement words which will be avoided

Examiners have been asked to avoid instructions which are imprecise or which may not specifically elicit an answer. The following words will not be used.

Consider	As candidates could do this without writing a word
Define	In the sense of stating exactly what a thing is, as CIMA wishes to avoid requiring evidence of rote learning
Examine	As this is what the examiner is doing, not the examinee
Enumerate	'List' is preferred
Identify	
Justify	When the requirement is not 'to state adequate grounds for' but 'to state the advantage of'
List	On its own, without an additional requirement such as 'list and explain'
Outline	As its meaning is imprecise. The addition of the word 'briefly' to any of the suggested action words is more satisfactory
Review	
Specify	
Trace	

SYLLABUS

The syllabus contains a weighting for each syllabus area, and a ranking of the level of ability required in each topic. The CIMA has published the following explanatory notes on these points.

Study weightings

A percentage weighting is shown against each topic in the syllabus; this is intended as a guide to the amount of study time each topic requires.

All topics in a syllabus must be studied, as a question may examine more than one topic, or carry a higher proportion of marks than the percentage study time suggested.

The weightings do not specify the number of marks which will be allocated to topics in the examination.

Abilities required in the examination

Each topic in the syllabus has been given a number to indicate the level of ability required of the candidate.

The numbers range from 1 to 4 and represent the following ability levels.

Appreciation (1)
To understand a knowledge area at an early stage of learning, or outside the core of management accounting, at a level which enables the accountant to communicate and work with other members of the management team.

Knowledge (2)
To have detailed knowledge of such matters as laws, standards, facts and techniques so as to advise at a level appropriate to a management accounting specialist.

Skill (3)
To apply theoretical knowledge, concepts and techniques to the solutions of problems where it is clear what technique has to be used and the information needed is clearly indicated.

Application (4)
To apply knowledge and skills where candidates have to determine from a number of techniques which is the most appropriate and select the information required from a fairly wide range of data, some of which might not be relevant; to exercise professional judgement and to communicate and work with members of the management team and other recipients of financial reports.

Aims of the Paper 13 syllabus

To test the candidate's ability to:

- evaluate the impact of different financial strategies on organisations
- select and evaluate funding choices in different organisations
- evaluate investment decisions
- identify and assess risk, using hedging methods to reduce such risks

Content and ability required

		Ability required
13(a) Financial strategy formulation	*(study weighting 15%)*	
(i)	Identifying, quantifying and achieving the financial objectives of the organisation: the distinction between long and short term	4
(ii)	Objectives of 'not for profit' organisations	3
(iii)	Internal constraints to policy formulation and action: funding and gearing	4
(iv)	External constraints to policy formulation and action: government legislation, accounting concepts, regulatory bodies, other stakeholders	4
(v)	Using both financial and non-financial published information in the formulation of strategy, eg balanced scorecard	4
(vi)	Risk analysis and setting out possible contingencies: simulation, sensitivity analysis, probabilities	4
(vii)	Illiquidity and corporate collapse	4
(viii)	Profit improvement schemes	3
13(b) Treasurership	*(study weighting 35%)*	
(i)	The efficient market hypothesis	2
(ii)	The operation of securities markets (stock exchanges); the role of merchant banks and other financial institutions	2
(iii)	The role of the treasury function	3
(iv)	Sources of capital and their advantages and disadvantages: equity, debt, mezzanine, leasing, venture capital, euro-finance	4
(v)	Cost of capital: equity, debt, weighted average, marginal cost	4
(vi)	Capital structure: traditional theory, Modigliani and Miller	4
(vii)	Dividend policy: theories and strategies of dividend policy, scrip issues	4
(viii)	Working capital management: aggressive/conservative strategies	3
(ix)	Cash management: cash forecasts and budgets, cash deficits, cash surpluses, cashflow models	4
(x)	Debtors management: factoring and invoice discounting	4
(xi)	Interest rate risk management	3

	Ability required
13(c) Investment decisions *(study weighting 30%)*	
(i) Evaluating and reporting on investment decisions: considering tax, inflation, all relevant cash flows, treatment of risk and post audit	4
(ii) Evaluating the impact of different sources of finance on an investment decision: leasing, adjusted present value using an adjusted discount rate	4
(iii) Assessing investments as options on future cash flows, including the option to abandon	4
(iv) Single period capital rationing eg use of profitability index	3
(v) Selecting an appropriate discount rate (eg cost of capital) following consideration of project risk	4
(vi) Portfolio theory, the capital asset pricing model and the arbitrage pricing model: uses and limitations	3
(vii) Valuation of businesses for mergers, acquisitions or disposal (eg management buyouts)	4
(viii) Corporate restructuring and its impact on financial statements and financial performance	4
13(d) International financial management *(study weighting 20%)*	
(i) Theoretical foreign exchange relationships	3
(ii) Risks and methods of reducing risks related to foreign operations: translation, economic, transaction and political risk	4
(iii) Use of hedging techniques to manage foreign exchange movements including derivatives	4
(iv) International capital budgeting and the impact of inflation and fluctuating exchange rates	4

CIMA SYLLABUS GUIDANCE NOTES 1999-2000

The Syllabus Guidance Notes below have been published by the CIMA.

The following guidelines have been drafted by the Chief Examiner for each of the subjects. They are intended to inform candidates and lecturers about the scope of the syllabus, the emphasis which should be placed on various topics and the approach which the examination papers will adopt.

The syllabus is concerned with the planning, operating and monitoring of the finance function and with understanding the effect these activities have on the organisation as a whole.

The main objective of financial management is often cited as maximisation of shareholder wealth. However, many of the principles and procedures of financial management are just as relevant to the public sector and not-for-profit organisations (such as charities) as they are to privately owned or listed companies. The scenarios used in examinations may use all forms of organisation, although it is fair to say that the emphasis will be on companies in the private sector, whether small, family-owned businesses or large enterprises with a stock market quotation and widespread share ownership.

In an examination, candidates will be expected to have some recall of subjects studied at earlier Stages. It will be particularly useful for candidates to revise the syllabuses for *Cost Accounting and Quantitative Methods* (Paper 2) and *Economic Environment* (Paper 3) at Stage 1 and *Business Taxation* (Paper 12) at Stage 3. However, it is *not* expected that candidates should be able to produce detailed calculations of, for example, advance corporation tax liabilities, or calculate standard deviations. They should, however, be able to recall the main principles and purposes of such methods and procedures.

Although the syllabus aims to test for practical applications of financial management, much of it is underpinned by theoretical concepts which need to be studied. The uses and limitations of the theories and the difficulties in linking them to practical aspects of corporate finance should also be understood.

Detailed accounting procedures will not be tested, although candidates are expected to be familiar with the aims and purposes of all extant SSAP and FRSs. In particular, they should know how the contents might affect a company's ability to raise and use funds. These are part of the external constraints on policy formulation.

Financial strategy formulation

Syllabus reference 13 (a)

Study weighting 15%

Questions on this section will typically be asked in conjunction with aspects of one of the other three main syllabus areas. For example, objectives of not-for-profit organisations combined with an investment appraisal; the effect of internal and external constraints on policy formulation in combination with raising new capital; or illiquidity and corporate collapse combined with working capital management.

This section specifically refers to not-for-profit organisations. As noted in the introduction, the basic principles and procedures of financial management are relevant to all types of organisations. However, the objectives may differ as may the detailed activities involved in achieving the objectives. For example, the differences between financial management in the private and public sectors are diminishing as government tries to make the public sector more commercially aware.

The main differences are how the operation is financed, what returns are required and how these returns are measured. These issues could be examined under objectives of not-for-profit organisations in section (a) or under cost of capital in section (b). Similarly, evaluating and reporting on investment decisions, covered in section (c), is not limited to profit making organisations and the principles could be applied to not-for-profit organisations.

Guidance notes

Section (e) on the SMM syllabus (corporate social responsibility and professional ethics) links closely to external constraints to policy formulation on the SFM syllabus. In SFM, the focus is likely to be on the issues surrounding the constraints on pursuing the maximisation of shareholder wealth as the sole objective of the firm.

Balanced scorecard is mentioned specifically in the syllabus. However, this subject, or aspects of it, could also feature in other papers, including MAA at Stage 3. The mention of balanced scorecard in SFM is useful for reminding students that financial strategy is not based solely on published and/or financial data.

In the examination, candidates may be required to:

- choose, and calculate, performance indicators to assess efficiency and effectiveness, including traditional measures such as profitability, liquidity etc, given a set of data. The ability to choose and interpret appropriate indicators will be given at least equal weighting with the ability to calculate the ratios correctly;
- understand the limitations of using historical data for forecasting purposes, and how non-financial data can influence forecasts;
- explain the principles of risk analysis, for example how sensitivity analysis and simulation exercises might be used to incorporate risk into an investment appraisal;
- explain how a company might manage a period of illiquidity;
- discuss the uses and limitations of models which can be used to predict corporate collapse, for example Altman's Z score;
- demonstrate some understanding of the issues involved in corporate governance;
- demonstrate an awareness of the Cadbury Report, its purpose and recommendations in outline.

The following items are *not* examinable:

- detailed knowledge of the contents of the Cadbury Report;
- large scale calculations of sensitivities or simulations.

Treasurership

Syllabus reference 13 (b)

Study weighting 35%

This section contains some of the most complex areas of financial management and requires careful study. In the examination, candidates may be required to:

- discuss and evaluate various sources of finance of varying durations, for example:

  Equity. This is the risk, and permanent, capital of a business, ie in balance sheet terms, ordinary share capital and reserves. The difference between book values, market values and nominal values of equity should be fully understood.

  Medium to long-term debt. This type of finance can take many forms, eg convertibles, debts with warrants, 'mezzanine' (which refers to unsecured loans often used in management buyouts), euro-bonds, government grants or assistance, and different types of leasing arrangements.

  Venture capital. This is a specialised form of finance provided for new companies, buy-outs and small growth companies which are perceived as carrying above average risk.

- understand the factors which might affect the cost of funds, eg the size of the business under review, a company's existing capital structure or government economic policy;

- demonstrate the ability to match sources of capital to a company's requirements and circumstances;
- demonstrate knowledge of theoretical explanations of capital structure, including Modigliani and Miller's propositions 1, 2 and 3;
- calculate the cost of the various components of capital structure, demonstrating an understanding of the various models available, eg the Dividend Valuation Model, the Earnings Growth Model and the Capital Asset Pricing Model (CAPM). The weaknesses of these models for practical purposes should be understood as well as the arithmetic involved in their calculations;
- demonstrate an understanding of the effect of capital structure on equity beta and the relationship of asset to equity betas, including taxation adjustments;
- demonstrate an understanding of adjusted present value techniques. Formulae for calculating adjusted cost of capital are included in the CIMA *Mathematical Tables*;
- discuss the role of financial institutions and the regulatory authorities. Knowledge of how these institutions affect the ability of a business to raise and manage funds is required as well as knowledge of how they operate;
- on the subject of interest rate risk management, demonstrate an understanding of the theories of the determination of interest rates and how companies manage the risk;
- discuss dividend policy, demonstrating a working knowledge of the various dividend policies available to a company in practice, including the information content;
- demonstrate an understanding of the principles of Modigliani and Miller's theory of dividend irrelevancy;
- on the subject of working capital management, answer numerical questions as well as provide a discussion of policy issues, eg calculations on cost of credit or cash management;
- demonstrate a knowledge of cash management models and the use of probability in cash and credit management;
- demonstrate an understanding of the forms of the Efficient Markets Hypothesis, its usefulness and limitations. Also an awareness that many aspects of corporate finance theory assume efficient markets for their validity, eg the Capital Asset Pricing Model.

The following items are *not* examinable:

- Miller's theories on the effects of personal taxation on capital structure and the cost of capital;
- the mathematical or graphical proof of Modigliani and Miller's theory of dividend irrelevancy;
- memorised formulae for cash management models. These are provided in CIMA's *Mathematical Tables* and questions will normally simplify the calculations required.

Investment decisions

Syllabus reference 13 (c)

Study weighting 30%

There has been a large amount of empirical research into the use of various methods of investment appraisal over the past fifteen years. Although it is not essential for candidates to be familiar with the results of these studies, familiarity with one or two of the most well-known and widely quoted (eg Richard Pike's work) would be a distinct advantage.

In the examination, candidates may be required to:

- identify the correct variables to include in an investment appraisal, incorporate inflation in the cash flows and adjust for risk;
- understand the use of the CAPM to determine risk-adjusted discount rates;
- understand other methods of risk adjustment such as certainty equivalents;
- understand the advantages and disadvantages of procedures for evaluating capital investment decisions when the company faces a period of capital rationing, including the use of a profitability index, and mathematical programming;
- demonstrate the impact of taxation on the investment decision, for example capital allowances (in the UK);
- understand the need to consider and quantify the social or environmental costs and benefits of an investment where possible;
- understand the principles and practices of project control, continuous evaluation and post-audit;
- understand the uses of limitations and modern portfolio theory (MPT) and the CAPM;
- understand the difference between portfolio theory and the arbitrage pricing model (APM) and how APM could be developed by companies using internal information;
- understand the benefits and limitations of using the share price as a benchmark guide in the valuation of a public listed company;
- understand alternative methods of valuation of different types of businesses and the difficulties involved in their application;
- demonstrate an understanding of the main provisions of the relevant accounting standards that cover the accounting treatment of mergers and acquisitions.

The following items are *not* examinable:

- in the context of linear and integer programming, the formulation of the objective function and the performance of simplex calculations;
- calculations of: betas from raw data; a two-asset portfolio variance; the APM;
- detail on the accounting treatment of mergers and acquisitions.

International financial management

Syllabus reference 13 (d)

Study weighting 20%

In the examination, candidates may be required to:

- demonstrate a good knowledge of foreign exchange arithmetic, eg how to calculate the net cost to a company of using different hedging techniques, as well as an ability to discuss risk management techniques;

- understand what types of foreign exchange risk may affect a company and what methods are available to minimise the risks, eg foreign currency hedging techniques;
- demonstrate a knowledge of both internal and external hedging techniques, and of when and how they might be used;
- demonstrate an understanding of how foreign exchange markets operate and of foreign exchange terminology, eg the meaning of spot and futures markets and the theories of interest rate parity and purchasing power parity;
- understanding the meaning of the term 'derivatives', and the circumstances in which derivatives may be worthwhile, for example the use of options and swaps;
- understand the two methods of applying NPV techniques to international investment appraisal;
- demonstrate a general knowledge of recent events in the economies and financial markets of countries outside the UK: students are encouraged to read appropriate journals such as *The Economist.* Overseas candidates may use their knowledge and experience of their own country and institutions when answering questions which appear to be UK-specific.

The following items are *not* examinable:

- Black and Scholes Option Pricing Model;
- detailed knowledge of the economy and financial institutions of specific foreign countries.

TABLES

The tables below are included in CIMA's *Mathematical Tables* which is made available to candidates in the exam.

Present value table

Present value of 1 = $(1+r)^{-n}$ where r = discount rate, n = number of periods until payment.

Periods	Discount rates (r)									
(n)	1%	2%	3%	4%	5%	6%	7%	8%	9%	10%
1	0.990	0.980	0.971	0.962	0.952	0.943	0.935	0.926	0.917	0.909
2	0.980	0.961	0.943	0.925	0.907	0.890	0.873	0.857	0.842	0.826
3	0.971	0.942	0.915	0.889	0.864	0.840	0.816	0.794	0.772	0.751
4	0.961	0.924	0.888	0.855	0.823	0.792	0.763	0.735	0.708	0.683
5	0.951	0.906	0.863	0.822	0.784	0.747	0.713	0.681	0.650	0.621
6	0.942	0.888	0.837	0.790	0.746	0.705	0.666	0.630	0.596	0.564
7	0.933	0.871	0.813	0.760	0.711	0.665	0.623	0.583	0.547	0.513
8	0.923	0.853	0.789	0.731	0.677	0.627	0.582	0.540	0.502	0.467
9	0.914	0.837	0.766	0.703	0.645	0.592	0.544	0.500	0.460	0.424
10	0.905	0.820	0.744	0.676	0.614	0.558	0.508	0.463	0.422	0.386
11	0.896	0.804	0.722	0.650	0.585	0.527	0.475	0.429	0.388	0.350
12	0.887	0.788	0.701	0.625	0.557	0.497	0.444	0.397	0.356	0.319
13	0.879	0.773	0.681	0.601	0.530	0.469	0.415	0.368	0.326	0.290
14	0.870	0.758	0.661	0.577	0.505	0.442	0.388	0.340	0.299	0.263
15	0.861	0.743	0.642	0.555	0.481	0.417	0.362	0.315	0.275	0.239

Periods	Discount rates (r)									
(n)	11%	12%	13%	14%	15%	16%	17%	18%	19%	20%
1	0.901	0.893	0.885	0.877	0.870	0.862	0.855	0.847	0.840	0.833
2	0.812	0.797	0.783	0.769	0.756	0.743	0.731	0.718	0.706	0.694
3	0.731	0.712	0.693	0.675	0.658	0.641	0.624	0.609	0.593	0.579
4	0.659	0.636	0.613	0.592	0.572	0.552	0.534	0.516	0.499	0.482
5	0.593	0.567	0.543	0.519	0.497	0.476	0.456	0.437	0.419	0.402
6	0.535	0.507	0.480	0.456	0.432	0.410	0.390	0.370	0.352	0.335
7	0.482	0.452	0.425	0.400	0.376	0.354	0.333	0.314	0.296	0.279
8	0.434	0.404	0.376	0.351	0.327	0.305	0.285	0.266	0.249	0.233
9	0.391	0.361	0.333	0.308	0.284	0.263	0.243	0.225	0.209	0.194
10	0.352	0.322	0.295	0.270	0.247	0.227	0.208	0.191	0.176	0.162
11	0.317	0.287	0.261	0.237	0.215	0.195	0.178	0.162	0.148	0.135
12	0.286	0.257	0.231	0.208	0.187	0.168	0.152	0.137	0.124	0.112
13	0.258	0.229	0.204	0.182	0.163	0.145	0.130	0.116	0.104	0.093
14	0.232	0.205	0.181	0.160	0.141	0.125	0.111	0.099	0.088	0.078
15	0.209	0.183	0.160	0.140	0.123	0.108	0.095	0.084	0.074	0.065

Cumulative present value table

This table shows the present value of £1 per annum, receivable or payable at the end of each year for *n* years.

Periods					Discount rates (r)					
(n)	**1%**	**2%**	**3%**	**4%**	**5%**	**6%**	**7%**	**8%**	**9%**	**10%**
1	0.990	0.980	0.971	0.962	0.952	0.943	0.935	0.926	0.917	0.909
2	1.970	1.942	1.913	1.886	1.859	1.833	1.808	1.783	1.759	1.736
3	2.941	2.884	2.829	2.775	2.723	2.673	2.624	2.577	2.531	2.487
4	3.902	3.808	3.717	3.630	3.546	3.465	3.387	3.312	3.240	3.170
5	4.853	4.713	4.580	4.452	4.329	4.212	4.100	3.993	3.890	3.791
6	5.795	5.601	5.417	5.242	5.076	4.917	4.767	4.623	4.486	4.355
7	6.728	6.472	6.230	6.002	5.786	5.582	5.389	5.206	5.033	4.868
8	7.652	7.325	7.020	6.733	6.463	6.210	5.971	5.747	5.535	5.335
9	8.566	8.162	7.786	7.435	7.108	6.802	6.515	6.247	5.995	5.759
10	9.471	8.983	8.530	8.111	7.722	7.360	7.024	6.710	6.418	6.145
11	10.37	9.787	9.253	8.760	8.306	7.887	7.499	7.139	6.805	6.495
12	11.26	10.58	9.954	9.385	8.863	8.384	7.943	7.536	7.161	6.814
13	12.13	11.35	10.63	9.986	9.394	8.853	8.358	7.904	7.487	7.103
14	13.00	12.11	11.30	10.56	9.899	9.295	8.745	8.244	7.786	7.367
15	13.87	12.85	11.94	11.12	10.38	9.712	9.108	8.559	8.061	7.606

Periods					Discount rates (r)					
(n)	**11%**	**12%**	**13%**	**14%**	**15%**	**16%**	**17%**	**18%**	**19%**	**20%**
1	0.901	0.893	0.885	0.877	0.870	0.862	0.855	0.847	0.840	0.833
2	1.713	1.690	1.668	1.647	1.626	1.605	1.585	1.566	1.547	1.528
3	2.444	2.402	2.361	2.322	2.283	2.246	2.210	2.174	2.140	2.106
4	3.102	3.037	2.974	2.914	2.855	2.798	2.743	2.690	2.639	2.589
5	3.696	3.605	3.517	3.433	3.352	3.274	3.199	3.127	3.058	2.991
6	4.231	4.111	3.998	3.889	3.784	3.685	3.589	3.498	3.410	3.326
7	4.712	4.564	4.423	4.288	4.160	4.039	3.922	3.812	3.706	3.605
8	5.146	4.968	4.799	4.639	4.487	4.344	4.207	4.078	3.954	3.837
9	5.537	5.328	5.132	4.946	4.772	4.607	4.451	4.303	4.163	4.031
10	5.889	5.650	5.426	5.216	5.019	4.833	4.659	4.494	4.339	4.192
11	6.207	5.938	5.687	5.453	5.234	5.029	4.836	4.656	4.486	4.327
12	6.492	6.194	5.918	5.660	5.421	5.197	4.988	4.793	4.611	4.439
13	6.750	6.424	6.122	5.842	5.583	5.342	5.118	4.910	4.715	4.533
14	6.982	6.628	6.302	6.002	5.724	5.468	5.229	5.008	4.802	4.611
15	7.191	6.811	6.462	6.142	5.847	5.575	5.324	5.092	4.876	4.675

FORMULAE AND SYMBOLS

Section 15 of the CIMA *Mathematical Tables* contains the formulae and symbols set out below.

SECTION 15: FINANCIAL MATHEMATICS

The numbered notes referred to below indicate which formulae are not relevant to the *SFM* syllabus and are to be found at the end of this section.

GENERAL

Annuity

The value of annuity of £1 per period for t years (t-year annuity factor) is:

$$PV = \frac{1}{r} - \frac{1}{r(1+r)^t}$$

Perpetuity

The value of a perpetuity of £1 per year is:

$$PV = \frac{1}{r}$$

Growing perpetuity (Gordon model)

If the initial cash flow is £1 at year 1 and if cash flows thereafter grow at a constant rate of g in perpetuity:

$$PV = \frac{1}{r-g}$$

Values and sums

The value, V, attained by a single sum X, after n periods at r% is $V = X(1 + r)^n$

The sum, S, of a geometric series of n terms, with first term A and common ratio R, is:

$$S = A + AR + AR^2 + AR^3 + \dots + AR^{n-1}$$

$$S = A\frac{(R^n - 1)}{R-1}$$

Equivalent annual cost

An asset with a life of t years has an equivalent annual cost of:

$$\frac{\text{PV costs}}{\text{t-year annuity factor}}$$

Interest rate parity

$$\frac{1 + r_{SFr}}{1 + r_{\$}} = \frac{f_{SFr/\$}}{s_{SFr/\$}}$$

Value of a right and ex-rights price

If N is the number of rights required to buy 1 share, the value of a right is:

$$\frac{\text{Rights-on price} - \text{issue price}}{N + 1} = \frac{\text{ex-rights price} - \text{issue price}}{N}$$

The ex-rights price is:

$$\frac{1}{N+1}\left((N \times \text{rights-on price}) + \text{issue price}\right)$$

Value of a future *(see Note 1)*

$$\frac{\text{Futures price}}{(1+r_f)^t} = \text{spot price} + \text{PV(storage costs)} - \text{PV (convenience yield)}$$

Value of lease *(see Note 2)*

If LCF_t is the lease's cash outflow in period t, the value of an N-period lease of an asset costing INV is:

$$INV - \sum_{t=0}^{N} \frac{LCF_t}{[1 + r(1 - T_c)]^t}$$

COST OF CAPITAL

Cost of equity (r)

(i) *CAPM*

$$E(r_j) = r_f + [E(r_m) - r_f]\beta_j$$

(ii) *Dividend valuation model*

$$r = \frac{d_1}{p_0} + g$$

Adjusted cost of capital *(see Note 3)*

If r is the cost of capital under all-equity financing, the adjusted cost of capital (r*) is:

MM formula

$$r^* = r(1 - T^*L)$$

where L = project's marginal contribution to the firm's overall debt ratio
T* = the net tax savings attached to debt interest payments

Miles-Ezzell formula

$$r^\star = r - Lr_D T^\star \frac{1+r}{1+r_D}$$

where r_D = the borrowing rate

Weighted average cost of capital formula

$$r^\star = r_D (1 - T_C) \frac{D}{E+D} + r_E \frac{E}{E+D}$$

where T_c = the marginal tax rate

RISK AND PORTFOLIO PERFORMANCE

Measures of risk

Variance of returns $= \sigma^2$

$= \text{expected value of } (\tilde{r} - r)^2$

Standard deviation of returns = σ

Covariance between returns of stocks 1 and 2

$= \text{Cov}_{1,2} = \text{expected value of } [(\tilde{r}_1 - r_1)(\tilde{r}_2 - r_2)]$

Correlation between returns of stock 1 and 2 = $\rho_{1,2} = \dfrac{\text{Cov}_{1,2}}{\sigma_1 \sigma_2}$

Beta of stock i = $\beta_i = \dfrac{\text{Cov}_{i,m}}{\sigma_m^2}$

where $\text{Cov}_{i,m}$ is the covariance between stock i's return and the market return and $\sigma^2{}_m$ is the variance of the market return.

Variance of portfolio returns *(see Note 4)*

The variance of returns on a portfolio with proportion x_i invested in stock i is:

$$\sum_{i=1}^{N} \sum_{j=1}^{N} x_i \, x_j \, \text{Cov}_{i,j}$$

Capital asset pricing model

The expected risk premium on a risky investment is: $r - r_f = \beta(r_m - r_f)$

Capital asset pricing model (certainty-equivalent form) *(see Note 5)*

The present value of a one-period risky investment is:

$$PV = \frac{C_1 - \lambda \text{Cov}(\tilde{C}_1, \tilde{r}_m)}{1 + r_f}$$

where

$$\lambda = \frac{r_m - r_f}{\sigma_m{}^2}$$

Measures of portfolio performance *(see Note 6)*

Gain from picking stocks (Jensen's measure) = $(r - r_f) - \beta(r_m - r_f)$

Net gain from picking stocks = $(r - r_f) - \frac{\sigma}{\sigma_m}(r_m - r_f)$

OPTIONS

Value of a call and a put

Value of call + present value of exercise price = value of put + share price

Black-Scholes formula for value of a call *(see Note 7)*

Present value of call option

$$= PN(d_1) - EXe^{-r_f t} N(d_2)$$

where

$$d_1 = \frac{\log(P / EX) + r_f t + \sigma^2 t / 2}{\sigma\sqrt{t}}$$

$$d_2 = \frac{\log(P / EX) + r_f t - \sigma^2 t / 2}{\sigma\sqrt{t}}$$

$N(d)$ = cumulative normal probability density function

EX = exercise price of option

t = time to exercise date

P = price of asset now

σ^2 = variance per period of (continuously compounded) rate of return on the asset

r_f = (continuously compounded) risk-free rate of interest

Binominal option valuation model *(see Note 7)*

Upside change = $u = e^{(\sigma\sqrt{h})} - 1$

Downside change = $d = e^{(-\sigma\sqrt{h})} - 1$

Probability of upside change in risk-neutral world = $p = \frac{r_f - d}{u - d}$

where σ = standard deviation of price changes per period

h = number of step jumps per period

Cash inventory models

Baumol model

Optimum amount of securities sold

$$= \sqrt{\frac{2 \times \text{annual cash disbursements} \times \text{cost per sale of securities}}{\text{Interest rate}}}$$

Miller-Orr model

Spread between upper and lower cash balance limits

$$= \quad 3\left(\frac{\frac{3}{4} \times \text{transaction cost} \times \text{variance of cash flows}}{\text{Interest rate}}\right)^{1/3}$$

BPP Notes

Note 1. The *value of a future* formula applies to futures in *commodities*, which are beyond the scope of the current *SFM* syllabus.

Note 2. Most well prepared students will be able to do a leasing question without having to look up a formula. The *value of lease* formula is included in the *Mathematical Tables* for those who might have need of it.

Note 3. The Examiner has indicated that the *MM formula* given for *adjusted cost of capital* is unlikely to be used often in examinations and that, if it is, clear guidance will be given on its application.

Note 4. In an article in *CIMA Student*, the *SFM* Examiner has written as follows.

'It is unlikely that students will be asked to calculate portfolio variances as the calculations are tedious and time-consuming. However, a question may ask for an explanation of what portfolio variances are and how they might be interpreted. The formula may therefore aid students in their explanations.'

Note 5. The Examiner has commented that although the standard form of the CAPM will feature regularly in exams, the *certainty-equivalent form* of the CAPM is unlikely to be tested but is included in the *Mathematical Tables* for general information.

Note 6. The Examiner has stated that 'it is unlikely these formulae *[Measures of portfolio performance]* will be needed for the *SFM* examination ... although the Jensen measure could be used in discussion if the performance of share prices was the subject of a question and the measure could be introduced into the discussion'.

Note 7. Knowledge of the *Black-Scholes formula* and the *binomial option valuation model* is not required for the *SFM* syllabus.

Question bank

DO YOU KNOW? - FINANCIAL STRATEGY FORMULATION

- *Check that you can fill in the blanks in the statements before you attempt any questions. If in doubt, you should go back to your BPP Study Text and revise first.*
- Strategy - whether short-term or long-term - involves action to achieve a specific objective. The decisions falling within the scope of financial strategy include those relating to:
  - ....
  - ....
  - ....
  - ....
- Plans are made within a framework of objectives. The theory of company finance is based on the assumption that the objective of management is to maximise the market value of the company. More specifically, the main objective of a company should be to ....
- All businesses operate within an environment of external (eg .... and ....) constraints, and must take that environment into account when making plans.
- There is the potential for conflict between business owners, directors, managers and other interest groups. .... theory sees employees and shareholders as individuals, each with their own objectives. Where different people's objectives can be met together, there is said to be ....
- The system of corporate governance - a responsibility of .... - should seek to ensure congruence between the objectives of the organisation and those of its teams or departments and individual team members.
- In the UK, a corporate governance 'supercode' combines elements of the ...., ..., and .... Reports

  TRY QUESTIONS 1-4
- The performance of a company is primarily assessed using *trends* and .... Time series of turnover and profits indicate whether a company is growing or declining. .... facilitate comparisons over time or between companies.
- Other sources of information should also be used in appraising a company's performance. These include the following.
  - ....
  - ....
  - ....
  - ....
  - ....
- Ratios and other information may be used to predict corporate failure.
- The methods of analysing risk and uncertainty include the following.
  - ....
  - ....
  - ....
  - ....
  - ....
- Cost control is concerned with keeping costs within acceptable limits. Cost .... is a planned and positive approach to reducing expenditure. Cost .... measures ought to be programmes to reduce costs rather than the result of panic action.
- One approach to cost reduction is ...., which attempts to maintain or improve the value of a product, but at a reduced cost.

  TRY QUESTIONS 5-12
- *Possible pitfalls*

  Write down the mistakes you know you should avoid.

DID YOU KNOW? - FINANCIAL STRATEGY FORMULATION

- *Could you fill in the blanks? The answers are in bold. Use this page for revision purposes as you approach the exam.*
- Strategy - whether short-term or long-term - involves action to achieve a specific objective. The decisions falling within the scope of financial strategy include those relating to:
  - **the sources from which funds are obtained**
  - **the amount which should be paid out by a company in dividends**
  - **financial aspects of asset replacement**
  - **a company's policies on allowing and taking up discounts**
- Plans are made within a framework of objectives. The theory of company finance is based on the assumption that the objective of management is to maximise the market value of the company. More specifically, the main objective of a company should be to **maximise the wealth of its ordinary shareholders**.
- All businesses operate within an environment of external (eg **governmental** and **regulatory**) constraints, and must take that environment into account when making plans.
- There is the potential for conflict between business owners, directors, managers and other interest groups. **Agency** theory sees employees and shareholders as individuals, each with their own objectives. Where different people's objectives can be met together, there is said to be **goal congruence**.
- The system of corporate governance - a responsibility of **the directors** - should seek to ensure congruence between the objectives of the organisation and those of its teams or departments and individual team members.
- In the UK, a corporate governance 'supercode' combines elements of the Cadbury, Greenbury and Hampel Reports.

  TRY QUESTIONS 1-4
- The performance of a company is primarily assessed using trends and **ratios**. Time series of turnover and profits indicate whether a company is growing or declining. **Ratios** facilitate comparisons over time or between companies.
- Other sources of information should also be used in appraising a company's performance. These include the following.
  - **Information in the accounts and in the notes to the accounts**
  - **The chairman's report**
  - **The directors' report**
  - **Press comments on the company or on the industry in which it operates**
  - **Published statistics on output and profitability in the relevant industry**
- Ratios and other information may be used to predict corporate failure.
- The methods of analysing risk and uncertainty include the following.
  - **Adjusting the discount rate to allow a premium on the cost of capital for risk**
  - **Expecting projects to pay back, or achieve a positive NPV, within a certain time limit**
  - **Simulation modelling**
  - **Using probability estimates of cash flows**
  - **Sensitivity analysis**
- Cost control is concerned with keeping costs within acceptable limits. Cost **reduction** is a planned and positive approach to reducing expenditure. Cost **reduction** measures ought to be programmes to reduce costs rather than the result of panic action.
- One approach to cost reduction is **value analysis**, which attempts to maintain or improve the value of a product, but at a reduced cost.

  TRY QUESTIONS 5-12
- *Possible pitfalls*
  - **Description of corporate objectives**
  - **Approaches to performance analysis**
  - **Ratio calculations**
  - **Describing effects of financial difficulties**

1 VARIOUS GOALS (11/94) *45 mins*

(a) Assume you are Finance Director of a large multinational company, listed on a number of international stock markets. The company is reviewing its corporate plan. At present, the company focuses on maximising shareholder wealth as its major goal. The Managing Director thinks this single goal is inappropriate and asks his co-directors for their views on giving greater emphasis to the following:

(i) cash flow generation;

(ii) profitability as measured by profits after tax and return on investment;

(iii) risk-adjusted returns to shareholders;

(iv) performance improvement in a number of areas such as concern for the environment, employees' remuneration and quality of working conditions and customer satisfaction.

Required

Provide the Managing Director with a report for presentation at the next board meeting which:

(i) critically evaluates the argument that maximisation of shareholder wealth should be the only true objective of a company; and

(ii) discusses the advantages and disadvantages of the MD's suggestions about alternative goals. **15 Marks**

(b) The company is already considering improving the methods of remuneration for its senior employees. As a member of the executive board, you are asked to give your opinions on the following suggestions:

(i) a high basic salary with usual 'perks' such as company car, pension scheme etc but no performance-related bonuses;

(ii) a lower basic salary with usual 'perks' plus a bonus related to their division's profit before tax;

(iii) a lower basic salary with usual 'perks' plus a share option scheme which allows senior employees to buy a given number of shares in the company at a fixed price at the end of each financial year.

Required

Discuss the arguments for and against *each* of the *three* options from the point of view of both the company and its employees. Detailed comments on the taxation implications are *not* required. **10 Marks**

Total Marks = 25

2 MAIN PRINCIPLES (11/95) *36 mins*

The main principles of financial management may be applied to most organisations. However, the role of the financial manager may be affected by the type of organisation in which he/she works.

Required

Describe the key characteristics of the financial management function and the role of the financial manager in each of the following types of organisation.

(a) Quoted, high-growth company
(b) Quoted, low-growth company
(c) Unquoted company aiming for a stock exchange listing

(d) Small, family-owned business
(e) Non profit-making organisation, for example a charity
(f) Public sector, for example a government department

Total Marks = 20

3 PUBLIC SECTOR OBJECTIVES (11/97) *36 mins*

The objective of a health authority (a public sector organisation) is stated in its most recent annual report as:

> 'To serve the people of the region by providing high-quality healthcare within expected waiting times.'

The 'mission statement' of a large plc in a manufacturing industry is shown in its annual report as:

> 'In everything the company does, it is committed to creating wealth, always with integrity, for its shareholders, employees, customers and suppliers and the community in which it operates.'

Required

(a) Discuss the main differences between the public and private sector which have to be addressed when determining corporate objectives, or missions. **8 Marks**

(b) (i) Describe three performance measures which could be used to assess whether or not the health authority is meeting its current objective. **6 Marks**

(ii) Explain the difficulties which public sector organisations face in using such measures to influence decision-making. **6 Marks**

Note. Candidates may draw on their knowledge and experience of the public sector in their own country when answering this question.

Total Marks = 20

4 COSTS AND BENEFITS (11/96) *36 mins*

(a) One of the most important elements of any decision is the specification of goals or objectives which the decision maker seeks to achieve. The literature on capital budgeting, or investment appraisal, generally assumes the goal of a company is the maximisation of shareholder wealth.

Required

Discuss the rationale for this assumption. Include in your discussion an explanation of alternative goals available to companies. **10 Marks**

(b) XYZ plc is a medium-sized company operating in the chemical industry. It is a profitable business, currently producing at below maximum capacity. It has one large factory located on the outskirts of a small industrial town. It is the region's main employer. The company is evaluating a project which has substantial environmental implications.

Required

Discuss the inclusion of environmental costs and benefits into the investment appraisal procedure and explain how this might be done. **10 Marks**

Total Marks = 20

5 TUTORIAL QUESTION: AIM COMPANIES

Your company is considering diversifying its activities by investing in a company engaged in computer services, notably software development and implementation. The United Kingdom market for such services is said to be growing at about 20% per annum. The business is seasonal, peaking between September and March.

Your attention has been drawn to two possible companies, X plc and Y plc, both of which have recently joined the Alternative Investment Market by way of placings.

An analyst has prepared for you the comparative data shown in the Appendix to this question.

You are required, in the light of this information:

(a) to compare the performance of the two companies;

(b) to give your reasons for selecting one of them as the company in which to invest.

It may be assumed that the difference in size of the two companies does not invalidate a comparison of the ratios provided.

Appendix

Data in this Appendix should be accepted as correct. Any apparent internal inconsistencies are due to rounding of the figures.

	X plc	*Y plc*
Date of formation	5 years ago, as the result of a management buyout	10 years ago
Current market price of ordinary shares	£1.15	£1.45
Financial year-end	30 June	30 September
Turnover in most recent year (£'000)		
Home	2,856	6,080
Export	2,080	1,084
Total	4,936	7,164
Index of turnover 19X9 (19X6 = 100)		
Home	190%	235%
Export	220%	150%
Total	200%	220%
Operating profit 19X9 (£'000)	840	720
Operating capital employed 19X9 (£'000)	625	1,895

Ratio analysis		*X plc*			*Y plc*		
		19X9	*19X8*	*19X7*	*19X9*	*19X8*	*19X7*
Return on operating capital employed	%	134	142	47	38	40	52
Operating profit: Sales	%	17	16	6	10	8	5
Sales: Operating capital employed	×	8	9	8	4	5	10
Percentages to sales value:							
Cost of sales	%	65	67	71	49	49	51
Selling & distribution costs	%	12	11	15	15	16	19
Administration expenses	%	6	6	8	26	27	25
Number of employees		123	127	88	123	114	91
Sales per employee	£'000	40	37	31	58	52	47
Average remuneration per employee	£'000	13	13	12	16	14	13
Tangible fixed assets							
Turnover rate	×	20	21	14	9	11	14
Additions, at cost	%	57	47	58	303	9	124
Percentage depreciated	%	45	36	20	41	60	72
Product development costs carried forward as a percentage of turnover	%	-	-	-	10	8	6
Debtors : Sales	%	18	18	22	61	41	39
Stocks : Sales	%	0	1	0	2	2	1
Cash : Sales	%	7	9	2	1	1	0
Trade creditors : Sales	%	2	2	3	32	21	24
Trade creditors : Debtors	%	11	14	15	53	50	62
Current ratio (:1)		1.5	1.3	1.2	1.1	1.1	0.9
Liquid ratio (:1)		1.5	1.3	1.2	1.0	1.0	0.9
Liquid ratio excluding bank overdraft		-	-	-	1.4	1.5	1.2
Total debt : Total assets	%	61	71	109	75	72	84
Prior-charge capital: Equity	%	10	46	480	81	75	132
Interest cover	×	18	13	3	6	12	5
Earnings per share	pence	4.5	2.9	0.4	13.2	8.6	4.2
Dividend cover	×	13.3	10.2	56.0	15.1	7.3	4.5

Approaching the question

1 This question has the advantage that ratios are provided. You need not spend much time on calculations and can concentrate on analysis instead. Think always of the practical implications of the data.

2 The key word in part (a) is 'compare'. Each of the two companies should be compared at each stage. This leads up to a summarisation of the analysis in part (b).

3 Time is wasted and no marks are earned for repeating data in the question, making calculations with no accompanying comment, and simply stating that one figure is higher or lower than another. The examiner may have a pretty good idea of what you meant to say, but you have to say it to earn the mark.

6 INDICATORS (5/96) *36 mins*

The list below provides a selection of performance and progress indicators. These indicators are generally associated with the private sector. However, management of the public sector is beginning to follow more closely private sector practices and procedures.

Required

(a) Briefly explain why organisations use performance and progress indicators.

4 Marks

(b) Choose *two* financial and *two* non-financial factors from the list below and discuss how they could be used to assess success in both the public and private sectors You should emphasise the differences and similarities between public and private sector usage of these factors and, where necessary, explain how they could, or should, be adapted for use by public sector organisations.

FINANCIAL	NON-FINANCIAL
Cash generation	Market share
Value added	Customer satisfaction
Profitability	Competitive position
Return on assets	Risk exposure

16 Marks

Total Marks = 20

7 **PDQ PLC (5/94)** *54 mins*

(a) The directors of PDQ plc have commissioned a firm of consultants to conduct a wide-ranging review of the company's public image and market position. Although this is not predominantly a financial review, the consultants need to examine the company's financial performance. The company has the following summary information for the last five years.

	Year 1	*Year 2*	*Year 3*	*Year 4*	*Year 5*
	£m	£m	£m	£m	£m
Turnover	51.2	58.3	63.9	75.2	78.2
Cost of sales	20.5	22.2	24.3	30.1	30.5
Salaries and wages	15.4	16.8	17.2	15.8	15.2
Other costs	6.1	7.9	9.9	16.3	17.9
Profit before interest and tax	9.2	11.4	12.5	13.0	14.6
Interest	1.5	1.6	1.3	0.3	0.2
Tax	2.5	3.2	3.7	4.2	4.8
Profit after interest and tax	5.2	6.6	7.5	8.5	9.6
Dividends payable	2.1	2.6	3.0	3.4	4.8
Average debtors	10.5	11.7	13.3	14.8	15.2
Average creditors	3.8	4.2	5.1	6.7	6.9
Average total assets	41.2	45.2	46.7	63.3	67.1
Shareholders' funds	26.2	30.2	34.7	59.8	64.6
Long-term debt	15.0	15.0	12.0	3.5	2.5
Number of shares in issue (millions)	6.0	6.0	6.0	8.0	8.0
P/E ratio:					
Company	8.0	8.5	9.0	9.2	9.5
Industry	8.5	9.0	9.1	9.0	9.1
Number of employees	1,720	1,750	1,820	1,720	1,690

Notes

1 Each P/E ratio is the average for the year.

2 The increased equity in year 4 was the result of a 1-for-3 rights issue at 1,000p per share which took place at the beginning of the year. Some of the money raised was used to reduce debt.

For the past five years, PDQ plc has stated its objectives as: 'To maximise shareholder wealth whilst recognising the responsibility of the company to its other stakeholders'.

As one of the consultants working on this assignment, you have been asked to assess whether the company has achieved its objectives in the five-year period under review and to discuss the key factors which have determined your assessment.

Required

(i) Discuss whether the company has met its objectives, based solely on the information available. **12 Marks**

(ii) Comment on what other financial information you would need in order to provide your client with a more accurate assessment. **8 Marks**

(b) On completion of this project, you are being assigned to work with a large, privately owned firm of architects, surveyors and building engineers to determine appropriate performance measures for their business. You have already given some thought to this assignment and have noted six dimensions under which you think performance measures can be developed for a service business such as this. These dimensions are:

(i) Competitiveness
(ii) Financial performance
(iii) Quality
(iv) Responsiveness to customer needs
(v) Resource utilisation
(vi) Innovation

Required

Describe and discuss *one* appropriate measure for *each* of the dimensions given above which could be used to assess the success of the client's business and to comment on the difficulties which might be experienced in determining performance measures in a service business.

Note

The requirement here is for *six* measures in total; *one* for *each* of the dimensions in the question. **10 Marks**

Total Marks = 30

8 BALANCED SCORECARD (5/99) *36 mins*

(a) The 'Balanced Scorecard' approach aims to provide information to management to assist strategic policy formulation and achievement. It emphasises the need to provide the user with a set of information which addresses all relevant areas of performance in an objective and unbiased fashion.

Required

(i) Discuss in general terms the main types of information which would be required by a manager to implement this approach to measuring performance; and

(ii) comment on three specific examples of performance measures which could be used in a company in a service industry, for example a firm of consultants. **10 Marks**

(b) *Quotation 1*

'The directors of all businesses must consider the wishes of all potential stakeholders for whose support they are competing - not just owners but employees, suppliers, customers, lenders, regulators and the community in which their business operates.'

Quotation 2

'Stakeholder theory is incompatible with business and its objectives and should be firmly resisted.'

Required

Discuss the opposing arguments in the two quotations given above, and explain how these views might be reconciled. **10 Marks**

Total Marks = 20

9 DIFFICULTIES (5/98) *36 mins*

(a) Companies may experience a period of financial difficulties.

Required

Describe three costs which may arise or increase during such a period of financial difficulty, and suggest strategies for minimising the impact of these costs on company financial performance. **10 Marks**

(b) 'Companies sometimes collapse in spectacular and unforeseen fashion. Models which use publicly available information to predict collapse, such as Altman's Z scores or Taffler's PAS scores, are often claimed by users to have strong predictive ability.'

Required

Discuss the reasons why companies might unexpectedly collapse even though the financial information is available to assist interested parties, such as analysts and shareholders, to forecast such events. **10 Marks**

Total Marks = 20

10 FORECASTING FAILURE (5/95) *36 mins*

(a) (i) Discuss the theories, or arguments, which suggest that financial analysis can be used to forecast the probability of a given firm's failure; and

(ii) explain why such an analysis, even if properly applied, may not always predict failure. **12 Marks**

(b) Discuss the following statement.

'It is always a sound rule to liquidate a company if its liquidation value is above its value as a going concern.' **8 Marks**

Total Marks = 20

11 STRATEGIC REVIEW (5/96) *36 mins*

(a) Assume you are the Finance Director of a medium-sized manufacturing company whose shares are listed on a recognised Stock Exchange. Your company is about to undertake its annual strategic review of all aspects of the business.

Required

(i) Explain how the following information might be used by your company as an aid to the development of its financial strategy.

(1) The interest yield curve, using a freehand graph to help illustrate your answer.

(2) Published government statistics and reports. You should include in your answer brief relevant comments on two government publications with which you are familiar, for example in the UK these could be *Business Monitor* or *Economic Trends*.

(3) Private and public data about the company's past performance.

(ii) Comment on what other information might be useful to your board during its discussions. **10 Marks**

(b) Assume that you are a financial manager about to prepare your company's cashflow forecast for the next two years. You have been provided with forecasts about product volumes, selling prices and costs.

Required

Describe the main characteristics of the following techniques, as applied to cashflow forecasting, and explain how they might be used to aid decision making. You should also comment on the main differences between the two methods and on their respective shortcomings.

(i) Monte Carlo simulation
(ii) Sensitivity analysis **10 Marks**

Total Marks = 20

12 FINANCIAL MODEL (5/94) *36 mins*

You are a qualified accountant working as assistant to the Finance Director of a medium-sized company engaged in the manufacture of kitchen and bathroom furniture. In your previous job you gained experience of preparing medium-term and long-term corporate and financial plans. Your present employers do not have a corporate planning department and are thinking of using a firm of outside consultants to prepare a five-year corporate financial plan. The Finance Director thinks this would be a very expensive exercise and, knowing your background, has suggested to the board that you be asked to co-ordinate this task, instead of using consultants. The board agrees to this suggestion.

Required

(a) List and briefly explain the steps you would take to construct the framework for a five-year corporate financial model and comment on the problems you might experience in its construction and use.

Note. You are not expected to discuss the *technical* processes involved in construction a *computer* model. **9 Marks**

(b) Describe *three* methods of incorporating the effects of uncertainty into the model. **6 Marks**

(c) Explain how mathematical programming or other computer models might assist your planning procedures and describe the dangers inherent in their use. **5 Marks**

Total Marks = 20

DO YOU KNOW? - THE TREASURY FUNCTION. SOURCES OF FINANCE. DIVIDEND POLICY

- *Check that you can fill in the blanks in the statements before you attempt any questions. If in doubt, you should go back to your BPP StudyText and revise first.*
- The functions of a treasurer include:
  - ....
  - ....
  - ....
  - ....
- Stock markets bring .... and .... together. Other sources of finance include ...., ... and ....
- Raising capital successfully means persuading investors that the returns are satisfactory. The main stock market ratios monitored by investors are:
  - ....
  - ....
  - ....
  - ....
  - ....
- The efficient market hypothesis can be proposed in different forms, in terms of different degrees of information processing efficiency: ...., ...and ....
- The period of an .... lease is less than the expected economic life of the asset and the full cost of the asset may not be paid for within the leasing period. With a .... lease, the lessee is responsible for maintaining the asset while the asset is leased for most or all of its expected life.

  TRY QUESTIONS 13-19
- The cost of equity can be calculated using either the .... model or the .... model. A weighted average cost of capital may be computed, usually weighting the sources of finance by their ....
- The proportion of a company's long-term finance in the form of loan capital is measured by the company's ....
  - The traditional view is that there is an optimum level of gearing for each company which will minimise its ....
  - The view of .... is that in the absence of taxation, gearing does not affect the value of a company. With taxation, the company's value is increased by the tax relief on the debt.
- Dividend policy may be affected by:
  - ....
  - ....
  - ....
  - ....

  TRY QUESTIONS 20-24
- *Possible pitfalls*

  Write down the mistakes you know you should avoid.

DID YOU KNOW? - THE TREASURY FUNCTION. SOURCES OF FINANCE. DIVIDEND POLICY

- *Could you fill in the blanks? The answers are in bold. Use this page for revision purposes as you approach the exam.*
- The functions of a treasurer include:
  - **advising on capital structure**
  - **managing cash flows to minimise associated costs**
  - **maintaining good banking relationships**
  - **managing foreign currency transactions to avoid risk**
- Stock markets bring **companies** and **investors** together. Other sources of finance include **banks**, **venture capitalists** and **leasing**.
- Raising capital successfully means persuading investors that the returns are satisfactory. The main stock market ratios monitored by investors are:
  - **dividend yield**
  - **earnings per share**
  - **price/earnings ratio**
  - **dividend cover**
  - **earnings yield**
- The efficient market hypothesis can be proposed in different forms, in terms of different degrees of information processing efficiency: **weak form**, **semi-strong form** and **strong form**.
- The period of an **operating** lease is less than the expected economic life of the asset and the full cost of the asset may not be paid for within the leasing period. With a **finance** lease, the lessee is responsible for maintaining the asset while the asset is leased for most or all of its expected life.

  TRY QUESTIONS 13-19
- The cost of equity can be calculated using either the **dividend growth** model or the **capital asset pricing** model. A weighted average cost of capital may be computed, usually weighting the sources of finance by their **market values**.
- The proportion of a company's long-term finance in the form of loan capital is measured by the company's **gearing**.
  - The traditional view is that there is an optimum level of gearing for each company which will minimise its **weighted average cost of capital**.
  - The view of **Modigliani-Miller** is that in the absence of taxation, gearing does not affect the value of a company. With taxation, the company's value is increased by the tax relief on the debt.
- Dividend policy may be affected by:
  - **the desire to have a stable policy**
  - **the availability of cash**
  - **the company's tax position**
  - **shareholders' preferences for income or capital gains**

  TRY QUESTIONS 20-24
- *Possible pitfalls*
  - **Understanding the treasury function**
  - **Describing debt instruments**
  - **Financing calculations**
  - **Cost of equity calculations**
  - **Understanding dividend policy trends**

13 POLICY DECISIONS (11/98)

36 mins

When determining the financial objectives of a company, it is necessary to take three types of policy decision into account - investment policy, financing policy and dividend policy.

Required

(a) Discuss the nature of these three types of policy decision, commenting on how they are inter-related and how they might affect the value of the firm (ie the present value of projected cash flows). **10 Marks**

(b) Describe the different functions of the treasury and financial control departments of an organisation and comment on the relative contributions of these two departments to policy determination and the achievement of financial objectives. **10 Marks**

Total Marks = 20

14 TREASURY DEPARTMENT (11/95)

36 mins

ABC plc is a UK-based service company with a number of wholly-owned subsidiaries and interests in associated companies throughout the world. In response to the rapid growth of the company, the Managing Director has ordered a review of the company's organisation structure, particularly the finance function. The Managing Director holds the opinion that a separate treasury department should be established. At present, treasury functions are the responsibility of the Chief Accountant.

Required

(a) Describe the main responsibilities of a treasury department in a company such as ABC plc and explain the benefits which might accrue from the establishment of a separate treasury function. **12 Marks**

(b) Describe the advantages and disadvantages which might arise if the company established a separate treasury department as a profit rather than a cost centre. **8 Marks**

Total Marks = 20

15 S PLC (5/92)

36 mins

S plc issues a debenture at par carrying a 9% coupon. The debenture is redeemable in five years and each unit of £100 is convertible into 20 ordinary shares at any time prior to redemption. At the date of issue the yield on comparable nonconvertible debentures is 12% and the company's shares are quoted at 400p.

Required

(a) Calculate the conversion premium on the debenture at the date of issue and explain in general terms the relationship between the conversion premium and the coupon rate on convertible debentures. **5 Marks**

(b) Assuming a 10% annual growth rate in share price, calculate the conversion value of the debenture three years after issue and explain why the debenture's market value is likely to exceed this figure. **5 Marks**

(c) Explain why the market value of a convertible debenture is likely to be affected by the dividend policy of the issuing company. **5 Marks**

(d) Explain what strategy a company might be pursuing when raising capital in the form of a convertible as distinct from raising straight debt or straight equity. **5 Marks**

Total Marks = 20

16 DEBT INSTRUMENTS (5/92) *45 mins*

The capital markets provide corporate treasurers with a variety of debt instruments among which are interest rate swaps, deep discounted bonds and commercial paper.

Required

(a) Describe briefly the operation of an interest rate swap and indicate the circumstances in which such a swap would be beneficial to the parties involved. **8 Marks**

(b) Outline the principal differences between a deep discounted bond and a conventional bond and indicate the circumstances in which a company might choose to issue a deep discounted bond rather than a conventional bond. **9 Marks**

(c) Describe briefly the characteristics of commercial paper and indicate the type of company which would be able to raise finance using this instrument. **8 Marks**

Total Marks = 25

17 TUTORIAL QUESTION: EFFICIENT MARKET HYPOTHESIS

A number of investigations have been undertaken into the use made by shareholders of the annual reports of companies in which they have invested. Several of these show that the annual report is regarded as an important source of information for making decisions on equity investment.

Other types of study indicate that the market price of the shares in a company does not react in the short term to the publication of the company's annual report.

How would you reconcile these findings with each other, and with the efficient market hypothesis?

Approaching the question

1 You should start by outlining the efficient market hypothesis in general, and you should then distinguish the three forms of the hypothesis.

2 You should then identify the form of the hypothesis relevant to published information such as companies' annual reports.

3 Finally, if you feel that form does not explain the observed facts set out in the question, consider whether another form, or some other facts, might do so.

18 MRF (11/96) *36 mins*

MRF is a charitable organisation and exempt from all taxes. It is about to acquire some new capital equipment for a special project. The President of the charity has been advised that it might be advantageous to acquire the equipment with a finance lease. The cost to the charity of the equipment, if it were purchased outright, would be £22.5 million. However, the leasing company would be able to negotiate a 20% discount on this price because of its long-term commercial relationship with suppliers of the type of equipment being purchased. This discount would not be available to the charity if it purchased the equipment with a bank loan.

The leasing company is nearing its year end and is keen to obtain the tax advantages denied to MRF because of its charitable status. It has therefore offered what it considers to be very favourable terms. Payments by MRF would be £7.5 million per annum for 6 years, payable at the end of each year of the lease contract.

Writing down allowances are available to the leasing company at 25 per cent on a reducing balance basis. At the end of year 6, it is estimated that the second-hand value of the equipment would be £4 million. Insurance and maintenance would be the responsibility of the charity, whether it leases or purchases the equipment.

The cost of a bank loan to the charity would be 12 per cent. The opportunity cost of capital for the leasing company would be 14 per cent.

Assume no time lag in tax payments or refunds.

You should work to two decimal places throughout.

Required

(a) Assume you are MRF's treasurer. Evaluate the financial aspects of the lease and recommend to the President whether the charity should purchase with a bank loan or use a finance lease. You should state the reasons for your recommendation and any assumptions you make in arriving at your decision. **8 Marks**

(b) Now assume that you are an account negotiator for the leasing company. You have been informed that MRF has decided to buy the equipment with a bank loan at 12 per cent interest. Your boss, Helen, has asked you to advise her whether the lease terms could be reduced so as to be competitive with the bank loan. The leasing company pays tax at the marginal rate of 33 per cent. Assume that the lease receipts from MRF are fully taxable.

Required

Write a short report advising Helen:

(i) of the annual lease payments required for the charity to be indifferent between the bank and the leasing company;

(ii) the effect on the leasing company's evaluation if the lease payments were reduced to the amount calculated above (if you are unable to calculate a figure, assume £5 million per annum);

(iii) of other actions which the company could take to rescue the deal.

Supporting calculations should provided where appropriate. **12 Marks**

Total Marks = 20

19 ABC PLC (Specimen paper) *45 mins*

ABC plc is classified as a small company for corporation tax purposes and is liable to tax at 21%. The company is considering the purchase of a new computer system. The Chief Executive has been advised that it might be advantageous to lease the computer system rather than buy with a secured bank loan. The before-tax cost of a bank loan to ABC plc would be 11½%. Apart from the possible financial benefits which might arise, he has been told that leasing provides a hedge against obsolescence.

The capital cost of the computer would be £50,000. The leasing company, which is not the supplier or manufacturer of the equipment, has offered what it considers to be very favourable terms for the lease of the computer. Payments would be £15,000 per annum for five years. The first payment would be made at the beginning of the lease contract. This would be followed by four further payments at the beginning of each of the next four years.

Insurance and maintenance of the computer would be the responsibility of the lessee. At the end of year 5, the second-hand value of the computer is expected to be £5,000.

The leasing company pays tax at the marginal rate of 31%. Writing down allowances are available on the computer at 25% on a reducing balance basis. The company's required rate of return on equity is 15% and it considers this deal to be of about the average risk of its commercial ventures. The lessor will be able to finance the purchase of the computer from retained earnings.

Required

(a) Evaluate the financial decision concerning the lease from the point of view of both the lessee and the lessor. **8 Marks**

(b) Write a report to the Chief Executive of ABC plc explaining the purpose and conclusions of your evaluation. Include in your report an explanation of the claim that leasing provides a hedge against obsolescence. **9 Marks**

(c) The Chief Executive of ABC plc claims that the evaluation is basically a capital budgeting exercise and that the company's weighted average cost of capital is a more appropriate rate to use as a discount rate.

Discuss the validity of the Chief Executive's comments. **4 Marks**

(d) ABC plc decides to buy the computer system with a bank loan and notifies the leasing company of its decision.

Comment on what action the leasing company could take to try and persuade ABC plc to reconsider its position. **4 Marks**

Total Marks = 25

20 POLICY CHANGE (5/95) *36 mins*

PDQ is a medium-sized listed company. The results to 31 December 19X4 have just been announced. Earnings per share (EPS) and declared dividends per share (DPS) for the last five years are shown below.

	19X4	*19X3*	*19X2*	*19X1*	*19X0*
EPS (pence)	140	136	131	127	122
DPS (pence)	82	81	79	78	77

Dividends are paid on 31 December each year and the dividend shown as declared in a particular year would have been or will be paid on 31 December the following year. If the current dividend policy is maintained, the directors of PDQ plc estimate that annual growth in earnings and dividends will be no better than the average growth in earnings over the past four years.

PDQ plc is reluctant to take on debt at the present time to finance growth. The company is therefore considering a change in its dividend policy and total investment programme to allow 50% of its earnings to be retained for identified capital investment projects which are estimated to have an average post-tax return of 15%. The market risk premium is expected to be 4% over the risk-free rate of 6%. The company's beta is currently quoted at 1.5 and is not expected to change for the foreseeable future.

Required

(a) Calculate the share price which might be expected by the market:

(i) if the company does not announce a change in dividend policy;
(ii) if the company does announce a change in dividend policy,

using whatever model(s) you think appropriate. **8 Marks**

(b) (i) Comment on the limitations of the model(s) you have used in your answer to part (a); and

(ii) discuss the reasons why the share price might react differently from the market's expectations. **12 Marks**

Formulae

Dividend valuation model	*Earnings growth model*	*Capital asset pricing model*
$P_o = \frac{D_1}{r_E - g}$	$P_o = \frac{E_0 \star (1 - b)[1 + (b \star r)]}{r_E - (b \star r)}$	$E_{rj} = R_f + \beta_j(R_m - R_f)$

Total Marks = 20

21 XYZ PLC (Specimen paper) *45 mins*

The table below shows earnings and dividends for XYZ plc over the past five years.

Year	*Net earnings per share*	*Net dividend per share*
	£	£
19W9	1.40	0.84
19X0	1.35	0.88
19X1	1.35	0.90
19X2	1.30	0.95
19X3	1.25	1.00

There are 10,000,000 shares issued and the majority of these shares are owned by private investors. There is no debt in the capital structure.

It is clear from the table that the company has experienced difficult trading conditions over the past few years. In the current year, net earnings are likely to be £10 million, which will be just sufficient to pay a maintained dividend of £1 per share.

Members of the board are considering a number of strategies for the company, some of which will have an impact on the company's future dividend policy.

The company's shareholders require a return of 15% on their investment.

Four options are being considered, as follows.

(a) Pay out all earnings as dividends.

(b) Pay a reduced dividend of 50% of earnings and retain the remaining 50% for future investment.

(c) Pay a reduced dividend of 25% of earnings and retain the remaining 75% for future investment.

(d) Retain all earnings for an aggressive expansion programme and pay no dividend at all.

The directors cannot agree on any of the four options discussed so far. Some of them prefer option (1) because they believe to do anything else would have an adverse impact on the share price. Others favour either option (2) or option (3) because the company has identified some good investment opportunities and they believe one of these options would be in the best long-term interests of shareholders. An adventurous minority favours option (4) and thinks this will allow the company to take over a small competitor.

Required

(a) Comment on the company's dividend policy between 19W9 and 19X3 and on its possible consequences for earnings. **5 Marks**

(b) Advise the directors of the share price for XYZ plc which might be expected immediately following the announcement of their decision if they pursued each of the four options, using an appropriate valuation model. You should also show what percentage of total return is provided by dividend and capital gain in each case. You should ignore taxation for this part of the question. Make (and indicate) any realistic assumptions you think necessary to answer this question. **8 Marks**

(c) Discuss the reliability you can place on the figures you have just produced and on the usefulness of this information to the company's directors. **6 Marks**

(d) The directors are still unable to come to an agreement on dividend policy and decide to ask the consultancy division of their auditors for advice. The consultants suggest two alternatives:

(i) pay no cash dividend but give shareholders bonus shares in lieu (ie pay a scrip dividend);

(ii) offer shareholders an alternative: a cash dividend which will be 50% of earnings or an issue of bonus shares to the value of 150% of the value of the cash dividend.

The directors are unfamiliar with the use of scrip dividends and are unsure about the advantages.

Required

Advise the directors on the arguments for and against the use of bonus shares in lieu of cash dividends, and on the possible consequences for investors of offering alternative (ii). **6 Marks**

Total Marks = 25

22 RG PLC (5/93) *45 mins*

The following financial data relate to RG plc.

Year	*Earnings per share* Pence	*Net dividend per share* Pence	*Share price* Pence
19W7	42	17	252
19W8	46	18	184
19W9	51	20	255
19X0	55	22	275
19X1	62	25	372

A firm of market analysts which specialises in the industry in which RG plc operates has recently re-evaluated the company's future prospects. The analysts estimate that RG plc's earnings and dividends will grow at 25% for the next two years. Thereafter, earnings are likely to increase at a lower annual rate of 10%. If this reduction in earnings growth occurs, the analysts consider that the dividend payout ratio will be increased to 50%.

RG plc is all equity financed and has one million ordinary shares in issue.

The tax rate of 30% is not expected to change in the foreseeable future.

Required

(a) Calculate the estimated share price and P/E ratio which the analysts now expect for RG plc, using the dividend valuation model, and comment briefly on the method of valuation you have just used. Assume a constant post-tax cost of capital of 18%. **10 Marks**

(b) Comment on whether the dividend policy being considered by the analysts would be appropriate for the company in the following two sets of circumstances.

(i) The company's shareholders are mainly financial institutions.

(ii) The company's shareholders are mainly small private investors. **8 Marks**

(c) Describe briefly *three* other dividend policies which RG plc could consider. **7 Marks**

Total Marks = 25

23 DIVS PLC (5/97) *36 mins*

DIVS plc is a large international company with widespread interests in advertising, media and various consultancy activities associated with sales promotion and marketing. In recent years the company's earnings and dividend payments, in real terms, have grown on average by 15% and 12% per year respectively. The company is likely to have substantial cash surpluses in the coming year, but a number of investment opportunities are being considered for the subsequent two years. The senior managers of the company are reviewing their likely funding requirements for the next two to three years and the possible consequences for dividend policy.

At present the company has a debt:equity ratio of 1:5, measured in market value terms. It does not want to increase this ratio at the present time but might need to borrow to pay a maintained dividend in the future.

The senior managers of the company are discussing a range of issues concerning financial strategy in general and dividend policy in particular.

Required

Assume you are an independent financial adviser to the Board of DIVS plc. Write a report to the board which discusses the following issues.

(a) The repurchase of some of the company's shares in the coming year using the forecast surplus cash, the aim being to reduce the amount of cash needed to pay dividends in subsequent years. Other implications of share repurchase for the company's financial strategy should also be considered. **9 Marks**

(b) The advisability of borrowing money to pay dividends in years 2 and 3. **7 Marks**

(c) The likely effect on the company's cost of equity if the company decides on share repurchase and/or further borrowing. **4 Marks**

Total Marks = 20

24 EXPANSION (11/98) *36 mins*

RH plc manufactures machine tools. It has 2 million ordinary £1 shares in issue, quoted at 168 pence each, and £1 million 10% secured debentures quoted at par. To finance expansion the directors of the company want to raise £1 million for additional working capital.

Cash flow from trading before interest and tax is currently £1 million per annum. It is expected to rise to £1.3 million per annum if the expansion programme goes ahead. To simplify placing a valuation on the company's equity, you should assume that:

- the forecast level of cash flow, and a tax rate of 33%, will continue indefinitely.
- the required rate of return on the market value of equity, 18% post tax, will be unaffected by the new financing.
- there is no difference between taxable profits and cash flow.

The company's directors are considering two forms of finance - equity via a rights issue at 15% discount to current share price, or 12% unsecured loan stock at par.

Required

(a) Calculate for both financing options, the expected

(i) increase in the market value of equity,
(ii) debt : debt + equity ratio
(iii) weighted average cost of capital. **10 Marks**

(b) Assume you are the financial manager for RH plc. Write a report to the board advising which of the two types of financing is to be preferred. Include in your report brief comments on non-financial factors which should be considered by the directors before deciding how to raise the £1 million finance. **10 Marks**

Total Marks = 20

DO YOU KNOW? - INVESTMENT AND PORTFOLIO MANAGEMENT. WORKING CAPITAL MANAGEMENT

- *Check that you can fill in the blanks in the statements before you attempt any questions. If in doubt, you should go back to your BPP Study Text and revise first.*
- A combination or .... of investments will have a risk and an expected return. Investors will have .... curves, with each curve indicating equally acceptable combinations of risk and return.
- Portfolios which give the best possible return for their levels of risk lie on the **efficient** frontier. The .... line touches the .... frontier and also meets the point (zero risk; return on risk free investments).
- By holding a diversified portfolio an investor can avoid .... risk, but he must still accept .... risk. Systematic risk is the risk of a rise or fall in returns because of a general rise or fall in the market.
- A security's beta factor measures its volatility relative to that of the market.
  - Risk-free securities have a beta factor of ....
  - The market as a whole has a beta factor of ....
- The Capital Asset Pricing Model shows how the .... risk of a security, measured by its beta factor, is related to the rate of return required from it by investors. Beta factors may be given for projects as well as for securities, and used to find required rates of return for projects.

  TRY QUESTIONS 25-30
- In managing working capital, Strict control must be maintained over debtors, to ensure that .... limits are not exceeded and that debtors pay by the due date.
- Stockholding should be kept under control, but not reduced to the point where shortages lead to ....
- Creditors should be paid just early enough to avoid ....or to secure ....
- The operating cycle, from payments to creditors through to receipts from debtors, summarises the flow of ....
- If a large surplus of cash is predicted, suitable .... should be sought.
- If a shortage of cash is predicted, one or more of the following actions should be taken to deal with the problem:
  - ....
  - ....
  - ....
  - ....
  - ....
  - ....

  TRY QUESTIONS 31-39
- *Possible pitfalls*

  Write down the mistakes you know you should avoid.

DID YOU KNOW? - INVESTMENT AND PORTFOLIO MANAGEMENT. WORKING CAPITAL MANAGEMENT

- *Could you fill in the blanks? The answers are in bold. Use this page for revision purposes as you approach the exam.*
- A combination or **portfolio** of investments will have a risk and an expected return. Investors will have **indifference** curves, with each curve indicating equally acceptable combinations of risk and return.
- Portfolios which give the best possible return for their levels of risk lie on the **efficient** frontier. The **capital market** line touches the **efficient** frontier and also meets the point (zero risk; return on risk free investments).
- By holding a diversified portfolio an investor can avoid **unsystematic** risk, but he must still accept **systematic** risk. Systematic risk is the risk of a rise or fall in returns because of a general rise or fall in the market.
- A security's beta factor measures its volatility relative to that of the market.
    - Risk-free securities have a beta factor of **0**.
    - The market as a whole has a beta factor of **1**.
- The Capital Asset Pricing Model shows how the **systematic** risk of a security, measured by its beta factor, is related to the rate of return required from it by investors. Beta factors may be given for projects as well as for securities, and used to find required rates of return for projects.

  TRY QUESTIONS 25-30
- In managing working capital, Strict control must be maintained over debtors, to ensure that **credit** limits are not exceeded and that debtors pay by the due date.
- Stockholding should be kept under control, but not reduced to the point where shortages lead to **lost sales**.
- Creditors should be paid just early enough to avoid **costly penalties** or to secure **discounts**.
- The operating cycle, from payments to creditors through to receipts from debtors, summarises the flow of **working capital**.
- If a large surplus of cash is predicted, suitable **investments** should be sought.
- If a shortage of cash is predicted, one or more of the following actions should be taken to deal with the problem:
    - **Overdraft facilities might be arranged;**
    - **Short-term loans might be taken out;**
    - **Fixed asset purchases could be postponed;**
    - **Fixed asset sales could be brought forward;**
    - **Collection from debtors could be speeded up;**
    - **Payments to creditors could be delayed.**

  TRY QUESTIONS 31-39
- *Possible pitfalls*
    - **Understanding of risk**
    - **Theory v practice**
    - **Cost of capital calculations**
    - **Credit control explanations**
    - **Working capital calculations**

25 RISK AND MARKET EFFICIENCY (5/95) *36 mins*

(a) You are the company accountant with a medium-sized, privately owned company. The company has surplus funds which it does not believe it will be able to invest in company operations for at least five years. The majority shareholders are also the directors of the company and they do not wish the surplus funds to be distributed as dividends. A board meeting has therefore been called to discuss the proposal that the funds be invested in a portfolio of medium to long-term securities.

Three of the directors have recently attended a short course at the local university on 'Investment and the Management of Risk'. They make the following comments at the meeting, based on their interpretations of what they have learnt on the course.

'If we hold a portfolio of stocks, we need only consider the systematic risk of the securities.'

'As a cautious investor we must always consider total risk.'

'We should not buy anything if the expected return is less than that on the market as a whole, and certainly not if it is below the return on the risk-free asset.'

Required

(i) Explain to the members of the board the meaning of systematic, unsystematic and total risk and advise them, briefly, how all three types of risk can be measured.

(ii) Discuss the directors' comment. **12 Marks**

(b) The following two comments were drawn from separate articles in a highly respected financial newspaper.

'Market efficiency does not mean that share prices can be forecast with accuracy.'

'The research department of a large firm of stockbrokers has developed a multiple regression model, based on data collected between 1964 and 1994, which is claimed to give statistically significant results for predicting share prices.'

Required

Discuss these comments and explain why they are not contradictory. **8 Marks**

Total Marks = 20

26 CAPITAL MARKET LINE (5/92) *36 mins*

(a) Two investors, X and Y, have portfolios which lie on the Capital Market Line. X has one third of his funds invested at the risk-free rate, which is 12%, and the remainder in a market portfolio of equities. The expected return on his total portfolio is 18% with a standard deviation of 12%. Y's expected return on his total portfolio is 24%. Both investors can lend and borrow at the risk-free rate.

Required

(i) Explain, with supporting calculations, the composition of the expected return of *both* portfolios in terms of equity returns and fixed interest. **6 Marks**

(ii) Give a freehand graphical representation of the Capital Market Line showing the position of each investor's portfolio. **4 Marks**

(iii) On the assumption that X wishes to keep his portfolio on the Capital Market Line, calculate what standard deviation he would have to accept in order to increase his expected return to 20% and explain how the composition of his portfolio would change. **3 Marks**

(b) You are required to discuss the characteristics of an efficiently diversified portfolio of equities and the reasons why efficient diversification reduces investor risk. **7 Marks**

Total Marks = 20

27 COMPANY'S PORTFOLIO (11/97) *36 mins*

Z plc is a long-established company with interests mainly in retailing and property development. Its current market capitalisation is £750 million. The company trades almost exclusively in the UK but it is planning to expand overseas either by acquisition or joint venture within the next two years. The company has built up a portfolio of investments in UK equities and corporate and government debt. The aim of developing this investment portfolio is to provide a source of funds for its overseas expansion programme. It is currently 1 December 19X7. Summary information on the portfolio is given below.

Type of security	*Value £ million*	*Average % return over last 12 months*
UK equities	23.2	15.0
US securities	9.4	13.5
UK corporate debt	5.3	8.2
Long-term government debt	11.4	7.4
3-month Treasury bonds	3.2	6.0

Approximately 25% of the UK equities are in small companies' shares, some of them trading on the Alternative Investment Market. The average return on all UK equities over the past 12 months has been 12%. On US equities it has been 12.5%.

Ignore taxation throughout this question.

Required

(a) Discuss the advantages and disadvantages of holding such a portfolio of investments in the circumstances of Z plc. **10 Marks**

(b) One of Z plc's corporate debt investments is £50,000 nominal in a convertible loan stock 19X7/X9, currently selling at £106.50 per £100 of stock. The coupon rate is 6%. If not converted, it is repayable on 31 December 19X9 at par. Interest is payable annually and has just been paid for 19X7. Bonds of similar risk without a conversion feature are currently selling to return 7%.

The 19X7 date for conversion is 31 December 19X7 at a conversion ratio of 20 shares per £100 of stock. The ratio applicable for conversion in 19X8 is 18 shares per £100 of stock. The market price of the ordinary shares is 540 pence. At the time the bonds were purchased by Z plc in 19X6, the equity share price was 480 pence. Assume that interest rates have remained unchanged since the bonds were purchased.

Required

(i) Explain what is meant by the terms *conversion premium* and *conversion discount.*

(ii) Advise the company's treasurer about the factors to consider before deciding whether to convert the loan stock in 19X7 or 19X8. Include all relevant calculations in your advice. **10 Marks**

Total Marks = 20

28 PMS (5/93) *45 mins*

PMS is a private limited company with intentions of obtaining a stock market listing in the near future. The company is wholly equity financed at present but the directors are considering a new capital structure prior to it becoming a listed company.

PMS operates in an industry where the average asset beta is 1.2. The company's business risk is estimated to be similar to that of the industry as a whole. The current level of earnings before interest and taxes is £400,000. This earnings level is expected to be maintained for the foreseeable future.

The rate of return on riskless assets is at present 10% and the return on the market portfolio is 15%. These rates are post-tax and are expected to remain constant for the foreseeable future.

PMS is considering introducing debt into its capital structure by one of the following methods.

(a) £500,000 10% Debentures at par, secured on land and buildings of the company
(b) £1,000,000 12% Unsecured loan stock at par

The rate of corporation tax is expected to remain at 33% and interest on debt is tax deductible.

Required

(a) Calculate, for *each* of the *two* options:

(i) values of equity *and* total market values;
(ii) debt/equity ratios;
(iii) cost of equity. **9 Marks**

(b) List the main problems and costs which might arise for a company experiencing a period of severe financial difficulties. **6 Marks**

(c) 'Capital structure can have no influence on the value of the firm.'

Discuss this statement and comment briefly on the practical factors which a company may take into account when determining capital structure. **10 Marks**

Total Marks = 25

29 LEISURE INTERNATIONAL PLC (11/92) *45 mins*

The following is an extract from the balance sheet of Leisure International plc at 30 June 19X2.

	£'000
Ordinary shares of 50p each	5,200
Reserves	4,850
9% preference shares of £1 each	4,500
14% debentures	5,000
Total long-term funds	19,550

The ordinary shares are quoted at 80p. Assume that the market estimate of the next ordinary dividend is 4p, growing thereafter at 12% per annum indefinitely. The preference shares, which are irredeemable, are quoted at 72p and the debentures are quoted at par. Corporation tax is 33%.

Required

(a) Use the relevant data above to estimate the company's weighted average cost of capital (WACC), ie the return required by the providers of the three types of capital, using the respective market values as weighting factors. **6 Marks**

(b) Explain how the capital asset pricing model would be used as an alternative method of estimating the cost of equity, indicating what information would be required and how it would be obtained. **7 Marks**

(c) Assume that the debentures have recently been issued specifically to fund the company's expansion programme under which a number of projects are being considered. It has been suggested at a project appraisal meeting that because these projects are to be financed by the debentures, the cutoff rate for project acceptance should be the after-tax interest rate on the debentures rather than the WACC. Comment on this suggestion. **6 Marks**

(d) Assume that instead of raising £5 million of 14% debentures, the company had raised the equivalent amount in preference shares giving the same yield as the existing preference capital.

(i) Demonstrate that the returns offered to investors in the two securities are consistent with investor risk aversion.

(ii) Calculate how Leisure International plc's equity earnings would have been affected if the preference shares had been issued instead of the loan capital.

Assume income tax at 25% where relevant. **6 Marks**

Total Marks = 25

30 4D PLC (5/96) *36 mins*

(a) Briefly explain the factors which a company's treasurer should consider before investing in marketable securities. **6 Marks**

(b) 4D plc is a manufacturing company whose shares are listed on the London Stock Exchange. It is expecting to have surplus cash resources available for at least 12 months. The board has decided to develop an investment portfolio of marketable securities. The company's financial advisers have recommended four securities for the board to consider. These are as follows.

Security 1: Regularly traded shares in a medium-sized UK retailing company. The equity beta is quoted as 1.2.

Security 2: Shares in a relatively small but rapidly growing UK company in a high-technology industry. The shares have an equity beta of 1.6.

Security 3: Shares in an American bank which are listed on US stock exchanges but not in the UK. They are currently quoted at US$25.50. An equity beta is unavailable but 4D plc's stockbroker estimates that the required rate of return on the shares is 12% per annum.

Security 4: Short-dated government bonds.

The expected return on Treasury Bills is 5% per year, and that of the market is 12%.

4D plc's own equity beta is 0.8 and this is not expected to change in the foreseeable future.

The board can invest in one or more of these securities in any proportion.

Required

(i) Calculate the risk and expected return of the investment portfolio assuming 30% of available funds is invested in each of securities 1 and 2 and 20% in each of securities 3 and 4. **4 Marks**

(ii) Write a report for the board advising which, if any, of the four securities listed above should be considered as suitable investments for a company such as 4D plc. Also comment on the types of marketable securities, other than those listed above which could be considered by 4D plc. **10 Marks**

Total Marks = 20

31 CW LIMITED (11/98) *36 mins*

(a) Explain the term 'risk management' in respect of interest rates and discuss how interest rate risk might be managed. **8 Marks**

(b) CW Limited invests temporary cash surpluses in short-term deposits. The treasurer of CW Limited has forecast the following cash movements, and associated probabilities, for the next two months. By the end of month 3, the company will have much lower cash surpluses and possibly cash deficits.

		Probability
Cash available now	£200,000	1.0
Net cash flow in month 1	+£400,000	0.4
	+£600,000	0.6
Net cash flow in month 2	–£650,000	0.5
	–£750,000	0.5

Assume that all movements of cash take place on the last day of each month.

The structure of short-term interest rates is currently as follows.

Maturity period	*Annual yield*
1 month	6.5%
2 months	6.6%

Economic forecasters expect interest rates to rise, and in one month's time they are expected to be 6.8% per annum for one-month deposits. Transaction costs are £150 per transaction below £600,000 and £200 per transaction in excess of this amount.

Required

(i) Calculate the estimated cash balances at the end of months 1 and 2.

(ii) Recommend, with reasons, how the cash surpluses available between now and the end of month 2 should be deposited to maximise before-tax income.

12 Marks

Total Marks = 20

32 RT PLC (Specimen paper) *45 mins*

(a) RT plc has forecast the following cash movements for the next six months.

Cash available now	£2,000,000
Inflow in two months	£4,000,000
Outflow in four months	£2,000,000
Outflow in six months	£4,000,000

Assume that all movements of cash take place on the last day of each two-month period.

The structure of short-term interest rates is as follows.

Current		*Expected in 2 months*		*Expected in 4 months*	
Maturity period	*Annual yield* %	*Maturity period*	*Annual yield* %	*Maturity period*	*Annual yield* %
2 months	7.3	2 months	8.0	2 months	8.3
4 months	7.4	4 months	8.1	4 months	8.4
6 months	7.5	6 months	8.2	6 months	8.3

The company invests surplus cash balances in marketable securities. Company policy is to hold such securities to maturity once they are purchased. Every purchase transaction of marketable securities costs £100.

Required

(i) Calculate which securities should be purchased to maximise before-tax income.

(ii) Discuss the criteria that would influence a company's procedure for selecting marketable securities. **13 Marks**

(b) *Required*

Comment on the following statements.

(i) 'Interest rates have a strong influence on the demand for liquidity and an apparently weak influence upon business investment.'

(ii) 'The highly sophisticated financial systems of developed countries have greatly reduced the need for companies to hold cash balances.'

(iii) 'Cash management models sound a good idea in theory, but they are of no practical use to most companies.' **12 Marks**

Total Marks = 25

33 RECENT RESEARCH (11/97) *45 mins*

(a) Recent research has shown that a large percentage of small company failures were due to poor financial management skills and poor credit management.

Required

Explain the problems faced by small companies in respect of credit management, and discuss internal actions which they could take to minimise the effects of these problems. **8 Marks**

(b) A medium-sized manufacturing company is suffering a fall in sales of many of its product lines. It is reviewing its business strategy and the heads of all departments have been asked to review their activities. The accounting department has been asked to review specifically the company's credit control policy. At present the company offers its goods to customers on 30 days' credit (from date of invoice), subject to satisfactory trade references. It does not offer a discount for prompt payment.

Required

Assume you are a management accountant working in the company's credit control department. Write a report to the Credit Manager which:

(i) discusses the contribution that credit control policy can make to overall business strategy;

(ii) assesses the advantages and disadvantages of introducing discounts for prompt payment. Include in your assessment a calculation and comment on the true cost of discounts. For the sake of your discussion you should assume a 1% discount for payment within 10 days if the normal credit period allowed continues at 30 days. **12 Marks**

Total Marks = 20

34 DISCOUNT (5/93) *45 mins*

(a) A company offers its goods to customers on 30 days credit, subject to satisfactory trade references. It also offers a 2% discount if payment is made within 10 days of the date of invoice.

Required

(i) Calculate the cost to the company of offering the discount, assuming a 365-day year.

(ii) Compare offering discounts to customers to encourage early settlement of bills with using debt factors.

(iii) Describe two methods, other than debt factoring, that a company might use to obtain finance by using debtors as security. **15 Marks**

(b) Two aspects of working capital policy which require managerial decisions are the level of current assets and the manner in which they are financed.

Required

Discuss aggressive, moderate and conservative policies in these areas. **10 Marks**

Total Marks = 25

35 V PLC (11/96) *36 mins*

V plc manufactures engineering equipment. The company has received an order from a new customer for 5 machines at £5,000 each. V plc's terms of sale are 10 per cent of the sales value payable with order. This deposit has been received from the new customer. The balance is payable 12 months after acceptance of the order by V plc.

V plc's past experience has been that only 60 per cent of similar customers pay within 12 months. Customers who do not pay within 12 months are referred to a debt collection agency to pursue the debt. The agency has in the past had a 50 per cent success rate of obtaining immediate payment once they became involved. When they are unsuccessful the debt is written off by V plc. The agency's fee is £500 per order, payable by V plc with the request for service. This fee is not refundable if the debt is not recovered.

You are an accountant in V plc's credit control department and, based on the company's past experience and on discussions with the sales and credit managers, you do not expect the pattern of payment and collection to change.

Incremental costs associated with the new customer's order are expected to be £3,600 per machine. 70 per cent of these costs are for materials and are incurred shortly after the order has been accepted. The remaining 30 per cent is for all other costs which you can assume are paid shortly before delivery, that is in 12 months' time. The company is not at present operating at full production capacity.

V plc's opportunity cost of capital is 16 per cent. Ignore taxation.

Required

Write a report to the Credit Control Manager which:

(a) evaluates, from a purely financial point of view, whether V plc should accept the order from the new customer on the basis of the above information; **9 Marks**

(b) comments on what other factors should be considered before a decision to grant credit is taken; **6 Marks**

(c) discusses, briefly, methods which might be used to evaluate the creditworthiness of this particular customer. **5 Marks**

Total Marks = 20

36 MP LIMITED (11/98) *36 mins*

MP Limited is a manufacturing company which trades with a large number of suppliers of raw materials, components etc. The company's financial manager has asked you, her assistant, to review the terms of trade and their associated costs. As part of the exercise, you randomly choose three regular suppliers of one particular component. They have the following terms:

Supplier A charges a fixed penalty of 2% of invoice value for late payment

Supplier B charges compound interest at 2% per 30-day period after the due date of payment

Supplier C offers a 2% discount if payment is made within 10 days of invoice date but charges simple interest at 10% per annum on the invoice value if payment is after the due date

Assume that the due date for payment in each case is 30 days but that MP Limited's current credit control policy is to take an average of 90 days to pay these suppliers' invoices.

To simplify your calculations, assume also that MP Limited purchases £1,000 worth of goods from each supplier every month.

Required

Write a report to the financial manager which includes:

(a) a calculation of the annualised interest rate (ie percent per annum) for each of the three suppliers. **8 Marks**

(b) a discussion of the arguments for and against using trade credit as a source of funds, in general and from MP Limited's point of view, given their current credit policy. **8 Marks**

(c) a discussion of the advantages and disadvantages to MP Limited of introducing standard terms of trade with which all suppliers will have to conform. **4 Marks**

Total Marks = 20

37 OVERDRAFT (11/94) *45 mins*

XYZ plc is an unlisted company which has been trading for almost 10 years. The board of directors is concerned about the cost and level of the company's overdraft which have been increasing over the past two years. The company's financial manager estimates the deterioration will continue into next year (19X5) and beyond unless action is taken. The directors agree that the company should take action to improve its liquidity and debt collection procedures and, as a consequence, reduce the overdraft. The options available are as follows.

(a) Offer a cash discount to all credit customers of 1.5% for payment within 10 days. The normal terms of trade allow for 60 days although many customers regularly exceed this limit. Approximately 70% of sales are on credit and all credit customers trade regularly up to their maximum credit limit. If this scheme is introduced, approximately half of all credit customers are expected to take advantage. Bad debts are expected to fall by 50%.

(b) Employ a debt factoring company. The factor has agreed to accept 90% of XYZ plc's credit customers and will charge a commission of 2% of acceptable debtors' value. Finance charges will be 11%, which is 5% over base rate. XYZ plc will take the maximum finance available and use it to turn the overdraft into a cash balance. The use of a debt factor is expected to result in a saving of £65,000 on XYZ plc's in-company credit management costs.

(c) Raise £500,000 by taking out a 10-year mortgage secured on the company's premises and use the proceeds to reduce the overdraft. The interest rate on this debt will be 9%.

XYZ plc pays overdraft interest at 4% over base rate. Its opportunity cost of capital is 12%. Summary financial information is as follows.

	19X5 Forecast £'000
Turnover	4,850
Cost of sales	2,862
Bad debts	48
Profit after tax	325
Stock	455
Trade debtors	850
Total current assets	1,305
Trade creditors	550
Overdraft	565
Total current liabilities	1,115
Net current assets	190
Shareholders' funds	1,575
Director's loan (13% unsecured 19Y0)	450

Required

Evaluate for *each* of the *three* options:

(a) the net financial benefit to the company

(b) the effect on current ratios and debtors' days

and recommend, with reasons, which should be chosen to meet the directors' objectives.

Total Marks = 25

38 KL LTD (11/95) *36 mins*

It is currently November 19X5. KL Limited is a privately owned manufacturer of sports equipment in the UK. Information about the company is as follows.

(a) The business is growing modestly at present but faster growth is planned.

(b) The business is seasonal with sales peaking in the autumn.

(c) KL Limited is anticipating cashflow problems as a result of its planned growth. It has prepared a cash budget for 19X6, details of which are given below.

(d) The current overdraft facility is £150,000. The bank has indicated it would be unwilling to increase this amount without a substantial increase in the interest rate payable, which is currently 5% over bank base rate.

(e) The company has 15 shareholders at present. Four of the shareholders are directors of the company, owning 60% of the share capital between them. The other shareholders take no interest in the running of the business and, although the company is unlisted, shares have changed hands on a few occasions.

(f) None of the director-shareholders will be in a position to invest capital in the business for the next 2 to 3 years.

Cashflow forecast for 19X6 (£'000)

	Jan	*Feb*	*Mar*	*Apr*	*May*	*June*	*July*	*Aug*	*Sept*	*Oct*	*Nov*	*Dec*	*Total*
Receipts from customers	175	135	115	75	50	50	65	75	90	150	215	295	1,490
Other income			45			45			45			45	180
Total inflows	175	135	160	75	50	95	65	75	135	150	215	340	1,670
Payments to trade suppliers	53	41	35	23	15	15	20	23	27	53	75	103	480
Wages and salaries	53	53	53	53	55	57	57	55	55	53	53	53	650
Other operating expenses	25	25	25	30	30	30	35	35	35	35	35	40	380
Capital expenditure			45			35			40				120
Dividends payable		100											100
Tax payable									65				65
Total outflows	131	219	158	106	100	137	112	113	222	141	163	96	1,795
Net cash inflow/ (outflow)	45	(84)	3	(31)	(50)	(42)	(47)	(38)	(87)	10	52	144	(125)
Opening bank bal	50	95	11	14	(17)	(67)	(109)	(156)	(193)	(280)	(271)	(219)	50
Closing bank bal	95	11	14	(17)	(67)	(109)	(156)	(193)	(280)	(271)	(219)	(75)	(75)

The following information is also available.

(a) All sales are on credit. The company's usual terms of trade allow 60 days' credit. Customers take, on average, 90 days to pay. This has been allowed for in the cash budget. Sales in the three months to the end of December 19X6 are expected to be £660,000. No increases in selling prices are planned.

(b) Production is evenly scheduled throughout the year and finished goods for stock are stored until the peak selling period. The company estimates stocks of finished goods will be £170,000 higher at the end of December 19X6 than at the beginning of the year.

(c) The company's premises are all owned by the company. Other income is rental from letting some of its premises.

(d) Suppliers, on average, allow KL Limited 6 weeks' credit although the company typically takes up to 90 days to pay. Purchases for the three months to the end of December 19X6 are expected to be £231,000. All other expenses are paid in the month in which they arise.

(e) The capital expenditure forecast for 19X6 is for the following items of expenditure.

March 19X6	New plant and machinery	£45,000
June 19X6	New motor vehicles	£35,000
September 19X6	Building renovations	£40,000

Further capital expenditure is planned in 19X7.

Required

(a) Estimate the profit before depreciation of the company for 19X6. Use whatever reasonable assumptions you think necessary, but state, briefly, what they are.

6 Marks

(b) Review the cash budget and advise the board of KL Limited on possible actions it may take to improve its budgeted cashflow for the year and the likely effect of these actions on the company's business. Make whatever reasonable assumptions you think necessary.

14 Marks

Total Marks = 20

39 MILLER-ORR MODEL (5/97) *36 mins*

(a) Explain the advantages and disadvantages to a company of paying suppliers by using an electronic funds transfer system instead of cheques by post. **5 Marks**

(b) The treasurer of a local government department is reviewing her cash management procedures. She plans to introduce the use of cash management models and has asked you to investigate their applicability to the department. The following information is available.

(i) The department has agreed with its bank that it will maintain a minimum daily cash balance of £15,000. Severe financial penalties will apply if this balance is not maintained.

(ii) A forecast of daily cash movements for the next twelve months shows a standard deviation of daily cash flows of £3,000.

(iii) The daily interest rate is at present 0.0236% and this is not expected to change for the foreseeable future.

(iv) The transaction cost for each sale or purchase is £25.

Assume you are a newly recruited accountant in the department.

Required

Write a report to the treasurer which discusses:

(i) the advantages and disadvantages of cash management models over more traditional methods of cash forecasting, making specific reference to their applicability to a public sector organisation such as a local authority; **6 Marks**

(ii) how one such model, the Miller-Orr, would operate in practice, using the information given above. Your report should include calculations of the upper and lower limits for cash balances and the return point. Assume a spread of £26,820. **9 Marks**

Note. The Miller-Orr formula is given in the CIMA *Mathematical Tables* booklet. You do not need it to calculate the spread as this is given above, but you should explain the terms used in the Miller-Orr model.

Total Marks = 20

DO YOU KNOW? - INVESTMENT DECISIONS

- *Check that you can fill in the blanks in the statements before you attempt any questions. If in doubt, you should go back to your BPP Study Text and revise first.*
- Key methods of evaluating capital projects are the .... method; the ....method; the .... method.
- With single period capital rationing and divisible projects, the projects which earn the highest .... should be selected. If projects are not divisible, trial and error must be used and the NPV available from different combinations of projects tested.
- The effect of undertaking a capital project will be to increase or decrease tax payments each year. These incremental cash flows should be included in the cash flows of the project for discounting to arrive at the project's NPV. When taxation is included in the cash flows, a .... required rate of return should be used.
- The .... can be used instead of the dividend valuation model to establish an equity cost of capital to use in project appraisal.
- .... is a technique which attempts to quantify non-economic social costs and benefits, translates them into monetary values and incorporate them into the evaluation of investment decisions. A 'social' discount rate rather than a financial discount rate should be applied to the cash flows.
- .... is a halfway house between .... and not assigning monetary values to social costs and benefits at all.

  TRY QUESTIONS 40-46
- There are many different ways of valuing a company, including the following.
  - ....
  - ....
  - ....
  - ....
  - ....
- To use the .... method, we must first establish a P/E ratio using listed companies in the same industry. Such a ratio may need adjusting, for example if the company being valued is unlisted.
- A takeover may involve an offer to shareholders in the target company of .... ; .... ; .... or some combination of these.
- In a ...., the ratio of exchange (for example two shares for five) must be acceptable to the shareholders of both companies.
  - Shareholders will be particularly concerned about post-takeover earnings per share and post-merger asset backing.
  - Holders of the shares valued on the lower P/E ratio will suffer a loss of earnings.
  - This loss of earnings may be compensated for by an increase in overall earnings because of synergy.
- Takeovers are subject to regulation by .... and to the ....Code.
- In a ...., a division of a company or the whole company is sold to a management team. Substantial external finance is often required, leaving the bought-out business with a heavy burden of interest payments.

  TRY QUESTIONS 47-51
- *Possible pitfalls*

  Write down the mistakes you know you should avoid.

DID YOU KNOW? - INVESTMENT DECISIONS

- *Could you fill in the blanks? The answers are in bold. Use this page for revision purposes as you approach the exam.*
- Key methods of evaluating capital projects are the **accounting rate of return** method; the **payback** method; the **discounted cash flow (DCF)** method.
- With single period capital rationing and divisible projects, the projects which earn the highest **NPV per £1 of capital invested** should be selected. If projects are not divisible, trial and error must be used and the NPV available from different combinations of projects tested.
- The effect of undertaking a capital project will be to increase or decrease tax payments each year. These incremental cash flows should be included in the cash flows of the project for discounting to arrive at the project's NPV. When taxation is included in the cash flows, a **post-tax** required rate of return should be used.
- The **CAPM** can be used instead of the dividend valuation model to establish an equity cost of capital to use in project appraisal.
- **Cost benefit analysis** is a technique which attempts to quantify non-economic social costs and benefits, translates them into monetary values and incorporate them into the evaluation of investment decisions. A 'social' discount rate rather than a financial discount rate should be applied to the cash flows.
- **Cost effectiveness analysis** is a halfway house between **cost benefit analysis** and not assigning monetary values to social costs and benefits at all.

  TRY QUESTIONS 40-46
- There are many different ways of valuing a company, including the following.
  - **Balance sheet value**
  - **Replacement cost of assets**
  - **Realisable values of assets**
  - **The dividend growth model**
  - **The P/E ratio model**
- To use the **P/E ratio** method, we must first establish a P/E ratio using listed companies in the same industry. Such a ratio may need adjusting, for example if the company being valued is unlisted.
- A takeover may involve an offer to shareholders in the target company of **cash**; **shares**; **loan stock** or some combination of these.
- In a **share exchange**, the ratio of exchange (for example two shares for five) must be acceptable to the shareholders of both companies.
  - Shareholders will be particularly concerned about post-takeover earnings per share and post-merger asset backing.
  - Holders of the shares valued on the lower P/E ratio will suffer a loss of earnings.
  - This loss of earnings may be compensated for by an increase in overall earnings because of synergy.
- Takeovers are subject to regulation by the **Competition Commission** (formerly the Monopolies and Mergers Commission) and to the **City** Code.
- In a **management buyout**, a division of a company or the whole company is sold to a management team. Substantial external finance is often required, leaving the bought-out business with a heavy burden of interest payments.

  TRY QUESTIONS 47-51
- *Possible pitfalls*
  - **Cash flow adjustments**
  - **Describing pros and cons of methods**
  - **Adjusting the discount rate**
  - **Structuring of a report**
  - **Share valuation calculations**

40 RP PLC (5/98) *36 mins*

Harry is Financial Manager of RP plc. He is nearing retirement. You have been appointed as his deputy with a view to taking over from him in 12 months' time.

The company is considering an investment in a new product which will cost £1,200,000 in new machinery and will result in profit before depreciation and tax of £375,000 per annum in real terms for five years. At the end of the five years, the machinery can be sold for its written-down book value. The investment will require working capital at the *beginning* of each year as follows (figures in real terms).

Year	*1*	*2*	*3*	*4*	*5*
Amount (£)	100,000	200,000	300,000	400,000	500,000

Harry is proposing to evaluate the investment using the company's (nominal) weighted average cost of capital (WACC) of 16%.

The following notes are relevant.

1 At the end of year 5, the total working capital can be released in cash back to the company.

2 Inflation is expected to be 4% per annum on all operating cash flows and working capital for the period under review.

3 The company pays tax at the rate of 33%. There is a 12-month time lag for tax payments or refunds.

4 Tax relief is available on capital expenditure at 25% on a reducing balance. The company also depreciates its plant and equipment on this basis.

5 Assume all cash flows occur at the end of the year *except* the purchase of fixed assets (that is, the new machinery) and working capital. Both these items of expenditure occur at the beginning of the year.

Required

(a) Evaluate the investment using the company's WACC, as suggested by Harry.
12 Marks

(b) Whatever your own answer to part (a), assume the results of your financial evaluation suggest the investment is not worthwhile (ie the NPV is negative). You think that some of Harry's assumptions are unrealistic. In particular, you are concerned about the uncertainty surrounding each year's cash flows and the use of the WACC as the discount rate.

Write a memo to Harry which explains how the evaluation might be refined, or developed, to overcome your concerns.

Note. You are not required to revise your calculations for part (a) of the question to answer part (b) of the question.
8 Marks

Total Marks = 20

41 ALTERNATIVE SITES *36 mins*

A company is considering a project involving the outlay of £300,000 which it estimates will generate cash flows over its two year life with the probabilities shown in the following table.

Cash flows for project

Year 1

Cash flow	*Probability*
£	
100,000	0.25
200,000	0.50
300,000	0.25
	1.00

Year 2

If cash flow in Year 1 is:	*there is a probability of:*	*that cash flow in Year 2 will be:*
£		£
100,000	0.25	Nil
	0.50	100,000
	0.25	200,000
	1.00	
200,000	0.25	100,000
	0.50	200,000
	0.25	300,000
	1.00	
300,000	0.25	200,000
	0.50	300,000
	0.25	350,000
	1.00	

All cash flows should be treated as being received at the end of the year.

The company has a choice of undertaking this project at either of two sites (A or B) whose costs are identical and are included in the above outlay. In terms of the technology of the project itself, the location will have no effect on the outcome.

If the company chooses site B it has the facility to abandon the project at the end of the first year and to sell the site to an interested purchaser for £150,000. This facility is not available at site A.

The company's investment criterion for this type of project is 10% DCF. Its policy would be to abandon the project on site B and to sell the site at the end of year 1 if its expected future cash flows for year 2 were less than the disposal value.

Required

(a) Calculate the NPV of the project on site A. **7 Marks**

(b) (i) Explain, based on the data given, the specific circumstances in which the company would abandon the project on site B.

(ii) Calculate the NPV of the project on site B taking account of the abandonment facility. **11 Marks**

(c) Calculate the financial effect of the facility for abandoning the project on site B stating whether it is positive or negative. **2 Marks**

Ignore tax and inflation.

Total Marks = 20

42 CBA LTD (5/97) *36 mins*

(a) Assume you are the new financial manager for CBA Ltd, a company which has always evaluated its investments using IRR as the selection criterion. The company's managing director thinks that NPV may be a better method, and is aware that some companies use multiple methods, for example NPV in combination with a non-discounting technique such as payback or accounting rate of return. He has asked for your opinion.

Required

Write a report to the managing director which:

(i) explains the theoretical differences between IRR and NPV and comments on any practical aspects which might explain CBA Ltd's past preference for IRR;

(ii) discusses the advantages and disadvantages of using multiple methods for the evaluation of investments. **10 Marks**

(b) Regulatory bodies are, typically, established to protect consumers and ensure monopoly or near monopoly suppliers do not abuse their position for financial gain. (Examples in the UK are Ofgas (gas industry) and Ofwat (water industry).)

Required

(i) Explain the factors a regulator might take into account when discussing pricing policies with the management of a regulated industry.

(ii) Describe two other activities a regulator might perform (in addition to price controls) and explain why it might be necessary to retain a regulatory body even when competition enters an industry (for example in telecommunications in the UK). **10 Marks**

Total Marks = 20

43 THREE OPPORTUNITIES (5/96) *36 mins*

The directors of XYZ plc wish to expand the company's operations. However, they are not prepared to borrow at the present time to finance capital investment. The directors have therefore decided to use the company's cash resources for the expansion programme.

Three possible investment opportunities have been identified. Only £400,000 is available in cash and the directors intend to limit their capital expenditure over the next 12 months to this amount. The projects are not divisible (ie cannot be scaled down) and none of them can be postponed. The following cashflows do not allow for inflation which is expected to be 10% per annum constant for the foreseeable future.

Expected net cashflows (including residual values)

Project	*Initial investment*	*Year 1*	*Year 2*	*Year 3*
	£	£	£	£
A	–350,000	95,000	110,000	200,000
B	–105,000	45,000	45,000	45,000
C	–35,000	–40,000	–25,000	125,000

The company's shareholders currently require a return of 15% nominal on their investment.

Ignore taxation.

Required

(a) (i) Calculate the expected net present value and profitability indexes of the three projects; and

(ii) comment on which project(s) should be chosen for investment, assuming the company can invest surplus cash in the money market at 10%. (*Note.* You should assume that the £400,000 expenditure limit is the absolute maximum the company wishes to spend.) **10 Marks**

(b) Discuss whether the company's decision not to borrow, thereby limiting investment expenditure, is in the best interests of its shareholders. **10 Marks**

Total Marks = 20

44 CP LIMITED (5/99) *36 mins*

The board of directors of CP Ltd is considering two investments, each of which is expected to have a life of five years. The company does not have either the physical capacity or the funds to undertake both investments. Forecast profits and other financial data for the two investments are as follows.

Investment 1

Year	*0*	*1*	*2*	*3*	*4*	*5*
	£'000	£'000	£'000	£'000	£'000	£'000
Fixed assets	(500)					
Working capital	(50)					
Forecast sales		370	500	510	515	475
Forecast costs		300	325	335	330	325
Finance charges		15	15	15	15	15
Depreciation		100	100	100	100	100
Profit before tax		(45)	60	60	70	35

Investment 2

Year	*0*	*1*	*2*	*3*	*4*	*5*
	£'000	£'000	£'000	£'000	£'000	£'000
Fixed assets	(450)					
Working capital	(50)					
Forecast sales		420	510	575	550	510
Forecast costs		310	385	420	400	350
Finance charges		15	15	15	15	15
Depreciation		80	80	80	80	80
Profit before tax		15	30	60	55	65

Additional information

- The company pays tax at 33%. Writing down allowances are available on the initial investment in both projects at 25% per year. Tax is payable/receivable one year in arrears.
- The data is in real terms, ie it contains no increases for inflation. This has been ignored on the grounds that both sales and costs are expected to increase by 5% per year.
- The company's nominal cost of capital is 12% per year. Its target accounting rate of return (average profit before tax as a percentage of average investment) is 25%.
- All cash flows may be assumed to occur at the end of the year except the initial capital cost and working capital.
- For each project the value of working capital expected to be released back to the project's cash flows at the end of year 5 is £50,000 nominal. There will be no other terminal value of the investment.

- The £50,000 left over if investment 2 is chosen (ie the difference between the initial investment of £550,000 in investment 1 and £500,000 in investment 2) could be invested in the money market at between 6% and 7%.

Required

Assume you are the financial manager with CP Ltd. Recommend to the board which investment, if either, should be selected using whatever methods of evaluation you think appropriate. Include in your report a discussion of the various methods of evaluation and any non-financial factors which might be relevant to the decision.

Note. Your cash flows should be presented in *nominal* (as opposed to *real*) terms.

20 Marks

45 ADJUSTED PRESENT VALUE (5/98) *36 mins*

DT plc is a quoted company. The directors have been evaluating a cost-saving project which will require £1.9 million capital expenditure on new machinery. The directors expect the capital investment to provide cost savings of £300,000 per annum indefinitely.

The company is at present all equity financed. The discount rate which it applies to investment decisions of this nature is 16%. The directors believe the current capital structure fails to take advantage of the tax benefits of debt and propose to finance the new project with undated debt secured on the company's assets. The current rate of interest required by the market on corporate debt of this risk and maturity is 9%. The costs of issue, which are not tax-deductible, are expected to be 5% of the gross proceeds of issue. The company intends to issue sufficient debt to cover the cost of capital expenditure and the costs of issue.

The company's marginal tax rate is 33%.

Required

(a) Using the information given for DT plc, calculate the adjusted present value of the investment and the adjusted discount rate, and explain the circumstances in which this adjusted discount rate may be used to evaluate future investments. **10 Marks**

(b) A finance lease is being considered as an alternative method of financing. DT plc has been told it could lease the machinery over 5 years. The terms would be 5 annual payments of £425,000 payable at the beginning of each year. Assume the payments are net of tax.

  (i) Calculate the net present value of the lease, using whatever discount rate(s) you think appropriate, given the information in the scenario, and comment briefly on your answer. **5 Marks**

  (ii) Discuss the advantages and disadvantages of leasing as compared with long-term debt, and comment on whether the choice of method should affect the investment decision. **5 Marks**

Total Marks = 20

46 MEGAPOWER PLC (11/92) *63 mins*

It is now 19X2. In 19W9 MegaPower plc began construction of MAGNAPHALL, the UK's first privately owned nuclear power station.

MAGNAPHALL's commercial viability was determined in 19W7 on the basis of a capital investment appraisal exercise which showed MAGNAPHALL achieving a pre-tax IRR of 17%, which is above the hurdle rate of 15% specified by MegaPower plc's capital investment appraisal rules.

A nuclear reactor generates heat from the fission of uranium fuel rods in a reactor chamber. The reactor chamber is cooled by water passing through the chamber in pipes. The super-heated steam which emerges from the pipes is used to power turbines which produce electricity.

A uranium fuel rod has a useful life of about four years. Upon being extracted from the reactor chamber at the end of its life as spent uranium, it must be stored for an indefinite period in an appropriate environment. One practical use for spent uranium is to reprocess it into a low grade form of plutonium for use in a variety of nuclear and conventional weapons systems.

By the end of 19X2, MAGNAPHALL is approaching completion. The turbines are in place and operational. The reactor still requires work costing £45 million to complete. It is forecast that MAGNAPHALL is capable of being completed and fully commissioned by 1 January 19X4. MAGNAPHALL would then operate at full capacity for twelve years delivering electricity to regional electricity distribution companies and private buyers. It is forecast that revenues from such deliveries will be £18 million per year.

Since 19W7 a variety of developments have occurred which have brought MAGNAPHALL's future into question. Practical experience gained in decommissioning nuclear reactors and storing spent uranium has revealed that these exercises cost far more than was originally anticipated. The end of the cold war has eliminated the demand for weapons grade plutonium.

MegaPower plc is now considering three options:

(a) completing and commissioning MAGNAPHALL as originally planned;

(b) abandoning MAGNAPHALL;

(c) converting MAGNAPHALL into a gas-fired power station. This would involve abandoning the reactor and constructing a gas furnace to power the turbines.

At the end of 19X2, MegaPower plc's Management Science Unit appraises the viability of MAGNAPHALL again. It is found that by the end of 19X2 costs of £180 million have been incurred. It is forecast that spent uranium storage costs will be £5 million per year from 19X8 onwards and the cost of decommissioning MAGNAPHALL at the end of its life will be £200 million.

The Management Science Unit reports that the analysis of marginal costs and revenues shows that MAGNAPHALL has a pre-tax IRR of 27% and that the project should proceed to completion.

The Inland Revenue will allow writing down allowances (on a 25% reducing balance) to be claimed only once MAGNAPHALL has commenced operations. However, if MAGNAPHALL is abandoned, then all capital costs incurred may be claimed as an immediate loss for tax purposes. The current rate of corporation tax is 33%, and for simplicity it may be assumed that tax is payable in the year in which profit is earned.

After he receives the Management Science Unit's report, MegaPower plc's Finance Director makes the following statement:

'Using a pocket calculator and the same figures supplied to the Management Science Unit, I have determined that the pre-tax IRR generated by MAGNAPHALL is 12% - and MAGNAPHALL should therefore be abandoned. I have never had much confidence in these people and I am sure that the mess we are now in with MAGNAPHALL is largely their fault.'

Required

(a) Explain and reconcile the two alternative IRRs referred to above. You may find it helpful to use a diagram (which need not be perfectly to scale). **11 Marks**

(b) On the basis of the information supplied, prepare a report for MegaPower plc's Board advising on appropriate rules for capital investment appraisal and stating whether MAGNAPHALL should be completed or abandoned. **17 Marks**

(c) Comment on a report in the *New Scientist* to the effect that if MegaPower plc adopts the third option (conversion of MAGNAPHALL to gas power) it will result in 'the most inefficient gas-fired power station ever built'. **7 Marks**

Total Marks = 35

47 TUTORIAL QUESTION: BASES OF VALUATION

The directors of Carmen plc, a large conglomerate, are considering the acquisition of the entire share capital of Manon Ltd, which manufactures a range of engineering machinery. Neither company has any long-term debt capital. The directors of Carmen plc believe that if Manon is taken over, the business risk of Carmen will not be affected.

The accounting reference date of Manon is 31 July. Its balance sheet as on 31 July 19X4 is expected to be as follows.

		£	£
Fixed assets (net of depreciation)			651,600
Current assets:	stocks and work in progress	515,900	
	debtors	745,000	
	bank balances	158,100	
			1,149,000
			2,070,600
Current liabilities:	creditors	753,600	
	bank overdraft	862,900	
			1,616,500
			454,100
Capital and reserves:	issued ordinary shares of £1 each		50,000
	distributable reserves		404,100
			454,100

Manon's summarised financial record for the five years to 31 July 19X4 is as follows.

Year ended 31 July	*19X0*	*19X1*	*19X2*	*19X3*	*19X4 (estimated)*
	£	£	£	£	£
Profit before extraordinary items	30,400	69,000	49,400	48,200	53,200
Extraordinary items	2,900	(2,200)	(6,100)	(9,800)	(1,000)
Profit after extraordinary items	33,300	66,800	43,300	38,400	52,200
Less dividends	20,500	22,600	25,000	25,000	25,000
Added to reserves	12,800	44,200	18,300	13,400	27,200

The following additional information is available.

(a) There have been no changes in the issued share capital of Manon Limited during the past five years.

(b) The estimated values of Manon's fixed assets and stocks and work in progress as on 31 July 19X4 are as follows.

	Replacement cost	*Realisable value*
	£	£
Fixed assets	725,000	450,000
Stocks and work in progress	550,000	570,000

(c) It is expected that 2% of Manon's debtors at 31 July 19X4 will be uncollectable.

(d) The cost of capital of Carmen plc is 9%. The directors of Manon Ltd estimate that the shareholders of Manon require a minimum return of 12% per annum from their investment in the company.

(e) The current P/E ratio of Carmen plc is 12. Quoted companies with business activities and profitability similar to those of Manon have P/E ratios of approximately 10, although these companies tend to be much larger than Manon.

Required

(a) Estimate the value of the total equity of Manon Ltd as on 31 July 19X4 using each of the following bases:

(i) balance sheet value;
(ii) replacement cost;
(iii) realisable value;
(iv) the Gordon dividend growth model;
(v) the P/E ratio model.

(b) Explain the role and limitations of each of the above five valuation bases in the process by which a price might be agreed for the purchase by Carmen plc of the total equity capital of Manon Ltd.

(c) State and justify briefly the approximate range within which the purchase price is likely to be agreed.

Ignore taxation.

Approaching the question

1 This may at first appear to be a long question, but part (a) is broken down into five small parts, and this will enable you to work through the data systematically.

2 The balance sheet value is simply the value of the shareholders' interest in the business as shown in the balance sheet. The values of certain assets must then be adjusted to get replacement cost (what it would cost to replace them) and realisable value (the amount of cash they could be turned into).

3 A formula for the Gordon dividend growth model is $\frac{D_1}{r-g}$, where D_1 is the dividend one year hence, r is the required return and g is the dividend growth rate. In this case, you have to estimate a growth rate. One possibility is to take the average growth rate over 19X0 to 19X4. This is found by taking the fourth root of the fraction 19X4 dividend/19X0 dividend.

4 The P/E ratio valuation is simply earnings × P/E ratio. The problem here is to select an appropriate ratio.

5 In part (b), you must evaluate critically the estimates made in part (a). You should be particularly concerned with the reliability of any estimates or predictions made, and with the relevance of the bases of evaluation to a purchaser intending to run the business as a going concern.

6 In part (c), you should identify the lowest price the vendors might accept and the highest price the purchaser might offer.

48 MR JONES (5/95) *36 mins*

(a) RD plc has made a takeover bid for LO plc. RD plc's share price has been performing well in recent months as the market believes its Managing Director, Mr Jones, has the ability to improve dramatically the company's earnings. The acquisition of LO plc, an erratic performer in recent years, seems to be a sensible move in commercial terms. However, the market does not react to the terms of the bid as Mr Jones expected and he finds RD plc's share price falls.

A summary of the financial data before the bid is as follows.

	RD plc	*LO plc*
Number of shares in issue	5 million	15 million
Earnings available to ordinary shareholders	£2.5 million	£7.5 million
P/E ratio	12.5	7.5

Mr Jones' estimated financial data post-acquisition:

Estimated market capitalisation	£125 million
Estimated share price	£8.33
Estimated EPS	£0.67
Estimated equivalent value of one old LO plc share	£5.55

The offer is 10 RD plc shares for 15 LO plc shares. At the time of the bid announcement, no information is related other than the bid terms and the comment by Mr Jones that he hopes to 'turn LO round'. The expected rate of return on RD plc's equity capital is 15% per annum constant.

Required

(i) Suggest how Mr Jones might have calculated post-acquisition values.

(ii) Write a short report suggesting a probable post-acquisition share price and advising shareholders in both RD plc and LO plc on whether the bid should proceed. **13 Marks**

(b) It is later announced that the proposed merger is expected to result in immediate administrative savings of £5 million. Sales of redundant assets by the end of the first year are expected to realise £10 million. Net income is expected to increase by £7.5 million per annum for the foreseeable future as a result of a more aggressive marketing policy for LO plc's business.

Note. You should assume all figures are net of tax.

Required

Explain how this new information would affect your estimate of a probable post-acquisition share price, and comment on how it might affect LO plc's bargaining position. **7 Marks**

Total Marks = 20

49 PROVINCIAL PLC (11/92) *45 mins*

Provincial plc is contemplating a bid for the share capital of National plc. The following statistics are available.

	Provincial plc	*National plc*
Number of shares	14 million	45 million
Share price	840p	166p
Latest equity earnings	£11,850,000	£9,337,500

Provincial plc's plan is to reduce the scale of National plc's operations by selling off a division which accounts for £1,500,000 of National plc's latest earnings, as indicated above. The estimated selling price for the division is £10.2 million.

Earnings in National plc's remaining operations could be increased by an estimated 20% on a permanent basis by the introduction of better management and financial controls. Provincial plc does not anticipate any alteration to National plc's price/earnings multiple as a result of these improvements in earnings.

To avoid duplication, some of Provincial plc's own property could be disposed of at an estimated price of £16 million.

Rationalisation costs are estimated at £4.5 million.

Required

(a) Calculate the effect on the current share price of each company, all other things being equal, of a two for nine share offer by Provincial plc, assuming that Provincial plc's estimates are in line with those of the market. **10 Marks**

(b) Offer a rational explanation of why the market might react to the bid by valuing National plc's shares at (i) a higher figure and (ii) a lower figure than that indicated by Provincial plc's offer even though the offer is in line with market estimates of the potential merger synergy. **5 Marks**

(c) Assume that Provincial plc is proposing to offer National plc shareholders the choice of the two for nine share exchange or a cash alternative.

Advise Provincial plc whether the cash alternative should be more or less than the current value of the share exchange, giving your reasons. **5 Marks**

(d) Assume now that Provincial plc, instead of making a two for nine share exchange offer, wishes to offer an exchange which would give National plc shareholders a 10% gain on the existing value of their shares.

Calculate what share exchange would achieve this effect, assuming the same synergy forecasts as before. **5 Marks**

Total Marks = 25

50 WT PLC AND SZ PLC (11/93) *54 mins*

WT plc is a manufacturer of car care products. It carries insignificant amounts of stock. Turnover and profits after tax for last year are £145 million and £40 million respectively.

WT plc's shares are currently quoted at 440 pence, the lowest price for five years. The directors believe that this is because the company is not growing as fast as the market expects. They believe that the fastest way to grow, and as a result improve the share price performance, is to acquire another company in a similar line of business with a lower P/E ratio. They are therefore evaluating SZ plc on the basis that its earnings can be 'bootstrapped', ie on the assumption that, once the merger has been completed, the combined company's P/E ratio will be the same as WT plc's current ratio.

SZ plc's results for the past three years and its directors' own estimate for this year are as follows.

Year to 31 December	*Turnover*	*Profit after tax*
	£ million	£ million
19X0 actual	95	12.1
19X1 actual	100	12.5
19X2 actual	106	13.5
19X3 estimate	120	14.0

SZ plc's dividend payout ratio has been maintained at 50% for the past eight years. The company pays only one dividend per year at the end of December. Its shares are currently being traded at 126 pence.

Summary balance sheets at 31 December 19X2 for the two companies are as follows.

	WT plc	*SZ plc*
	£ million	£ million
Fixed assets (net of depreciation)	60.0	75.0
Net current assets	30.0	25.0
Total assets less current liabilities	90.0	100.0
Capital and reserves		
Called up share capital	25.00[1]	50.00[2]
Reserves	65.00	50.00
	90.00	100.00

1 100 million ordinary shares of 25p

2 100 million ordinary shares of 50p

If the merger goes ahead, some fixed assets of SZ plc will not be needed following the merger and will be sold at the end of the first year of operations. The estimated sales receipts from these assets at the time of sale is £25 million, which will also be the written down book value at that time. No other savings or synergies have been identified by the directors of WT plc at this stage.

WT plc's financial advisors believe that its directors are over-valuing SZ plc's future earnings post-tax. They advise that, in their opinion, the merged company should be more prudently valued and suggest that SZ plc's growth for the foreseeable future is likely to be maintained at no more than the average of the last four years.

The cost of capital for WT plc is 14% and for SZ plc is 12%.

Required

(a) Estimate the maximum price, in total and per share, that WT plc might bid for the whole of the share capital in SZ plc under both of the following assumptions:

(i) the directors of WT plc are correct,

(ii) the financial advisors are correct,

and comment briefly on the weaknesses of the methods of valuation you have used.

10 Marks

(b) Advise the directors of WT plc on an initial bid price and a maximum price which they should offer for the shares of SZ plc. **6 Marks**

(c) Describe four possible defence tactics which the directors of SZ plc might use if they decide to resist the bid from WT plc. **6 Marks**

(d) The bid is eventually agreed at £176 million. The directors of WT plc are now considering the most appropriate method of financing the bid and two options have been suggested. The first is a share exchange and the second is an issue of £176 million undated 12% secured loan stock at par. At present the return on the market is 12%; the return on the risk-free asset is 8%.

Corporation tax is currently payable at 33% and this is not expected to change in the foreseeable future. All figures given above are post-tax with the exception of the coupon rate on the loan stock.

Required

Calculate, on the basis of your answers to (a) and (b) above, the cost of equity and the weighted average cost of capital of the merged firm which might be expected under each of the two financing options, using any reasoned assumptions you consider necessary. **8 Marks**

Total Marks = 30

51 FINANCIAL ANALYST (5/99) *36 mins*

(a) One theoretical method of valuing a company's shares is to calculate the present value of future dividends using a discount rate that reflects the risk of the business. In respect of large, listed companies, current evidence suggests that this is far too simplistic a view of how company values and share prices are determined.

Required

Comment on the reasons why share prices may be substantially different from the level suggested by theory. Include brief comments on the relevance of P/E ratios and net asset values in share price determination. **5 Marks**

(b) ML plc is an expanding clothes retailing company. It is all equity-financed by ordinary share capital of £10 million in shares of 50p nominal. It is currently May 19X9. The company's results to the end of March 19X9 have just been announced. Pre-tax profits were £4.6 million. The Chairman's statement included a forecast that earnings might be expected to rise by 5% per annum in the coming year and for the foreseeable future.

CO plc, a children's clothes group, has an issued ordinary share capital of £33 million in £1 shares. Pre-tax profits for the year to 31 March 19X9 were £5.2 million. Because of a recent programme of re-organisation and rationalisation, no growth is forecast for the current year but subsequently constant growth in earnings of approximately 6% per annum is predicted. CO plc has had an erratic growth and earnings record in the past and has not always achieved its often-ambitious forecasts.

ML plc has approached the shareholders of CO plc with a bid of 2 new shares in ML plc for every 3 CO plc shares. There is a cash alternative of 135 pence per share.

Following the announcement of the bid, the market price of ML plc shares fell while the price of shares in CO plc rose. Statistics for ML plc, CO plc and two other listed companies in the same industry immediately *prior* to the bid announcement are shown below. All share prices are in pence.

19X8		*Company*	*Dividend yield*	*P/E*
High	*Low*		%	
225	185	ML plc	3.4	15
145	115	CO plc	3.6	13
187	122	HR plc	6.0	12
230	159	SZ plc	2.4	17

Both ML plc and CO plc pay tax at 33%.

ML plc's cost of capital is 12% per annum and CO plc's is 11% per annum.

Required

- Assume you are a financial analyst with a major fund manager. You have funds invested in both ML plc and CO plc.
- Assess whether the proposed share-for-share offer is likely to be beneficial to the shareholders in ML plc and CO plc, and recommend an investment strategy based on your calculations.
- Comment on the other information that would be useful in your assessment of the bid. Assume that the estimates of growth given above are achieved and that the new company plans no further issues of equity.

State any assumptions that you make. **15 Marks**

Total Marks = 20

DO YOU KNOW? - INTERNATIONAL FINANCIAL MANAGEMENT

- *Check that you can fill in the blanks in the statements before you attempt any questions. If in doubt, you should go back to your BPP Study Text and revise first.*
- In relation to foreign operations, a company may be exposed to:
  - .... risk
  - ....risk
  - ....risk
  - ....risk.
- A company may avoid ....risk by buying or selling currency forward. This fixes the exchange rate for a transaction in the future.
  - The difference between a .... rate (for a transaction now) and a .... rate reflects the difference in interest rates between the two countries concerned.
  - The forward rate is quoted as a spot rate plus a discount or minus a premium.
- Alternatives to forward purchases and sales include .... and ....
- A variety of financial instruments are available for reducing exposure to interest rate risk. An interest rate .... may be used to exchange obligations with another company.
- .... (FDI) will generally be undertaken if exporting is more costly than overseas production. However, difficulties in repatriating profits and other political factors complicate the issue.
- International portfolio .... brings advantages resulting from differences in the economies of different countries.
- The CAPM can be extended to cover international portfolio risk, but in practice .... and ....also need to be considered.
- The appraisal of foreign projects involves a number of complexities which do not arise in the case of domestic projects, including .... and ....
- There are various methods of providing export and import finance.
  - .... provides all the advantages of factoring generally and is especially useful in assessing credit risk.
  - .... and .... provide medium-term finance for imports of capital goods.
- The exporter might obtain finance from the foreign buyer (by insisting on ....) and the importer might obtain finance from the foreign supplier (by means of normal trade credit, perhaps evidenced by a ....).
- .... is the general term for a complex and possibly expensive means of trading by barter and similar deals with poor and less developed countries.
- The international .... and .... markets provide various possibilities in the form of financial instruments which the treasurer of large companies may use for borrowing or for financial investment.

  TRY QUESTIONS 52-60

- *Possible pitfalls*

  Write down the mistakes you know you should avoid

DID YOU KNOW? - INTERNATIONAL FINANCIAL MANAGEMENT

- *Could you fill in the blanks? The answers are in bold. Use this page for revision purposes as you approach the exam.*
- In relation to foreign operations, a company may be exposed to:
    - **translation** risk
    - **economic** risk
    - **transaction** risk
    - **political** risk.
- A company may avoid **foreign exchange** risk by buying or selling currency forward. This fixes the exchange rate for a transaction in the future.
    - The difference between a **spot** rate (for a transaction now) and a **forward** rate reflects the difference in interest rates between the two countries concerned.
    - The forward rate is quoted as a spot rate plus a discount or minus a premium.
- Alternatives to forward purchases and sales include **foreign currency options** and **foreign currency futures**.
- A variety of financial instruments are available for reducing exposure to interest rate risk. An interest rate **swap** may be used to exchange obligations with another company.
- **Foreign direct investment** (FDI) will generally be undertaken if exporting is more costly than overseas production. However, difficulties in repatriating profits and other political factors complicate the issue.
- International portfolio **diversification** brings advantages resulting from differences in the economies of different countries.
- The CAPM can be extended to cover international portfolio risk, but in practice **foreign exchange fluctuations** and **market imperfections** also need to be considered.
- The appraisal of foreign projects involves a number of complexities which do not arise in the case of domestic projects, including **international tax complications** and **differential rates of inflation**.
- There are various methods of providing export and import finance.
    - **Export factoring** provides all the advantages of factoring generally and is especially useful in assessing credit risk.
    - **International credit unions** and **forfaiting** provide medium-term finance for imports of capital goods.
- The exporter might obtain finance from the foreign buyer (by insisting on **cash with order**) and the importer might obtain finance from the foreign supplier (by means of normal trade credit, perhaps evidenced by a **term bill of exchange**).
- **Countertrade** is the general term for a complex and possibly expensive means of trading by barter and similar deals with poor and less developed countries.
- The international **money** and **capital** markets provide various possibilities in the form of financial instruments which the treasurer of large companies may use for borrowing or for financial investment.

  TRY QUESTIONS 52-60
- *Possible pitfalls*
    - **Discount rate adjustments**
    - **Distinction between transaction risk and translation risk**
    - **Understanding of risk management methods**

52 EXPO PLC (11/97) *36 mins*

Expo plc is an importer/exporter of textiles and textile machinery. It is based in the UK but trades extensively with countries throughout Europe. It has a small subsidiary based in Germany. The company is about to invoice a customer in Germany 750,000 Deutschmarks, payable in three months' time. Expo plc's treasurer is considering two methods of hedging the exchange risk. These are:

Method 1

Borrow DM 750,000 for three months, convert the loan into sterling and repay the loan out of eventual receipts.

Method 2

Enter into a 3-month forward exchange contract with the company's bank to sell DM 750,000.

The spot rate of exchange is DM 2.3834 to £1.
The 3-month forward rate of exchange is DM 2.3688 to £1.
Annual interest rates for 3 months' borrowing are: Germany 3%, UK 6%.

Required

(a) Advise the treasurer on:

(i) which of the two methods is the most financially advantageous for Expo plc, and

(ii) the factors to consider before deciding whether to hedge the risk using the foreign currency markets.

Include relevant calculations in your advice. **14 Marks**

(b) Assume that Expo plc is trading in and with developing countries rather than Europe and has a subsidiary in a country with no developed capital or currency markets. Expo plc is now about to invoice a customer in that country in the local currency. Advise Expo plc's treasurer about ways in which the risk can be managed in these circumstances.

Note: No calculations are required for this part of this question. **6 Marks**

Total Marks = 20

53 EASTASIA (11/95) *36 mins*

A professional accountancy institute in the United Kingdom is evaluating an investment project overseas - in Eastasia, a politically stable country. The project involves the establishment of a training school to offer courses on international accounting and management topics. It will cost an initial 2.5 million Eastasian dollars (EA$) and it is expected to earn post-tax cashflows as follows.

Year	1	2	3	4
Cashflow (EA$'000)	750	950	1,250	1,350

The following information is available.

(a) The expected inflation rate in Eastasia is 3% a year.

(b) Real interest rates in the two countries are the same. They are expected to remain the same for the period of the project.

(c) The current spot rate is EA$ 2 per £1 Sterling.

(d) The risk-free rate of interest in Eastasia is 7% and in the UK 9%.

(e) The company requires a sterling return from this project of 16%.

Required

(a) Calculate the £ Sterling net present value of the project using *both* the following methods.

(i) By discounting annual cash flows in £ Sterling.

(ii) By discounting annual cash flows in Eastasian $. **12 Marks**

(b) The Chief Finance Officer of the institute has noted that borrowing rates in Scandinavia are below those in most other countries and suggests that the institute should borrow Scandinavian currency to finance the project.

Required

Discuss the main methods of finance for overseas operations and the issues the company should consider before making a decision about whether to borrow Scandinavian currency. **8 Marks**

Total Marks = 20

54 OVERSEAS INVESTMENT (Specimen paper) *45 mins*

(a) The financial press recently listed the following information about two currencies, the Westland dollar ($W) and the Eastland mark (Em).

Spot rates:	2.0725 Em/$W
	0.4825 $W/Em
90 day rates:	2.0687 Em/$W
	0.4834 $W/Em

The Westland prime interest rate on the same day was 9.5%.

Note. Use a 365-day year.

Required

(i) Explain what is implied about the Eastland interest rate.

(ii) Calculate and comment on the Eastland interest rate if the forward exchange rate was 0.4795 $W/Em.

(iii) Calculate and comment on the 90-day forward rate on Em/$W if the Eastland interest rate was 8%. **7 Marks**

(b) It is currently 19X4. In the late 19W0s R plc, a manufacturing company based in the United Kingdom, developed a substantial market for its products in Eastern Europe. The board decided to establish a subsidiary in Hungary. The assets needed for the new subsidiary were mainly buildings. Plant and equipment were provided from the UK. Most of the raw material for production was, and still is, sourced in the UK. Local labour is used, except for senior managers who are seconded from the UK parent for 2 to 3 years.

Required

Assuming the UK company wished to minimise its exposure to exchange risk:

(i) discuss the options which were available to the parent company management for financing the new subsidiary. Assume that the parent company did not need to raise new long-term capital to finance this new venture;

(ii) explain how the UK parent could have minimised its exchange losses arising from either operating transactions or a decline in the value of Hungarian Forints (HUF). **10 Marks**

(c) R plc went ahead with the overseas investment in June 19X2 when the exchange rate was 150 HUF = £1. In October 19X2 the UK government was forced to devalue the pound sterling and leave the European Exchange Rate Mechanism. The exchange rate of HUF to the pound at the end of 19X2 was 125 = £1.

Required

Discuss how the devaluation of the pound against the HUF might have affected the cash flows generated by the subsidiary and how the parent company could have managed the situation. **8 Marks**

Total Marks = 25

55 CANADA (5/99) *36 mins*

PG plc is considering investing in a new project in Canada which will have a life of four years. The initial investment is C$150,000, including working capital. The net after-tax cash flows which the project will generate are C$60,000 per annum for years 1, 2 and 3 and C$45,000 in year 4. The terminal value of the project is estimated at C$50,000, net of tax.

The current spot rate of C$ against the pound sterling is 1.7. Economic forecasters expect the pound to strengthen against the Canadian dollar by 5% per annum over the next 4 years.

The company evaluates UK projects of similar risk at 14%.

Required

(a) Calculate the NPV of the Canadian project using the following two methods:

(i) convert the currency cash flows into sterling and discount the sterling cash flows at a sterling discount rate;

(ii) discount the cash flows in C$ using an adjusted discount rate which incorporates the 12-month forecast spot rate;

and explain briefly the theories and/or assumptions which underlie the use of the adjusted discount rate approach in (ii). **12 Marks**

(b) The company had originally planned to finance the project with internal funds generated in the UK. However, the Finance Director has suggested that there would be advantages in raising debt finance in Canada.

Required

Discuss the advantages and disadvantages of matching investment and borrowing overseas as compared with UK-sourced debt or equity.

Wherever possible, relate your answer to the details given in this question for PG plc. **8 Marks**

Total Marks = 20

56 SWISS MULTINATIONAL (5/98) *36 mins*

(a) Assume you are the treasurer of a medium-sized manufacturing company which trades throughout Europe. At a recent meeting to discuss the company's policy on foreign exchange management, the managing director, a non-accountant, makes the following statements.

Statement 1

'Translation risk is concerned only with the effect of exchange rate changes on financial statements and is mainly an accounting issue. There is no need to hedge this risk unless we are close to our foreign currency borrowing limits.'

Statement 2

'Transaction risk can easily be hedged using the forward market although I am inclined either not to hedge at all or to use internal hedging methods as they are cheaper.'

Required

(i) In respect of statement 1, explain what the MD means when he says that there is no need to hedge unless the company is close to its foreign currency borrowing limits. **4 Marks**

(ii) In respect of statement 2, comment on whether the MD is right to consider not hedging as an appropriate strategy, and discuss, briefly, three internal hedging techniques which the company could consider. **6 Marks**

(b) Assume you are the treasurer of a multinational company based in Switzerland. Your company trades extensively with the United States of America. You have just received US$1 million from a customer in the USA. As the company has no immediate need of capital you decide to invest the money in either US$ or Swiss Francs for 12 months. The following information is relevant:

- The spot rate of exchange is SFr 1.3125 to US$ 1
- The 12-month forward rate is SFr 1.275 to US$ 1
- The interest rate on a 1-year Swiss Franc bond is $4\,^{9}/_{16}\%$
- The interest rate on a 1-year US$ bond is $7\,^{5}/_{8}\%$

Assume investment in either currency is risk-free and ignore transaction costs.

Required

Calculate the returns under both options (investing in US$ or Swiss Francs) and explain why there is so little difference between the two figures. **10 Marks**

Total Marks = 20

57 SWAPS (11/96) *36 mins*

(a) Discuss the usefulness of interest rate swaps and currency swaps to the financial manager of a fast growing business which is just beginning to trade internationally. **8 Marks**

(b) Assume you are the treasurer of G Ltd, an importer of goods mainly from Germany. You have received the following memo from your managing director, who is not an accountant:

'I have been reading the *Financial Times* and note that the current spot rate for Deutschmarks is 2.234 DM to the £ Sterling. The six-month forward rate is 2.196 and for 12 months it is even lower. I also note that interest rates in Germany are only 3.25% per annum whereas in the UK they are much higher. I have three suggestions:

1. If we buy Deutschmarks on the spot market as and when we need them to pay for our imports, rather than taking out forward contracts, as is our present policy, it should surely save us a lot of money.

2. An alternative policy, if you think that Sterling will depreciate over the next 12 months, is to buy Deutschmarks on the spot market now and place them on deposit until we need them.

3. Would it not be in our interests to borrow Deutschmarks and pay off our Sterling loans? This would save us money on interest payments.

Please let me have your views.'

Required

Write a report to the managing director responding to each of his suggestions.

12 Marks

Total Marks = 20

58 FREIMARKS (5/90) *45 mins*

F plc, a merchandising company operating mainly in the UK, undertakes export and import transactions with firms in a less well developed country, Freiland. Many of these transactions are necessarily conducted in the local currency, the Freimark (Fm).

F plc also has a small subsidiary company in Freiland, concerned wholly with servicing equipment sold in that country.

The sterling value of the Freimark has fluctuated frequently over the past 12 months between Fm 12.50 and Fm 27.50 = £1. The exchange rate currently stands at 25.00.

The treasurer of F plc has prepared the following cash flow forecast of transactions in Fm over the next six months.

	Month 1	*Month 2*	*Month 3*	*Month 4*	*Month 5*	*Month 6*
	Fm'000	Fm'000	Fm'000	Fm'000	Fm'000	Fm'000
Receipts in respect of sales invoiced from the UK	37,400	48,500	35,000	77,300	62,600	46,700
Remittances from subsidiary company: balances in excess of agreed float	3,200	1,600	2,000	2,700	2,400	1,800
Total receipts	40,600	50,100	37,000	80,000	65,000	48,500
Payments for goods imported from Freiland	38,200	55,500	44,200	36,800	53,000	49,500
Purchase of fixed assets in Freiland for subsidiary company				40,000	4,000	
	38,200	55,500	44,200	76,800	57,000	49,500
Net receipts/ (payments)	2,400	(5,400)	(7,200)	3,200	8,000	(1,000)

Required

(a) State and explain the various factors that should be taken into account before the company decides to take any action to reduce its foreign exchange transaction exposure. **10 Marks**

(b) Describe three techniques of exposure management that might be available to F plc under the circumstances of this question. **10 Marks**

(c) Explain the meaning of 'economic exposure' and distinguish it from transaction exposure. **5 Marks**

Total Marks = 25

59 X AND Y (5/91) *45 mins*

X Limited (incorporated in England) and Y (Pty) Ltd (a South African company) are two private companies of approximately the same size, working together in the same field. They have been co-operating well for some years and the directors of both companies are proposing to put this co-operation on a more formal footing by amalgamating the companies. It is thus hoped to facilitate international marketing of both of their product ranges.

Neither company is quoted.

The rand/sterling exchange rate has oscillated between 4.92 and 6.04 over the last year.

X Limited's directors wish to set up XY (International) Limited when equity would be allocated to the existing owners of each company on a 50/50 basis.

Y (Pty) Ltd's board would prefer a mutual exchange of shares so that half of X Limited and half of Y (Pty) Ltd is owned by the shareholders of the other company.

Required

(a) Outline the advantages and disadvantages of the two approaches referred to. **12 Marks**

(b) Discuss what might be gained were each of the companies to issue loan stock to each other and to describe how the results of X Limited would be affected by such an arrangement. **8 Marks**

(c) Explain how the control of remittances by a government overseas may affect a foreign investor. **5 Marks**

Total Marks = 25

60 OJ LTD (5/97) *36 mins*

OJ Ltd is a supplier of leather goods to retailers in the UK and other western European countries. The company is considering entering into a joint venture with a manufacturer in South America. The two companies will each own 50% of the limited liability company JV (SA) and will share profits equally. £450,000 of the initial capital is being provided by OJ Ltd, and the equivalent in South American dollars (SA$) is being provided by the foreign partner. The managers of the joint venture expect the following net operating cash flows which are in nominal terms.

	SA$'000	*Forward rates of exchange to the £ Sterling*
Year 1	4,250	10
Year 2	6,500	15
Year 3	8,350	21

For tax reasons JV (SA), the company to be formed specifically for the joint venture, will be registered in South America.

Ignore taxation in your calculations.

(a) Assume you are a financial adviser retained by OJ Ltd to advise on the proposed joint venture.

Required

(i) Calculate the NPV of the project under the two assumptions explained below. Use a discount rate of 16% for both assumptions.

Assumption 1

The South American country has exchange controls which prohibit the payment of dividends above 50% of the annual cash flows for the first three years of the project. The accumulated balance can be repatriated at the end of the third year.

Assumption 2

The government of the South American country is considering removing exchange controls and restrictions on repatriation of profits. If this happens all cash flows will be distributed as dividends to the partner companies at the end of each year.

(ii) Comment briefly on whether or not the joint venture should proceed based solely on these calculations. **8 Marks**

(b) During a meeting to discuss the joint venture, the following questions are raised by the managers of OJ Ltd.

'In reality we will exchange our SA$ cash flows into Sterling at the spot rate prevailing at the end of each year. How reliable are forward rates of exchange as predictors of spot rates?'

'If exchange controls exist we will not get much of our cash for three years. Surely we should be using a higher discount rate for Assumption 1?'

'Under either assumption we havc to accept substantial exchange rate risk. Could we use a currency swap to help us minimise this risk?'

Required

Comment on the three questions raised by the managers of OJ Ltd and advise them of any other practical issues which should be considered before they decide to proceed. **12 Marks**

Total Marks = 20

Case study questions

61 DOBSON LTD (5/99) *108 mins*

Background

Dobson Limited is a medium-sized private company which manufactures and sells office equipment. The company is expanding into different product lines to meet the changing needs of the market. The market is becoming increasingly competitive and customers are able to negotiate very favourable credit terms. This is putting considerable strain on the company's working capital.

Current situation: credit terms and invoicing

UK customers (70% of sales)

Dobson Limited offers a cash discount of 1.5% for payment within 10 days to all UK customers. The normal terms of trade allow for 30 days. Approximately 50% of customers take advantage of the early payment discount. The remaining customers who are not 'bad' take the full period of credit allowed. Historically, bad debts have averaged 1% of total sales value.

Overseas customers (30% of sales)

All sales are on credit. Customers are required to pay 20% deposit with order and the balance within 60 days. All customers pay in accordance with these credit terms. To date, no overseas customers have failed to pay, The company invoices all customers, wherever their location, in pounds sterling.

Financing of working capital

Dobson Limited currently finances working capital using an overdraft facility of £150,000. This is likely to be insufficient for the company's requirements next year. The bank will not extend this facility at current interest rates unless the company can provide security. If this is not possible, the interest rate on the entire overdraft will rise by 2%.

Forecast sales and cost information

The company is forecasting sales of £2.5 million for the next 12 months, an increase of £400,000 over the previous year. Sales are made evenly throughout the year. The proportion of UK and overseas sales is not expected to change. Additional information is as follows.

- Cost of goods sold averages 40% of sales value. All the company's costs are in pounds sterling and the company has negotiated 45 days' credit, on average, from its suppliers.
- Cash payments for other operating and administration expenses are expected to be £750,000 for the year.
- Other cash outgoings during the year are expected to be £700,000. Payments are mainly for tax, capital expenditure and dividends.
- The company currently pays interest on overdraft at 5% over base rate, which is currently 6%. Assume that interest is charged annually in arrears. The company's opportunity cost of capital is 16%.
- Opening balances on working capital accounts at 1 April 19X9 were:

Overdraft	£135,000
Debtors	£163,400
Creditors	£145,000

Assume no change in stock levels during the year.

Proposals

The company is considering three policy alternatives in respect of working capital.

Alternative 1

Continue with existing policies.

Alternative 2

Employ a debt factor. Preliminary discussions indicate that a non-recourse factor will accept 85% of Dobson Limited's UK customers and charge a commission of 2% of acceptable debtors' value. The use of a debt factor is expected to result in a saving of £25,000 per annum on in-company credit administration costs, although there will be a one-off redundancy cost of £35,000.

The factor will take over existing UK debts. The company will continue to allow 30 days' credit to the remaining 15% of customers not accepted by the factor, but will discontinue its discounts for early payment.

Alternative 3

Use the invoice discounting facility of the company's bankers. This essentially involves Dobson Limited using its debtors as security for a loan. The bank has agreed to provide finance against 90% of the average total debtors' balance at an interest rate of 10% per annum. Dobson Limited will take the maximum finance available and will continue to operate its existing credit policies with all customers.

Note

Assume a 365-day year and that the decision on the most appropriate is taken today (25 May 19X9) and implemented immediately.

Required

(a) Calculate:

(i) debtors' days

- at 31 March 19X9 and
- expected at 31 March 19Y0 for each of the three proposed alternatives;

4 Marks

(ii) forecast overdraft balance at 31 March 19Y0 assuming alternative 1; **8 Marks**

(iii) the incremental effect on cash flows at 31 March 19Y0 for alternatives 2 and 3 compared with alternative 1. **12 Marks**

(b) Assume you are the financial manager of the company.

Write a report to the board of Dobson Limited recommending a working capital policy, using your answers to part **(a)** above, and any additional ratios you think appropriate to support your arguments.

Include in your report specific comments on:

- the financial and non-financial advantages and disadvantages of the three methods of financing debtors:
- the effect on the company's debt capacity of all three alternatives;
- alternative financing methods which might be considered for working capital. **22 Marks**

(c) Because it invoices in sterling, and because exchange rates are volatile, Dobson Limited may lose overseas customers to competitors who invoice in the customer's own currency. The company's directors are therefore considering changing its policy to invoice in currencies other than sterling.

Discuss:

- the implications of invoicing overseas customers in their own currency;
- the usefulness of the foreign currency markets in the management of overseas debtors;
- alternative methods of managing exchange risk which do not use the foreign currency markets. **14 Marks**

Total Marks = 60

62 SPEARHEAD PLC (11/98) *180 mins*

Background to the company and selected financial information

Spearhead plc, a company based in the United Kingdom, manufactures high-technology landing and airport control equipment which it sells worldwide, mainly to government departments. The company was owned by the government of the United Kingdom until 1988 and has demonstrated strong growth since privatisation, although it is not the market leader in the industry.

In its last financial year, the company had earnings of £360 million and earnings per share (EPS) of 60 pence. The current share price is 950 pence compared with 825 pence a year ago. The company's equity beta is quoted at 1.5.

Company objectives

Financial objectives

(i) investing in projects which yield a positive NPV when discounted at an appropriate discount rate,

(ii) maintaining an annual return on assets at 25%.

Other objectives

The company aims to be the leading UK supplier of airport control equipment within the next 10 years and retains a large proportion of its earnings for future investment. It pays a relatively low annual cash dividend and aims to top this up with a scrip dividend each year.

Information on major contracts

Spearhead plc is examining two potential contracts which will each require substantial capital investment. The timing of the bids, the amount of capital investment required, and the need for highly-specialised design staff mean that it can bid for only one of the two contracts. Details are as follows.

CONTRACT 1

The customer is a Western European government. The contract is for the supply of radar-controlled landing equipment over a period of four years to a value of DM2,000 million. Spearhead plc must agree a fixed price in Deutschmarks for the duration of the contract.

The forecast cash flows, in nominal terms, are:

Initial capital expenditure	£300 million
Estimated residual value at the end of the project	£50 million
Income from sales	DM 500 million per annum
Contract costs	£75 million per annum

The bidding for this contract was expected to be fiercely competitive. Despite the need for a fixed-price clause in the contract, the company classifies this investment as low risk.

CONTRACT 2

The customer is the government of a country in the Middle East. The contract is in two stages. The first stage is for the provision of a single delivery of a major piece of equipment worth US$2,000 million. The terms are that a 50% deposit is to be paid when contracts are signed: the balance will be paid on delivery at the end of year 2. Payments for stage 1 will be in US$. A penalty of 10% of the contract value is payable if the contract overruns.

The second stage of the contract, starting in year 3, involves the supply of a large number of smaller pieces of equipment over a 3-year period. No additional capital investment will be required for this work, which is estimated to be worth £600 million. Payment for stage 2 will be in pounds sterling.

The second stage of the contract is relatively low risk, but there are high risks associated with the first stage. For example, the initial piece of equipment is state-of-the-art technology. This requires the full-time involvement of many of the company's design staff, and will mean the loss of some other business currently being considered by Spearhead plc. The incremental cash flows (net of any saving in capital outlay) associated with this lost business are estimated at £175 million in year 1 and £150 million in year 2.

The forecast cash flows, in nominal terms, are:

Stage one of contract 2

Initial capital expenditure	£500 million. This can be used on the second stage of the contract if it is awarded, but otherwise there is no residual value.
Sales income	As per contract details above.
Contract costs	£350 million in year 1 and £150 million in year 2.

Stage two of contract 2 (starting in year 3)

Sales income	£200 million per annum
Contract costs	£100 million per annum

Other information

- Estimated inflation rates per annum: UK 3%; Germany 2%; USA 4%.
- Real interest rates in all countries are expected to remain the same. The risk-free rates are: UK 6%; Germany 5%; USA 7%.
- The expected return on the market is 12% per annum.
- The current spot rates are DM3 to £1 and US$1.6 to £1.
- All cash flows occur at year end except where otherwise indicated.
- All raw materials and other costs associated with the supply of the equipment are sourced and paid for in the UK.
- The evaluation method used by Spearhead plc is to translate the foreign currency income into sterling and discount the cash flows at the appropriate sterling opportunity cost of capital.
- The company depreciates capital equipment on a straight-line basis over the life of the equipment, after adjusting for any estimated residual value.
- The company calculates its costs of equity using the CAPM and uses this to evaluate all sterling-denominated investments. However, because of the difficulties in determining discount rates for international investments, it uses a 'rule of thumb' approach and adjusts its cost of equity by a percentage for the estimated amount of risk involved, as follows.

High risk projects	cost of equity 5%
Medium risk	cost of equity plus 2%
Low risk	cost of equity

Parts (b) and (c) of this question relate specifically to the case details. Part (a) of the question should be answered in general terms, although your answer may use the case details for illustration if you wish.

Ignore taxation throughout this question, including the calculation of capital allowances, in all aspects of your calculations.

Required

(a) Discuss the factors which need to be considered when determining discount rates for evaluating international investment decisions.

Comment specifically on the difficulties which would be involved in using the CAPM to calculate international discount rates. **8 Marks**

(b) Calculate, using the information given in the case:

(i) the cost of equity;

(ii) the exchange rates to apply to the foreign currency cash flows of each of the contracts;

(iii) the net present value and annual return on assets of each of the contracts.

Make (and state in your answer) whatever assumptions you think necessary.

Work to the nearest million units of currency (pounds sterling, DM, US$).

22 Marks

(c) Assume you are a financial manager with Spearhead plc. Write a report to the board of Spearhead plc which recommends, with reasons, which contract, if either, should be chosen. You should include in your report comments on:

(i) how each contract might contribute to the achievement of the company's objectives;

(ii) how the company has incorporated risk into its evaluation, and alternative methods of risk management which could be considered by the company;

(iii) the difficulties involved in evaluating mutually-exclusive projects of unequal risk and unequal lives;

(iv) methods of hedging the risks associated with trading internationally.

30 Marks

Note. If you have not been able to complete part (b) of this question, or think you have arrived at incorrect NPVs, answer part (c) in general terms but relate your answer to the company details in the case wherever possible.

Total Marks = 60

63 IBSEN PLC (5/98) *108 mins*

Background

Ibsen plc is a privately-owned toy manufacturing company which has been trading for 12 years. It has 15 shareholders who each own an equal number of shares. Two of the shareholders are full-time managers in the company. The shareholders have discussed the possibility of a public flotation of shares on a number of occasions over the past five years, but have each time decided against the idea because it would conflict with many of their personal objectives for the company. However, some of the shareholders would now like to liquidate a proportion of their investment and believe the time might be right for a quotation on the London Stock Exchange.

Recent financial information

It is currently May 19X8. The company's accounting year ends on 31 December. Summary financial information for the five years 19X3-19X7 and forecast for 19X8 is shown below (all figures in millions of pounds Sterling).

Profit and loss account (extracts)

	19X8 forecast	*19X7*	*19X6*	*19X5*	*19X4*	*19X3*
Turnover	220.0	215.0	170.0	150.0	125.0	115.0
Profit before tax and interest	36.0	25.0	27.0	26.0	23.0	21.0
Interest	4.0					
Taxation	10.6	8.2	8.9	8.6	7.6	7.0
Profit after interest and tax	21.4	16.8	18.1	17.4	15.4	14.0
Dividend payable	17.5	17.5	17.5	9.0	9.0	9.0

Balance sheet (extracts)

Assets						
Fixed	124.0	85.0	66.0	60.0	55.0	50.0
Current (net of liabilities)	48.0	35.0	30.0	34.0	30.0	28.0
	172.0	120.0	96.0	94.0	85.0	78.0
Less: long-term creditors						
10-year bank loan	45.0	-	-	-	-	-
	127.0	120.0	96.0	94.0	85.0	78.0
Financing						
Authorised and issued ordinary share capital	30.0	30.0	30.0	30.0	30.0	30.0
Par value 50p						
Reserves	97.0	90.0	66.0	64.0	55.0	48.0
	127.0	120.0	96.0	94.0	85.0	78.0

Notes

- The fixed assets were valued in 19X7.
- The average P/E ratio for companies in Ibsen plc's industry is currently 11.
- The company's marginal and average tax rate is 33%.
- The bank loan was taken out on 1 January 19X8. It is secured on the firm's premises and carries a variable rate of interest. The interest rate on similar loans made to companies with the same risk characteristics as Ibsen plc averaged 10% throughout 19X7.
- The company's weighted average cost of capital is currently 14% after adjusting for tax.

Developments 19X8 to 19Y2

Note. The information in this section of the scenario relates *only* to requirement (c) of the question.

The company is floated on the Stock Exchange during 19X8 at 300 pence per share. Assume it is now the year 19Y2 and the company wishes to raise £250 million for the development and marketing of new products. The following information is relevant:

- There has been no change in issued ordinary share capital during the five years and no new debt has been raised. Earnings after interest and taxes in the year to 31 December 19Y1 were £45 million.

- The original shareholders now own 20% of the issued shares; a further 20% is owned by three large institutional investors and the remaining 60% by a large number of small, private investors.
- P/E ratios have been as follows over the past 9 months.

	Ibsen plc	*Industry*
Present	18	16
3 months ago	15	16
6 months ago	14	15
9 months ago	16	15

The company is considering raising the £250 million by means of either a rights issue at 15% discount to the prevailing share price, or issuing convertible debt which would be convertible into ordinary shares in five years' time.

Required

(a) Explain the main characteristics of the following methods by which a company can obtain a quotation for its shares on a recognised stock exchange, and comment on the most appropriate method for a small company such as Ibsen plc:

- Private placing
- Offer for sale by fixed price or tender **8 Marks**

(b) Assume you are a financial advisor to Ibsen plc *prior to flotation* in 19X8. Write a report to the Board which:

(i) explains the advantages and disadvantages of a public flotation, in general circumstances and also in the circumstances described in the scenario; **8 Marks**

(ii) recommends an issue price for the company if it decides to seek a stock market quotation.

You should estimate the price using three methods: the dividend valuation model (using your own assessments about the growth rate), net asset value, and on a P/E basis, and explain the reasons for your formal recommendation.

Assume no change in issued share capital before flotation and that the existing shareholders are each prepared to sell 49% of their holding; **15 Marks**

(iii) discusses the difficulties of setting a new issue price and recommends what other information should be considered by the company before deciding whether to proceed with the flotation. **7 Marks**

(c) The company was floated in 19X8 at an issue price of 300 pence per share. Assume it is now 19Y2 and you are advising the company on its need for new capital. Write a report to the Board which:

(i) advises a suitable rights issue price and calculates the theoretical ex-rights price; **6 Marks**

(ii) advises on the conversion terms for the issue of convertible debt. The return on unsecured debt is 10% in 19Y2; **10 Marks**

(iii) explains, briefly, the main advantages and disadvantages to a company such as Ibsen plc of raising finance via either a rights issue or convertible debt. Using your assumptions and calculations in (i) and (ii) above, recommend which of the two methods of financing is to be preferred by Ibsen plc in the circumstances. **6 Marks**

Total Marks = 60

64 PREMOCO PLC (11/97) *108 mins*

Background information

It is currently November 19X7. Premoco plc operates in oil and related industries. Its shares are quoted on the London Stock Exchange. In its retailing operations the company has concentrated on providing high-quality service and facilities at its service stations rather than competing solely on the price of petrol. Approximately 75% of its turnover and 60% of its profits are from sales of petrol, the remainder coming from other services (car wash and retail sales from its convenience stores which are available at each service station).

The company has been highly profitable in the past as a result of astute buying of petroleum products on the open market. The company does not enter into supplier agreements with the major oil companies except on very short-term deals. However, profit margins are now under increasing pressure as a result of intensifying competition and the cost of complying with environmental legislation.

Future strategy

The managing director of the company, David Wong, is assessing three possible acquisitions which would help the company increase the percentage of its non-petroleum revenue and profits.

Option 1. Nafco plc owns fifteen service stations in the south of England. These sites are of poor image, the company having, in the past, aimed at selling petrol at the lowest possible prices and providing little in the way of other services. However, the sites are in good locations and therefore suitable for renovation and development. The institutional investors in Nafco plc are known to be dissatisfied with the company's recent performance and can be expected to support a bid if the terms are right. Nafco plc's service stations are too small for the major oil companies to want to operate, so Premoco plc foresees little competition from alternative buyers. One of Premoco plc's suppliers of petroleum products has indicated it might be willing to provide development finance for up to 50% of the acquisition cost at only 5% interest per annum, repayable over ten years. However, this would involve Premoco plc entering into a long-term supply agreement for all fifteen sites.

Option 2. Oiltrans plc specialises in oil distribution from the depots owned by the major oil companies to their retail outlets. Its shares have been quoted on the Alternative Investment Market for the past two years. It operates a fleet of oil tankers, some owned and some leased. Premoco plc has used Oiltrans' services in the past and knows it has an up-to-date and well-managed fleet. However, a bid for Oiltrans plc would almost certainly be regarded as hostile and, as 40% of the shares are owned by the directors and their families, a successful bid is far from assured.

Option 3. Carsals Ltd owns six car showrooms in prestige locations, all of which operate the franchise of a major motor manufacturer. It is a long-established family-owned business. The managing director and major shareholder is planning to retire shortly and his children have shown no interest in taking over the business. He has therefore approached David Wong, whom he has known for some years, asking if Premoco plc would be interested in buying Carsals Ltd.

Premoco plc's financial advisors have produced estimates of the expected NPV and the first full-year post-merger earnings of Premoco plc with each of the three acquisition options. These are as follows.

	Estimated post-merger earnings in first full year following merger	*Estimated NPV of combined organisation*
	£ million	£ million
Premoco plc plus Nafco plc	32	512
Premoco plc plus Oiltrans plc	35	595
Premoco plc plus Carsals Ltd	23	368

Financial statistics and other information on Premoco plc and the three possible acquisitions are shown below.

Extracts from Premoco plc's balance sheet at 30 June 19X7

	£ million	*£ million*
Fixed assets (NBV)		140.00
Current assets:		
Stock and debtors	120.00	
Bank and cash	80.00	
Less: current liabilities	(90.00)	
Net current assets		110.00
		250.00
Ordinary £1 share capital:		
(authorised £30 million)		
Issued		20.00
Reserves		180.00
Secured loan stock 8% 19Y5		50.00
		250.00

Summary financial statistics

	Premoco plc	*Nafco plc*	*Oiltrans plc*	*Carsals Ltd*
Last year end	30.6.X7	30.6.X7	30.6.X7	31.3.X7
Shares in issue (millions)	20	10	12	0.5
Earnings per share (pence)	103	75	85	160
Dividend per share (pence)	31	55	42	112
Share price (pence)	1,648	675	1,530	n/a
Net asset value (£ million)	250	60	65	6
Debt ratio (outstanding debt as % of total market value)	13.0	30.0	15.0	0
Forecast annual growth rate %	11	5	14	9
Beta co-efficient	1.2	0.9	1.3	1.25

(1) The forecast growth rates have been provided by Premoco plc's financial advisors. They are based on publicly available information and assume all companies continue to operate independently and that dividend policies, capital structure and risk characteristics remain unchanged.

(2) The beta shown for Carsals Ltd is the equity beta of a larger, quoted company in a similar line of business. This company has a gearing ratio (debt : debt + equity) of 20%. Assume a debt beta of zero.

Note. Parts (b) and (c) of this question relate specifically to the case details given. Part (a) of the question should be answered in general terms, although your answer may use the case details for illustration if you wish.

You should ignore any taxation issues throughout this question.

Required

(a) Comment on the services which might be provided during the acquisition process by a bidding company's merchant bank and stockbroker. **8 Marks**

(b) Calculate, for Premoco plc and, where relevant, for the three acquisition options before the merger:

(i) the current market value and P/E ratio;

(ii) the cost of equity using the CAPM;

(iii) the prospective market value using the constant growth dividend valuation model,

assuming the return on the market is 12% and the return on the risk-free asset is 6%. **10 Marks**

(c) You now have up to three values for each company as an independent entity. These are the current market value and the value using the Dividend Valuation Model (as you have calculated for part (b)), and asset value (given in the scenario).

Discuss the usefulness and limitations of each of these methods of company valuation to Premoco plc in its acquisition decision. **12 Marks**

(d) Assume you are working as one of Premoco plc's financial advisors. Write a report to David Wong, the managing director, which addresses the following issues for *each* acquisition option:

- the price to be offered to the target company's shareholders. You should recommend a range of terms within which Premoco plc should be prepared to negotiate;
- whether cash or a share exchange would be the most appropriate method of financing the bid;
- the business implications (effect on existing operation, growth prospects, risk etc).

You should recognise that there is no single correct solution to the issues raised in this part of the case. The exercise is to assess and analyse the information available (state any assumptions you make), and then use your judgement to offer credible advice. **30 Marks**

Total Marks = 60

65 LAVINIA PRODUCTS PLC (5/97) *108 mins*

Lavinia Products plc manufactures toys and other goods for children. It has been trading for three years. The shares in the company are owned by five people, all of them employed full time in the business. The company is doing well and now needs additional capital to expand operations.

Assume you are a consultant working for Lavinia Products plc. It is now May 19X7. You have been assigned to the company to advise on its objectives and financial situation. As well as being provided with financial statements for the year to 31 December 19X6, the company's accountant gives you the following information.

(1) Sales and cost of sales are expected to increase by 10% in each of the financial years ending 31 December 19X7, 19X8 and 19X9. Operating expenses are expected to increase by 5% each year.

(2) The company expects to continue to be liable for tax at the marginal rate of 33%. Assume tax is paid or refunded 12 months after the year end.

(3) The ratios of *debtors to sales* and *creditors to cost of sales* will remain the same for the next three years.

(4) The fixed assets are land and buildings which are not depreciated in the company's books. Capital allowances on the buildings may be ignored. All other assets used by the company (machinery, cars etc) are rented.

(5) Dividends will grow at 25% in each of the financial years 19X7, 19X8 and 19X9, as per the company's objectives.

(6) The company intends to purchase new machinery to the value of £500,000 during 19X7 although an investment appraisal exercise has *not* been carried out. It will be depreciated straight line over ten years. The company charges a full year's depreciation in the first year of purchase of its assets. Capital allowances are available at 25% reducing balance on this expenditure.

(7) Additional stock was purchased for £35,000 at the beginning of 19X7. The value of stock after this purchase is likely to remain at £361,000 for the foreseeable future.

(8) No decision has been made on the type of finance to be used for the expansion programme. However, the company's directors think they can raise new medium-term secured debt if necessary.

(9) The average P/E ratio of listed companies in the same industry as Lavinia Products plc is 15.

The company's objectives include the following.

- To earn a pre-tax return on the closing book value of shareholders' funds of 35% per year.
- To increase dividends per share by 25% per year.
- To obtain a quotation on a recognised stock exchange within the next three years.

A summary of the financial statements for the year to 31 December 19X6 is set out below.

LAVINIA PRODUCTS PLC
SUMMARISED PROFIT AND LOSS ACCOUNT
FOR THE YEAR TO 31 DECEMBER 19X6

	£'000
Turnover	1,560
Cost of sales	950
Gross profit	610
Operating expenses	325
Interest	30
Tax liability	84
Net profit	171
Dividends declared	68

SUMMARISED BALANCE SHEET AT 31 DECEMBER 19X6

	£'000
Fixed assets (net book value)	750
Current assets	
Stock	326
Debtors	192
Cash and bank	50
Current liabilities	
Trade creditors	(135)
Other creditors (including tax and dividends)	(152)
Total assets less current liabilities	1,031

Financing	£'000
Ordinary share capital (ordinary shares of £1)	500
Retained profits to 31 December 19X5	128
Retentions for the year to 31 December 19X6	103
10% debenture redeemable 19Z0	300
Total financing	1,031

Required

(a) Discuss the specific problems encountered by small and medium-sized enterprises (SMEs) in raising finance for expansion. **10 Marks**

(b) Using the information in the case:

(i) prepare forecast profit and loss accounts for the years 19X7, 19X8 and 19X9, and calculate whether the company is likely to meet its stated financial objective (return on shareholders' funds) for these three years; **14 Marks**

(ii) prepare cash flow forecasts for the years 19X7, 19X8 and 19X9, and estimate the amount of funds which will need to be raised by the company to finance its expansion. **10 Marks**

Notes

(1) You should ignore interest or returns on surplus funds invested during the three-year period of review.

(2) This is *not* an investment appraisal exercise; you may ignore the timing of cash flows within each year and you should not discount the cash flows.

(3) Ignore inflation.

(c) Write a report to the directors of Lavinia Products plc which:

(i) discusses the key aspects and implications of the financial information you have obtained in your answer to part (b) of the question, in particular noting whether the company is likely to meet its stated objectives; **10 Marks**

(ii) discusses whether the objectives as stated are suitable for the company at the present stage of its development, and discusses alternative objectives which the directors could consider; **9 Marks**

(iii) recommends additional methods of financial forecasting which could be used with advantage by the company's management. You should assume that the only forecasts prepared by the company at present are similar to those you have prepared for your answer to part (b) of this question. **7 Marks**

Total Marks = 60

66 DP PLC (11/96) *108 mins*

DP plc is a family-owned company in the motor trade and had a turnover in 19X5 of £12 million. It has two main services - car body repairs and breakdown recovery. A few years ago Alan, the Managing Director of DP plc, was considering a public flotation for the company. However, in the past two years the rate of growth of both operations has slowed, particularly the car body repairs. This appears to be due to two main factors - increased competition for recovery services and a change of policy by insurance companies which has made car body repairs less profitable.

Comments on the balance sheet

Table 1 provides a summary balance sheet for DP plc at 31 December 19X5. The ordinary and preference shares are all held by family members and their associates. The preference dividend had not been paid for 19X5. The bank loan is secured by a charge on the company's total fixed assets.

Problems current at today's date (19 November 19X6)

The book value of DP plc's assets increased by £1 million in 19X5 over their book value at the end of 19X4. This was primarily a consequence of:

(a) an increase in debtors. Prior to 19X5, debtors had represented about 40 days' turnover. At the end of December 19X5 they represented 65 days, and the situation is deteriorating;

(b) an increase in stocks;

(c) a failure to cancel an order for new recovery vehicles in 19X5.

The supplier of the new recovery vehicles, EF plc, has not been paid. Payment had been due in April 19X6. The supplier has, however, obtained a floating charge on DP plc's current assets and has now, reluctantly, commenced court proceedings against DP plc to recover its money.

Of the bank loan, 50 per cent (ie £300,000) was due to be repaid on 30 September 19X6. The balance is due on 31 March 19X7. The September payment was not made and, as a consequence, the senior loan officer of the bank called in the directors of DP plc to discuss the problem. At this meeting, the bank agreed to allow DP plc to repay the entire amount of the loan at the end of March 19X7.

Future prospects and problems

Despite the current problems, the directors of DP plc are confident of an upturn in business. They are negotiating new contracts with two major insurance companies which will be worth approximately £1.5 million per year in additional gross revenue. However, time is against them and they must now consider a capital reconstruction and pay off the main creditors - the bank, EF plc and a number of smaller suppliers - to avoid liquidation.

Possibilities of injection of new capital

DP plc's bank is not prepared to advance any more money, but it has put the company in touch with a merchant bank which may be prepared to buy into the company. The merchant bank has now conducted an appraisal of DP plc and has concluded the following.

(a) The fixed assets are estimated to be worth £1 million less than the 19X5 balance sheet value.

(b) Stock would realise in the market place no more than 50 per cent of its book value at 31 December 19X5.

(c) Bad debts are estimated at 10 per cent of the 31 December 19X5 debtors' value. Invoicing and collections are expected to be roughly equal throughout 19X6.

(d) All other assets and liabilities are considered to be worth their 19X5 book values.

(e) If the company is liquidated, the administration costs are likely to be 20 per cent of the gross liquidation value.

(f) If the company can be rescued, earnings after interest and taxes are likely to be £320,000 for 19X7. A prospective P/E ratio of 12 is estimated, based on the average for companies in similar trades and on expected growth for DP plc after the reorganisation.

The merchant bank decides it is willing to invest in DP plc provided it gains control of 51 per cent of the voting share capital. However, the merchant bank makes three conditions:

(a) the family would have to agree to retire the preference stock without compensation;

(b) the family would have to forgo preference dividend arrears;

(c) some shares currently owned by the family would have to be cancelled and reissued to the merchant bank to provide it with the required 51 per cent ownership of DP plc.

The merchant bank's intention would be to hold DP plc's shares as a medium-term investment, defined as 5-7 years, and then float the company on the Alternative Investment Market (AIM).

Table 1

DP plc

Balance sheet at 31 December 19X5

	£'000	£'000
Total fixed assets (net book value)		4,350
Stock	825	
Debtors	2,150	
Cash	5	
Total current assets		2,980
Unsecured creditors	(750)	
EF plc (secured creditor)	(300)	
Tax payable	(150)	
Bank loan	(300)	
Preference dividend	(100)	
Total current liabilities		(1,600)
Total assets less current liabilities		5,730
Mortgage	(2,500)	
Bank loan due 31 March 19X7	(300)	
		(2,800)
Net assets attributable to shareholders		2,930

Financed by:

	£'000
Issued share capital	
Ordinary £1 shares	2,500
Retained earnings/(loss) carried forward	(820)
Preference shares (undated)	
£1 shares 8 per cent	1,250
	2,930

Required

(a) Explain the role of merchant banks in the provision of new capital. **8 Marks**

(b) Discuss the advantages and disadvantages to both DP plc and EF plc (the vehicle supplier) of DP plc being forced into liquidation. **8 Marks**

(c) (i) Calculate the estimated market value of DP plc's equity. Base your answer on the merchant bank's estimate of future earnings, assuming the company is rescued. **2 Marks**

(ii) Calculate the book value of net assets attributable to DP plc's shareholders as at today's date (19 November 19X6), assuming the merchant bank's conditions are met. In addition to the information provided in the case, you should assume that:

(1) all current liabilities are paid, with the exception of the portion of the bank loan not yet due;

(2) the values of fixed assets, stock and debtors are as per the merchant bank's estimates;

(3) the cash balance is cash on hand plus cash received from the merchant bank minus cash paid out;

(4) the merchant bank agrees to pay 140 pence per share for its shareholding. **7 Marks**

(iii) Comment briefly on the difference between the values you have found in answer to parts (i) and (ii) above. **3 Marks**

(d) Assume you are employed by the merchant bank to advise on the rescue operation for DP plc and subsequently to assist the company in improving its profitability. Write a report to the bank's board, on the basis of the information provided in the case, which:

(i) critically reviews the investment and exit strategies from the point of view of the bank;

(ii) recommends what financial controls should be implemented as a condition of mounting the operation;

(iii) advises on methods of profit improvement which could be applied to DP plc's operations. **32 Marks**

Total Marks = 60

67 TUTWILER PLC (5/96) *108 mins*

It is currently May 19X6. Tutwiler plc manufactures musical instruments. It has been quoted on the Alternative Investment Market (AIM) in the United Kingdom for 12 months. The latest dealings have been in the region of 200p per share. The company exports around 60% of its output. Customers are dispersed around the country and there is no concentration in one particular area.

Tutwiler plc's turnover has been growing at around 20% per annum over the past five years and it now needs to consider extending its premises or moving to a new location. The present premises are rented from the local government authority. The rental agreement is due for renewal on 1 January 19X7. The company spent £500,000 on renovations to the property three years ago to provide a more suitable manufacturing environment for its products. The renovations are structural and could not be removed if Tutwiler plc decides to relocate.

The company is considering three alternatives.

1 Renegotiate the rental agreement and extend the existing premises with the approval of the landlords.

or

2 Buy a much larger property which is available a few miles from the current premises and which is around 20 years old.

or

3 Build a new factory and office premises in an 'enterprise' zone approximately 150 miles away.

The information available on these three alternatives is as follows.

Alternative 1: rent and extend

The rental terms would be £500,000 per annum in real terms as at 1 January 19X7. Rent will be payable at the end of each of the years 19X7 to 19Y1. Rates are included with the rental payments. The agreement allows for an increase in the annual rental payments in line with inflation of 5% per annum. Extensions to the premises would cost £950,000 (nominal), payable at the end of 19X7. You should assume extension costs can be written off, for tax purposes, in the year in which they are incurred. The local authority (the landlord) has indicated it would be willing to purchase the extension from Tutwiler plc at the original nominal cost at the end of 19Y1.

Alternative 2: buy larger, locally

The purchase costs at £2.5 million payable on 1 January 19X7. Rates will be fixed at £250,000 per annum, payable at the end of each year from 19X7 to 19Y6 inclusive. Renovations and removal costs payable at the end of the first year (19X7) are estimated at £750,000 nominal. The company thinks these premises will be large enough until the end of 19Y6. After that, it may have to sell and move again as there is no possibility of extending these premises. You should assume that writing down allowances for tax purposes are available on the full purchase cost of the new premises at 4% straight line. The realisable value of the premises at the end of 10 years is estimated as £5 million nominal. (*Note:* Assume the application of indexation allowance at the time of sale will result in there being no balancing charge or balancing allowance.)

Alternative 3: build new

The land will cost £1 million which will be paid at the beginning of the evaluation period (1 January 19X7). Building costs are estimated at £1.25 million. They will be paid at the end of 19X7. While building is in progress, the company will remain in its existing premises at an agreed annual rental of £500,000 payable on January 19X7. No rates will be payable on the new premises for the years 19X7 to 19X9 inclusive. From 19Y0 onwards they are expected to be £150,000 per annum indefinitely, payable at the end of each year. The company estimates that 50% of the workforce will relocate. Removal and relocation costs at the end of 19X7 will be £250,000. Recruitment and training costs of the new staff are estimated as £350,000, also payable at the end of 19X7. Assume all costs in this alternative are in nominal terms.

The cost of land will not attract any tax allowances. The cost of the buildings, being in an enterprise zone, will attract 100% first year allowance.

For purposes of evaluation, assume a 15-year life of the land and buildings from the commencement of the evaluation under this alternative.

Notes

1. Assume the starting date for the evaluation is 1 January 19X7.
2. All costs other than those noted above are expected to be the same under all three alternatives. The choice of location is not expected to affect sales.
3. The company pays tax at 33%. This rate is not expected to change. Tax relief is available on 100% of all expenses and costs except land in Alternative 3, and buildings in Alternative 2 which attract writing down allowances as indicated. You should assume that there is no time lag for tax payments or refunds.
4. The company currently has 5 million shares in issue and £2 million debt. The debt is a 15-year bank loan at 15% fixed rate of interest, secured by personal guarantees of the directors. It was taken out in 19X5.

5 If Alternative 1 is chosen, Tutwiler plc can finance it out of operating cashflows. If Alternative 2 or 3 is chosen, new finance must be raised. The most likely method would be a five-year debenture secured on the building. The interest rate payable on debt of this maturity is 11.5%.

6 The accountant advising Tutwiler plc suggests using the Capital Asset Pricing Model (CAPM) to estimate the company's cost of capital, which can then be used as the discount rate. A competitor company, which is quoted on the London Stock Exchange, and which has a debt:equity ratio (based on market values) of 1:3, has a published equity beta of 1.2. This is unlikely to change in the foreseeable future.

You should assume a debt beta of 0.2. The expected return on 3-month Treasury Bills is 8%. The expected return on the market is 13%. Assume all these figures in note 6 are after adjusting for tax.

7 You should work in round £'000s and, if necessary, round your calculated discount rate to the nearest percent and use the discount tables provided.

Required

(a) Calculate the company's cost of capital using the Capital Asset Pricing Model (CAPM) (as per details in Note 6 of the scenario). **4 Marks**

(b) Calculate the NPV and equivalent annual costs for each project, using the discount rate obtained in your answer to (a). Make whatever assumptions you think necessary but base them wherever possible on information provided in the scenario.

Note. If you have been unable to answer part (a), you may assume a rate of 13% after tax. **15 Marks**

(c) Assume you are the company's management accountant. Write a report to the Finance Director, based on your calculations in answer to part (b) of the question, recommending which project should be chosen and why. You should include in your report an explanation of your method of ranking and choice of discount rates. You should also comment on the risks, financial and non-financial, involved in choosing between the three alternatives. **15 Marks**

(d) Explain the shortcomings of using the CAPM to arrive at risk-adjusted discount rates in the circumstances of the scenario presented here, and comment on an alternative method of evaluating uncertain cash flows. **8 Marks**

(e) The Finance Director later suggests that there is greater uncertainty attached to Alternative 1 because of a cancellation clause in the contract, exercisable at the option of the landlord. He therefore suggests that at a discount rate 2% higher than the one used in the original calculations is more appropriate to evaluate Alternative 1.

(i) Comment on the logic of adjusting the discount rate by a notional percentage to allow for uncertainty; and

(ii) comment on the difference between risk and uncertainty. **8 Marks**

(f) The decision is eventually taken to build new (Alternative 3) but the company fails to get the required permission from its bankers to finance the investment by its preferred method of a five-year debenture. The Finance Director suggests the company could consider raising the money via a venture capital company.

Discuss the advantages and disadvantages of raising new capital by this method in the circumstances of the scenario compared with medium-term debt or a rights issue. **10 Marks**

Total Marks = 60

68 TS PRODUCTS PLC (11/95) *108 mins*

Background and history

It is now November 19X5. TS Products plc is a manufacturer of scientific instruments and other products for the health and medicine markets. The company was formed in 19W2 by Terry, a former doctor in a large teaching hospital, and Susan, a manufacturing process engineer. Their combined skills allowed them to find and exploit a growing market for precision scientific instruments in both the United Kingdom and overseas. The company was floated on the Unlisted Securities Market in 19W7 and obtained a full listing on the Stock Exchange in 19X2. Each of the two founders owns 26% of the share capital, a further 10% is held by other directors and 38% is owned by other individual and institutional investors. Summary financial statements for the company are shown below.

Profit and loss accounts for years to 30 September

	19X4	*19X5*
	£'000	£'000
Turnover	27,500	34,000
Total costs (excluding interest)	19,985	24,140
Profit before interest	7,515	9,860
Interest payable (on long-term debt)	630	1,000
Profit before tax	6,885	8,860
Tax on profit at 33%	2,272	2,924
Profit for the financial year	4,613	5,936
Dividends	2,000	2,300
Retained profit for the financial year	2,613	3,636

Balance sheets at 30 September

	19X4	*19X5*
	£'000	£'000
Fixed assets (NBV)	20,900	26,500
Net current assets	2,964	4,000
Total assets	23,864	30,500
Financed by		
Ordinary share capital (50p shares)	5,000	5,000
Retained profit	11,864	15,500
Long-term debt: 9%	7,000	
Long-term debt: 10%		10,000
Total financing	23,864	30,500
Share price at 30 September	400p	560p

Development of new production method and effect on sales

Although the company has achieved reasonable growth, and profit before interest and taxes from existing operations is expected to grow by 15% in 19X6, Terry and Susan think there is still great potential for their products in a variety of markets. The company has developed an innovative production method for manufacturing scientific instruments which would allow them to produce products of the highest quality at a lower average price than their competitors. The instruments will be sold in packs of 10. Sales are estimated as follows.

Sales (number of packs)	*Probability*
5,000	0.1
12,500	0.3
20,000	0.4
25,000	0.2

The estimated selling price is £500 per pack.

New capital investment and need for financing

Although the variable costs of production are likely to be substantially lower than with older methods, the fixed costs are likely to be high. Extension of the premises will be necessary. An initial capital investment of £14 million is needed plus additional working capital of £6 million. The new production methods will incur fixed costs, including depreciation, of £2.5 million per year and average variable costs of £200 per pack of instruments.

How the investment might be financed: debt versus equity

To finance its expansion, TS Products plc can use debt, equity (ordinary shares) or a combination of the two. Terry and Susan and their fellow directors now have to make a final decision about the method of financing. At a recent meeting two views were presented. The Finance Director recommends that the company should choose debt financing at this time as she believes that inflation is likely to increase in the next few years. Although debt financing might increase the risk of the company, she explains that most investors hold diversified portfolios.

An opposing view is taken by a non-executive director who thinks interest rates may soon fall. He also comments that the success of any new project may be much riskier than anticipated and, as investors generally are risk-averse, lower share prices are found in highly geared companies undertaking risky projects. If additional ordinary shares were issued, the company's financial position would be stronger. Should demand for the product exceed expectations, the company would then be in a better position to issue lower cost debts at a later date.

These opposing views are not entirely resolved in the meeting and it is suggested that further advice should be sought.

Capital structure and its effect on share valuation

TS Products plc currently has outstanding £10 million of long-term debt which carries an interest rate of 10%. If the company wished to raise a further £10 million or £20 million in addition to the existing debt, the interest rates payable are likely to be 12% or 14% respectively. The Board agreed that they should maintain a minimum of £10 million of long-term debt. To go below this amount would forgo tax relief obtained on debt interest payments.

After consulting with their financial advises, estimates on how increasing their debt:total asset ratio might affect the price earnings ratio were eventually agreed as follows.

Debt:total asset ratio	*Estimated P/E ratio*
Up to 30%	10.5
Over 30% and up to 40%	10.0
Over 40% and up to 50%	9.2
Above 50%	8.5

Financing options

Three financing methods are being considered to raise the capital needed for the new production process. These are:

(1) £20 million equity (2) £10 million debt plus £10 million equity (3) £20 million in debt

The financial advisers indicate that ordinary shares will need to be issued at a discount of around 15% to their current market price if the issue is to stand any chance of success. Debt will be issued at par. Issue costs should be ignored. The company's P/E ratio, today, is 9.0. Assume that profit after interest and taxes will increase in years after 19X6 only by the rate of inflation which is expected to remain constant. Tax rates are not expected to change in the foreseeable future.

Required

(a) Calculate:

(i) earnings per share and return on closing shareholders' funds for 19X4 and 19X5,

(ii) today's share price,

(iii) estimates of sales volume and sales value of the new product for 19X6.

5 Marks

(b) Calculate, for *all three* potential capital structures:

(i) the estimated ordinary share price;
(ii) the market value of equity; and
(iii) the combined market value of debt and equity;

which might be expected in 19X6, using only the information provided in the question.

Note. You are *not* required to apply Modigliani and Miller's or Miller's theories of capital structure to the scenario. **20 Marks**

(c) Write a report to Terry and Susan using your findings in part (a) of this question, to explain which of the three capital structure alternatives being considered should be accepted by TS Products plc.

Include in your report:

(i) a comment on the opposing views of the Finance Director and the non-executive director; *and*

(ii) a discussion of what other information would be used before a final decision is made.

Assume that the maximisation of shareholder wealth is the company's main objective. **20 Marks**

(d) During the meeting to discuss the report, the Finance Director says 'clearly the investing public is not aware of our proposed new product'.

(i) Explain the reasoning behind the Finance Director's comment; *and*

(ii) discuss whether it would be to the company's advantage to try and inform investors, and by what method.

Assume the public is not aware of the new proposals. **10 Marks**

(e) You later discover that the directors and some senior managers hold share options on the company's shares.

Explain how this might affect the decision to be taken by the board of TS Products plc. **5 Marks**

Total Marks = 60

69 GLOBAL TELECOMMUNICATIONS INC (5/95) *108 mins*

(a) Zenobia is a developing country situated on the coast of Africa. Its government, now democratically elected, has produced a programme of economic reforms aimed at promoting investment in the country and reducing its dependence on foreign aid. A major feature of this programme is the privatisation of companies and corporations which are currently 100% owned by the government, for example hotels, breweries and coffee production. For the time being, the government is not considering privatising services such as post, railways or the provision of basic telecommunications (this is mainly the fixed line, voice telephony service). It does, however, wish to attract private capital to provide new services such as cellular (mobile) telephones and data communication.

Global Telecommunications Inc (GTI) is a company registered in the USA but with global business interests. Its shares are not listed on a stock exchange, but industry sources estimate that it could command a market capitalisation of around US$200 million. It has established itself as a specialist in the provision of mobile telephone (cellular) services. It is currently negotiating with the government of Zenobia (GoZ) for a licence to provide such services in the country and has already spent US$0.5 million in surveys and miscellaneous expenses. If GTI were successful in the negotiations, it would be the company's first experience of working in a developing country.

Based on a recent World Bank report, GTI estimates that there is a market for between 10,000 and 15,000 customers in a rectangular geographical area bounded by the capital city and three other main towns. The proposed cellular service will operate in this relatively prosperous 'urban rectangle' but the poorer, rural areas outside the rectangle will not be covered.

The market for 10,000 lines is, apart from potential disaster, virtually guaranteed. GTI estimates that the initial investment for this number of lines will be US$25 million. The company has asked the GoZ for a five-year exclusivity period (a period when no other company will be allowed to enter the market to compete). Net operating cashflows, based on a network of 10,000 lines, are forecast to be:

Year	*1*	*2*	*3*	*4*	*5*
Net operating cashflows (US$ million)	3.5	4.8	5.6	6.8	7.2

Cashflows are after interest and tax payments and are shown in US$ equivalents at today's exchange rate.

In year 6, competitors are likely to enter the market and cashflows are expected to fall to around US$6million per annum. For the purposes of evaluation, GTI assumes this annual net cashflow will maintain indefinitely from year 6 onwards on a network of 10,000 lines.

The GoZ is aware that there are other telecommunications companies which are considering investment in the country although to date none has formally declared an interest. It is therefore not prepared to offer a licence based on GTI's terms and has made two counter-proposals for GTI to consider.

Option 1

GTI must provide at least 20% of the 10,000 lines to rural areas and charge rural customers lower rental and call charges than urban customers. In return, the GoZ will allow a ten-year period of exclusivity to GTI. GTI estimates this option will involve US$30million in initial capital costs, and annual net operating cashflows are likely to fall US$0.5 million below those forecast above. However, the ten-year period of exclusivity means that further investment in the network might be advantageous. In considering this option, GTI estimates that an additional investment to provide between 2,000 and 5,000 additional lines at the end of year 3 may be worthwhile. The following information is relevant to GTI's decision.

The capital cost of each additional line is estimated at US$2,000. The average net operating cashflow for each additional line is estimated as US$600 from year 4 onwards. The probabilities for additional demand are:

Number of additional lines	*Probability*
2,000	0.60
3,000	0.30
5,000	0.10

Note. You should assume that the additional lines will be connected simultaneously at the end of year 3.

Option 2

GTI will be allowed a five-year period of exclusivity, a tax holiday for that five-year period and other cost concessions by the GoZ. In return for these concessions, the GoZ requires a 20% shareholding in GTI's Zenobia subsidiary. Dividends will not be payable on this 20% and GTI may remit all profits during this five-year period free of tax. However, GTI will not be permitted to expand the network during the five-year period and at the end of five years GTI will be required to sell 100% of its Zenobia interests on the Zenobia stock market, which is planned to be operational by that time. GTI estimates that this option will reduce the initial investment needed to US$20million, and increase annual net operating cashflows by 10% over the company's original forecasts. The terminal value of GTI's Zenobia subsidiary is estimated as the capitalised value of year 5's net operating cashflows.

There is some dispute between GTI's directors about the discount rate to be used for the evaluations of this project. The company's cost of capital is 15% per annum constant and this is the rate which is being suggested. However, the Managing Director thinks this is a particularly risky project, not least because all calculations and negotiations with the GoZ are in US$, but also because much of the cash inflow will be in local currency. The Technical Director says that, as the project increases international diversification, it actually reduces the company's risk, so a lower rate should be used. The Financial Director says that, as the three options being evaluated have different life spans, different discount rates should be used to evaluate the three options. He also notes that the cashflows for each year are highly correlated with those of the previous and subsequent years.

Required

(i) Advise the board of GTI of the methods available for evaluating international investment decisions, and on how an appropriate discount rate should be determined for the evaluation of a project such as this. Your discussion should be based on, but not necessarily limited to, the comments of the three directors given in the last paragraph above. **10 Marks**

(ii) Provide the board of GTI with a report which evaluates the net present value of the company's own proposal and the two options suggested by the GoZ. You should also provide in your report reasoned recommendations for which, if either, of the Government of Zenobia's offers should be accepted. You should assume that all cashflows occur at the end of each year, with the exception of the initial investment. Assume also that the board of GTI has agreed on a discount rate of 20% to evaluate all three options for the project.

Note. You should ignore taxation in your calculations. **25 Marks**

(b) GTI is at present all equity financed. The company has sufficient cashflows from other projects to enable it to finance the Zenobia deal internally. However, the IFC (the World Bank's sister company which provides finance for investment in developing countries) is prepared to offer 10% fixed interest rates on loans of up to

US$20 million for investments of this nature. Capital is repaid at the end of the loan period which must be a minimum of five years. Interest is paid annually. No early repayment of the loan is permitted without severe financial penalties. If GTI were to raise a similar amount of debt in the capital markets it would currently be obliged to pay 12.5% interest. GTI will be eligible for tax relief at 40% on loan interest payments.

Required

Discuss the advantages and disadvantages of financing the project with an IFC loan. **10 Marks**

(c) A regulatory body for the telecommunications industry in the country, the Zenobia Office of Telecommunications (Zoftel), is being established.

Required

(i) Explain the objectives and main activities of a regulatory authority. **10 Marks**

(ii) Comment on how Zoftel might influence negotiations between GTI and the GoZ. **5 Marks**

Total Marks = 60

70 GARDEN WORLD PLC (Specimen paper) *90 mins*

Garden World plc is a company specialising in horticultural and botanical products. It has two wholly product-centred divisions and a corporate head office. Its business to date has concentrated mainly on supplying retailers of garden products (garden centres), landscape gardeners and other major users and retailers of its products.

A summary balance sheet at 31 December 19X3 for the company is as follows.

	£ million
Fixed assets (net of depreciation)	50.0
Net current assets	20.0
Total assets less current liabilities	70.0
Capital and reserves	
Called-up share capital - 50 million shares of 50p each	25.0
Reserves	25.0
12% debentures 19Y5	20.0
	70.0

The debentures are secured on some of the company's land and buildings.

The shares are currently trading at 250 pence per share. The company's shareholders currently require a return of 15% on their investment.

Garden World plc is now considering a major investment programme. This will involve the creation of a new wholly owned retail subsidiary to operate a chain of garden centres in selected locations throughout the United Kingdom.

As Chief Accountant you have been asked to evaluate the proposed investment. You ask your Assistant Accountant to prepare a schedule of expected cash flows and total working capital requirements as a staring point for your appraisal.

Year	0	1	2	3	4
	£'000	£'000	£'000	£'000	£'000
Land and buildings	5,000				
Fittings and equipment	1,000				
Working capital	500	600	750	800	800
Gross turnover		1,750	3,250	5,250	6,250
Direct costs		1,500	2,300	3,100	3,300
Marketing/advertising		300	450	400	400
Office overhead		250	250	250	250

Note. All expenditure should be assumed to take place at the end of each year, with the exception of capital expenditure and opening working capital which will take place immediately.

You discuss these figures with your assistant and ask her to obtain further information which you will need before you proceed with your investment appraisal. The following day she provides you with the following notes.

(a) Taxation is at present 33% and is expected to remain at this rate for the foreseeable future. The company will claim capital allowances on fittings and equipment at 25% on a reducing balance basis. Capital allowances are not available on land and buildings. Tax is paid one year in arrears.

(b) The company also depreciates its fittings and equipment at 25% on a reducing balance. It does not depreciate land and buildings.

(c) 50% of office overhead is an allocation of head office operating costs which will be charges to the new subsidiary.

(d) The cost of land and buildings includes £250,000 which has already been spent on surveyors' and other advisors' fees.

(e) The parent company expects to be able to sell the subsidiary at the end of year 4. It would expect to receive a sum equal to the book value of land and buildings, the written-down value of fittings and equipment and working capital plus three times year 4's post-tax profits.

(f) Forecast inflation for trading income and all costs and expenses is 4% per annum.

(g) The risk-free rate of interest is at present 8%. You may assume this rate will not change during the life of the project.

You are keen to provide the worth of the investment as you have been told by the Managing Director that the company intends to promote you to be Finance Director of the new subsidiary if the investment goes ahead. However, you are aware that you appraisal must be realistic as it will be judged not only on the actual performance of the subsidiary but also on the comparison of actual with your forecasts.

You are therefore concerned that the appraisal should take adequate account of the risks of the new venture. After assessing the various methods available for incorporating risk into the investment decision, you decide to use the certainty equivalent approach. Based on the probabilities used to estimate the expected cash flows for each year of the project's life, and your estimates of the rates of return which investors require for investments of different levels of risk, you calculate the following certainty equivalents.

Year	*Certainty equivalent*
1	0.90
2	0.85
3	0.80
4	0.75
5	0.70

Required

(a) Advise the board of Garden World plc whether to proceed with this new venture. Base your advice solely on the information presented so far in the case and ignore any possible group tax effects such as rollover relief or capital losses brought forward. **16 Marks**

(b) The information provided for part (a) of this question is necessarily simplified for examination conditions.

(i) Describe how your appraisal might differ in real life from the one you have just produced.

(ii) Comment on any judgmental factors which should be taken into account by the board before it takes the investment decision. **8 Marks**

(c) The use of certainty equivalents is one method of adjusting for investment risk.

Discuss, briefly, two other methods which you might have used. **6 Marks**

(d) The company decides to proceed with the venture and the directors discuss how it will be financed. The Managing Director would like to finance it with equity because he believes this minimises the overall risk. The Finance Director agrees with the Managing Director's comment on risk but suggests that, as the company is substantially equity-financed at present, an increase in the amount of debt in the capital structure would be quite acceptable to the market and could have a favourable effect on the share price. The Finance Director produces the following table of types of medium to long-term debt and the associated average costs.

	%
Medium-term borrowing (1 to 5 years)	8.5
Long-term borrowing (over 5 years)	9.5
Convertibles with conversion dates between 5 and 10 years	9.0
Preference shares	9.5

Discuss the suitability of each of these types of borrowing in the circumstances of this case. **8 Marks**

During the period of the company's evaluation of the investment and method of financing, interest rates start to rise as a result of economic and political factors. The equity market however appears strong and set to improve further over a period of 12 to 18 months. The company is now undecided about whether to issue debt or equity and calls in a merchant bank to advise on the decision.

Required

(e) Explain what services a merchant bank might provide to Garden World plc in connection with an issue of new capital. **6 Marks**

(f) Describe the factors which should be considered in establishing:

(i) the method of issue; and
(ii) the issue price,

if the company decides to finance the investment with equity. **6 Marks**

Total Marks = 50

Answer bank

1 VARIOUS GOALS

> **Pass marks**. In part (a) it is helpful to discuss corporate objectives in the context of stakeholder theory. It is also helpful to discuss the way in which the primary objective is achieved when looking at some of the alternative proposals put forward. In part (b) it may be helpful to set out the factors that must be taken into account in setting a remuneration policy and then to evaluate the options in this context.
>
> **Examiner's comment**. A definition of shareholder wealth is desirable at the beginning of the answer as all else stems from this. It has been argued that shareholder wealth is the only true objective of the firm. Jensen in particular has argued that the interests of shareholders, as owners of the firm, are paramount. However, this is an extreme view and many companies now establish objectives which aim to maximise shareholder wealth whilst recognising the constraints, legally enforceable or voluntary, imposed by society.

(a) REPORT

To: Managing Director
From: Finance Director Date: 17 November 19X5
Subject: Definition of corporate objectives

Introduction

1 This report has been drafted for use as a discussion document at the forthcoming board meeting. It deals with the validity of continuing to operate with the single major goal of **shareholder wealth maximisation.** The remaining sections of the report contain an analysis of the advantages and disadvantages of some of the alternative objectives that have been put forward in recent discussions.

Maximisation of shareholder wealth

2 The concept that the **primary financial objective** of the firm is to maximise the wealth of shareholders, by which is meant the net present value of estimated future cash flows, underpins much of modern financial theory. However, there has been some recent debate as to whether this should or can be the only true objective, particularly in the context of the multinational company.

3 The **stakeholder view** of corporate objectives is that many groups of people have a stake in what the company does. Each of these groups, which include suppliers, workers, manager, customers and governments as well as shareholders, has its own objectives, and this means that a compromise is required. For example, in the case of the multinational firm with a facility in a politically unstable third world economy, the directors may at times need to place the interests of local government and economy ahead of those of its shareholder, in part at least to ensure its own continued stability there.

4 While the relevance of the wealth maximisation goal is under discussion, it might also be useful to consider the way in which this type of objective is defined, since this will impact upon both parallel and subsidiary objectives. A widely adopted approach is to seek to **maximise the present value of the projected cash flows**. In this way, the objective is both made measurable and can be translated into a yardstick for financial decision making. It cannot be defined as a single attainable target but rather as a criterion for the continuing allocation of the company's resources.

Cash flow generation

5 The validity of **cash flow generation** as a major corporate objective depends on the timescale over which performance is measured. If the business maximises the net present value of the cash flows generated in the medium to

long term, then this objective is effectively the same as that discussed above. However, if the aim is to maximise *all* cash flows, then decisions are likely to be disproportionately focused on short-term performance, and this can work against the long-term health of the business. Defining objectives in terms of long-term cash flow generation makes the shareholder wealth maximisation goal more clearly definable and measurable.

Profitability

6 Many companies use **return on investment (ROI)** targets to assess performance and control the business. This is useful for the comparison of widely differing divisions within a diverse multinational company, and can provide something approaching a 'level playing field' when setting targets for the different parts of the business. It is important that the measurement techniques to be used in respect of both profits and the asset base are very clearly defined, and that there is a clear and consistent approach to accounting for inflation. As with the cash flow generation targets discussed above, the selection of the time frame is also important in ensuring that the selected objectives do work for the long-term health of the business.

Risk adjusted returns

7 It is assumed that the use of **risk adjusted returns** relates to the criteria used for investment appraisal, rather than to the performance of the group as a whole. As such, risk adjusted returns cannot be used in defining the top level major corporate goals; however they can be one way in which corporate goals are made congruent with operating decisions. At the same time, they do provide a useful input to the goal setting process in that they focus attention on the company's policy with regard to making risky investments. Once the overall corporate approach to risk has been decided, this can be made effective in operating decisions, for example by specifying the amount by which the cost of capital is to be augmented to allow for risk in various types of investment decisions.

Performance improvement in non-financial areas

8 As discussed in the first section of this report, recent work on corporate objectives suggests that firms should take specific account of those areas which impact only indirectly, if at all, on financial performance. The firm has responsibilities towards many groups in addition to the shareholders, including:

(i) **employees:** to provide good working conditions and remuneration, the opportunity for personal development, outplacement help in the event of redundancy and so on;

(ii) **customers:** to provide a product of good and consistent quality, good service and communication, and open and fair commercial practice;

(iii) **the public:** to ensure responsible disposal of waste products.

9 There are many **other interest groups** that should also be included in the discussion process. Non-financial objectives may often work indirectly to the financial benefit of the firm in the long term, but in the short term they do often appear to compromise the primary financial objectives.

Conclusions

10 It is very difficult to find a comprehensive and appropriate alternative primary financial objective to that of **shareholder wealth maximisation**. However, achievement of this goal can be pursued, at least in part, through

the setting of specific **subsidiary targets** in terms of items such as return on investment and risk adjusted returns. The definition of non-financial objectives should also be addressed in the context of the overall review of the corporate plan.

Signed: Finance Director

(b) The choice of an appropriate remuneration policy by a company will depend, among other things, on:

(i) **cost:** the extent to which the package provides value for money;

(ii) **motivation:** the extent to which the package motivates employees both to stay with the company and to work to their full potential;

(iii) **fiscal effects:** government tax incentives may promote different types of pay. At present there are tax benefits in offering share options and profit-related pay schemes (although the phasing-out of PRP schemes in the UK started in 1998). At times of wage control and high taxation this can act as an incentive to make the 'perks' a more significant part of the package;

(iv) **goal congruence:** the extent to which the package encourages employees to work in such a way as to achieve the objectives of the firm - perhaps to maximise rather than to satisfice.

In this context, Option (i) is likely to be **relatively expensive** with no payback to the firm in times of low profitability. It is unlikely to encourage staff to maximise their efforts, although the extent to which it acts as a **motivator** will depend on the individual psychological make-up of the employees concerned. Many staff prefer this type of package however, since they know where they are financially. In the same way the company is also able to budget accurately for its staff costs.

Provided that the scheme qualifies, the firm will be able to gain **fiscal benefits** from operating a profit-related pay scheme (Option (ii)). It also benefits from the fact that **costs** will be lower, though not proportionately so, during a time of low profits. The effect on motivation will vary with the individual concerned, and will also depend on whether it is an individual or a group performance calculation. There is a further risk that figures and performance may be manipulated by managers in such a way as to maximise their bonus to the detriment of the overall longer term company benefit.

A share option scheme (Option (iii)) carries fiscal benefits in the same way as the performance related pay above. It also minimises the cost to the firm since this is effectively borne by the existing shareholders through the dilution of their holdings. Depending on how pricing is determined, it may assist in achieving goal congruence. However, since the share price depends on many factors which are external to the firm, it is possible for the scheme to operate in a way which is unrelated to the individual's performance. Thus such a scheme is **unlikely to motivate directly** through links with performance. Staff will continue to obtain the vast majority of their income from salary and perks and are thus likely to be more concerned with maximising these elements of their income than with working to raise the share price.

2 MAIN PRINCIPLES

Pass marks. The organisations discussed in the question can each cover a very wide range of situations, and you should address this issue in your answer. You may find it helpful for each of the organisations to consider the source of funds, the objectives of the organisation, and the way in which performance is evaluated.

Examiner's comment. Few scored very high marks but most answers were at least satisfactory. The main weakness was an inability to discuss the *differences* between the financial management function in the various types of organisation.

(a) **Quoted, high growth company**

(i) **Strong management accounting function** with staff involved in the evaluation of strategic opportunities including expansion of existing businesses, product/market diversification and merger and acquisition work. If the capital structure is changing, then this will demand attention to be given to the determination of the cost of capital.

(ii) A relatively large amount of time may be spent on **statutory and listing requirements,** particularly if the company is growing by acquisition.

(iii) The **demands of growth** are likely to impose the need to be constantly developing and adapting management information and accounting systems to meet the needs of the business.

(iv) **Strong treasury skills** will be required to secure both the short and long-term financing for the company and to contribute to capital structure decisions.

(v) The financial manager must be able to adapt to a **continually changing environment** and to contribute to the strategic decisions facing the business.

(b) **Quoted, low growth company**

(i) The department must be capable of dealing efficiently with the **statutory and listing requirements.**

(ii) If growth is slow due to market constraints, there is likely to be a higher degree of attention paid to the improvement of profit by means of **cost control,** and therefore the financial management must be able to select and implement appropriate budgetary and cost control systems and to provide management information in a concise and relevant form.

(iii) If the focus is on cost control, then the **finance department** itself must be run as effectively and efficiently as possible.

(iv) If the company is growing, albeit slowly, the financial managers must be able to make a significant contribution to the evaluation of **strategic opportunities** as described above.

(v) If the slower rate of growth means that the company is cash generative, the financial management will be concerned with the best **ways in which to use the funds,** whether this involves investment in new business opportunities or repayment to shareholders in the form of dividends or a buy-back of shares.

(c) **Unquoted company aiming for a stock exchange listing**

(i) The financial management must understand the **listing requirements** and be able to liaise with the banks and institutions advising on the flotation. They must also be able to provide information on the likely valuation of the shares and to advise on the proposed capital structure of the quoted company.

(ii) If the flotation is being made due to the need for **access to a wider pool of funds** to finance expansion, then many of the points made in part (a) will also be relevant.

(iii) If the purpose of the flotation is to enable the owners to realise the value of their investment then the financial managers must be able to **persuade potential investors** that the company will be as successful under a new ownership and control structure as it was as a private company.

(iv) The managers must be good at **communicating information** about the company to the wider public, and must be able to present financial information in a clear and accessible format.

(d) **Small family owned business**

(i) The precise role of the financial manager will depend to some extent on the position and nature of the company. For instance, is it growing or is it facing competitive pressure and liquidity problems? **Different business situations will place different demands** upon the financial managers.

(ii) In a small company, the financial manager must be able to turn his hand to a much **wider range of activities** than in a large company. For example, if office staff are absent then he may find himself making up wage packets, followed by a meeting with the bank to discuss the overdraft, followed by a time of both producing and interpreting the monthly management information. He must therefore be much more of a generalist and understand the details of a wide range of financial specialisms.

(iii) The financial manager must be able to **communicate effectively** with a wide range of people, including the owners of the business, providers of finance, tax officers and shopfloor workers.

(e) **Non profit-making organisation, eg a charity**

(i) The fundamental difference between a non profit-making organisation and a commercial business is that **resources are allocated** not on the basis of cash flow generation, but **on the basis of value to those providing the funds**. Thus the financial manager will be more concerned with providing an appropriate way of measuring 'value' in the context of the aims of the organisation than with measuring cash flow.

(ii) The financial manager will need to be involved in the **fund-raising process**, whether this is targeted at individuals, other charitable institutions or various public sector bodies such as the Ministry for Overseas Development, the National Lottery or EU funds. This is obviously quite different from the way in which a commercial organisation raises funds in the form of equity and debt.

(iii) Since funds are donated, there is likely to be a strong emphasis on **cost control** and the efficient use of allocated resources.

(iv) The financial manager must have a good knowledge of **tax law** as it affects charities, for example in certain VAT exemptions and in the recovery of tax on money covenanted in various ways.

(f) **Public sector, eg a government department**

(i) In terms of expenditure, the work of the financial manager is likely to be similar to that in a non profit-making organisation, the emphasis being on '**value**' rather than cash flow. This is likely to demand an understanding of the techniques of cost benefit analysis.

(ii) Unless the department concerned is the Treasury, the financial manager will have little or no concern with the way in which the funds are raised since there is generally a **separation** in the public sector **between sourcing of funds and expenditure.**

(iii) Unlike the private organisation where some attempt will be made to look at the longer term, most of the budgeting in a government department is concerned with the **one year timespan** and is **framed in revenue terms.**

3 PUBLIC SECTOR OBJECTIVES

Pass marks. The private sector includes non-profit seeking organisations, just as the public sector has profit seeking ones but, for ease of discussion, the main thrust of our answer to part (a) is comparing the profit-making private sector against the non-profit making public services. This question is not easy to discuss: it is too easy to lapse into the prejudices of one's own viewpoint. Try to maintain a balanced view. A few amusing examples can be given of dysfunctional public service performance measures.

Examiner's comment. In answer to part (b) of the question few candidates were able to discuss satisfactorily the difficulties in using the measures to influence decision making. Many simply repeated what they had said in part (a) rather than focusing on the more important difficulties.

(a) A **private sector** organisation is owned by private shareholders whereas a **public sector** body is owned by a government, whether national, local or international. Both sectors can have profit-making and non-profit organisations. Most of this discussion, however, is concerned with the comparison of the profit-seeking private sector with non-profit seeking public services.

Some of the **main differences between private sector and public sector organisations,** which need to be addressed when determining corporate objectives or missions, are discussed below.

Public sector objectives are usually detailed in a statute or other regulatory document. Private sector bodies will have objectives decided by their owners or by directors acting as agents for the owners. It is easier for private sector objectives to adapt to changing circumstances.

Private sector organisations will usually not survive unless they earn adequate profits for their owners. Public services are not charged with making profits but with producing the maximum effective high-quality output for the minimum unit cost within the allowed budget. This difference is explored below. Other than this, the objectives of the two types of organisation may be very similar, involving consideration for the various stakeholders, such as customers, suppliers, employees and the wider community.

Private sector organisations nearly always have outputs which can be expressed in monetary terms (eg sales value). Public service outputs cannot be or are not valued in monetary terms. For example, one of the outputs of a public sector hospital will be a patient with a mended leg but the equivalent output of a private sector hospital is a patient with a mended leg and an invoice in his pocket.

This difference between the two types of organisation is fundamental when trying to set objectives. Private sector businesses always have a profit-based measure as one of their major objectives. Often it will be the over-riding objective. It might be profit or return on capital employed or shareholder value, but if the organisation fails to achieve the required financial returns for its owners, it will fail to survive.

Public service organisations cannot measure profit because their outputs are non-financial. Their financial objectives are always concerned with input costs only, whereas output objectives are set in terms of non-financial quality and efficiency measures.

The sanctions on failing to meet public service objectives are weaker than in the private sector. Except in extreme cases, the organisation cannot be closed down and it is often more difficult to change the management. The most severe sanction that can be imposed is to starve the organisation of cash in an attempt to force efficiency improvements.

Until recently, public sector organisations have used cash-based accounting systems which make it more difficult to estimate the resources used in service provision. The introduction of resource accounting in the UK and other countries enables the setting of objectives and targets which are easier to monitor against the actual out-turn and hence allows comparison with equivalent private sector service providers.

(b) (i) The health authority has as its **objective** the provision of high quality healthcare within expected waiting times. This should be quantified by the setting of **performance targets.**

Many **performance measures** can be devised. Three examples are as follows.

Waiting times

- Average time taken for an ambulance to arrive at the scene of an emergency
- Average time spent waiting for a particular type of non-urgent operation

Quality

- Percentage of successful operations for a given type of surgery

All of these measures can be compared against the national average, or another benchmark figure.

(ii) **Decision making** in public sector bodies is often difficult because of conflicting objectives and performance measures. Some of the performance measures are ambiguous or motivate dysfunctional behaviour whereas others are constrained by limited resources.

For example:

(1) a long waiting list for a hospital operation may arise because the hospital is slow and inefficient, or alternatively because the operation is very popular at that particular hospital as it is done so well

(2) to evaluate quality of surgery by success rates encourages the rejection of cases where there is more chance of failure, in other words rejection of the most needy cases. Similarly, schools will try to reject poorly performing pupils and police forces find that their statistics look much better when crimes are simply not reported

(3) a hospital clearly does not want to operate a long waiting list but may be forced to, simply because there is a limit to the funds available

Private sector organisations probably face as many **conflicts in their decision making** as public sector organisations, but in the end the final judge for the private sector is the market place. Many high quality companies have failed because they over-emphasised the wrong objectives. So maybe the problem for public service organisations is not the conflict between objectives but the fact that there is no overall dispassionate judge to tell them whether their decisions are right or wrong. In a rationing decision somebody has to make a difficult decision. If a harsh decision is made by market forces, nobody is to blame. If a public sector administrator makes a harsh decision, the criticism is seemingly endless.

4 COSTS AND BENEFITS

Pass marks. In part (a) you may find it helpful to consider the capital structure of the firm as a means of approaching the question of the definition of the primary financial objective. Discussion of the definition of shareholder wealth and the timescale over which this is to be measured is also helpful. This can be followed up with a discussion of other approaches to corporate objectives, such as the stakeholder theory.

In part (b) you may find it helpful to consider a concrete example of a project with environmental implications and to base your discussion around this, rather than to write of environmental costs and benefits in general terms.

Examiner's comment. Common failures in part(a) were to ignore cultural influences (although some did mention the differences between the aims of companies in Japan and those in the West), and limiting an answer to a discussion of shareholder wealth as the sum of dividends plus capital gains. A common weakness in part (b) was to focus on employment issues and ignore other benefits such as public image or technological spin-offs.

(a) The concept that the primary financial objective of the firm is to **maximise the wealth of the ordinary shareholders** underpins much of **modern financial management theory**. A company is financed by ordinary shareholders, preference shareholders, loan stock holders and other long-term and short-term creditors. All surplus funds, however, belong to the legal owners of the company, its ordinary shareholders. Any retained profits are undistributed wealth of these equity shareholders. The wealth of the shareholders in a company comes from dividends received and the market value of the shares, and it is the maximisation of the sum of these two elements that is generally seen as the aim of a firm's strategic activities.

In financial management theory, **shareholder wealth** is generally defined as being the wealth that accrues to the shareholders as a direct result of their equity stake in the firm and, in this context, the approach most widely adopted is to seek to maximise the present value of the projected cash flows. Such a definition and approach renders the objective measurable, and means that it can be used as a yardstick for financial decision making. However by its very nature, shareholder wealth maximisation cannot be defined as a single attainable target, but rather as a criterion for the continuing allocation of the company's resources.

It is also important to consider the **timescale** over which the objective is to be pursued and measured. Policies directed at maximising short-term wealth will have quite different implications from those directed at longer term performance. Maximisation of short-term profits and cash flows can result in longer term strategic opportunities being missed and may not be in the best long-term interests of the company and its shareholders.

Recent debate has questioned whether the maximisation of shareholder wealth should or can be the only true objective. The stakeholder theory of corporate objectives contends that **many groups of people** have a stake in what the company does. Each of these groups, including workers, managers, suppliers, customers, the local community and government, as well as shareholders, has its own objectives. Thus in practical terms, the goal of shareholder wealth maximisation must be seen as a primary objective within a whole matrix of objectives, the relative importance of which will vary from location to location and from time to time.

Some examples of these non-financial objectives are as follows.

(i) **The welfare of the employees**. A company might try to provide good wages and salaries, attractive and safe working conditions, good training and career development and good pensions. While such policies are likely to improve morale and impact favourably on financial performance, it may be unrealistic to expect them to generate a positive financial return on investment.

(ii) **Fulfilment of responsibilities to suppliers**. Large companies may be able to exert considerable pressure on suppliers, both in terms of prices and payment terms. This power should not be used unfairly.

(iii) **Responsibilities to society**. Some companies, such as The Body Shop, take seriously their responsibilities to society and devote resources both to initiatives in their local community and to wider social campaigning.

Thus in practice, companies operate with a whole range of financial and non-financial objectives. Although maximisation of shareholder wealth may well be the primary objective, this is likely to be constrained to some degree by the **other aims** of the firm.

(b) The way in which **environmental costs and benefits** are included in the appraisal process will depend on the nature of the environmental implications, and the way in which the company intends to approach them. One method is to include in the appraisal only those elements of environmental cost that are **directly attributable** to undertaking the project, and to evaluate any further actions that the company may wish to undertake as a separate issue. In some cases, this may be relatively simple, particularly if legislation exists that defines the environmental standards to be applied. For example, if the process under consideration produces significant volumes of trade effluent, the Environment Agency must be informed and it will then impose a discharge consent on the company that defines the acceptable composition of discharge to sewer in terms of parts per million of contaminating substances.

The company will then be faced with a variety of **technological options** that it could use to reduce the contamination to the required levels; for example, if volumes are large enough, it may be appropriate to build a treatment plant to decontaminate the effluent - alternatively it could enter into an agreement with a waste treatment company to tanker away the waste and dispose of it off site. Each of these options will have a definable cost which can be evaluated and incorporated into the overall project appraisal. In this situation, there are no quantifiable benefits as such, since the environmental issues take the form of a constraint on the project. The costs arise as a direct result of undertaking the project, and as such must be incorporated into the appraisal.

The problems arise where the company sees the opportunity to go beyond its statutory duties and to act in such a way as to maximise the environmental benefits. In the example cited above, it may be that the most cost effective method from the point of view of the company is to tanker the waste to a remote treatment plant. However, it may view this as unacceptable on the grounds that it wishes to minimise the disturbance to the area around the site, and thus not to generate high volumes of tanker traffic in the local area. In this situation, the higher cost option of on-site treatment may become more attractive, although this is not a direct requirement of the project being undertaken. The benefits that arise are difficult to quantify and will not accrue directly to the company undertaking the investment.

In this situation, two approaches are possible.

(i) The company could decide that its own environmental standards form a financial constraint upon the project, and thus that the project should be **evaluated at its full environmental cost**.

(ii) Alternatively, it could decide that the additional costs of on-site treatment over and above the cost of meeting the statutory requirements represent a **separate environmental investment**. If the company sets aside a budget for environmental and social issues, these excess costs could then be taken away from the project and allocated against this environmental budget.

Both approaches are valid and will depend on the objectives and policies of the company with regard to environmental issues.

5 TUTORIAL QUESTION: AIM COMPANIES

(a) X plc is the **more profitable** company, both in absolute terms and in proportion to sales and to operating capital employed. This may indicate that X plc is much better managed than Y plc, but this is not the only possibility, and a study of the other data shows that Y plc's profitability, while at present lower, may be more sustainable.

A higher percentage of Y's sales are to the home market, while it has still achieved fairly substantial export sales. This suggests that Y could have done better in exploiting the export market, but also that Y is less exposed than X to exchange rate fluctuations and the possible imposition of trade barriers. The prospects for the home market appear good, and should give scope for adequate growth. Y has achieved higher growth in total turnover than X over the past three years.

While Y appears to be making **worse use** of its assets than X, with asset turnover ratios lower than X's and falling, this seems to be largely because Y has recently acquired substantial new assets. It may be that within the next few years X will have to undertake a major renewals programme, with consequent adverse effects on its asset turnover ratios. While X may be making better use of its assets (subject to the reservations set out above), Y is making sales per employee about 50% higher than X, and has consistently done so over the past three years. In favour of X, it could be pointed out that Y has been established twice as long as X; on the other hand, X shows no sign of catching up, despite the fact that its total number of employees has recently fallen slightly. The modest rises in sales per employee over the past three years in both X and Y may be due largely to inflation.

Y seems to be significantly better than X at **controlling cost of sales** (49% of sales in Y, and 65% in X), though X has made improvements over the past three years while there has been little change in Y. On the other hand, X's administration expenses have been only 6% of sales, while Y's have been 26% of sales. This contrast between the two types of cost suggests that different categorisations of costs may have been used. If we combine cost of sales and administration, then for X they total 71% of sales and for Y they total 75% of sales. There is thus little difference between the companies, though X has shown improved cost control while Y has not. X has also had lower selling and distribution costs. One must however bear in mind that X will have had a lower depreciation element in its costs than Y, because Y has recently invested substantially in fixed assets. Y's costs will also be increased by its higher salaries, which may pay off in better employee motivation and hence higher sales per employee. On the other hand, Y's costs have been kept down by the carrying forward of an increasing amount of product development costs, an accounting policy which may well be regarded as imprudent.

In **working capital management**, X has the edge. Y has very high debtors, and these have recently risen sharply as a proportion of turnover. Y also carries rather more stock than X, and has very little cash. While both companies have tolerable current and liquid ratios, X's are certainly safer. Y achieves a liquid ratio of 1:1 almost entirely by relying on debtors. If it suffers substantial bad debts, or if the bank should become concerned and call in the overdraft, Y could suffer serious liquidity problems. It also depends heavily on trade credit to finance debtors. While it is sensible to take advantage of trade credit offered, Y may depend too much on the continued goodwill of its suppliers. This, and Y's deteriorating (though still adequate) interest cover may indicate the need for a fresh injection of equity.

X's **interest cover** has risen sharply, as its debt has fallen. Presumably the substantial borrowings needed for a management buyout are now being repaid. Returns to equity, measured by earnings per share, have increased significantly in both companies, though much faster in X than in Y. **Dividend cover** has shown good growth in Y, paralleling that in earnings per share and showing that dividends have hardly changed, perhaps because of liquidity problems. After paying virtually no dividend in 19X7, X seems to be settling down to a dividend policy appropriate to a company which is no longer new. The ample dividend cover leaves plenty of room to improve dividends when retention of most of the profits is no longer necessary.

(b) X is recommended, for the following reasons.

(i) Its **liquidity position** is far safer than Y's.

(ii) It appears to have greater **potential for growth**, so long as the high motivation of the management and staff following the management buyout can be sustained. However, substantial funds may need to be invested for little short term return, while the company develops.

(iii) Y's management appear to have lost interest in efficient **working capital control** and **cost control**, and the company may be losing its way.

(iv) X has come to the AIM after five years, while Y took ten years to reach that stage. This suggests that X has **investors' confidence**, and so further capital should be readily obtainable if it is needed.

6 INDICATORS

> **Pass marks**. In part (a) it is helpful to set the use of performance indicators into the context of the planning and control process. For part (b), remember that the public sector is now much more diverse than it was previously, for example it contains areas being prepared for privatisation and areas with a developing internal market, as well as the more traditional areas. For completeness, our solution covers *all* factors from the list.
>
> **Examiner's comment**. Marking was flexible as a wide range of approaches is possible. Candidates who clearly worked in, or were familiar with, the public sector did particularly well. However, many candidates did not appear to know anything about developments in the public sector. Many answers simply stated that since the public sector was a monopoly and obtained its money from government, none of the ratios were relevant.

(a) Performance and progress indicators can be approached from the angle of the **planning and control process.**

There are three main components of this process:

(i) setting targets for performance
(ii) measuring and evaluating actual performance
(iii) corrective action where necessary

Indicators to measure progress and performance therefore provide an essential link between the processes of planning and control.

A company with a well developed planning and control process will set targets and measure performance in all areas of its activities, including areas such as research and development and human resources. Clearly, pure financial indicators will be inadequate in these areas, and thus a range of more appropriate indicators to measure performance and progress have been, and continue to be, developed. Examples include measures of customer satisfaction, product innovation and environmental standards.

(b) **Cash generation.** In the private sector this is a key measure of financial performance related to the liquidity and solvency of the organisation. It can be measured in a number of ways, one of the simplest being the excess of receipts (from customers, tax etc) over expenditure (to suppliers, workers, shareholders, government etc). In reasonably profitable companies, this is only likely to become a constraint when additional cash is needed to finance further expansion in some form.

In the public sector, cash generation is generally measured in terms of cash absorption in annual terms, and this is often the principal constraint on a service provider. Since cashflow measures make no distinction between capital and revenue expenditure, the effect of this is to encourage an excessive concern with short term performance.

Value added. This is a measure used in the private sector that seeks to relate cashflow generation to throughput, and it is valuable in making decisions about product mix, pricing etc. One of its key drivers is the unit price of the product, and for this reason it has been little used in the public sector. However, it can be argued that a public sector variant of this which is being increasingly used is cost benefit analysis which seeks to maximise the amount of benefit generated per unit of scarce resource (generally cash).

Profitability. In the private sector profitability is one of the most widely used performance indicators. It is generally defined as the ratio of profit to sales or to capital employed, and it is used among other things to make decisions on the allocation of resources between different product and market segments.

In the **public sector,** the concept has been relatively little used in the past but is now increasing in importance, particularly in those organisations being prepared for transfer to the private sector, such as British Rail and the Royal Mail. As in the private sector, the implications for resource allocation are considerable, and may lead to a change in emphasis away from the target of providing a **universal service** to a target of providing an **economic service.**

Return on assets. This is similar in definition to some of the measures of 'profitability' as discussed above. It seeks to relate the profit for a period to the value of the underlying assets used to generate that profit. It suffers many of the limitations of measures that are based on purely accounting figures, such as the emphasis on historical performance, and tangible assets, and one of the main dangers is that if there is an emphasis on maximising short term performance the effect of concentrating attention on return on assets will be to restrict investment. This is unlikely to be in the best long-term interests of the business.

Despite its limitations, this measure is being increasingly used in the public sector, particularly in the evaluation of performance in the NHS where it is one of the key approaches to comparing the performance of the different NHS trusts.

Market share. Market share measures the percentage of a total market that a company supplies for a given product. It is therefore a measure of the success of the sales performance, pricing strategy and product quality.

Since the majority of public sector organisations have, at least until recently, been in a monopoly position, this measure has been largely irrelevant. However, with the drive to create competition, for example by the creation of the internal market in the NHS, it is likely that market share will gain increasing importance in some areas of the public sector. For example, it could be used as a measure of the success of different NHS trust hospitals in attracting patients from the GPs in their area.

Customer satisfaction. This is concerned with the extent to which a company has succeeded in satisfying the full range of its customers' requirements, and may be measured by customer survey or in some circumstances by managers posing as customers. It is important in that it measures areas of product and service quality, for example the quality of technical support provided for a particular product, which cannot be assessed in any other way, but which are significant elements in the purchasing decision.

For the same reasons as with market share, this measure has until recently been relatively unimportant in the public sector. However, the introduction of competition, allied to the development of the Citizens' Charter has resulted in an increasing amount of attention being focused on this area. Measurement approaches will generally be very similar in the two sectors.

Competitive position. This is a wider measure than the preceding two, being concerned with the company's overall capabilities in terms of innovation, flexibility, product quality and price etc. There are no clearly defined universally applicable approaches to measurement, but at the same time the competitive position of an organisation is seen as of vital importance in its long term survival and growth. It is not likely to be of the same significance in the public sector, except in those areas which are being subjected to a degree of competition.

Risk exposure. Exposure to risk will be evaluated in the private sector in a number of areas, for example when capital investment alternatives are being considered, in relation to exchange rates, interest rates etc. Such decisions will be faced to a lesser extent in the public sector where the service targets and operating constraints are more closely defined. Various hedging techniques are available for certain types of risk, but in general, the approach taken will depend largely on the attitude of the management to risk. In the majority of cases, public sector organisations are much more risk averse than private companies.

7 PDQ PLC

Pass marks. Part (a) requires an evaluation of performance in terms of stated objectives. It is worth commenting on the validity of the objective in relation to the appraisal process due to its 'fuzziness' in definition. In part (ii) take into account information external to the firm and financial projections as well as the more obviously helpful detailed management accounts.

Part (b) requires an understanding of the dynamics of a service business and gives you the opportunity to think creatively about performance measurement in this context. It may be helpful in some areas to consider the different elements of the business separately since it is unlikely that one measure is likely to be appropriate to all the types of work undertaken.

Examiner's comment. Most candidates successfully identified that shareholder wealth is increased by both dividends and capital gains. However, a large number did not fully understand the concepts of shareholder wealth and thought this should be measured entirely by changes in share prices, irrespective of changes to the capital structure.

(a) (i) A numerical analysis of the **financial performance** of PDQ is shown below. The figures provide the basis for making a traditional evaluation of the performance of the company from the point of view of the shareholders. However, there is only limited information on which to assess performance from the standpoint of the other stakeholders.

Calculation of key variables

	Year 1	2	3	4	5
Shareholders' ratios					
(1) Payout ratio (%)	40.38	39.39	40.00	40.00	50.00
(2) Dividend per share	£0.35	£0.43	£0.50	£0.43	£0.60
(3) Share price P/E × earnings/no of shares in issue	£6.93	£9.35	£11.25	£9.77	£11.40
(4) Dividend yield (%)	5.05	4.63	4.44	4.35	5.26
(5) Earnings/share	£0.87	£1.10	£1.25	£1.06	£1.20
(6) Market capitalisation (£'000)	41,600	56,100	67,500	78,200	91,200
Profitability					
(1) Post tax profit/sales (%)	10.16	11.32	11.74	11.30	12.28
(2) ROCE (PBIT:total assets) (%)	22.33	25.22	26.77	20.54	21.76
(3) Sales growth (%)		13.87	9.61	17.68	3.99
(4) PBIT growth (%)		23.91	9.65	4.00	12.31
(5) Interest:debt (%)	10.00	10.67	10.83	8.57	8.00
Working capital					
(1) Debtor days	75	73	76	72	71
(2) Creditor days (based on cost of sales)	68	69	77	81	83
Average wages/person	£8,953	£9,600	£9,451	£9,186	£8,994

From the point of view of the shareholders, financial performance has been good. The **payout ratio** has been maintained at 40% and in year 5 increased to 50%. **Dividend per share** has increased throughout the period with the exception of year 4 when their was some dilution due to the rights issue. This reflects the overall trend of growth in sales and profits, albeit somewhat more erratic than the dividend performance. However, **return on capital employed** fell after the rights issue although it shows signs of renewed improvement in year 5.

It appears that in the earlier part of the period under review, growth in earnings was achieved from growth in sales. The figures suggest that the part of the proceeds of the rights issue not used to redeem debt was invested in assets which may have been used to generate the further sales growth in year 5. At the same time there was a significant reduction both in the number of people employed and the average level of remuneration in years 4 and 5, which may suggest that PDQ has been replacing labour by capital to achieve both sales growth and cost savings. The drop in the average earnings level could also suggest either a switch to more part time working (assuming that the number employed figure is not a full time equivalents figure) or that there has been rationalisation in the management structure which has reduced the proportion of more highly paid employees.

The actual **return to the shareholders** over the period can be calculated as follows.

	£m
Increase in market capitalisation (£91.2m – £41.6m)	49.6
Less cost of rights issue	(20.0)
Dividends (Yrs 1-4)	11.1
	40.7

This equates to a total return over four years of 82%.

Other stakeholders in the business include customers, suppliers, employees, providers of debt finance and the tax authorities. The performance of PDQ from their points of view can be evaluated as follows.

(1) **Customers.** The volume of goods and services provided has increased by 52.7% over the period, presumably to their benefit. However, the period of credit allowed has reduced from 75 to 71 days.

(2) **Suppliers.** The volume of business has also increased by 50% based on the cost of goods sold. However, the period of credit taken by PDQ has increased from 68 to 83 days, presumably to the detriment of the suppliers.

(3) **Employees.** The numbers employed increased from years 1 to 3 before being cut back. Average earnings similarly increased to year 3 before falling back. Assuming that there was some degree of wage inflation in the economy during the period, the employees do not appear to have fared particularly well. Possible reasons for the movement in the figures were outlined above.

(4) **Providers of debt finance.** There has been a steady repayment of debt capital during the period with the major repayment being made at the same time as the rights issue in year 4. At the same time the average rate of interest paid has reduced from 10% to 8%.

(5) **Tax authorities.** They have benefited from payments of £18.4m over the five year period.

In conclusion, it can be seen that the major benefit over the period has accrued to the **ordinary shareholders**. Some assessment of the position of the other stakeholders has been made but it is not possible to make a full evaluation of their relative position from the information given. Since the objective is not expressed in quantitative terms it is not possible to provide a definitive appraisal as to whether or not it has been successfully met.

(ii) The other financial information that would be helpful include the following areas.

(1) **Financial projections and investment proposals.** The wealth of the shareholders as represented by the market value of the shares is very dependent upon future earnings and dividend projections. It would

therefore be helpful to have access to more detailed information on these areas in order to assess the likely movements in both financial performance and the share price. The fact that the P/E ratio has been increasing at a faster rate than the industry average suggests that the market takes a positive view of PDQ's current performance and projections.

(2) **Factors external to the firm.** These include factors such as the current rates of interest and inflation which would allow a better appraisal to be made of the performance of the company in real terms from the point of view of the shareholders. It would also be helpful to have information on the size and projected growth of the markets in which PDQ operates, its current and projected market share and the competitive structure of the industry.

(3) **Detailed management accounts and reports.** It would be helpful to have access to a more detailed analysis of the customer and supplier base, the breakdown of the sales figures by market sector, volume and price, credit policies etc. Similar information on the status of the fixed asset base would also be helpful. Human resources information on the grading, turnover and salary levels of the various groups of employees would enable a better analysis to be made of the position of this particular stakeholder group.

The objective as stated is not expressed in terms of measurable targets. It would therefore be helpful to have any internal information relating to any internal targets that are set, as well as discussion documents relating to this process. A further stakeholder group that has not been mentioned so far is the wider community and the environment; details of charitable giving, social and environmental projects would allow an appraisal to be made of performance in this area.

(b) (i) The most obvious statistic on which to measure **competitiveness** is market share; however this may be difficult to obtain in practice. A more helpful measure of ongoing performance might therefore be a simple conversion rate of quotes issued to business received.

(ii) One of the traditional measures of **financial performance** is return on capital employed. However this is unlikely to be appropriate in a service business such as this, and therefore it may be more helpful to focus on simple measures of profit, both in absolute terms and as a percentage of sales.

(iii) There are various approaches to **quality** in a service business. It can be evaluated from the negative point of view of number of complaints; another alternative is to seek to maximise the proportion of repeat business.

(iv) The first step towards measuring performance in **responsiveness to customer needs** is to establish the factors that customers believe to be important in selecting an architect, surveyor or engineer. One simple measure would be to record response time, ie the number of days to provide a client with a survey report from the time the survey was requested. However, a truly meaningful measure can only be developed after communication with the client base, and the most appropriate yardstick may be different for an architect than for a building engineer.

(v) The key resource in this type of business is the professionally trained staff. One appropriate measure of **resource utilisation** might therefore be the proportion of each individual's time spent on work directly connected with client business, or sales per hour.

(vi) **Innovation** is difficult to quantify directly since there are no obviously identifiable 'products' that can be seen to be developing. As with responsiveness to customer needs, the measure may need to be different in different areas of the business. One possibility in the architects' department might be to measure the number of new buildings types quoted representing an extension of the range of the work undertaken.

For performance measures to be effective they need to be objective and measurable, and ideally directly related to the strategic plans of the business. The problem in service businesses is to identify key performance parameters and to set realistic and measurable targets against these. As the examples above demonstrate, this is easier in some areas than other - resource use is relatively easy to measure, but it is likely to be extremely difficult to develop a truly meaningful an realistic measure of innovation.

It is also likely that improvements in one area may result in a deterioration of performance in another. For example, improvements in financial performance may be at the expense of quality. It may be appropriate to attempt to score performance on the chosen variables and then to seek to maximise the overall score rather than to try to maximise on all variables which is unlikely to be possible in practice.

8 BALANCED SCORECARD

Pass marks. These questions are straightforward requests for explanations of alternatives approaches to performance measurement and corporate governance. It is always much easier to collect your thoughts on short discussion questions like this if you have previously made a list of relevant bullet points, while making your revision notes.

Examiner's comments. The question was generally answered well, part (a) in particular, although some candidates thought that the 'balanced scorecard' and 'stakeholder theory' were the same thing.

(a) (i) Kaplan and Norton (1992) devised the 'balanced scorecard' as a way of improving the use of organisational performance measures. The approach recognises that performance improvement results from taking action on a range of activities, only some of which are measurable in financial terms.

Four perspectives are considered as follows.

The customer perspective. How do customers see us? Have customers' needs been met? Measures include price, demand, quality, customer loyalty and customer satisfaction.

The internal business perspective. What must we excel at? What are our key business processes? How do we compare with best practice? (benchmarking). Measures of efficiency, resource utilisation, quality, effectiveness etc.

The innovation and learning perspective. Can we continue to improve and create value? How many new products have we developed and successfully launched? Are we exploring new markets? Are we embracing new technologies?

Financial perspective. How do we look at shareholders? Therc are many financial measures of performance. However, most can be only be improved by considering non-financial activities.

There will be conflicts between these four perspectives when attempting improvements in performance measures. For example, an over-concentration on the financial perspective can result in short-term actions which harm the organisation's longer term future. The 'balanced scorecard' attempts to combine the performance measures by weighting them suitably for each organisation.

(ii) **Examples of performance measures in a firm of consultants**

Customer perspective

Proportion of customers who have placed further business.

The success of any service industry depends on customer satisfaction, and repeat customers are often more profitable than first-time customers.

Internal business perspective

Utilisation of consultants: proportion of 'idle time'. Success of a consultancy business depends on having the consultants 'charged out' to clients for a high proportion of their time. Caution must be exercised however, because it is necessary to allocate the right people to each job.

Innovation and learning perspective

Proportion of jobs done which are associated with techniques or technologies not offered five years ago.

Care must be taken with this measure, as the firm does not want to embrace new techniques at the expense of ignoring its core skills and expertise.

(b) Quotation 1 puts forward the view that a firm is run for the benefit of a number of stakeholder groups, all of which are necessary for the continuing success of the business. In some versions of this description, each group will require a minimum reward for their involvement, and if the business generates surpluses in excess of these requirements, stakeholders will bargain as to who receives the excess rewards. The quotation implies that if stakeholder groups are ignored, the business will suffer.

Quotation 2 takes the traditional view that businesses are run for the benefit of their owners (shareholders) and that other stakeholder groups are secondary. The business objective is to maximise shareholder wealth and, if this objective is pursued, then the welfare of society will also be maximised, provided that society (eg governments or charities) take action to eliminate market imperfections and undesirable corporate behaviour.

The two quotations appear at first sight to put forward very different viewpoints. Quotation 1 seems to favour a democratic organisation in which employees and customers, for example, have as much right as company directors and shareholders in determining corporate objectives and direction. Quotation 2, on the other hand, appears to relegate all stakeholder groups other than shareholders to the level of minimum feasible rewards.

However, both of these two interpretations would lead to sub-optimal performance. The dangers of the over-democratic organisation are that costs may rise and strategic direction might be uncertain, whereas a business run to maximise short-term profit for shareholders is likely to anger all other stakeholders to the point that they choose to be associated with alternative organisations.

The key to reconciling the two statements is in realising that shareholders can assist in maximising their own *long-term* benefits by (i) ensuring that other stakeholders are treated fairly, and (ii) attempting to align the goals of other stakeholders with their own. Employees who are treated fairly will remain in their job and may work more efficiently. Those whose pay is partly related to company performance may become more motivated. Customers for whom extra costs are spent on producing customised products are likely to make repeat purchases. The key to these attempts to align stakeholder goals is a reward system for directors to ensure that they make decisions which are sensible for long-term shareholder wealth. Share options have proved successful in this respect.

Thus although shareholders, and their agents the directors, remain in firm control of organisations, it is clear that maximisation of business value can only take place if the needs of all stakeholders are considered.

9 DIFFICULTIES

> **Pass marks.** Part (a) is concerned with the **effects** rather than the **causes** of financial difficulties, and the **strategies** rather than the **tactics** that should be used to deal with them. In part (b) you could choose to think about some of the business collapses that you have read about in the press, and to consider whether they could have been predicted in a quantitative way. This may help you to develop a structure for your discussion.

(a) Additional costs that a company is likely to incur during a period of financial difficulties include the following.

(i) **Increased maintenance costs**

Companies facing financial difficulties are unlikely to have either the confidence or the cash resources to undertake major items of plant replacement. As a result, they continue to operate with plant that has exceeded its realistic lifespan, and one consequence of this is that the costs of maintaining worn out plant are likely to be higher than those of maintaining newer equipment. A further problem is that productivity may be reduced due to a larger amount of down time than should be expected.

(ii) **Reduced competitiveness**

If the company lacks the resources to invest in new technology, it is likely fall behind its competitors in the level of quality and service that it is able to provide. As a result it may be forced to compete strongly on price, and this in turn will impact upon the margins that it is able to achieve and hence on profitability.

(iii) **Loss of confidence by customers and suppliers**

If the company is perceived to be in financial difficulties, this may result in a loss of business as customers turn to alternative suppliers for all or part of their requirements in order to ensure their own continuity of supply. Similarly, suppliers may be less willing to trade on generous terms, and the company may face a reduction in the level of credit available and a reduction in the quality of service received, all of which will generate additional costs.

Other areas that could be addressed include the problems of recruiting and retaining quality staff, resulting in higher administration and training costs, and the probability that lenders will also take a more cautious approach.

The approach required to deal with these problems will depend on their fundamental cause, and the nature of the financial problems. Possible options include the following.

(i) It may be that the underlying business is sound and well run, and that the problems are due to over-ambitious expansion plans. In this case the best approach would be to improve the quality of the capital base, either by seeking additional long-term capital in the form of debt or through a rights issue, or by taking on medium-term finance to cover the period until the operational cash flow grows in response to the new investment.

(ii) Although the underlying business may be sound, the company may be suffering from weak management resulting in the inefficient use of working capital and other resources. In this situation a tightening up of the management performance should resolve the problems in the long term, although a short-term cash injection may be needed to finance this process.

(iii) A more serious situation arises when the business has lost strategic direction. For example, it may be operating in a declining market, which has left it with resources, and structures that are no longer appropriate to the current scale of operations. In this situation it can either seek new areas into which to expand, or decide to adapt to being a niche supplier. Both options will require additional capital, although if the latter route is chosen, this should only be of a short-term nature in order to finance the restructuring of the company to a smaller scale level of operations. During this process, funds should be released through the sale of surplus assets, and the cost base reduced so as to enable the company to operate profitably once again. If the former route is chosen, a larger investment is likely to be needed and there will be no reduction in scale, in which case longer-term capital is likely to be required.

(b) There are two fundamental problems in the use of available financial information to predict failure, as follows.

(i) The information is often **out-of-date**. Significant events can take place between the end of the financial year and the publication of the accounts. An extreme example of this would be the collapse of the Barings merchant bank. A further feature of the Barings case that is worthy of comment is the fact that the factors that led up to the collapse were essentially internal to the business and would never have become apparent in the published accounts.

(ii) The information is essentially **backward looking** and takes no account of current and future situations. Another extreme example would be the Central American banana producers. There would be nothing in their published accounts to predict the effect on their businesses of Hurricane Mitch.

Other contributory factors may include the use of **creative, or even fraudulent, accounting**. Polly Peck was the fastest growing company in the UK at one time, but eventually and catastrophically it failed when accounting manipulation could no longer conceal its true financial position. Similarly, the pressure to deliver earnings growth may result in companies making poor decisions that eventually lead to their downfall. It is arguable that the recent deterioration in the performance of BTR (now Invensys) is attributable to its policy of aggressive acquisition followed by price increases and stringent cost reduction. Although this delivered growth in earnings for a while and made it a highly regarded company in which to invest, the effects of this policy are now being felt in a shrinking customer base and the consequences of a lack of investment in the underlying businesses.

Business is not an exact science, and the use of apparently objective models can foster the illusion that it can be reduced to a set of numerical ratios. In practice, it is the decisions and actions of subjective and fallible human beings that create businesses, which must always operate under conditions of inadequate and imperfect information. Given this, it is not surprising that deterministic models of failure prediction only ever appear to meet with partial success.

10 FORECASTING FAILURE

Pass marks. Part (a) is not asking for a detailed description of the models available for failure prediction, but rather of the validity of using these models at all. In approaching this, it may be helpful to consider the way in which such models are derived, the way they are used and the assumptions on which they are based. In part (b) you should consider the other alternatives that may be available to the company as well as the position of a poorly performing subsidiary within a group structure.

Examiner's comment. This question was very well answered by some candidates, but was clearly a desperation choice by others. Those who made poor attempts generally failed to understand what the question required and, at best, limited their answer to a discussion of financial analysis without relating it to the question.

(a) (i) There are a variety of approaches that have been used to attempt to predict **company failure**. One of these is the use of the 'Z-score' developed by Altman on the basis of the analysis of a relatively small sample of US firms, both failed companies and going concerns. In this analysis, five factors emerged as being key factors in determining the financial soundness of a company, and these five factors could then be weighted to produce a single Z-score which could be used to predict the likelihood of failure. Other approaches focus on the use of **ratio analysis** to predict instability.

All these approaches are developed by attempting to correlate failure with the financial profile of the company immediately prior to failure. They are thus all clearly historic in approach and are descriptive rather than explanatory. Although the results at times seem to give some empirical success in predicting failure, it is unreasonable to expect a given formula or approach to be capable of predicting failure in economic and commercial situations which are significantly different from those under which the formula was derived.

The historical approach is only valid if the data to which the formula is applied can reasonably be expected to form the basis of a valid projection of the future. In practice, this is often not the case, a given set of financial relationships only being a snapshot from one angle of the firm at one given point in time.

A further factor to be considered is the way in which an attempt to predict failure can become a self-fulfilling prophecy. If a bank monitors the performance of its clients against a certain set of yardsticks and in so doing believes it has identified one which is on the brink of collapse, it may decide on this basis to withdraw its support. This action may in itself then bring about the failure of the company which might otherwise have survived.

(ii) Reasons why even properly applied models may not predict failure correctly include the following.

(1) Failure is often apparently catastrophic due to the concealment of the true financial situation through **manipulation of the accounts**.

(2) Good management may mean that the company is able to analyse the problems itself and take avoiding action, in other words to use the analysis to **prevent** the predicted outcome from taking place.

(3) Certain companies and industries may have a **unique combination of financial structure and trading conditions** which mean that ratios which would generally indicate problems are not in fact dangerous. For example, food retailers can operate with apparently very low current and quick ratios due to the fact that the majority of their customers pay cash while they receive credit from their suppliers.

(b) This statement derives from the fact that it is generally accepted that the principal financial objective of a company is to maximise the wealth of the ordinary shareholders. Thus if the liquidation value is above its value as a going concern it would appear that liquidation is indeed the best way of serving this objective.

However, this statement assumes that there are only two choices open to the company, ie to **liquidate** or to **carry on in the existing form**. This is a very simplistic approach, and in practice other options may be available which would be in the better interests of the shareholders.

(i) It may be possible to **sell all or part of the business** and so realise more than the liquidation value.

(ii) It may be possible to **dispose of a particularly poorly performing area** and so improve the going concern value of the remainder of the business.

(iii) It may be possible to **improve the operating cost base** of the existing business and so improve the going concern value.

(iv) A **change in the direction of the business,** for example by the successful penetration of a new market area, could also improve performance.

The situation is further complicated if the company in question is a **subsidiary of a larger group**. In this case its liquidation may have a significant effect on the performance of the group as a whole which results in an overall worsening of the position of the ordinary shareholders. For example, the subsidiary may be supplying key components which are not only more expensive if bought in, but whose quality and reliability of supply are critical to the performance of the group. The board must also consider what other effects the liquidation could have on the performance of the group, for example through the impact on employee morale if it is closed.

11 STRATEGIC REVIEW

Pass marks. In part (a) it is helpful to relate the different sources of information to the practicalities of the strategic review process. In particular it is important to distinguish between historic and forecast data.

Examiner's comment. Most candidates provided a reasonable yield curve graph, although the axes had to be labelled to gain full credit. Many candidates failed to discuss private and public data about a company's past performance and also omitted to comment on what other information might be useful to the board ((a)(ii)).

(a) (i) (1) **The interest yield curve**. This represents the relationship between yield to maturity and years to maturity of fixed interest securities at a given point in time. The securities used should be identical in all respects other than the maturity date, and for this reason the curve is usually constructed using risk free government bonds. The shape of the curve will depend on the prevailing economic conditions and the demand for credit of different maturity. In practice, the most common situation is an upward-sloping curve, and this means that yields are higher on long-term securities, and suggests that there is a greater level of demand relative to supply for short-term securities than there is for long-term securities.

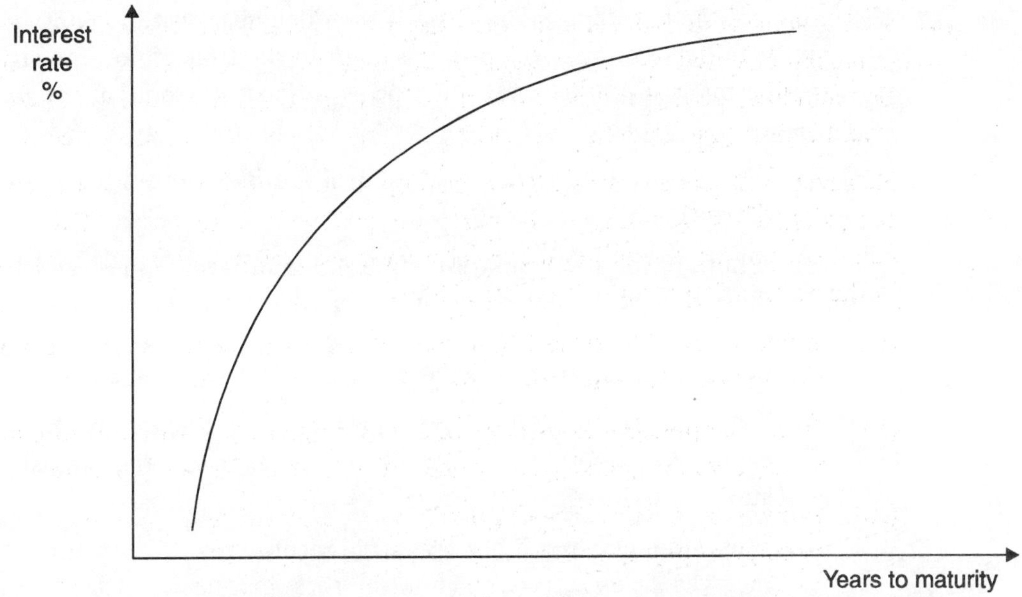

The significance of this for a company developing its financial strategy is that it provides an indicator of the relationship between the required rate of return and the timescale of the investment being considered. For example, an upward sloping curve would suggest that the company should be prepared to accept a lower rate of return on its short-term investments than on its long-term investments. The shape of the curve can also assist in forecasting other areas such as exchange rate movements (via the interest rate parity theory), and deciding the most appropriate capital structure.

(2) **Published government statistics and reports**. Business information published by the government will either be historical in nature (eg Social Trends), provide forecasts of activity (eg Economic Trends) or be prescriptive (eg Competition Commission reports). Publications that fall into the latter two categories will be the most useful to a company seeking to make strategic decisions about the future.

Two examples of their use are as follows.

- **Economic Trends**. This includes both historical statistics and forecasts of future trends within the economy. An example of a potential application is the use of inflation forecasts in negotiations with employees, customers and suppliers.
- **Competition Commission reports**. These provide lengthy studies of the competitive structure of an individual industry. They may provide useful insights into areas of market opportunity and existing barriers to entry, and their recommendations may in themselves create new opportunities.

(3) **Private and public company data**. This form of information provides useful material for monitoring performance. For example it may be noted that increasing the size of the sales force was associated with an increase in the total level of sales. However, such information is essentially descriptive, and cannot be used to prove the existence of a causal relationship. It is also historical in nature, and should not therefore be used indiscriminately to attempt to predict future performance.

(ii) Much of the foregoing information is essentially backward looking in nature and is unlikely to form the primary input to the strategic review process. It will be more appropriate for the process to focus on some of the following areas:

(1) Where does the company wish to **position** itself within both its existing and its potential markets?

(2) What are the **key operating strengths and weaknesses**, and how can these best be exploited within the markets that the company seeks to serve? Similarly, how can the **internal operating environment** be improved and better aligned to meet customer requirements?

(3) What are the perceived **opportunities and threats** in the external environment, both within the market segments that the company serves and within the wider economy?

(4) What **financial and other operating resources** will be required to meet the strategic objectives, and how can these best be sourced?

Much of this information will be gained informally from market sources and from potential suppliers of goods, services and finance, rather than from published sources?

(b) (i) The **Monte Carlo approach** seeks to consider all possible combinations of outcomes and to focus them into a single 'expected value'. The practical steps involved are as follows.

(1) **Model the project**. Create a set of equations for each of the variables in the cash flow, taking into account the interdependencies between the variables and the effect of forecast errors.

(2) **Specify the probabilities**. Derive patterns of the possible forecast errors for each of the variables defined in the model.

(3) **Sample using random numbers.** Sample from the distributions of the forecast errors using random numbers. When this process has been repeated many times it will be possible to generate a probability distribution of the project cash flows.

The output from the simulation takes the form of a **probability distribution of expected cash flows** for each time period, to which standard deviations can be applied to provide a measure of the likely range of outcomes.

A benefit of this approach is that it requires that an attempt be made to understand the uncertainties and interdependencies inherent in the cash flows in a structured way. Once the model has been constructed it can be used to evaluate the effect of modifications to the circumstances. Weaknesses include the subjectivity involved in defining the probabilities and interdependencies and the complexity of the calculations involved.

(ii) **Sensitivity analysis** is a similar technique in that it seeks to investigate the effect of changes in the cashflow projections on the expected outcome. However, rather than combining the results into a single expected value, it seeks to address the likely implications of different scenarios on the final result (for example, what would be the effect on the cash flow if costs turned out to be x% higher than predicted). The technique compares the effect of a percentage change in one variable with the percentage change in the final outcome to determine the relative level of sensitivity of the cash flow to changes in the different variables. As with the Monte Carlo approach, it is important to determine the interdependencies that exist in arriving at the different scenarios.

The principal weakness of sensitivity analysis is that it does not examine the probability that any particular variation in costs and revenues might occur. It is also difficult in practical terms to incorporate all the interdependencies into the model. Its main attraction is that it provides management with a number of alternative scenarios that can be assessed, rather than with a single expected value and a set of probabilities.

12 FINANCIAL MODEL

Pass marks. The question is concerned with the theory and practice of the corporate planning process. Do not focus solely on the planning process itself, but take into account the key parameters for ensuring its success, such as the objective setting process. In part (c) it is helpful to distinguish between mathematical approaches and the widely used arithmetical modelling techniques.

Examiner's comment. In part (a), most candidates recognised that the first step in constructing a corporate financial model was to identify corporate objectives. In part (b), most candidates identified three methods of allowing for uncertainty, but frequently provided only a list and did not attempt even a brief description.

(a) The first stage in constructing the framework for a five year corporate plan is that of **business review and assessment**, including the appraisal of corporate **strengths and weaknesses**. A detailed appraisal of the market situation and the key competencies needed to succeed in the chosen markets will also be made at this stage. The review will enable a forecast to be made of likely changes in sales, profitability and capital requirements. This can then be compared with the restatement of the company's objectives in order to identify the 'gap' which must be overcome strategically. This stage is very important in establishing some of the parameters for the financial model, including the following.

(i) Defining the primary objective, for example to achieve a certain level of net present value (NPV) return to equity.

(ii) Establishing initial forecasts of sales activity, production bottlenecks and so on.

(iii) Establishing the cost of capital to be used, taking account of the company's attitude to risk.

(iv) Quantifying the interrelationships between different variables such as price sensitivity, volume/cost, and any constraints which may exist for example, technical capacity.

(v) Defining the effect of probable external influences for example changes in fiscal policy and legislation.

Other issues that need to be addressed in developing the model include the following.

(i) The choice of appropriate hardware, software and reporting formats.

(ii) Defining the time frame, including establishing the start and end points and the time intervals between.

(iii) The way in which performance against the plan will be monitored and reported.

(iv) The number of alternative scenarios that can be handled and the way in which these will be constructed.

Problems that are likely to be encountered include the following.

(i) Getting the main objectives defined in an unambiguous and quantifiable way.

(ii) Different people will take different views of the future - some will be very optimistic while others may be very pessimistic - this can make it difficult to establish what the expected outcome of a given set of circumstances really is.

(iii) Some people will be very wary of making any projections at all for fear of being held to them in the future.

(iv) Antipathy towards the entire planning process from individuals who believe it to be a waste of time.

(v) Establishing the correct degree of detail at which to work.

(b) Methods for incorporating the **effects of uncertainty** include the following.

(i) The simplest approach is to use the statistically expected value for all the variables and to add a premium to the cost of capital to reflect the degree of risk aversion of the business.

(ii) It is possible to prepare a probability distribution for the range of different possible outcomes in relation to given variables, for example sales growth rate. These can then be used to prepare forecasts of the expected values and to calculate the probability distribution of the expected values.

(iii) Sensitivity analysis can be used to determine the effect on business performance of variables differing by varying amounts from the expected value (ie asking 'what if?' questions). The difficulty with this approach is isolating the extent of interdependency between the different variables. Neither does sensitivity analysis take into account the probability of a given variation in a cost or revenue occurring.

(c) **Mathematical modelling techniques** include the use of algebra and differential calculus to describe the relationships between different variables and to optimise the combination of different input variables. An example of an area where this can be used is in defining the relationship between price and volume (price elasticity). These techniques tend to be appropriate for constructing different parts of the model and for approximating relationships to be included in the overall model. This latter however is generally built on simple arithmetical principles for ease of handling and understanding, and in order that it is compatible with the accounting information with which managers in the business are familiar and which they understand.

The principal benefit of computer modelling is that it significantly increases the volume of data that can be handled and the speed with which information can be processed. As a result it may be possible to undertake a more thorough analysis of the effects of uncertainty than would otherwise be possible.

Examples of computer models that could be used include the following.

(i) Those built by the user on spreadsheet software.

(ii) Those built by the user on relational database software such as Dataease. The advantage of these is that data entry can be simplified, and a large volume of data can be handled more easily than with a spreadsheet.

(iii) Financial modelling applications software which may be integrated with the financial reporting system such as IMRS.

The main problem in using computer modelling techniques arises from a preoccupation with the model rather than with the quality of the data which may lead to a belief in the infallibility of the model. However, if there were deficiencies in the initial data, then the results of a sophisticated model will be no better than those of a simple one. Similarly, the appearance of detail and accuracy may obscure the fact that much of the data, particularly the sensitivities may have been derived subjectively.

13 POLICY DECISIONS

Pass marks. This question deals with some of the basics of financial management, both in general terms, and in relation to different elements of the finance function. The questions asked are quite specific, and you should be careful to address the issues as requested, and not merely to write all you know about the topics involved.

Examiner's comment. This was by far the most popular of the optional questions, and the only one of the four that required no calculations. Most candidates made a satisfactory to good effort at part (a), although not many managed to discuss the interrelationships of the three policies and how they affected the value of the firm. Many spent far too long discussing dividend policy to the detriment of the answer as a whole. Some brief comments on MM's theories of dividend irrelevancy and capital structure were expected, but near-essays on the topics were not required.

Answers to part (b) of the question were varied. Most candidates recognised the major functions of the two departments, but these were often provided as a list with no discussion of the relative contributions to the achievement of financial objectives.

(a) Maximising the wealth of the ordinary shareholders generally implies aiming to maximise profits in a way that is consistent with long-term stability. On occasion this means that short-term gains must be sacrificed in the interests of the long-term profitability of the company. There are three major types of decisions that must be faced in the context of this overall financial objective.

Investment decisions

Investment decisions involve committing funds to:

(i) **internal investment** projects (and being prepared to withdraw funds from these projects in the event of their proving to be unprofitable);

(ii) **external investment** decisions that involve the takeover of another company or a merger;

(iii) **disinvestment decisions,** which involve selling or liquidating an unwanted part of the business such as an unprofitable subsidiary.

The outcome of investment decisions directly affects the level of earnings that the firm makes, and this is thus a major determinant of the value of the firm where this is defined as the present value of projected cash flows.

Investment decisions involve the commitment of funds in various ways. The ways in which these funds are raised, and the form in which they are held, form the basis of the second type of major policy decision:

Financing decisions

The assets of a company will be financed by a combination of:

- Share capital
- Reserves
- Long-term liabilities
- Short-term liabilities

The choice of the appropriate mix of finance involves balancing the following factors.

- The relative cost and ease of sourcing additional funds of different types

- The effects on the net worth of the business of using a particular source of funds
- The effect on the overall financial risk of the business of using a particular source of funds
- Maintaining an appropriate level of liquidity

Financial management is concerned with obtaining funds for investment, and investing those funds profitably so as to maximise the value of the firm. It is not enough to invest at a profit – the company must be able to pay its investors at least the rate of return that they require, otherwise they will take their funds elsewhere. Investments must therefore earn at least the **opportunity cost of finance**.

Dividend decisions

Dividends must be paid out of earnings, and the level of earnings is directly related to the outcome of the investment decisions made by the company. At the same time, the value of a company's shares will be related to the amount of dividends that the company has been paying, and also to the expectations of future dividends. Thus dividends themselves also have an impact on the value of the firm. The level of dividends is also further related to financing decisions since retained earnings are one of the most important sources of new funds for companies.

(b) **Treasury**

The CIMA definition of **treasurership** is 'the function concerned with the provision and use of finance. It includes provision of capital, short-term borrowing, foreign currency management, banking, collections and money market investment'. Thus, of the three types of policy decision discussed above, the treasury department is primarily concerned with financing policy at a high level within the organisation. The department is likely to be involved both in the determination of policy in this area, and in the achievement of the related financial objectives. While the treasurer may have an input to investment policy, this will not be one of his key roles. Treasury will also be involved to some extent in the determination and implementation of dividend policy since, as explained above, this is closely related to both short-term and long-term financing decisions.

The **functions of the treasury department** may include the following.

(i) Input to the determination and implementation of financial aims, strategies and policies.

(ii) Implementation of the appropriate financial and treasury systems.

(iii) Undertaking liquidity management to ensure that the company has the liquid funds it needs, and that it invests any surplus funds, even for very short terms.

(iv) Banking relationships and arrangements, and the day to day management of money.

(v) Arranging the best mix of debt finance, including leasing and factoring agreements.

(vi) Management of foreign currency operations, including exposure policies and procedures, exchange dealing, international monetary economics and exchange regulations.

(vii) Corporate finance in relation to equity capital management, business acquisitions and divestments, project finance and joint ventures.

(viii) Corporate taxation.

(ix) Risk management and insurance.

(x) Pension fund investment management.

Financial control

Financial management can be defined as the management of the finances of an organisation in order to achieve the financial objectives of the organisation. In general terms, there are two aspects to financial management:

- Financial planning
- Financial control

The financial control function is concerned with monitoring performance to determine the extent to which the various activities of the organisation are meeting their financial objectives. This involves the use of existing budgets, actual results and financial forecasts to evaluate performance.

The financial control department is therefore primarily concerned with the area of investment policy, although it may also deal with financing policy in evaluating the way in which funds are being raised and used, and the relative costs of finance. The direct input of this department to **policy determination** is relatively low, but it does make an important contribution to the **achievement of policy**. Good financial control will mean that mistakes may be made once, but not repeated; that investments that are not achieving their objectives are identified and action taken to remedy the situation; and that forthcoming problems are identified quickly and dealt with appropriately.

14 TREASURY DEPARTMENT

> **Pass marks**. In your discussion of the treasury function you should relate it as far as possible to the service based multinational in question.
>
> **Examiner's comment**. This question was quite well answered. However, a significant minority of candidates was ignorant of the treasury's role and confused the job's functions with those of the financial manager or controller.

(a) The official CIMA and Association of Corporate Treasurers definition of **treasury management** is 'the corporate handling of all financial matters, the generation of external and internal funds for business, the management of currencies and cash flows, and the complex strategies, policies and procedures of corporate finance'. The **main responsibilities** of such a department in a service-based multinational company are likely to include the following.

(i) It will make a significant contribution to the definition of corporate financial objectives, including strategies, policies and systems.

(ii) It will be responsible for liquidity management, ensuring that the company has the liquid funds it needs and that it invests any surplus funds, even for the very short term. This will involve:

(1) managing working capital and the transmission of funds within the group;

(2) maintaining banking relationships and arrangements for short term borrowings and investments;

(3) money management.

(iii) It will carry out funding management, including funding policies and procedures, and the sources and types of funds to be used. This involves the negotiation of all forms of borrowing and alternative sources of funds such as leasing.

(iv) In a multinational company, currency management will be a very important role. This includes:

(1) exposure policies and procedures;
(2) exchange dealing, including futures, options and derivative products;
(3) international monetary economics and exchange regulations.

(v) The department will have an input to corporate finance decisions including items such as:

(1) equity capital management - the form in which further equity should be raised;
(2) dividend policy;
(3) financial information for management;
(4) mergers, acquisitions and divestments;
(5) project finance and joint ventures;
(6) corporate taxation;
(7) risk management and insurance;
(8) pension fund investment management.

(vi) It will be responsible for liaising with the management of associated companies on treasurership matters.

Although treasury functions are currently the responsibility of the Chief Accountant, it is not clear whether these functions are carried out in a centralised or a decentralised manner. For the purposes of this discussion it will be assumed that much of the responsibility currently lies with the operating units. The **benefits of a separate centralised treasury function** are likely to include the following.

(i) Liquidity management can be improved by allowing bulk cash flows and therefore lower bank charges, and by avoiding the proliferation of small local surpluses and overdrafts.

(ii) The centralisation of cash surpluses means that larger amounts are available for short-term investment thus giving better investment opportunities.

(iii) Borrowings can be arranged in bulk at lower interest rates than for smaller amounts.

(iv) Foreign currency risk management is likely to be improved since it will be possible to match receipts and payments made in a given currency across all the subsidiaries. This means that the need for more expensive hedging methods such as forward rate agreements is minimised.

(v) A specialist department can employ experts with knowledge and experience of corporate treasurership, derivative products and so on.

(vi) The centralised precautionary balance is likely to be lower than the sum of the local precautionary balances.

(vii) It is easier to measure the performance of the treasury team in financial terms, for example by way of the net interest cost.

(viii) Multilateral netting between subsidiaries may be possible, depending on the regulations of the countries concerned. This should result in reduced transaction costs because there will be a reduced level of transfers between different currencies.

(b) The advantages of operating a separate treasury department as a **profit centre** rather than a cost centre include the following.

(i) Some companies, particularly those with a high level of foreign exchange transactions, are able to make significant **profits** from their treasury activities. Treating such departments as profit centres recognises the fact that some activities may earn revenues for the company and may as a result make treasury staff more motivated.

(ii) Recognition of the department as a profit centre may allow the company to introduce an element of **performance related pay** should it wish to do so.

The possible disadvantages of operating the treasury department as a profit centre include the following.

(i) Operating the department as a profit centre may encourage a more **aggressive attitude to risk** which may be difficult to reconcile with the directors' requirements. In addition it means that a good system of controls must be in place to prevent speculation.

(ii) If it is a true profit centre, then **market prices** should be charged for the treasury service to other departments. It may be difficult to put realistic prices on some services such as the arrangement of finance or general financial advice. If the charges are viewed as too high by the subsidiaries they may be tempted to seek outside advice instead and thus the advantages of a centralised treasury function will be lost.

(iii) Even with a profit centre approach it may be difficult to measure the success of a treasury department because successful treasury activities sometimes involve **avoiding the incurring of costs**. For example, a successful currency hedge during a period of strong currency movements may prevent the company from incurring a substantial loss.

15 S PLC

Pass marks. This question required only very simple calculations to be made. In approaching the discussion of the relationships between convertible debenture values and share prices and dividends it is helpful to view the convertible as a form of delayed equity rather than as loan stock.

Examiner's comment. Few candidates demonstrated a real understanding of the nature of convertibles despite the fact that convertible securities of various kinds are in vogue.

(a) At the date of issue, the market value of each share to be received is 400p. Therefore to convert the debenture to 20 shares would mean that the value of the shares received would be 20 × 400p = £80.00. Since the debenture price was £100.00, this implies a **conversion premium** of £20.00 (£100 – £80), or 25% (100 × 20 ÷ 80).

The fact that a conversion premium exists, and that the coupon rate on convertibles is frequently less than that on irredeemable stocks reflects expectations of share price movements. It is expected that the share price will increase between the date of issue of the stock and the date of conversion in such a way as to mean that conversion on the due date will allow the debenture holder to obtain shares at a discount to the prevailing market price.

(b) If the market price of the shares grows at 10% per annum, then the price after three years will be 532.4p (400p × 1.1 × 1.1 × 1.1). If the debenture is converted at that date, then the value of the shares received will be £106.48 (532.4p × 20).

It is likely that the market value of the debenture will exceed this because investors will be expecting to see continued growth in the price of the shares, in excess of the cost of the funds tied up in the debenture, and therefore the terminal value of the debenture will be considerably higher. The debentures will reflect these expectations by trading at a higher price than the current conversion value.

(c) Dividend policy is one of the major factors which determines the share price. Under the **dividend valuation model**, the share price is held to be directly related both to the current dividend and to the expected future growth in dividends:

$$p_0 = \frac{d_0(1+g)}{(r-g)}$$

where: p_0 = market price of shares
d_0 = current level of dividend
r = required rate of return
g = expected annual growth in dividend

Thus it can be seen that dividend growth is important in determining the likely market value of the shares. As has already been discussed above, the market value of the shares is very important in determining the price of convertibles, and therefore the dividend policy of the company will have an important effect on the value of convertible stock.

(d) Companies normally issue convertibles in the expectation that the **holders will exercise their options**. Convertibles can therefore be seen as a form of **delayed equity**. They are attractive to the firm when the price of the ordinary shares is abnormally low at the date of issue, and at times when to issue a further tranche of equity would result in a significant drop in earnings per share. However they also carry the risk that the share price will not rise in line with expectations at the time of issue and that holders will not therefore convert. If the debentures are dated, then the company must have funds in place to allow redemption on the due date. Convertibles also have a short term benefit in that interest payments are allowable against tax.

Convertibles therefore may form part of the strategy of a company whose objective is to raise new equity, but which for various reasons does not wish to go directly to the market in the short term. They are often preferable to straight loan stock since they **do not commit the company indefinitely** to the payment of large interest bills. They further allow the company to **widen the investment base** by attracting investors looking for a guaranteed short term income plus the possibility of a capital gain at a later date. They have also recently formed a part of the strategy of companies that wished to manipulate their reported gearing and earnings per share, since they could choose whether to show them as equity or debt. However, this loophole has now been closed.

16 DEBT INSTRUMENTS

Pass marks. This question requires a knowledge of the features of some of the different forms of debt finance available to a company. Restrict your answer to the terms of the question. Do not become sidetracked, in part (a) for example, into the characteristics of other forms of hedging.

Examiner's comment. Some candidates confused currency swaps and interest rate swaps.

(a) An **interest rate swap** is a mechanism by which two organisations swap their interest rate commitments with each other. The effect of this is to allow each company to take advantage of different rates of interest in different markets. Thus a company which is borrowing at a fixed rate of interest may exchange its commitments with a company borrowing at a variable rate of interest. This may be valuable when its incomes are tied to variations in rates, thus allowing a more effective matching of income and expenditure.

The interest rate swap does not alter the company's obligation to the original lender - if its partner defaults on the payments it will still be liable. In practice, such arrangements are not normally made directly between companies, but instead through financial intermediaries. Other benefits are that they are flexible, cheap and simple to arrange.

As with foreign exchange **hedging** techniques, interest rate swaps can also be used as a method of financial **speculation**. This can have unfortunate consequences, as in the case of swaps undertaken by some local authorities in the recent past.

(b) **Deep discounted bonds** and **conventional bonds** are two forms of loan stock that may be issued by a company. An investor in these bonds will normally receive a return which is made up partly of interest payments and partly of capital growth, although the proportions will vary from bond to bond. Deep discounted bonds lie at one extreme end of this spectrum. They are issued at a price which is at a large discount to the nominal value of the stock, and will be redeemable at or above par when the bond eventually matures. However they carry a much lower rate of interest than other loan stock. Thus they are attractive to the investor who would prefer a large capital gain to regular interest payments.

From the point of view of the company, they are useful when there are specific cash flow requirements. Servicing costs are low during their lifetime due to the low rate of interest paid, while the cost of redemption on maturity is high. Thus they provide a means of matching the periodic cost of finance to the revenues generated.

(c) **Commercial paper** is a means by which a large company can raise short-term finance. It takes the form of unsecured promissory notes with a fixed maturity of between seven and 364 days (in practice, usually less than three months) in bearer form and issued on a discount basis whereby the rate of return is implied in the sale value. It is thus effectively a form of short-term debt.

Its advantages are **flexibility** - the issuer can select the period to maturity and schedule borrowing for the times when they expect interest rates to be favourable - and **cheapness** - the interest rate payable should be slightly lower than if the money were borrowed directly from the bank. Commercial paper is an example of **disintermediation** ie dispensing with financial intermediaries, which is perceived as lowering the cost of short-term finance.

Companies with assets of at least £25m can take advantage of commercial paper issues. Companies do not have to be formally rated, although they will not be able to obtain rates as favourable as those which are rated. A market has been developed by the banks in commercial paper which improves its liquidity; however this means that issues need to be of a reasonable size for the market to function effectively.

17 TUTORIAL QUESTION: EFFICIENT MARKET HYPOTHESIS

The **efficient market hypothesis** describes an efficient market as one where security prices fully and speedily reflect available information: in other words, the market is efficient in terms of information processing. The result is the product of the actions of market participants actively competing with each other. The content of any new information becoming available will be quickly digested by market participants and, if the information causes them to change their opinion of the security's intrinsic value, their subsequent actions will rapidly cause an equivalent change in the security's market price.

The hypothesis takes three forms depending upon the extent of the information deemed available to market participants.

(a) **Weak form**. Information available is restricted to details of past share prices, returns and trading volumes. Hence future prices cannot be predicted from historical price data alone and trading rules based only on such price and volume data, ie the chartist approach, cannot consistently produce excess returns if the hypothesis is correct.

(b) **Semi-strong form**. Share prices reflect all publicly available information. Reaction to public announcements will not produce excess returns as the information content of such announcements is reflected in share prices.

(c) **Strong form**. Share prices reflect all information whether publicly available or not.

Since the question refers to published annual reports, it is the **semi-strong form** of the hypothesis that is in question. This form of the hypothesis is in accord with the results of the first set of investigations, which indicated that the annual report is an important source of information for investment decisions, but appears to conflict with the studies which indicate that market prices of equity do not react in the short term to the publication of the annual report.

There are a **number of factors** which may explain the apparent discrepancy.

(a) Much information contained in the annual report will already have been published in the financial press before the report appears.

(b) If the strong form of the hypothesis is valid, share prices may be influenced by information which has not been published. Investors in possession of such information will take action accordingly and if they are large, for example institutional investors, their actions may influence the market price.

(c) It is possible that reactions to the annual report take time to affect share prices. This might be because time is needed to weigh up the contents of the report or because investors need time to gather together the funds necessary to give effect to their reactions. Studies based on the short term would then be inadequate as a guide to the effect of the annual report on market prices.

18 MRF

> **Pass marks**. You should state clearly the reasons for your choice of discount rates, and your assumptions as to the tax position of the rates chosen. In the final part of the question you should consider other methods of making the deal attractive to MRF. It is helpful to draw attention to the effect of the different tax positions of the two organisations on the calculations.
>
> **Examiner's comment**. Generally, candidates recognised the need to apply different discount rates to the lessee and lessor and quick marks could have been gained by recognising that annuity tables (or cumulative NPV tables) could be used to short-cut the calculations. Many candidates were confused about the treatment of interest payments.

(a) REPORT

To: MRF President
From: MRF Treasurer — Date: 19 November 19X6
Subject: Financial evaluation of project financing

The purpose of this paper is to evaluate the alternatives of buying the new capital equipment using a bank loan and acquiring the equipment under a finance lease. Since MRF has charitable status, no writing down allowances are available if the equipment is purchased, and no tax relief will be available on payments made to the leasing company. Since the cost of the bank loan would be 12%, it is proposed to **evaluate the alternatives** at this rate since this is effectively the **marginal cost of capital** for the project.

Purchase using bank loan

If the equipment is purchased, there are two relevant cash flows that arise. These are the payment for the equipment at the start of the project, and the receipt on the sale of the equipment at the end of year 6:

		£
Year 0	(£22.5m × 1.000)	22.50m
Year 6	(£4.0m × 0.507)	(2.03m)
Net cost of project		20.47m

Finance lease alternative

In this case, MRF would make annual payments of £7.5m at the end of each of the years one to six. The PV cost of this can therefore be found by applying a six year annuity at 12% to the annual cost:

£7.5m × 4.111 £30.83m

Conclusions

On financial grounds, purchase of the equipment using the bank loan has a much lower PV cost over the life of the project. Insurance and maintenance costs will be unaffected by this decision.

Signed: Treasurer

(b) REPORT

To: Account Manager
From: Account Negotiator Date: 19 November 19X6
Subject: MRF leasing proposal

The purpose of this report is to evaluate the options available to us in order to gain the MRF business. This will include the calculation of the **annual lease payments** that we would need to offer in order to gain the business, the effect of such a **reduction** in leasing payments on our evaluation of the project, and a discussion of other options that we could consider in order to rescue the deal.

Annual lease payments required by MRF

For the charity to be indifferent between the bank and the leasing company, the annual payments would need to be reduced to the point where the PV cost of the payments over six years at 12% was the same as the PV cost of purchase using the bank loan. This can be found using the following expression, where 'a' = the annual lease payment made by MRF:

$$a \times 4.111 = £20.47m$$
$$a = £4.98m$$

This represents a reduction in the annual payment of £2.52m.

Financial implications of the reduction in payments

The calculation of the effect of this reduction in payments on the position of the leasing company is contained in the Appendix to this report. For the purposes of the evaluation it is assumed that the opportunity cost of capital of 14% is a net of tax figure, and the figure to be used in the evaluation. It is further assumed that the **writing down allowances** (WDAs) will be claimed from year 1, and that the balancing charge will be incurred in year 6. Tax payments are assumed to be made in the year in which the revenue/expenditure arises.

The figures show that the NPV of the lease on this basis is £0.17m, in other words, about breakeven.

Other factors to be considered

It has been shown that offering the equipment to MRF at an annual leasing figure of £4.98m offers little financial benefit. However, it may be possible to offer other incentives to MRF in conjunction with a higher lease cost. These include the following.

(i) We may be able to structure a deal that offers a beneficial maintenance contract to MRF.

(ii) It is not clear what MRF's intentions are at the end of the six year period. The calculations assume that the equipment is disposed of. However, it may be beneficial for MRF to continue to use the equipment which could then be offered at a lower cost for a secondary period.

(iii) It may be possible to structure the annual payments in such a way as to offer MRF other cash flow benefits.

The **opportunity cost of capital** of 14% has been used, but it may be that a lower rate could be more appropriate to the specific risks associated with this project. If this is the case, then there may be more flexibility that the figures suggest in the MRF proposal.

Conclusions

It will be difficult for us to put together a package that is both attractive to MRF and financially beneficial to ourselves due to the different tax positions of the two organisations, even taking into account the discount available to us from the supplier. However, it has been shown that there are a number of other options that could be considered should we decide to pursue the deal.

APPENDIX

The first step is to calculate the net-of-tax cash flows.

Year	*0*	*1*	*2*	*3*	*4*	*5*	*6*
	£m	£m	£m	£m	£m	£m	£m
Capital expenditure	(18.00)						4.00
WDA		4.50	3.38	2.53	1.90	1.42	0.27
33% tax on WDA		1.49	1.12	0.83	0.63	0.47	0.09
Income from MRF		4.98	4.98	4.98	4.98	4.98	4.98
Net of tax income		3.34	3.34	3.34	3.34	3.34	3.34

The annual cash flow can now be calculated and discounted at 14% to find the present value of the lease.

Year	*0*	*1*	*2*	*3*	*4*	*5*	*6*
	£m	£m	£m	£m	£m	£m	£m
Capital expenditure	(18.00)						4.00
33% tax on WDA		1.49	1.12	0.83	0.63	0.47	0.09
Net income		3.34	3.34	3.34	3.34	3.34	3.34
Cash flow	(18.00)	4.83	4.46	4.17	3.97	3.81	7.43
Discount factor	1.000	0.877	0.769	0.675	0.592	0.519	0.456
PV cash flow	(18.00)	4.24	3.43	2.81	2.35	1.98	3.39
Cumulative PV	(18.00)	(13.76)	(10.33)	(7.52)	(5.17)	(3.19)	0.20

An annual lease revenue from MRF of £4.98m therefore yields a net present value of £200,000 for the lease as a whole.

19 ABC PLC

> **Pass marks**. The calculations for part (a) are quite simple, but make sure you state clearly the assumptions made about the discount rate used in the evaluation and the timing of the tax payments. Your answer to part (b) should be in the form of a report with an introduction, main section(s) and conclusion. If necessary, refer to the calculations made in part (a).
>
> *Other points.* Part (c) offers the chance to demonstrate an understanding of the two-stage nature of some capital investment decisions.

(a) The discount rate to be used is 9% which is the approximate **after tax cost of borrowing** at 11½%. It is assumed that tax is paid one period after that in which it arises. It is also assumed, in the absence of information about depreciation policies, that the **lease payments** are allowable in full for tax purposes.

Lease

Year	*Lease payments*	*Tax at 21%*	*Cash flow*	*Discount at 9%*	*PV cost*
	£	£	£		£
0	(15,000)		(15,000)	1.000	(15,000)
1	(15,000)	3,150	(11,850)	0.917	(10,866)
2	(15,000)	3,150	(11,850)	0.842	(9,978)
3	(15,000)	3,150	(11,850)	0.772	(9,148)
4	(15,000)	3,150	(11,850)	0.708	(8,390)
5		3,150	3,150	0.650	2,048
NPV cost of leasing					(51,334)

The NPV cost of leasing exceeds £50,000. Because of writing down allowances, the NPV for the purchase option will be less than £50,000. On financial grounds leasing is therefore the preferred option.

The situation from the point of view of the leasing company is as follows.

Year	*Revenue*	*Capital costs*	*Tax*	*Net cash flow*	*Discount at 15%*	*PV*
	£	£	£	£		£
0	15,000	(50,000)		(35,000)	1.000	(35,000)
1	15,000		(775)	14,225	0.870	12,376
2	15,000		(1,744)	13,256	0.756	10,002
3	15,000		(2,470)	12,530	0.658	8,245
4	15,000		(3,015)	11,985	0.572	6,855
5		5,000	(3,424)	1,576	0.497	783
6			2,128	2,128	0.432	919
NPV of leasing agreement						(4,200)

Working: tax computation

Year	*Revenue*	*WDA*	*Taxable*	*31% tax*	*Year of tax flow*
	£	£	£	£	
0	15,000	(12,500)	2,500	775	1
1	15,000	(9,375)	5,625	1,744	2
2	15,000	(7,031)	7,969	2,470	3
3	15,000	(5,273)	9,727	3,015	4
4	15,000	(3,955)	11,045	3,424	5
5		(6,866)	(6,866)	(2,128)	6

The leasing company makes a net gain on the deal of £4,820 in present value terms. This is much less than the savings that ABC plc could make if it purchased rather than leased the equipment.

(b) REPORT

To: Chief Executive
From: Management Accountant Date: 12 May 19X4
Subject: Computer system financing options

Introduction

This report deals with the **relative merits of buying and leasing** the new computer system. Detailed supporting calculations can be found attached [see (a)].

Financial position

The calculations show that purchase of the equipment is a much **more financially advantageous** option than leasing. This assumes that it will continue to be possible to borrow at 11½% to finance the purchase. If we feel that it is likely that interest rates will rise, then the possibility of taking out a fixed rate loan should be considered. Alternatively it may be possible to hedge through a mechanism such as an interest rate swap or by the use of futures.

Other factors

Although, if the system is leased, the leasing company will be responsible for insurance and maintenance, we are effectively **locked into the deal** for the duration of the lease. We are therefore exposed to the risk that the equipment becomes obsolete during this period. To terminate the lease and to switch to new equipment is likely to carry heavy financial penalties. This sort of flexibility could only be found by taking out an operating lease, and this is almost certain to be even more expensive than a finance lease. A further alternative would be a turnkey operation involving facilities management, but this too would be very expensive.

Conclusions

The calculations show that the **relative financial loss** to us in the leasing situation is very great when compared with the financial gain that would be made by the leasing company. There is therefore little point in trying to negotiate a better deal. The discrepancy arises due to the different tax position of the two companies and our ability to use all our capital allowances. It is therefore recommended that the system should be purchased outright although we may need to do further work to identify the best way to finance the transaction.

Signed: Management Accountant

(c) It is important to appreciate that there are effectively two stages in the decision making process.

(i) The first step is to **evaluate the benefit to the company** of acquiring the system. This involves calculating the marginal cash flows that will result from the use of the system and then discounting these at the weighted average cost of capital.

(ii) Once the fact that the investment in the system should be undertaken has been established, the next step is to **evaluate the alternative methods of financing the acquisition**. This involves calculating the relative costs of the different methods of finance which are available.

In the calculations above, it is taken as given that the system will add value to the business and should be acquired. It is the second stage of the process that is being undertaken, and therefore it is the relative costs of finance which are important and not the weighted average cost of capital.

(d) The calculations above show that the leasing company has little room for manoeuvre in cutting the leasing payments that it would charge to ABC. This is due to the difference in the tax position of the two companies and the fact that ABC is able to use fully all its capital allowances. The only way in which the leasing company might be able to offer significantly improved terms is to **renegotiate its own deal** with the manufacturer of the equipment.

20 POLICY CHANGE

Pass marks. Use the CAPM to estimate the cost of equity. This can then be used in the dividend growth model to find the theoretical share price. In part (a)(ii) there is more than one possible approach to the effect of the increase in retentions on earnings, and it is therefore important to explain your assumptions.

Examiner's comment. Part (a) was generally answered well. Detailed comments on the CAPM were not required for part (b) although candidates who provided an answer which did discuss this model were given credit.

(a) The first step is to calculate the **cost of equity capital** (r_E) to PDQ. This can be estimated using the CAPM:

$$r_E = r_f + (r_m - r_f)\,\beta_j$$
$$= 6\% + (10\% - 6\%) \times 1.5 = 12\%\text{ pa}$$

Under the current dividend policy, dividend growth will match the average growth in earnings over the last four years.

The average rate of annual growth in earnings over the last four years has been as follows.

19X1	4.10%
19X2	3.15%
19X3	3.82%
19X4	2.94%
Average	3.50%

(i) If the annual rate of growth in dividends tracks that of earnings at 3.5% pa, and the cost of capital remains constant at 12% pa, then the expected share price can be estimated using the dividend growth model:

$$p_o = \frac{d_1}{r_E - g}$$

d_1	=	expected dividend in Yr 1	=	84.87p
r_E	=	cost of equity	=	12%
g	=	rate of dividend growth	=	3.5%

$$p_o = \frac{84.87p}{12\% - 3.5\%} = £9.98$$

(ii) It is assumed that the growth in earnings is cumulative and that the earnings rate of 15% applies to all of the funds retained and not only to the incremental retentions. If this is the case, then the annual rate of growth in dividends would be expected to be 15% × 50% = 7.5%. If the cost of equity remains constant at 12% then the expected price can again be calculated using the **dividend growth model**:

$$p_o = \frac{d_1}{r_E - g}$$

d_1	=	expected dividend in Yr 1 ((140p × 50%) + 7.5%)	=	75.25p
r_E	=	cost of equity	=	12%
g	=	rate of dividend growth	=	7.5%

$$P_0 = \frac{75.25p}{12\% - 7.5\%} = £16.72$$

(b) (i) Although the dividend growth model was used, the same result would have been obtained from the **earnings growth model** since they are mathematically equivalent. The limitations on the model arise from the assumptions upon which it is based, as follows.

(1) The dividends from the new projects will be of the same risk class as those from existing operations. If this is not true then the model will not hold.

(2) In practice it is unlikely that the cost of capital will remain constant over time.

(3) It is unlikely that the effect of increasing retentions will really have such a dramatic immediate effect on the rate of growth in earnings and dividends. In reality it is more probable that the rate of growth will increase at different rates in different years. This can be accounted for in the model but the calculations become more complicated.

(4) In practice, taxation may have a distorting effect.

(ii) Although the dividend valuation model does provide an effective method of estimating share prices, and in particular the relative levels of prices of different securities, the actual level on any given day is also influenced by a number of **other factors**. These include the following.

(1) The price of a share is influenced by the amount of funds available for investment and the overall level of supply and demand for shares.

(2) Investor confidence in the market as a whole will influence the general level of share prices. When investors expect the economy to grow, share prices will tend to rise as a result of an expectation of growth in earnings.

(3) Catastrophic market events such as the stock market crash of 1987 can result in large movements in share prices even though the earnings prospects for the individual firm have not changed.

(4) The preferences and tax position of individual investors will affect the attractiveness of an individual security and hence its price.

Thus although the earnings prospects and cost of equity to the individual company are important in determining the price of its shares, there are a number of other factors which also come into play and over which the directors have no control.

21 XYZ PLC

Pass marks. Part (b) involves the use of the dividend valuation model. It is most important to explain exactly what assumptions you have had to make in arriving at your answer since the information provided in the question is extremely limited. In part (c) it is helpful to consider some of the other factors that influence the share price, as well as addressing the investment decisions that surround the choice of dividend policy.

(a) During this period, **earnings per share** have declined by 10.7% while at the same time **dividend per share** has increased by 19.0%. The **payout ratio** has increased from 60% in 19W9 to 80% in 19X3, and thus the proportion of earnings retained has fallen to 20%. If it is assumed that the capital structure has not changed over the period, then it can be seen that both **actual earnings** and the **return on capital employed** have declined over the period.

One possible implication of this policy is that insufficient earnings have been retained to finance the investment required to at least maintain the rate of return on capital employed. If this means that the company is falling behind its competitors, then this could have a serious impact on the long-term profitability of the business.

(b) For the purposes of calculation it is assumed that any new investment will earn a rate of return equivalent to that **required by the shareholders** (ie 15%), and that this will also be the level of return that is earned on existing investments for the foreseeable future. It is further assumed that investors are indifferent as to whether they receive their returns in the form of dividend or as capital appreciation.

Option 1. The amount of dividend per share is £1 with no growth forecast. The rate of return required by shareholders is 15%. The theoretical share price can be estimated using the dividend valuation model.

$r = d_1/p_o$

where r = Rate of return on equity
d_1 = Dividend per share
p_o = Market price per share

$15\% = 1.00/p_o$

p_o = £6.67, or £7.67 cum div

100% of the total return is provided in the form of dividend.

Option 2. Under the assumptions relating to earnings stated above, the share price will be the same as that calculated for option 1, ie £6.67 per share. However in this case 50% of the expected return is in the form of dividend and 50% as capital appreciation.

A numerical example will clarify the position.

The rate of growth of dividends g may be expressed as:

$g = rb$

where r = required rate of return
b = proportion of profits retained

In this case therefore, with dividends at 50 pence per share:

$$g = 0.15 \times 0.5 = 0.075$$

$$p_0 = \frac{d_1}{r - g} = \frac{0.50 \times 1.075}{0.15 - 0.075} = £7.17$$

£7.17 plus 50p dividend at t_o = £7.67 cum div.

Option 3. This is the same as for option 2, but 25% of the expected return is in the form of dividend and 75% as capital growth.

$$g = 0.15 \times 0.75 = 0.1125$$

$$p_0 = \frac{0.25 \times 1.1125}{0.15 - 0.1125} = 7.42$$

£7.42 plus 25p dividend at t_0 = £7.67 cum div

Option 4. In this case, for a share price of £6.67, investors would need to believe that retained profits will be invested in projects yielding annual growth of 15% and that the share price will grow at this rate. 100% of the expected return is provided in the form of capital appreciation under this option.

(c) The figures calculated above assume that the **share price** is wholly dependent on the **rate of return required by shareholders** and that the shareholders are indifferent as to the form which the return takes. In practice, this is but one element in the range of factors which influence share prices. Other significant influences include the following.

(i) The **level of funds available for investment**
(ii) **Investor confidence**
(iii) The **tax situation and income requirements of investors**
(iv) The **availability of alternative investments**

The figures calculated are helpful to the directors only in so far as they direct attention away from the share price: they demonstrate that it is the level of returns and the rate of return required by investors which drive the share price.

It would be more helpful for the directors to look in detail at the options available to them in terms of investment and to assess these against the **cost of capital**, taking account of the differing **degrees of risk** entailed. For the share price to be maximised in the long term, it is the effect of investment policy on the net worth of the business which is important, ie the net present value of operating cash flows. This may mean that in the short term the share price declines, but the directors may decide that this is a worthwhile sacrifice to make for the long-term profitability of the business. They may also need to consider whether the company needs a further injection of capital in addition to an increase in retentions in order to fund its development.

(d) If the company is to offer a **scrip dividend**, it will have to make a small share issue which capitalises distributable profits in the form of extra shares. The shareholders can then decide whether to retain the shares or to sell them on the market for cash. The main advantage of a scrip dividend is that there is no payment of cash and thus liquidity is preserved. Another effect is that distributable reserves are converted into permanent capital thus restricting the scope for future dividend payments.

The second alternative does not represent a simple equal value choice between shares and cash since it is biased in favour of the scrip issue: shareholders will receive a higher value dividend if they take it in the form of shares. This means that even those shareholders who would prefer to receive their dividend in the form of cash will take it as shares and then accept the transaction costs involved in liquidating them. Those who take this course of action will thus suffer a **dilution in their holding** in the company.

22 RG PLC

Pass marks. Many candidates had problems with part (a) of this question which requires the dividend valuation model to be applied in circumstances where there is a change in the growth rate.

Part (b) provides the opportunity to display your knowledge of recent developments in the discussion of dividend policy from the financial press. Examples of the more extreme policies can be given, together with examples of pronouncements made by some of the institutions.

(a) **Forecast earnings and dividends**

	Earnings	*Dividends*
	p	p
19X2 (plus 25%)	77.50	31.25
19X3 (plus 25%)	96.88	39.06
19X4 (earnings plus 10%; div 50% of earnings)	106.56	53.28
19X5 (plus 10%)		58.61

Dividend valuation model

$$\text{Value at 19X4 (when growth becomes constant)} = \frac{\text{19X5div}}{r - g} = \frac{58.61}{0.18 - 0.10} = 732.6\text{p}$$

Value at 19X1

	Time	*Description*	*pence*	*18% factor*	*Present value*
19X2	1	Dividend	31.25	0.847	26.47
19X3	2	Dividend	39.06	0.718	28.04
19X4	3	Div + MV (53.28 + 732.6)	785.88	0.609	478.60
		Total PV			533.11

$$\text{P/E ratio} = \frac{\text{Market price per share}}{\text{Earnings per share}} = 533.11 \div 62 = 8.6$$

The dividend valuation model includes a number of assumptions as follows.

(i) **Future dividends** will be of the same risk class as existing dividends.

(ii) Shareholders can be viewed as a **homogeneous group** ie there are no variations in their information, attitude to risk and so on.

(iii) **Transaction costs** can be ignored.

Its major weakness relates to the assumption that the **level of business risk** will not change as the firm develops. If this assumption cannot be met then it might be more appropriate to use a different approach to valuation such as the **capital asset pricing model.**

(b) The policy being put forward is consistent with the basic accounting concept that dividends should only be paid if there are **sufficient distributable profits** available to cover the payout. However, profits vary from one accounting period to the next, and companies face the conflicting demands of maintaining a constant payout ratio and level of dividend cover against maintaining a consistent level of actual dividend payments. This conflict has been brought to public attention in the recent recession where some firms have adopted a conservative policy and severely cut the dividend, while others have maintained the level of payments in line with their view of longer term future prospects rather than short-term current performance. ICI is an example of a company which has paid an **uncovered dividend.**

(i) Financial institutions tend to prefer **dividend income** to **capital growth** because cash flows are required to meet their liabilities and, if these cash flows are in the form of dividend payments, they can avoid the transaction costs involved in realising capital gains. It is therefore likely that institutional shareholders would prefer the increased payout ratio in the period of reduced growth. There has been pressure on companies recently from institutions such as the Prudential to ensure that dividend levels are maintained during periods of reduced profit performance.

(ii) The **position of small private investors** will vary. Where they are investing through an Individual Savings Account (ISA) or fall below the income tax threshold then they too are likely to express a preference for an increased payout ratio. However these tax advantages are not available to other investors, who are likely to prefer capital gains since they are able to take advantage of the indexation allowances and the additional annual exemption for capital gains tax. They will also be able to time their realisation of capital gains in order to minimise their tax liability.

(c) There are a number of **other options** available to RG, including the following.

  (i) The company could decide not to set a defined long-term payout ratio but could instead make a review of its shareholders each year to decide what would be most appropriate and to follow the trends being set by other firms.

  (ii) Instead of managing the payout ratio, the company could decide to try to maintain a constant real level of dividends regardless of the profit performance in an individual year.

  (iii) RG could decide not to make any distributions at all but to aim for investors interested in capital growth, and to use retained earnings as a major source of finance.

23 DIVS PLC

Pass marks. This is a topical question about the use of surplus cash for share buy-backs compared with increasing dividends or retaining the cash. The most difficult part to handle is part (a), which requires careful thought to cover the points in a logical order. By contrast, 7 marks is probably too many for part (b) and part (c) is a straightforward explanation of the effect of gearing on the cost of equity capital.

Examiner's comments. Most candidates who chose to answer the question had a reasonable understanding of the subject. In part (a) most candidates omitted to discuss strategic financial implications of share buy-backs beyond dividend policy. Neither did they discuss the method of share purchase (open market versus private arrangement).

To: The Directors of DIVS plc
From: IFA Financial Advisers — Date: 15 May 19X7
Subject: Dividend policy and share buybacks

We set out below our comments on the matters we talked about at our recent meeting.

(a) *Implications of share repurchase*

Before deciding on a **share repurchase**, you must clarify the company's overall cash requirements for the foreseeable future. Our assumption in this discussion is that the company will have a substantial temporary surplus of funds this year but that, if this is distributed to shareholders, additional funds will be needed for the subsequent two years.

Your first decision is whether to retain the cash until it is needed next year, or to distribute it to shareholders, or to retain a proportion, distributing the balance. **Retained cash** could be placed on deposit or invested in a suitable financial portfolio. Secondly, if you decide to distribute the cash to shareholders, this can be done either as a dividend or by buying back some shares.

The argument against retaining too much cash is that it can give the impression that the directors have 'run out of ideas' for expanding the company's operations. This may cause the share price to drop and attract unwanted takeover bids. On the other hand, the retention is logical if the company can invest the cash short term at a higher interest rate than individual shareholders. Any such retention of cash must be accompanied by careful explanations to the market of the company's investment plans over the following two years.

If the surplus cash is distributed to shareholders as a **dividend,** this will cause a big percentage increase in dividend this year. Shareholders will be happy with the cash received but, in the absence of further explanations, will become confused by what the company is trying to 'signal' by this dividend increase. Some may assume that further large increases in dividend can be expected in future years, and may develop over-optimistic expectations of the company's prospects.

Most finance directors take the view that it is best to increase dividends at a steady rate which **signals the company's long-run growth prospects.** If you agree with this view and you wish to make an above-average distribution to shareholders, you may consider using the balance of surplus cash to buy back some of the company's shares. For example, GEC plc, which for many years was criticised for holding too much cash, has more recently adopted a policy of share buy-backs.

The share buy-back requires provision in the company's **Articles of Association** and approval in general meeting. It can be arranged as a series of purchases on the open market or as a private purchase from a number of large shareholders. Assuming that the buy-back is at market price, the share price should be unaffected, whereas if a dividend payout is made, the share price will fall (from cum div to ex div). With a buy-back, the remaining shares will effectively be worth more, reflecting the higher future earnings per share.

Share buy-backs are sometimes made for **strategic reasons** separate from the dividend policy considerations outlined above. These include:

(i) the wish to re-privatise a business (as in the case of Richard Branson's Virgin Group); in this case all the shares were bought back from investors;

(ii) to make shares available for employee share option schemes;

(iii) as a defence against a hostile takeover bid;

(iv) to increase the company's gearing.

(b) *The advisability of borrowing money to pay dividends in years 2 and 3*

Borrowing money to pay dividends is legal provided that the dividends are **covered by the accumulated balance of distributable profits.** The question is whether it is financially advisable.

In theory, if cash is invested and dividends are reduced, this should not worry shareholders provided that they can see the prospect of increased future dividends. In practice, for 'signalling' reasons mentioned above, it is believed that shareholders are happiest when they receive a steady stream of dividends increasing from year to year. This is an argument in favour of borrowing in order to maintain the dividend growth. Shareholders receive more cash in years 2 and 3 but less in future years because of the need to repay the loans with interest.

Given that the company is not highly geared we recommend that the company borrows as much as is needed to maintain dividend growth in line with long-term earnings growth.

(c) *The effect on the company's cost of capital*

If shares are repurchased, the total value of equity goes down by the amount of cash paid out while debt remains unchanged. This **increase in gearing** will cause the cost of equity to rise because of the increased financial risk (volatility of equity earnings) experienced by the shareholders.

In the same way, if the company increases its borrowings in order to pay dividends, the gearing will increase and the **cost of equity capital** will rise.

However, DIVS is operating at a low level of gearing. The increase in the cost of equity is likely to be outweighed by the cheap after-tax cost of debt compared with equity. The tax savings resulting from debt interest will mean that, even though the cost of equity goes up, the weighted average cost of capital will be reduced.

I hope these notes address the points you have raised with us. If you require any further clarification please contact us at any time.

Signed: IFA Financial Advisers

24 EXPANSION

Pass marks. When discussing the financing alternatives, it is helpful to consider why the need for funds has arisen, and the likely timescale of this requirement. When assessing the figures, you may find it useful to bear in mind the theory of how the WACC changes with the level of gearing.

Examiner's comment. Most candidates who attempted this question were able to calculate the market value of the firm, the EPS and the number of shares required for a rights issue to raise £1 million. A few incorrectly used nominal values to calculate the number of shares to be issued. Few candidates understood the need to use the increased figure for cash flow before interest and tax of £1.3 million.

Part (b) of the question was generally poorly answered. Few candidates were able to note that the value of the firm is maximised under option 1, financing with equity, and theory suggests that this is the main criterion. However, EPS has a key position in company objectives and in practice the dilution effect of new equity cannot be ignored. This was a point correctly observed by many candidates.

(a) **Financing using equity via a rights issue**

(i) The market value of the equity is currently **£3.36m** (2m × £1.68). This approximates to that which would be expected using the dividend valuation model and assuming that all available earnings are paid out as dividends:

MV = d/r

where MV = market value of equity

D = current level of dividends

R = cost of equity

In the case of RH, the current level of **earnings attributable to equity** is as follows:

	£
Profit before interest and tax	1,000,000
Interest (£1m × 10%)	100,000
	900,000
Tax at 33%	297,000
Earnings attributable to equity	603,000

Therefore MV = £603,000 ÷ 18% = £3.35m

After the rights issue, the earnings will increase to £1.3m per annum, and the interest charge will be unchanged. The earnings attributable to equity will therefore become:

	£
Profit before interest and tax	1,300,000
Interest (£1m × 10%)	100,000
	1,200,000
Tax at 33%	396,000
Earnings attributable to equity	804,000

Therefore MV = £804,000 ÷ 18% = £4,466,667.

The market value of the equity has therefore increased by **£1,116,667**.

(ii) The **gearing ratio**, based on market values and assuming that the market value of the debentures is unchanged, will be:

$$\text{Debt : debt + equity} = \frac{£1\text{m}}{£1\text{m} + £4.467\text{m}} = \mathbf{18.3\%}$$

(iii) The **weighted average cost of capital (WACC)** will be found using market value weightings. The post tax cost of equity will be unchanged at 18%. The post tax cost of debt will be 6.67% (10% × (1 – 0.33)). The WACC can be found using the formula:

$$\text{WACC} = K_e \frac{E}{(E+D)} + K_d \frac{D}{(E+D)}$$

where K_e is the cost of equity (18%)
K_d is the cost of debt (6.67%)
E is the market value of equity (£4.467m)
D is the market value of debt (£1m)

$$\text{WACC} = 18\% \times \frac{4.467}{(4.467+1)} + 6.67\% \times \frac{1.0}{(4.467+1)}$$

WACC = **15.9%**

Financing using unsecured 12% loan stock

(i) After the rights issue, the earnings will increase to £1.3m per annum, and the interest charge will also increase as shown below. The **earnings attributable to equity** will therefore become:

	£
Profit before interest and tax	1,300,000
Debenture interest (£1m × 10%)	100,000
Loan interest (£1m × 12%)	120,000
	1,080,000
Tax at 33%	356,400
Earnings attributable to equity	723,600

Therefore MV = £723,600 ÷ 18% = £4,020,000.

The market value of the equity has therefore increased by **£660,000.**

(ii) The **gearing ratio**, based on market values and assuming that the market value of the debentures is unchanged, will be:

$$\text{Debt : debt + equity} = \frac{£2\text{m}}{£2\text{m} + £4.02\text{m}} = \mathbf{33.2\%}$$

(iii) The **WACC** will be found using the same method as above. The after tax cost of the loan stock will be 8% (12% × (1 – 0.33)).

$$\text{WACC} = 18\% \times \frac{4.02}{(4.02+2)} + 6.67\% \times \frac{1.0}{(4.02+2)} + 8\% \times \frac{1.0}{(4.02+2)}$$

WACC = 14.5%

(b) To: Board of Directors, RH plc

From: Financial Manager

Date: 15 November 19X8

Subject: **Alternatives for financing additional working capital**

The company currently requires an additional £1m of working capital to finance its expansion plans. The alternatives under consideration are the use of additional equity raised through a rights issue, and an issue of unsecured 12% loan stock. This report will deal with the relative merits of each of these two options, as well as highlighting some of the other factors that should be taken into consideration in arriving at a decision.

Rights issue

Under this option, the new shares would be issued at a discount of 15% to the existing share price, giving an issue price of £1.43. Therefore it would be necessary to issue 699,300 shares in order to raise the required amount of money. While this might have the effect of depressing the share price in the short term, the additional earnings generated mean that in the longer term the total value of the equity should rise to £4.467m, suggesting a theoretical share price of £1.65 per share, which is close to the current level. At the same time, the gearing would fall to a very low level of 18.3%, suggesting that the company would have a very low level of financial risk.

The weighted average cost of capital is currently:

$$WACC = K_e \frac{E}{(E+D)} + K_d \frac{D}{(E+D)}$$

where K_e is the cost of equity (18%)
K_d is the cost of debt (6.67%)
E is the market value of equity (£3.36m)
D is the market value of debt (£1m)

$$WACC = 18\% \times \frac{3.36}{(3.36+1)} + 6.67\% \times \frac{1.0}{(3.36+1)}$$

WACC = **15.4%**

After the rights issue, this would increase to approximately 16%. This reflects the very low gearing and the fact that the company is taking little opportunity of the tax advantages arising from debt financing and the lower cost of debt. Thus although this would be a very safe option, the cost of capital would increase as a consequence.

Loan stock issue

The effect of the loan stock issue would be to increase the gearing to 33.2%. However, this is still a perfectly acceptable level assuming that earnings will continue to be steady. At the same time, the theoretical share price should increase to £2.01 per share (£4.02m ÷ 2m shares), and the WACC should fall to 14.5%. This reflects the fact that the company would be gaining additional benefits from the tax relief on the loan interest and the lower cost of debt. Given the fact that the gearing is currently very low, this is likely to be the preferred option on financial grounds.

Other factors

The following are among the other factors that should be considered in making this decision.

- The effect of the financing choice on the structure of ownership and control. In this case, since the choice is between a rights issue and debt, the preemption rights of the existing shareholders are not affected, and there should be little change.

- It should be considered whether at least a part of the additional funds required could be generated efficiently, for example either by rescheduling capital expenditure, or through efficiency savings.
- Are there any borrowing restrictions in the Articles of Association, or any covenants on the existing debenture stock that affect the company's ability to raise further debt finance, albeit unsecured?
- How will forecast external events affect the financing decision? For example, how are interest rates expected to move in the coming years?
- Will the loan stock require redemption at some date in the future, and if so, how is this to be financed?

25 RISK AND MARKET EFFICIENCY

Pass marks. Part (a) demands an understanding of the different types of risk, how they are measured, and their implications for investment strategy. In part (b) it is helpful to consider the relationship of the statements to time: are they explaining the past, describing the present or predicting the future?

Other points. This question aimed to examine candidates' knowledge and understanding of different types of risk, the relationship between them and how they can be measured. It further examined for an understanding of market efficiency and how historical information can be related to future periods.

Examiner's comment. Marking was flexible between parts (a)(i) and (a)(ii) of the question as there was scope for discussing the issues of risk in both sub-sections of the question.

(a) MEMORANDUM

To: Board of Directors
From: Management Accountant Date: 23 May 19X5
Subject: Portfolio risk

The purpose of this paper is to provide a definition of the different types of **portfolio risk** and an explanation of their measurement, and to relate them to the recent board discussions on this subject.

There are three elements to be considered in this context.

(a) Systematic risk
(b) Unsystematic risk
(c) Total risk

Each of these will be considered separately below.

Total risk

The total risk of an investment is the sum of the systematic and the unsystematic elements. It is measured by the standard deviation of the returns on the investment.

Systematic risk

This is that element of risk that cannot be avoided by diversification. It must therefore be accepted by the investor unless he invests entirely in risk-free investments. He will expect to earn a return which is higher than the return on a risk-free investment in return for accepting systematic risk. The amount of systematic risk in an investment varies between different types of investment. Some industries by their nature are more risky than others, for example compare the restaurant business with the retailing of basic foodstuffs. Similarly, some individual projects will be more risky than others:

compare the building of the Channel Tunnel with the replacement of a fleet of car ferries, which can be sold for use on alternative routes if necessary.

The **capital asset pricing model** (CAPM) is concerned with the measurement of systematic risk. It seeks to relate the premium on returns required by investors to the systematic risk of the company via a measure known as the beta factor. A beta factor in excess of 1.0 indicates that the share carries a higher level of systematic risk than the average for the market and vice versa.

Unsystematic risk

This is that element of risk which it is possible to eliminate through diversification. Therefore if an investor holds a well diversified portfolio he will be able to avoid unsystematic risk. The simplest approach to quantifying the unsystematic risk is indirectly in relation to the total risk and the systematic risk of the portfolio. Since the total risk is defined as the sum of the systematic and the unsystematic risk, it follows that the unsystematic risk element can be found by subtraction.

Implications for investment strategy

Since unsystematic risk can effectively be removed from the portfolio through diversification, it is true to say that if the portfolio is fully diversified then only systematic risk needs to be considered. However, it would be dangerous to ignore the total risk insofar as this provides an indicator as to whether the portfolio is in fact sufficiently diversified.

It may be the case that the price of a share indicates a return that is below that of the market or even of the risk-free asset. In theory, if the beta is lower as a result, the lower return makes the share worth investing in because of lower uncertainty.

Signed: Management Accountant

(b) An **efficient market** can be defined in terms of **information processing** as one in which the prices of traded securities reflect all the relevant information which is available to participants, where no individual or group of individuals dominates the market, and where transaction costs are insignificant. Thus it will be supposed that share prices respond quickly to all new information about future prospects. Since it is postulated that prices already reflect all the available information, it follows that at any one point in time future price movements cannot be forecast, since future information is not known and therefore the corresponding price movement is not known. The efficient market hypothesis thus provides a means of explaining the current level of share prices and not of forecasting their future levels. The implication for investors is that it is not possible for an investor consistently to outperform the market.

Mathematical models which attempt to predict movements in share prices are generally, as in this particular case, based on the analysis of a large volume of data over a long period of time. However, they are only likely to be able to predict the future with accuracy if the economic, financial, corporate and political framework that governed the period in question remains stable into the future. In practice, such conditions are in a constant state of change and therefore the predictive value of such models degrades quickly over time thus rendering such models of limited value. However, in the short term they may in themselves become an influence on the market since if sufficient people have faith in them they may influence buying behaviour and hence become something of a self-fulfilling prophecy. In the longer term though, prices will adjust back to their 'underlying' or 'real' values and the utility of the models will decline.

Neither statement claims to be able to predict the price of a given security with significant accuracy for a given point in time, and therefore to this extent they are not contradictory. Similarly, both statements are in fact concerned more with the historical movements in share prices than with their prediction into the future.

26 CAPITAL MARKET LINE

> **Examiner's comment**. Part (a) of the question requires the construction of simple equations to calculate the mix of equities and risk free investments in the two portfolios. It also requires a knowledge of the linear expression which describes the capital market line, since this must be used to calculate the new standard deviation in (iii). In (a)(ii), the axes of your graph should be labelled clearly. Part (b) requires only a discussion of risk in the context of portfolio theory. Other factors, such as the personal financial and tax situation of the investor, can be ignored.

(a) (i) X's overall expected return is 18%. We know that one-third of his investments are at the risk free rate of 12%. It is therefore possible to calculate the **overall return** being earned by his equity investments as follows.

Let:			
	Overall expected return	=	r
	Return on equities	=	r_e
	Risk free returns	=	r_f

$$r = r_f/3 + 2r_e/3$$
$$18 = 4 + 2r_e/3$$
$$14 = 2r_e/3$$
$$r_e = 21\%$$

Assume that the market portfolio held by Y is similar to that of X and yields a return of 21%. For Y to achieve an overall return in excess of this implies that he must be augmenting his funds by borrowing at the risk free rate.

Let:			
	Overall expected return	=	r
	Funds borrowed as a proportion of existing investment	=	F
	Return on equities	=	r_e
	Risk free returns	=	r_f

$$r = r_e(1 + F) - (r_f \times F)$$
$$24 = 21(1 + F) - 12F$$
$$24 = 21 + 21F - 12F$$
$$3 = 9F$$
$$F = 1/3$$

Y has therefore borrowed at 12% to increase his funds by one third. All his funds are invested in equities.

(ii)

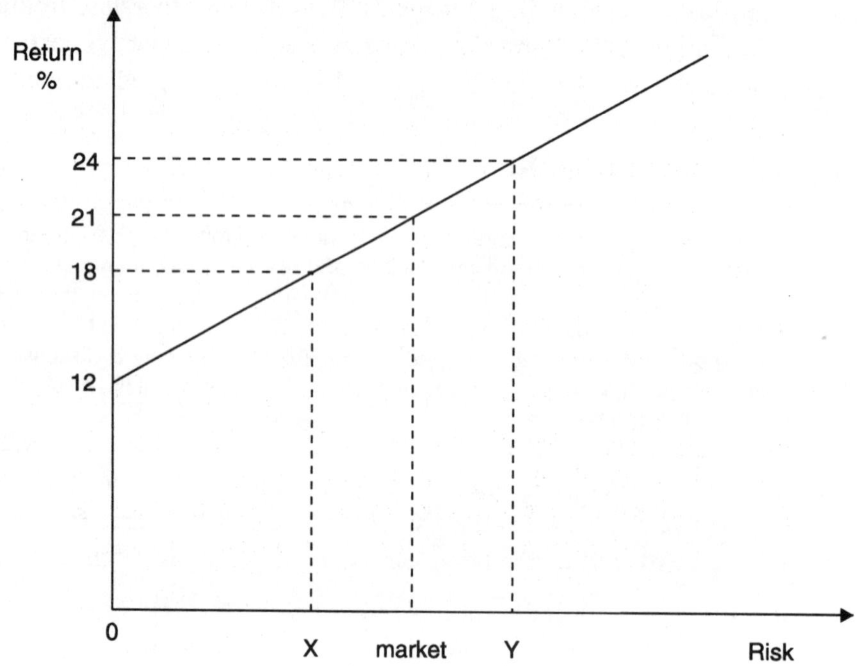

(iii) The formula for the capital market line is:

$$Y = r_f + b\sigma$$

where:

Y = Overall rate of return

r_f = Risk free rate of return

b = Slope of capital market line

σ = Standard deviation of portfolio

Using the existing data for the portfolio it is possible to calculate b:

$$18 = 12 + 12b$$
$$b = 0.5$$

This can then be used to calculate the new standard deviation of the portfolio if the required return increases to 20%:

$$Y = r_f + b\sigma$$
$$20 = 12 + 0.5\sigma$$
$$\sigma = 16\%$$

The composition of the new portfolio can also be calculated.

Let:

r = Overall rate of return

r_f = Risk free rate of return

r_e = Rate of return on equities

P = Proportion invested in risk free investments

$$r = Pr_f + r_e(1 - P)$$
$$20 = 12P + 21(1 - P)$$
$$20 = 12P + 21 - 21P$$
$$9P = 1$$
$$P = 1/9$$

Thus the proportion of equities in the portfolio would have to increase to 8/9, with a corresponding rise in the risk (as represented by the standard deviation) of the portfolio, in order to achieve an overall rate of return of 20%.

(b) The risk attaching to an equity investment can be divided into two parts.

(i) **Systematic risk** is the part of the risk which is broadly common to all securities and is dependent upon general economic and market conditions. This element of risk is largely unavoidable and cannot be reduced by diversification.

(ii) **Unsystematic risk** is also known as **business risk** and is that element of risk which is specific to a given type of business activity. For example, sales of cold drinks will be adversely affected by a poor summer. Unsystematic risk can be offset by selecting securities which are either negatively correlated, for instance sales of wellington boots are likely to move in the opposite direction to those of cold drinks, or which are in totally unrelated economic segments. An example of the latter case is bananas and socks.

Thus it can be seen that unsystematic risk can be reduced by diversification, and empirical studies have shown that most unsystematic risk can be eliminated by holding around thirty securities in the portfolio. In the efficiently diversified portfolio, these securities will be as different as possible from each other in terms of their product type, technology, and market positions.

27 COMPANY'S PORTFOLIO

Examiner's comment. Answers to part (b) of the question were generally very poor. Few candidates understood the meaning of conversion premium and conversion discount and virtually no candidates could provide the correct calculations (or even any calculations) for part (b)(ii).

(a) Z plc wishes to build up a fund for foreign investment which will be spent within the next two years. There are **two main points** to consider.

(i) The rate of return from invested funds must always be reviewed against the risk of the investment. In the long term, equity investments show a higher rate of return than government securities and corporate debt but they suffer from the risk that in the short term the stock market might fall, severely reducing the funds available for investment.

(ii) Ideally the funds should be accumulated in the currency of the country where they will eventually be spent.

Below, we expand on these points in relation to Z plc's case.

Z plc has investments in UK and US equities. At the time of writing, both of these stock markets have been performing well, but to maintain more than 60% of the fund in equities is taking a risk of over-reliance on equities.

The portfolios of UK and US equities have shown higher rates of return than the stock market average for these countries. This is very good news but it probably indicates that the portfolios have an above-average proportion of high-beta shares. Such shares will tend to do very well when the stock market is rising but are likely to fall more than average if there is a stock market collapse. A similar point can be made about the small companies' shares which can be very volatile.

Because of the principle of **liquidity preference**, long-term debt instruments tend to show a higher average rate of return than short-term bonds. However the long-term government bonds suffer from the same problem as equities: there is a risk that they might have to be sold at a point when their value is low. The 3-month Treasury Bonds do not suffer from this risk.

The investment in UK corporate debt shows a higher rate of return than the UK government debt. However there is higher default risk on corporate debt.

On balance then, Z plc's portfolio is a long way from being risk-free. With less than two years to go before the money is spent, it is probably wise to transfer some of the money out of equities into low-risk deposits. The proportion in deposits can be gradually increased as the date gets nearer.

As a hedge against currency risk, investments or deposits should now be made in the currencies in which the eventual investment will take place. With the pound at a high level against most currencies in the world, now is probably a good time to effect this change.

(b)

> **Pass marks**. Convertible loan stock is an interesting investment, having the return and risk characteristics of an option. This is a good question, except that the convertible is trading at a discount below the underlying share price, which is unrealistic in the scenario given. The decision maker must choose between selling now, converting now, converting after one year, or holding to redemption.

(i) The **conversion premium** is the difference between:

- the current market price of the convertible loan stock, and
- the current market value of the equivalent shares if the conversion was made

In other words, a premium indicates that the value of the stock is higher than that of the underlying shares. This is because the convertible loan stock is normally a better investment than the underlying shares. It will enable the holder to gain from any increase in the share price but protects against a collapse in share price by having a minimum value as loan stock.

If, however, the market price of the convertible is less than that of the equivalent shares, there is a **conversion discount**.

(ii) The treasurer has four options:

- Sell the stock now at £106.50 (31 December 19X7)
- Convert now (31 December 19X7)
- Convert in one year's time (31 December 19X8)
- Hold the stock to redemption (31 December 19X9)

Option 1: Selling the stock now will give cash of 50,000/100 × £106.50 = £53,250.

Option 2: Converting now will give 50,000/100 × 20 = 10,000 shares with a current value of £54,000.

Option 4: Holding to redemption will give 6% interest for 2 years and a redemption value of £50,000. Discounting at 7%, the appropriate rate for debt of this risk:

Year		£	*7% factor*	*Present value* £
1-2	6% interest	3,000	1.808	5,424
2	Redemption	50,000	0.873	43,650
				49,024

The present value of holding to redemption is £49,074.

Looking at these three options, the stock is at a discount to the value of the equivalent shares which means that **converting now** (option 2) gives the best value, £54,000.

Option 3 will give interest after one year of £3,000 and 50,000 × 18/100 shares, ie 9,000 shares. The present value of the interest at 7% is £2,805.

So, if option 3 is to be better than option 2, the present value of the share value in one year's time must be more than £54,000 – £2,805 = £51,195, which is £5.69 per share.

£5.69 is 5.4% higher than the current share price.

On the basis of the figures, therefore, and ignoring brokerage fees, the decision is to convert the loan stock to shares now, receiving £54,000, unless it is expected that the present value of the share price in one year's time will be more than £5.69, which would require a growth in the share price of 5.4% above the cost of equity capital.

The decision cannot be made purely on the basis of these figures, however, because the different options have different levels of risk attached to them. If the loan stock is converted now and the shares are held, they might collapse in value over the next two years. If, on the other hand, the shares are sold for cash, the opportunity of share price growth is lost. If the convertible is held until the last date for conversion it provides a protection against share price collapse and the opportunity of gaining from a share price increase. The decision is ultimately a subjective one, based on the Treasurer's attitude to risk.

Pass marks. As already mentioned, the idea that the convertible stock can be at a discount on a conversion day, as in this question, is unrealistic! The best decision would in fact be to convert the stock to shares, immediately sell them for £54,000 cash and buy more convertible stock for £53,250, making a risk free gain of £750 (1.4%). This arbitrage process could be repeated until the cost of the stock rose sufficiently so that transaction costs prevented any further gains.

28 PMS

Pass marks. In part (a) make clear the theoretical basis for your calculations. The traditional view and the Modigliani/Miller (MM) approach have different implications for company values at different levels of gearing. It is also helpful to state any assumptions made about the dividend policy. It is helpful to calculate the income statement under the different scenarios as a preliminary to finding the market values and cost of equity.

Examiner's comment. Some excellent answers were given to part (b). Part (c) requires an outline of the alternative views of capital structure and an understanding of how theory becomes distorted by practical issues. Part (c) seemed to be answered either very well by those candidates familiar with MM, or very badly by those who failed to understand what was being asked.

(a) The purpose of raising the money is not stated. In the absence of details of a project, we assume that it is for restructuring. The first step is to calculate the present cost of equity using the **capital asset pricing model** (CAPM):

$$E(r_j) = r_f + [E(r_m) - r_f]\,\beta$$

where	$E(r_j)$	=	cost of equity (expected return)
	r_f	=	risk free rate of return (10%)
	β	=	beta value (1.2)
	$E(r_m)$	=	market rate of return (15%)

In this case: $E(r_j) = 10 + (15 - 10) \times 1.2$
$= 16\%$

This cost of equity can now be applied in the **dividend valuation model** to find the total market value of the firm. It is assumed that all earnings are distributed as dividend; earnings and therefore dividends do not grow.

$$p_o = d_o/r$$

where p_o = market value
d_o = current level of dividends (post tax)
r = cost of equity

$$p_o = 400 \times 0.67/0.16 = £1.675m$$

(i) The situation under the different scenarios can be summarised as follows.

	Current	*Scen 1*	*Scen 2*
	£'000	£'000	£'000
Profit before interest and tax	400.0	400.0	400.0
Less interest	0.0	50.0	120.0
	400.0	350.0	280.0
Less tax at 33%	132.0	115.5	92.4
Distributable profits	268.0	234.5	187.6

According to the basic theory of capital structure developed by **Modigliani and Miller**, the market value of a firm is independent of capital structure. When tax is introduced into the calculations, the market value of the firm will increase as debt is added to the capital mix because of the present value of the **tax shield** on interest payments. This can be expressed as:

$$V_g = V_u + DT_c$$

where V_g = market value of the geared company
V_u = market value of the ungeared company
D = market value of debt
T_c = rate of corporation tax

In this case:

	Current	*Scen 1*	*Scen 2*
	£'000	£'000	£'000
V_u	1,675	1,675	1,675
D	0	500	1,000
T_c	33%	33%	33%
	£'000	£'000	£'000
$D \times T_c$	0	165	330
Total market value	1,675	1,840	2,005

The value of the equity can now be found:

$E = V_g - D$

Scenario 1: £1.84m – £0.5m = £1.34m
Scenario 2: £2.005m – £1.0m = £1.005m

(ii) The ratio of **debt to equity** is given by D/E:

Scenario 1: 500/1,340 = 37.3%
Scenario 2: 1,000/1,005 = 99.5%

(iii) Assuming that all distributable profits are paid as dividends, the **cost of equity** can be found using:

	r	=	d_0/p_0
where:	r	=	cost of equity
	d_0	=	dividend (distributable profit above)
	p_0	=	market value of equity
Scenario 1: 234.5/1,340		=	17.5%
Scenario 2: 187.6/1,005		=	18.7%

(b) The main areas in which **problems** will be experienced are those which are linked to cash flow. These include the following.

(i) The company may find it difficult to meet large payments as they become due, for example an additional week's holiday pay for production workers. As a result of this it may become increasingly difficult to attract and retain staff of a good calibre at all levels.

(ii) Suppliers may become more cautious in extending credit. This may be felt in higher prices, a shorter credit period or a lower credit limit. The company may no longer receive the same level of priority from its suppliers.

(iii) The bank may start to exercise stricter controls, restricting the overdraft level, demanding higher interest rates, looking for regular detailed financial reports from the company, and possibly requiring a say in the management of the business.

Effects will also be felt in **other areas.**

(i) Customers may become fearful of an interruption in supplies and may start to source some of their products from other manufacturers.

(ii) Money will be unavailable for activities which are essential for the long term health of the business such as training and research and development.

(iii) Additional legal costs may be incurred if it becomes necessary to undertake some form of financial restructuring.

(iv) It will be difficult to raise additional long term finance and if a source can be found it is likely to be expensive.

(v) Staff motivation and morale is likely to be weakened and this will impact on the operational performance.

(c) The contention that capital structure is irrelevant to the value of the firm was first put forward by **Modigliani and Miller**. Until that point the **traditional view** was that there is an optimal mix of debt and equity that minimises the weighted average cost of capital (WACC).

The key difference between these two approaches is related to the behaviour of the rate of return required by shareholders as the gearing level rises. The traditional view is that the cost of equity remains at a constant level at low levels of gearing, causing the WACC to fall. Beyond a certain point however, the shareholders begin to demand a higher rate of return in compensation for the higher level of financial risk and the WACC begins to rise.

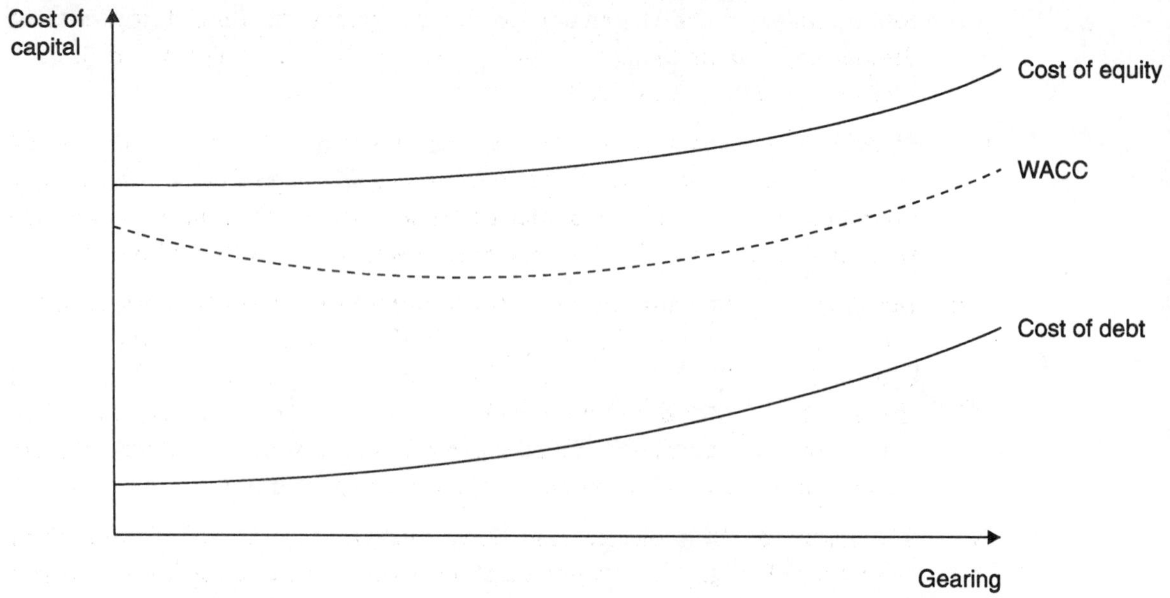

The implications of the traditional view of the value of the firm are illustrated below.

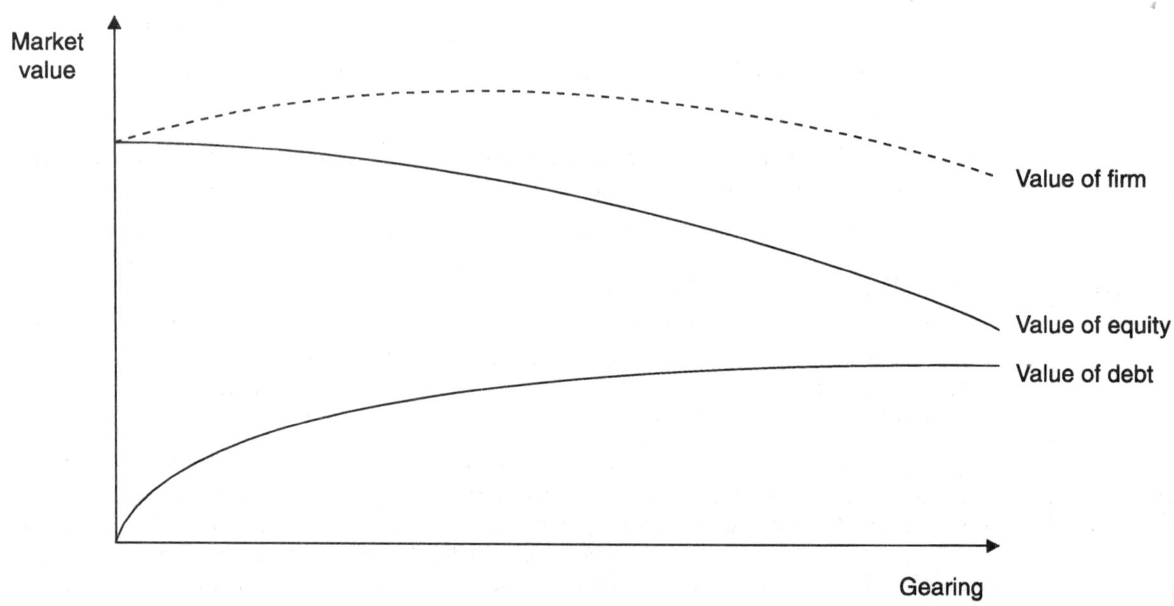

Modigliani and Miller showed that the value of the firm was determined by the income generated from its business activities, and that the way this income was split between the providers of capital was irrelevant. If the shares of two firms with the same level of business risk but different gearing levels were traded at different prices, then shareholders would move from the overvalued to the undervalued firm and adjust their level of personal borrowing through the market to maintain their financial risk at the same level. This **arbitrage process** would force the total price of the two firms to a common equilibrium value.

The above discussion would suggest that capital structure is irrelevant. However in practical terms this is not the case and other factors come into play.

(i) Both **corporate and personal taxation** distort the theory and can cause a bias in favour of debt into the capital structure.

(ii) **Agency problems** may restrict the level of debt taken on. Agency costs arise from ensuring that the agents ie the company management act in the best interests of the principals ie the providers of debt. It is increasingly common for covenants to be placed on loans, for example to restrict the level of dividend payments to prevent the capital base being run down and thereby increasing the risk of the lenders.

(iii) The **nature of the asset base** has been shown empirically to affect the capital structure. Companies with a high level of tangible assets find it easier to take on debt since they are able to offer better security in the event of bankruptcy than firms with a high level of intangible assets such as software house.

(iv) Managers may have a **preference for one sort of finance over another**. In the UK there is often a preference for retained earnings over debt finance and equity issues. This is partly due to the transaction costs involved in raising the finance, but has also to do with the balance of ownership and control. The use of retained earnings causes the minimum disruption to the existing balance of control and is often preferred for this reason.

(v) The nature of the projected cash flows will affect the ability of the firm to raise debt. The greater the **potential variability in the cash flows**, the less easy it will be for the firm to borrow.

(vi) **Interest rate fluctuations** may deter firms from taking on a high level of borrowings.

(vii) If the firm has significant **international operations**, it may need to take on loans denominated in foreign currencies in order to minimise its exchange exposure.

(viii) There may be a **clause in the Articles of Association** with restricts the ability of the firm to borrow.

29 LEISURE INTERNATIONAL PLC

> **Pass marks**. This generally well answered question is testing your knowledge of the different theories relating to the cost of capital, as well as testing your ability to calculate the cost of capital correctly taking into account the effects of taxation.
>
> In part (c) you are required to demonstrate the way in which the cost of capital should be used by the company in assessing individual projects. It may be helpful to approach this from the point of view of the effect of the new funding and investments on the overall capital structure of the firm, and the implications of this for raising finance in the future.

(a) It is assumed that the market prices of the shares and debentures are quoted excluding dividend and interest. Since the WACC is to be calculated based on market values, the cost of reserves can be ignored.

Cost of equity. The dividend valuation model taking into account growth will be used.

$$r = \frac{d_1}{p_0} + g$$

where:	r	=	cost of equity
	d_1	=	annual level of dividends
	g	=	annual rate of growth in dividends
	p_0	=	market price of shares (ex div)
In this case:	r	=	4/80 + 0.12
		=	17.0%

Cost of preference shares

$$r = d_1/p_o$$

where:

r = cost of preference shares
d_1 = preference dividend (9p)
p_o = market price of shares (72p)
r = 9 / 72
= 12.5%

Cost of debentures. It is assumed that the debentures are irredeemable. The after tax cost to the company will be calculated.

$$r_D = \frac{i(1-T_c)}{p_o}$$

where:

r_D = cost of debentures
I = annual interest payment (14p)
p_o = market price of debentures (100p)
T_c = rate of corporation tax (33%)

$$r_D = \frac{14(1-0.33)}{100}$$
= 9.4%

Weighted average cost of capital (WACC)

	No in issue £	*Market price* £	*Market value* £	*Cost* %	*Weighted cost*
Equity	10,400,000	0.80	8,320,000	17.0	141,440
Preference shares	4,500,000	0.72	3,240,000	12.5	405,000
Debentures	5,000,000	1.00	5,000,000	9.4	470,000
			16,560,000		2,289,400
WACC (2,289,400 / 16,560,000)					13.82%

(b) The **capital asset pricing model** (CAPM) provides an alternative to the dividend valuation model in calculating the cost of equity. Unlike the dividend valuation model, the CAPM seeks to differentiate between the various types of risk faced by a firm and to allow for the fact that new projects undertaken may carry a different level of risk from the existing business.

The model focuses on the level of **systematic risk** attaching to the firm, in other words, that element of risk which is common to all investments and which cannot be avoided by diversification. The model uses the **beta factor** as a measure of an individual share's volatility of expected returns as against the market average. A beta factor of less than 1.0 indicates that the expected volatility is less than that of the market as a whole, and vice versa.

The model can be formulated as follows:

$$r = r_f + [E(r_m) - r_f]\,\beta_j$$

where:

r = cost of equity capital
β_j = beta factor for the firm
$E(r_m)$ = market rate of return
r_f = risk free rate of return

Thus the additional information that would be required is as follows.

Beta factor. This can be calculated statistically from historical records of:

(i) the returns earned by the share in terms of capital gains/losses and dividends;
(ii) the overall returns earned by the market.

It can be formulated as follows.

$$\beta_i = \frac{Cov_{i,m}}{\sigma^2_m}$$

where: β_i = beta factor of stock i

$Cov_{i,m}$ = covariance between the return on Leisure International shares and the market return

σ^2_m = variance of the market return

Market rate of return. The average annual rate of return on the securities market as a whole. This can be calculated from historical records.

Risk free rate of return. This is generally taken to be the rate of return on government stocks.

(c) It is not usually correct to regard the **required rate of return** for an individual project as the cost of the actual source of funds that will be used to finance it, even where the funds can be traced directly. Debt is cheaper than equity only because there is an equity base which takes the risk - if the equity funds were not there then the company could not borrow. Each year some profits should be retained to increase the equity base, thus allowing further borrowing to take place. The borrowing is not independent of equity funds, and thus it is appropriate to combine the two in arriving at the cost of capital to be used in project appraisal.

The WACC reflects the company's long-term capital structure, and therefore capital costs. The capital structure generally changes only very slowly over time, and therefore the marginal cost of new capital should be approximately equal to the WACC. The **WACC** is therefore a more appropriate yardstick for the evaluation of new projects.

(d) (i) As calculated above, the existing preference shares are yielding 12.5% net. Based on the single income tax rate given in the question of 25%, this represents a gross yield of 16.67%, as compared with 14% on the debentures. In the event of Leisure International being wound up, the debenture holders would rank above the preference shareholders for repayment of capital. Similarly, preference dividend will only be paid in a given year if sufficient funds are available after the debenture holders have been paid. Thus holders of preference shares carry a greater burden of risk than do the debenture holders, and it is consistent that they should expect to receive a higher rate of return in compensation for this.

(ii) The net payment made by the company on the debentures is:

£5m × 14% × 0.67 = £469,000

In order to raise the £5m through a preference share issue, the company would need to offer the shares at a discount. To yield 12.5% to the investor, the shares would therefore need to be priced at the same level as the existing preference shares ie 72p per share. 6,944,445 shares would need to be issued at 72p in order to raise £5m. The annual cost in terms of dividends can be calculated either as 12.5% of £5m, or as 9.0% of the nominal value (£6,944,445). In either event, the cost to the company is £625,000.

Thus if preference shares are issued instead of debentures, the annual equity earnings would be reduced by £156,000 (£625,000 – £469,000).

30 4D PLC

Pass marks. In part (a) it is necessary to define the likely investment criteria before going on to consider the individual factors to be taken into account. In part (b)(ii) you should consider both the systematic and unsystematic risk components of the proposed portfolio, and seek to relate these to the objectives of the company and to its existing risk position.

Examiner's comment. Many candidates misunderstood part (a) and discussed investment appraisal or even portfolio theory. The question was about the management of cash surpluses. The criteria for investment are therefore different from those necessary for long-term investments. In part (b) many candidates over-complicated the risk calculation. The main failure was not understanding what the betas for securities 3 and 4 should be.

(a) When selecting marketable securities in which to invest, the treasurer will normally be doing so with the aim of **maximising the return on short-term cash surpluses**. In this situation, the criteria are likely to include the following.

(i) The amount of funds available for investment will influence the type of security that will be appropriate.

(ii) Since the company is not seeking a speculative gain, the level of risk should be as low as possible. However, he must ensure that funds which are intended for specific future purposes do not lie idle.

(iii) The level of return should be as high as possible within the class of risk which the company is prepared to accept.

(iv) The level of transaction costs and the complexity of administration should be kept to a minimum.

(v) The securities should be easily marketable so that if the funds are required at an earlier date than anticipated this can be achieved without a significant loss of revenue.

(b) (i) The **risk of the portfolio** can be calculated using a weighted average of the beta values of the different securities. It is assumed that in the case of security 3, the required rate of return is a sterling figure. If this is the case, then this corresponds with the market average which means that the beta can be assumed to be 1.0.

	Proportion	*Beta*	*Weighted*
Security 1	30%	1.2	0.36
Security 2	30%	1.6	0.48
Security 3	20%	1.0	0.20
Security 4 (risk free)	20%	0.0	0.00
			1.04

Assuming that the historical performance of these securities will continue into the future, this beta value can be used in the CAPM to calculate the expected return for the portfolio:

$$r = r_f + (E(r_m) - r_f)\,\beta_j$$

where

r = expected return

β_j = beta value (1.04)

r_f = risk free rate of return (5%)

r_m = market rate of return (12%)

$$r = 5\% + (12\% - 5\%) \times 1.04$$
$$= 12.28\%$$

(ii)

REPORT

To: Board of Directors
From: Management Accountant Date: 15 May 19X6
Subject: Investment portfolio of marketable securities

Introduction

The purpose of this report is to consider the choice of marketable securities for 4D for the coming twelve months. The securities already proposed will be considered, together with other available alternatives.

Proposed portfolio

The securities selected must meet the Board's criteria in terms of **risk profile, liquidity, return** and **transaction and administration costs**. The proposed portfolio would offer a level of risk slightly in excess of the market level of risk, with a return similarly slightly above the market rate of return. In the context of the purpose for which the investment is being made, and assuming that the funds will be required in full at the end of the twelve month period, one might consider that this is too high a level of risk to accept for such a portfolio. In fact, the beta of the portfolio is significantly in excess of our own beta which suggests that the portfolio may not conform to our financial objectives.

When the individual securities are considered, it is apparent that the portfolio beta is only brought down to its existing level by the inclusion of 20% short-dated government bonds; the remainder of the portfolio carries a level of risk significantly above that of the market. Although the US shares carry an apparently lower beta, their inclusion in the portfolio would introduce a level of exchange rate exposure, thus increasing their real level of risk. The UK equity investments are also relatively risky, particularly the small high technology company.

A further factor to be considered is the spread of the portfolio. It is generally considered that a portfolio of at least twenty securities is required in order to eliminate unsystematic risk, but in this case, only four securities are being considered. It is not as yet clear what the exact amount of the funds available for investment will be, and it may be that if the amount is relatively low, the benefits of diversification could be outweighed by the higher level of transaction costs.

Alternative options

A number of other options are available. These include:

(1) other UK equities
(2) loan stock or debentures
(3) commercial paper
(4) bank deposits
(5) local authority bonds
(6) bills of exchange
(7) investments that offer a spread themselves, such as unit trusts

Conclusions

The Board should give consideration to the investment criteria in terms of risk, return and transaction costs that it wishes the portfolio to meet. The proposed portfolio carries a relatively high level of systematic risk and is unlikely to succeed in eliminating unsystematic risk. A number of other alternatives are available, and it is suggested that further consideration should be given to these before the final decisions are made.

Signed: Management Accountant

31 CW LIMITED

Pass marks. The first part of the question requires a straightforward explanation of the various hedging techniques that are available to manage interest rate risk. However, it would be easy to write more than is strictly necessary on these areas and thus to leave insufficient time for the second part of the question. You should therefore be careful to limit your discussion to the key points, which is all that is really required.

In part (b) it is helpful to draw a decision tree showing the closing cash balance for each month (starting with month 0) as an aid to calculation. Note that the interest rates given are **annual** and not **monthly** rates.

Examiner's comment. Most candidates who answered this question made a creditable attempt at part (a), although many confused exchange rate risk with interest rate risk. There are, of course, close similarities and the two are connected, but the question required a focus on interest rates. In part (b), very few candidates understood the need to apply conditional probabilities to cash flows in month 2 or that there were two options for investing the cash surpluses. Another common failure was to show the cash movement in the month, which gained some credit, but not the cash balance at the end of the month, as required by the question. Presentation of the answers to this question was generally poor and it was difficult to follow what some candidates intended.

(a) Interest rate exposure arises when a company's borrowing is such that a change in interest rates might expose it to interest charges that are unacceptably high. For example, if a company has a large tranche of debt at a fixed rate of interest that is due for repayment in the near future, and the loan is to be replaced or renegotiated, the company would be vulnerable to a sudden increase in market interest rates. Risk management in this context involves using hedging techniques to reduce or 'cover' an exposure. However, hedging has a cost, which will either take the form of a fee to a financial institution or a reduction in profit, and this must be weighed against the reduction in financial risks that the hedge achieves. The extent to which the exposure is covered is known as the 'hedge efficiency'. A perfect hedge has an efficiency of 100%.

Methods of managing interest rate risk include the following.

Forward interest rate agreements (FRAs)

A FRA is an agreement, usually between a company and a bank, about the interest rate on a future loan or deposit. The agreement will fix the rate of interest for borrowing for a certain time in the future. If the actual rate of interest at that time is above that agreed, the bank pays the company the difference, and vice versa. Thus the company benefits from effectively fixing the rate of interest on a loan for a given period, but it may miss the opportunity to benefit from any favourable movements in rates during that time. A FRA is simply an agreement about rates – it does not involve the movement of the principal sum – the actual borrowing must be arranged separately.

Futures

A financial future is an agreement on the future price of a financial variable. Interest rate futures are similar in all respects to FRAs, except that the terms, sums involved, and periods are standardised. They are traded on the London International Futures and Options Exchange (LIFFE). Their standardised nature makes them less attractive to corporate borrowers because it is not always possible to match them exactly to specific rate exposures. Each contract will require the payment of a small initial deposit.

Interest rate options

An interest rate guarantee (or option) provides the right to borrow a specified amount at a guaranteed rate of interest. The option guarantees that the interest rate will not rise above a specified level during a specified period. On the date of expiry of the option the buyer must decide whether or not to exercise his right to borrow. He will only exercise the option if actual interest rates have risen above the option rate. The advantage of options is that the buyer cannot lose on the interest rate and can take advantage of any favourable rate movements. However, a premium must be paid regardless of whether or not the option is exercised. Options can be negotiated directly with the bank or traded in a standardised form on the LIFFE.

Caps and collars

These can be used to set a floor and a ceiling to the range of interest rates that might be incurred. A premium must be paid for this service. These agreements do not provide a perfect hedge, but they do limit the range of possibilities and thus reduce the level of exposure.

Swaps

Interest rate swaps are transactions that exploit different interest rates in different markets for borrowing, to reduce interest costs for either fixed or floating rate loans. A swap is an arrangement whereby two companies, or a company and a bank, swap interest rate commitments with each other. Thus a company could convert a fixed rate liability into a variable rate liability; however the parties to a swap retain their obligations to the original lenders, and this means that they must accept counterparty risk.

Swaptions

This is a hybrid hedging instrument that is traded on the market, and which allows the purchasing of an option to buy an interest rate swap.

(b) (i) A decision tree can be used to express the probabilities.

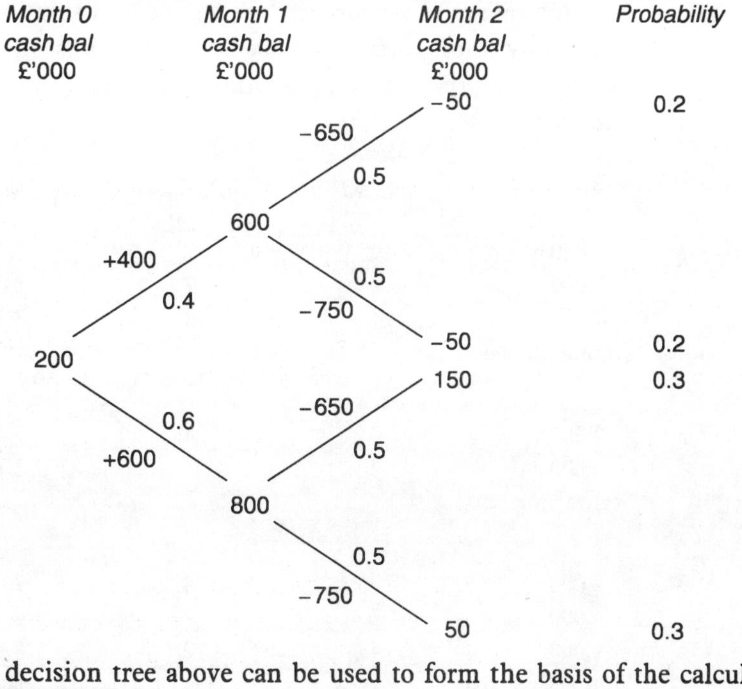

The decision tree above can be used to form the basis of the calculations of the expected cash balances as follows:

Month 1 cash balance = (£600,000 × 0.4) + (£800,000 × 0.6) = £720,000

Month 2 cash balance = (50,000 × 0.3) + (150,000 × 0.3) – (150,000 × 0.2) – (50,000 × 0.2) = £20,000

(ii) CW will have £200,000 to invest at the start of month 1 and is likely to have £720,000 to invest at the start of month 2. It therefore has two investment options, as follows.

(1) Invest £200,000 at the start of month 1 in a deposit with a one month maturity, and £720,000 at the start of month 2 in a deposit with a one month maturity.

Sum invested	*Rate pa*	*Interest*	*Transaction cost*	*Net interest*
£	%	£	£	£
200,000	6.5	1,083	150	933
720,000	6.8	4,080	200	3,880
				4,813

(2) Invest £200,000 at the start of month 1 in a deposit with a two month maturity, and £520,000 at the start of month 2 in a deposit with a one month maturity.

Sum invested	*Rate pa*	*Interest*	*Transaction cost*	*Net interest*
£	%	£	£	£
200,000	6.6	2,200	150	2,050
520,000	6.8	2,947	150	2,797
				4,847

Option 2 should yield the highest net return, and is therefore the preferred choice on financial grounds. Even if CW is risk averse to the extent that it is unwilling to tie up £200,000 for two months, the forecast suggests that even in the worst case scenario there will be £600,000 available for investment at the start of month 2.

32 RT PLC

(a) (i) Since interest rates are forecast to rise, the best solution is likely to be one in which only **short-term deposits** are made, thus allowing advantage to be taken of the rise in rates. Options structured in this way include the following.

	Amount £'000	*Month invested*	*Period* Months	*Rate*	*Income* £
1	2,000	0	2	7.3%	24,333
	6,000	2	2	8.0%	80,000
	4,000	4	2	8.3%	55,333
	Transaction costs				(300)
					159,366
2	2,000	0	4	7.4%	49,333
	4,000	2	4	8.1%	108,000
	Transaction costs				(200)
					157,133
3	2,000	0	4	7.4%	49,333
	4,000	2	2	8.0%	53,333
	4,000	4	2	8.3%	55,333
	Transaction costs				(300)
					157,699

	Amount	Month invested	Period	Rate	Income
	£'000		Months		£
4	2,000	0	2	7.3%	24,333
	2,000	2	2	8.0%	26,667
	4,000	2	4	8.1%	108,000
	Transaction costs				(300)
					158,700
5	2,000	0	6	7.5%	75,000
	2,000	2	4	8.1%	54,000
	2,000	2	2	8.0%	26,667
	Transaction costs				(300)
					155,367
6	2,000	0	6	7.5%	75,000
	4,000	2	2	8.0%	53,333
	2,000	4	2	8.3%	27,667
	Transaction costs				(300)
					155,700

It can be seen that Option 1 yields the best return.

(ii) When selecting marketable securities, the company is normally doing so with the aim of **maximising the return on short-term cash surpluses**. With this aim in mind, the criteria are likely to include the following.

(1) The level of risk should be as low as possible since the company is not seeking a speculative gain, but to ensure that funds which are intended for specific purposes in the future do not lie idle.

(2) The level of return should be as high as possible within the class of risk which the company is prepared to accept.

(3) The level of transaction costs and the degree of complexity of administration should be as low as possible.

(4) Ideally the securities will be easily marketable so that if the funds are required at an earlier date than anticipated this can be achieved without significant loss of revenue.

(5) The amount of funds to be invested will influence the types of security that will be appropriate.

(b) (i) Long-term business investment tends not to be driven by the **availability of funds** but rather by the **opportunities in which to invest**. In practice, if a company perceives an investment opportunity, it will firstly evaluate it against its cost of capital to determine whether or not the project will enhance the net worth of the company. Thus the interest rate is only important at this stage in so far as it forms a component of the hurdle rate used by the company.

When interest rates are relatively very high this may mean that the availability of funds to invest is limited and this may mean that the company is unable to finance projects which it would like to undertake. Thus high interest rates can act as a constraint on investment, but relatively low rates are unlikely to act directly and proportionately to increase the rate in investment.

In terms of **liquidity**, when interest rates are high companies will try to keep short-term borrowings at as low a level as possible by putting pressure on to speed up the transmission of cash through the cycle. When rates are low, there will be less pressure to do this, and thus it is likely that the liquidity position of companies does relate more closely to the level of interest rates.

(ii) In general, the **development of technology** has caused companies to reduce the operating cycle by reducing the amount of stock held within the manufacturing process. This effect has also been felt in the financial markets where transactions, even the complex ones have been speeded up. The result of this is that delivery and lead times have been reduced and thus the degree of uncertainty has also been reduced. Thus there is in theory less need to hold large cash balances as a buffer against uncertainty. In practice however, some companies still do stockpile cash, both to protect themselves against uncertainty and also to be able to take advantage of opportunities that may arise.

(iii) The type and use of **cash management models** differs with the size and complexity of the organisation. In small companies, the weekly or monthly cash forecast can be very helpful in order to ensure the best timing of payments, and can also act as a spur to debt collection.

In large organisations, models are much more sophisticated and allow all free funds to be placed on deposit whenever possible, minimising the costs of holding cash.

Models such as that of **Miller and Orr**, which triggers the buying or selling of securities when cash balances reach an upper or lower limit, can help to free up management time which might otherwise be spent responding to day-to-day fluctuations in cash balances.

Cash management models can also be used to evaluate the relative costs and benefits of switching between alternative short-term investments.

Thus cash management models can be useful to companies at a variety of levels although it is unlikely that in practice they will be used to their fullest extent: in many cases, large cash movements which are predictable, as with tax and dividend payments, can be best managed without using a formal model.

33 RECENT RESEARCH

> **Pass marks**. With the exception of a very small computation, this question is entirely narrative. It really covers most of the syllabus for credit control and management of debtors and shows that, in this paper, a broad grasp of the problems and principles is as valuable as detailed knowledge, provided that you can explain the concepts in words under exam conditions.

(a) Small companies face a number of **problems in respect of credit management**, as follows.

(i) Small companies are often under pressure from large customers to give over-generous credit facilities. Sometimes these customers negotiate long payment periods and sometimes they just take them. The average small company has little bargaining power to resist such pressures.

(ii) The business is too small to justify the appointment of a skilled credit controller. If the job is only part of someone's overall responsibilities, it may be shelved behind other more pressing tasks. It is not always obvious to employees that prompt collection of cash has an impact on profitability and the situation may be allowed to drift until the company reaches its overdraft limit.

(iii) Small companies do not usually have documented systems on their credit control policies. Neither do they invest much in training their staff in financial skills and awareness of credit problems. This may result in the granting of credit to high-risk customers.

(iv) Many small companies are undercapitalised and operate with a bank overdraft as the main source of external finance. Consequently poor cash collection will quickly result in the overdraft limit being reached and recurrent problems with the bank.

The following actions could be taken to minimise the effects of these problems.

(i) Ensure that all top management are adequately trained in the importance of cash and credit management to the profitability, liquidity and survival of the company.

(ii) Obtain benchmark figures for payment periods and bad debts to determine how efficient the company is compared with others in the same industry.

(iii) Analyse the company's strengths and weaknesses to see whether it is able to exercise more bargaining power with large customers. A company with above-average products and services will be able to operate a stricter credit control policy than one which is only average.

(iv) Decide whether credit control should be managed in-house or whether it should be passed to an external expert, such as a factoring company or even a freelance credit consultant.

(v) If credit is to be managed internally, invest in designing and documenting a proper system, assigning clear responsibilities and training the appropriate staff. Ensure that customers are informed of the new rules.

(vi) Consider discount schemes for prompt payment.

(vii) Consider a strategic alliance with a larger company in order to gain more bargaining power with large customers.

(b) To: Credit Manager
From: Management Accountant Date: 11 November 19X7
Subject: Credit control policy and discounts for prompt payment

(i) Credit control has an impact on many aspects of business strategy, including **marketing, production** and **financial strategy**.

In formulating marketing strategy, emphasis is rightly given to achieving growth through customer satisfaction. Credit control may be seen as a boring operational job which has little to do with the company's strategic plans. It is important for you to refute these assumptions. Cash, after all, is the life-blood of the company and in these volatile times no sale can be regarded as safe until the cash is collected.

When deciding which customers to target, their ability to pay is of major concern. A review of the creditworthiness of the existing customer base may result in a revised target clientele.

On the other hand, the extension of credit periods or the granting of prompt payment discounts as special offers can act as a positive marketing tool (see (ii) below).

The costs of collecting late debts and writing off bad debts can be viewed as one of the costs of the product itself. In order to achieve cost efficiency and effective pricing, the company must have strategic plans for credit control.

The need to ensure prompt payment of debts will also motivate the organisation to produce products of above-average quality so that late payment can be more easily countered by the threat of cutting off the supply. In this way, credit control has an impact on product design and manufacture and can be seen to form part of a total quality management programme.

Credit control has an obvious impact on financial strategy. The company needs to be able to forecast its debtor levels as accurately as possible in order to determine its financing requirements.

Since credit policy impacts on marketing, production and finance, it is important to elevate it to the level of strategic planning so that the company's resources are properly co-ordinated.

(ii) The **advantages of introducing prompt payment discounts** are as follows.

(i) If customers are attracted by the discount, there will be an immediate cash inflow which will lower the company's interest costs by, for example, lowering the overdraft requirement.

(ii) Total sales will increase if customers view the discount as a price reduction.

(iii) Bad debts are likely to be reduced, because default risk increases with the time a debt is outstanding.

The disadvantages are as follows.

(i) The cost of the discount itself often has to be substantial to induce prompt payment.

(ii) The effect on customers who miss the prompt payment period is that sometimes they will delay payment more than they otherwise would.

To illustrate the cost of the cash discount, imagine that our company offers a 1% discount for payment within 10 days when the normal credit period is 30 days. In other words, cash is received 20 days earlier in return for a cost of 1%. A rough estimate of the effective annual cost is $1\% \times 365/20 = 18.25\%$. The true annual compound rate of interest will be higher than this. This is an expensive discount, but it is likely to increase demand for our products if customers regard it as a price reduction.

Signed: Management Accountant

34 DISCOUNT

Pass marks. Part (a)(i) requires an understanding of the relative costs of offering a trade discount as against accepting a longer payment period. Do not forget to mention the less easily quantifiable aspects such as the effect of a longer credit period on the risk of default.

The remainder of part (a) is testing your knowledge of the various ways of managing the debtors ledger and the ways in which it can be used to generate additional finance.

Part (b) is looking for a broader discussion of the conflicting objectives that must be held in balance when determining working capital policy. Define how you are interpreting the terms 'aggressive' and 'conservative' since these can be used in different ways.

(a) (i) The company is offering its customers a 2% discount in return for the loss of 20 days credit. This represents an annualised rate of interest of $1.02^{365/20} - 1 = 0.435$, ie 43.5%. The cost of offering the discount must be compared with the opportunity cost of capital in deciding whether the policy is appropriate.

Other factors must also be taken into account such as any potential improvements in bad debts which might result from speeding up payments.

(ii) A **debt factoring organisation** manages the debts owed to a client on the client's behalf. Services offered by a factor may include:

(1) administration of invoicing, sales accounting and debt collection;

(2) credit protection, whereby the factor undertakes to take over the risk of bad debts;

(3) provision of finance to the client secured on the outstanding debts.

Factoring can therefore provide a significant source of credit to a business and can reduce the overheads associated with debt collection. However there is a cost for the service and it may well be more economic to continue to operate the sales ledger directly.

A company may be unable to avoid offering some form of settlement discount if this is common practice in the industry. An efficient sales administration system is essential to ensure that discounting does produce its full potential cash flow benefits. It should also be borne in mind that the sales administration department can be an important point of contact with the customer and can glean information essential to maintaining the smooth running of the account, as well as fostering a good long-term relationship.

(iii) Other sources of finance secured on debtors include the following.

(1) **Invoice discounting**, whereby invoices can be sold at a discount to raise cash. This service is offered by many factoring companies. Sales administration is not transferred. Typically the discounter will advance 75% of the value of the invoices at the start of the period, with the balance being transferred at the end of the period if payment has been received. Charges are higher than for factoring since the discounter has no role in the collection process and is therefore taking on more risk.

(2) **Overdraft facilities,** which can be secured on a guaranteed minimum level of debtors (or general working capital). The company will have to make regular reports to the bank on the status of its debtors ledger.

(b) It is assumed that the degree of **aggression** or **conservatism** in the management and financing of current assets relates to the degree of risk which the company is prepared to accept. This can be assessed by taking each element of the current asset base in turn.

(i) **Cash and marketable securities**. All companies will require a certain amount of cash to be available for their day to day operations - to pay suppliers, wages, expenses and so on. The precise amounts required will be determined by means of a regularly updated short-term cash flow forecast which will highlight peaks and troughs in cash demands. A company with a conservative cash policy will probably maintain a bank balance which is sufficient to cover the normal peaks in demand. The cash forecast will be updated less often, perhaps twice a month, and the company will accept that there is likely to be some idle cash in the account.

A company with an aggressive policy will monitor the cash position throughout the day and will seek to minimise the amount held in the bank account. Wherever possible surplus funds will be transferred to other accounts and investments, or alternatively placed on overnight deposit to ensure that interest is maximised. The downside of such a policy is that there will be an overhead incurred in monitoring the situation and moving the funds around. There is also the risk that if forecasts are inaccurate the company may need to call on other reserves at short notice and so incur a loss of interest. It may even face the embarrassment and loss of confidence of its suppliers if mistakes result in some of its cheques being bounced.

(ii) **Stock and work in progress**. The first decision to be faced by a company is whether to manufacture to order or to supply from stock. If it chooses the latter option it must then decide on the level of stock it should carry, and to do this it will need to make demand forecasts. The key problem is that all such forecasts are subject to some degree of error and the company must decide what level of buffer stock is appropriate to minimise the risk of a stock out occurring. Although models are available which attempt to quantify the relative costs of carrying excess stocks as against a stock out, it is very difficult to estimate what the effect of a stock out will be on future business. A company which chooses an aggressive policy in the sense of being prepared to accept a higher level of risk will probably choose to stock at a lower level than one which adopts a more conservative policy.

(iii) **Debtors**. An **aggressive** policy in respect of debtors could be one of two things. If aggression is to be defined in terms of attitude to risk, then a company with an aggressive policy is likely to have a high level of debtors, being generous in allowing credit in order to achieve the maximum level of sales. A more **conservative** company would be more cautious in both granting credit to a customer and in the size of the credit limit applied and this may mean that some sales are sacrificed as a result.

Alternatively, an aggressive approach to the level of debtors might mean that the company seeks to minimise the amount of capital tied up by debtors. In this situation the aggressive policy would be to allow the minimum amount of credit to customers, to chase up payments as soon as they become due and to place 'on stop' customers who exceed their credit limit or who are late with their payment.

The traditional view is that short-term assets should be financed from short-term sources of capital such as the bank overdraft. However it is commonly accepted that in practice working capital is unlikely to fall below a certain amount and that this level can be regarded as semi-permanent requiring a longer term more secure source of finance. The more aggressive company is likely to try to minimise interest costs by using a source of finance which can be varied in amount to match the fluctuations in requirements, rather than committing itself to a longer term loan. It is also likely to try maintain a high level of trade creditors and to use this as a source of finance, although such a policy obviously carries a risk of interruption of supply or litigation if creditors' terms are not complied with.

35 V PLC

Pass marks. In the first part of the question, it is a good idea to structure the cash flows by year, rather than by revenues and costs. These can then be discounted at the cost of capital, and probabilities applied to obtain an expected NPV for the order.

In part (b) it is helpful to consider both internal policies on debt collection and external methods of improving the management of debtors such as the use of bills of exchange.

Examiner's comment. Few candidates correctly applied probabilities in part (a) and many did not even discount cash flows payable or receivable in the future. A common approach was to calculate the profitability of the sale. this approach gained marks but it was not what was required.

Marking was flexible between parts (b) and (c) as a number of candidates discussed creditworthiness in part(b) instead of part (c).

(a) REPORT

To: Credit Control Manager
From: Accountant Date: 19 November 19X6
Subject: Credit control implications of order from new customer

Introduction

The purpose of this report is to examine the financial implications of accepting the order from our new customer, given the fact that our record in achieving 100% collection is poor. Other commercial and factors will also be considered.

Method

The method used will be to examine the cash flows arising on acceptance of the order, and at the end of twelve months. The **opportunity cost of capital** (16%) will be used to discount future cash flows. Where probabilities are available these will be used to arrive at an 'expected value' for the order - however, these will not be applied until the final stage of the calculations so that the full implications of the different scenarios are apparent.

Financial evaluation

Cash flows on receipt of order:

		£
Deposit from customer	(£5,000 × 5 × 10%)	2,500
Incremental material costs	(£3,600 × 5 × 70%)	(12,600)
Net cash flow		10,100

Cash flows at end of twelve months:

The net receipt from the customer will either be £22,500 or £22,000 if a debt collection agency is used and is successful in obtaining payment. If payment is not received, there is a net additional cost of £500.

The incremental costs of the order will be £3,600 × 5 × 30% = £5,400. Revenues and costs at the end of the year must be discounted at 16% by applying the discount factor of 0.862.

The expected cash flows for the order as a whole can now be tabulated.

Probability	*Receipt year 1*	*Cash flow year 1*	*DCF year 1*	*Net DCF of order*	*Expected value*
	£	£	£	£	£
60%	22,500	17,100	14,740	4,640	2,784
20%	22,000	16,600	14,309	4,209	842
20%	(500)	(5,900)	(5,086)	(15,186)	(3,037)
					589

The figures indicate that acceptance of the order produces a small positive expected net present value of £589, and on this basis the order should be accepted. However, it is also apparent that there is a 20% probability that V plc will make a substantial loss on the order of £15,186, and it is recommended that steps should be taken to minimise this risk before the order is undertaken.

(b) **Other factors to be considered**

As well as considering the previous collection record for similar orders from other customers, it is important that an investigation should be made of the creditworthiness of this particular customer. Specific methods for assessing this will be discussed in the final section of the report.

In addition to considering the collection record for this type of order, and the credit worthiness of the individual customer, it is proposed that a review should be made of the methods used to obtain collection. Factors to be considered include the following.

(i) 70% of the costs of the order are incurred at the outset, but a deposit of only 10% is required from the customer. It is therefore reasonable to argue that customers should be asked to pay a larger deposit when the order is placed.

(ii) In addition to increasing the size of the deposit, it might be possible to request additional stage payments during the first year which reflect more closely the degree of completion of the order.

(iii) It is not clear at what point in time the machines are delivered to the customer. If delivery takes place before the balance of the debt becomes due, then it could be possible to require customers to pay the balance, or a significant proportion of the balance, just before delivery of the equipment.

(iv) Depending on the type of customer, it may be possible to obtain guarantees of payment from the directors.

(v) If an individual customer is expected to present a particular credit risk, then it could be worth requiring them to undertake a bill of exchange or a letter of credit that would provide for payment to be made by their bank on the due date.

(vi) For large customers another alternative would be to take out some form of credit insurance to cover the risks of non-payment.

(vii) The collection agency currently being used requires payment of a flat fee regardless of the size of the debt or the success of the agency in achieving collection. It may be possible to renegotiate the fees so as to provide the agency with a greater incentive to achieve payment, for instance, by paying a percentage of the debt recovered to the agency, and reducing the amount payable in the event of non-collection.

(viii) Account should also be taken of the effect on the business of not undertaking the order, for example the cost of any redundancies that might be incurred.

(c) **Assessing creditworthiness**

A number of approaches can be used to assess the **creditworthiness of the individual customer.**

(i) New customers should give two good references, including one from a bank, before being granted credit.

(ii) Credit ratings can be checked using agencies such as Dun and Bradstreet.

(iii) For large value customers, a file should be maintained of any available financial information, including an analysis of the company's annual report and accounts. Relevant press comments are also useful and provide up-to-date information on current performance.

(iv) The DTI can give advice on overseas companies and markets.

(v) Staff should visit the potential customer to get a first hand impression of the company and its prospects.

Signed: Accountant

36 MP LIMITED

> **Pass marks.** This is a slightly unusual question in that it relates to a company that is taking a surprisingly long credit period on a regular basis. You should think through the practical implications of implementing such a policy as well as the financial costs involved when drafting your answer
>
> **Examiner's comment.** Performance on section (a) of this question was surprisingly poor. Very few candidates managed to calculate the three annualised interest rates. Many gave answers in absolute money terms rather than percentages. Calculations for supplier A and supplier B were rarely done correctly. The rate for supplier C was fairly obvious as it was given in the question although many failed to spot this. There was, however, an opportunity cost of the lost discount which was recognised by a few candidates.
>
> The answers to sections (b) and (c) were done rather better, although many candidates said simply that trade credit was 'cheap', providing no real discussion and no understanding that it is often not at all cheap. However, a few candidates correctly commented that many firms take the discount and pay late anyway, noting that few suppliers will chase a customer for a relatively small amount of money owed in this way.

To: Financial Manager
From: Assistant Financial Manager
Date: 15 November 19X8
Subject: **Review of the policy concerning trade credit terms**

The purpose of this report is to evaluate the costs of our existing trade credit policy, and to discuss the arguments for and against using trade credit as a source of funds. The final section of the report will deal with the advantages and disadvantages of introducing standard terms of trade for all suppliers.

Evaluation of the existing policy

MP's current policy is to take 90 days credit on all supplier invoices. The result of this is that we routinely incur a variety of penalties and charges from a number of our suppliers for exceeding their terms of trade. An **analysis of the costs** in relation to three randomly chosen suppliers is outlined below. For the purposes of calculation it is assumed that we purchase £1,000 worth of goods from each supplier every month.

Supplier A charges a fixed penalty of 2% of invoice value for late payment. This penalty does not increase with the length of the credit period taken. Since under our existing policy, all invoices are paid late, the cost per invoice is £20, and the cost per year is £240. The average amount by which we exceed the supplier's terms at any one time is £2,000 (two months invoices), and therefore the annualised cost in percentage terms is 12% (240/2,000).

Supplier B charges compound interest at 2% per 30-day period after the due date of payment. Each invoice is paid two months late, and therefore the cost per invoice is as follows:

			£
Month 2	£1,000 × 2%	=	20.00
Month 3	£1,020 × 2%	=	20.40
			40.40

The cost per year is therefore £484.80, and the annualised percentage cost on an average credit level of £2,000 is 24.2%.

Supplier C charges simple interest at 10% per annum on the invoice value if payment is late. We always forego the opportunity to receive settlement discount. Each invoice is outstanding for two months, and therefore the cost per invoice is £1,000 × 10% × 2/12 = £16.60. The cost per year is £200.00, and the annualised percentage cost is 10% (200/2,000).

For the suppliers chosen, the cost of trade credit can be seen to vary from 6.7% to 16.2%, the average being 10.3%.

The use of trade credit as a source of funds

Taking credit from suppliers is a normal feature of business. It is a source of short-term finance because it helps to keep working capital down. If the purchaser keeps to the terms of trade, it will be a cheap source of finance because in this situation suppliers rarely charge interest. However even in this situation there is some cost where settlement discounts are foregone, as in the case of Supplier C above. In this case the cost can be estimated using the formula:

$$\frac{d}{100-d} \times \frac{365}{t}$$

where d is the size of the % discount (in this case, 2)

t is the reduction in the payment period in days which would be necessary to obtain the early payment discount (in this case, 30 – 10 = 20)

The cost of foregoing the discount is therefore 37.2%.

The situation is different when credit periods taken regularly **exceed the terms of trade.** Many suppliers now impose a cost for the additional credit taken, as demonstrated above, and this should be compared with the cost of alternative short-term sources of funds to ensure that the cost of trade credit is not in fact greater than that of other funds. There are also further disadvantages to taking long credit periods, including the following.

- The company's credit rating will be reduced.
- It may be difficult to obtain additional credit from suppliers.
- The company may rank behind other customers due to its payment record if shortages of materials arise.
- The goodwill between the company and its suppliers will be eroded. This may damage the business in other ways, for example, it may be difficult to get extra goods at short notice.
- Extra administrative costs will arise from the fact that suppliers will be continually chasing for payment.
- Staff morale may be eroded if those who are regularly deal with suppliers feel that they are unable to do an efficient job due to the payment policy in place.

In general therefore, it is recommended that trade credit should be used judiciously as a source of finance, but it is inadvisable for a variety of reasons greatly to exceed suppliers' terms on a regular basis.

The merits of standard terms of trade

The introduction of standard terms of trade for suppliers has a number of merits.

- It greatly simplifies the administrative processes for dealing with supplier invoices
- It makes cash flow forecasting more straightforward.
- If the terms are communicated clearly to suppliers and formally agreed, the relationship between customer and supplier will be smoother, and the number of payment queries reduced.

However, it is important that the terms are both reasonable and flexible and not imposed unilaterally. Possible problems that could arise include the following.

- There will always be some suppliers for whom different terms will be required, for example, telephone accounts normally have to be settled within ten days, and there must be procedures for dealing with these situations.
- The company must ensure that it does not forego valuable settlement discount opportunities in the process. Where such opportunities exist, they must be evaluated in financial terms, and the system must be able to deal with earlier payments if necessary.
- There must be procedures in place to ensure that even within the policy, credit opportunities are maximised, for example, credit notes should be taken immediately where they relate to earlier invoices, and not also held for the standard credit period.

37 OVERDRAFT

> **Pass marks**. Be careful to make the calculations in relation to credit customers only and not to total sales. Show clearly how the ratios have been calculated. When making recommendations, take into account the objectives of the firm. You may wish to comment on the practicalities of your recommendation.
>
> **Examiner's comment.** This question was not well answered by those who attempted it. Most candidates got into a dreadful muddle over the calculations and failed completely to make any recommendations.

The three options are evaluated below as (a), (b) and (c) respectively.

(a) (i) The first step is to calculate the forecast level of credit sales for 19X5:

£4,850,000 × 70% = £3,395,000

If it is assumed that the closing debtors figure is representative of the 'normal' level of debtors, then the average collection period can be found.

£850,000 ÷ (£3,395,000/365) = 91.4 days

If 50% of the customers take advantage of the discount scheme, the average debtor days will fall to:

(91.38 ÷ 2) + (10 ÷ 2) = 50.7 days.

Thus the average level of debtors will fall to:

(£3,395,000/365) × 50.7 = £471,580.

This represents a reduction of £378,420.

The **financial effect of the proposal** can now be evaluated.

	£
Reduction in interest costs on overdraft	
£378,420 × (11% – 5% + 4%)	37,842
Reduction in level of bad debts	24,000
Cost of discount	
£3,395,000 × 50% × 1.5%	(25,462)
Total annual savings	36,380

By the end of the first year, the overdraft should have fallen to £565,000 – £378,420 – £36,380 = £150,200.

(ii) The **current ratio**, if no action is taken, is projected as:

$$\frac{£455{,}000 + £850{,}000}{£550{,}000 + £565{,}000} = 1.17$$

Under these proposals it would improve to:

$$\frac{£455{,}000 + £471{,}580}{£550{,}000 + £150{,}200} = 1.32$$

As calculated above, the debtor days would fall from 91.4 to 50.7 days.

(b) (i) The factor would enable 90% of the debtors to be converted into cash, thus releasing capital amounting to:

£850,000 × 90% = £765,000

This would give rise to a cash surplus of £765,000 – £565,000 = £200,000. If it is assumed that these funds can be invested at, say base + 3% ie 9%, the financial effect of this proposal can be estimated as follows.

	£
Saving in overdraft interest	
£565,000 × 10%	56,500
Interest on cash surplus	
£200,000 × 9%	18,000
Saving in administration costs	65,000
Factor's commission	
£3,395,000 × 90% × 2%	(61,110)
Finance charge	
£765,000 × 11%	(84,150)
Net cost of proposals	(5,760)

By the end of the first year, the cash surplus should therefore amount to £200,000 – £5,760 = £194,240.

(ii) Assuming the cash surplus is treated as a current asset, the current ratio can be calculated as follows.

$$\frac{£455{,}000 + £194{,}240 + £85{,}000}{£550{,}000} = 1.33$$

The appropriate average debtor days would become:

£85,000 ÷ (£3,395,000/365) = 9.1

However, it could be argued that this ratio should be calculated in relation to the actual sales to which the remaining debtors relate, in which case the ratio would be unchanged at 91.4 days.

(c) (i) It must be assumed that the base rate remains constant at 6% for the duration of the mortgage in order to calculate the full effect of this proposal. In the first year:

	£
Saving in overdraft interest	
£500,000 × 10%	50,000
Cost of mortgage interest	
£500,000 × 9%	(45,000)
Net benefit	5,000

By the end of the first year, the overdraft will have fallen to £565,000 – £500,000 – £5,000 = £60,000.

(ii) The current ratio will become:

$$\frac{£455,000 + £850,000}{£550,000 + £60,000} = 2.14$$

The debtor days will be unchanged at 91.4 days.

The preferred course of action to be taken by XYZ will depend on its detailed **financial circumstances** and the importance of the **ratios**. Assuming that the level of the ratios will not materially affect its cost of borrowing, the choice can be made on the basis of the impact of the various options on the total value of the firm. The first option is the one which maximises the total value, giving annual savings of £36,380, and it is therefore recommended that the discount scheme should be implemented. However, this does assume that the projected effects on customer behaviour are realistic - that at least 50% of the customers will pay within 10 days and that the average collection period for those who do not opt for the discount is not longer than the existing average. It is also suggested that XYZ should encourage its customers to adhere more closely to their credit terms in the future.

38 KL LTD

Pass marks. In the suggested answer to part (a), interest has been calculated and included in the profit and loss account. However it could be argued that this is unnecessary in arriving at the profit before depreciation. If you choose to follow the latter course then the fact that you have excluded interest should be stated. In part (b) it is helpful to calculate the application of funds for KL since this provides a method of structuring your discussion of the methods of improving the cashflow position.

Examiner's comment. Most managed to arrive at the correct profit figure for part (a). Common errors were to ignore the stock increase and to treat capital expenditure (and even dividends) as costs in arriving at a profit figure. Part (b) was, on the whole, much better answered. However, higher marks were only available for candidates who discussed the likely *effects* of their suggestions, as required by the question. It was not sensible to suggest the company should be floated on the stock market to solve what might be a short-term liquidity problem, particularly as the company has a turnover of less than £2 million.

(a) KL LIMITED
ESTIMATED PROFIT AND LOSS ACCOUNT FOR 19X6

	£'000	£'000
Sales		1,725
Purchases	(582)	
Wages and salaries	(650)	
		(1,232)
Stock movement		170
Gross profit		663
Other operating expenses	(380)	
Other rental income	180	
Interest	(13)	
		(213)
Profit before depreciation		450

Workings

	£'000
Sales	
Receipts for year	1,490
Less: January	(175)
February	(135)
March	(115)
Add: October to December sales	660
Total	1,725

Purchases. It is assumed that the actual amount of credit taken (90 days) has been used in the calculation of the cash flow.

	£'000
Payments for year	480
Less: January	(53)
February	(41)
March	(35)
Add: October to December purchases	231
Total	582

Wages and salaries. Since KL is a manufacturing company, it is assumed that the wages and salaries are primarily direct costs. It is further assumed that they are all paid in the month in which they arise.

Interest. Assuming a base rate of 7%, interest will be payable on the overdraft at 12%. This will be calculated on the average balance for each month. It is assumed that no interest is paid on credit balances.

Month	*O/bal*	*C/bal*	*Av bal*	*Interest*
	£'000	£'000	£'000	£'000
Jan	50	95	73	0.0
Feb	95	11	53	0.0
Mar	11	14	13	0.0
Apr	14	(17)	(2)	0.0
May	(17)	(67)	(42)	(0.4)
Jun	(67)	(109)	(88)	(0.9)
Jul	(109)	(156)	(133)	(1.3)
Aug	(156)	(193)	(175)	(1.7)
Sep	(193)	(280)	(237)	(2.4)
Oct	(280)	(271)	(276)	(2.8)
Nov	(271)	(219)	(245)	(2.5)
Dec	(219)	(75)	(147)	(1.5)
Total				(13.5)

(b) REPORT

To: Board of Directors, KL Limited
From: Management Accountant Date: 21 November 19X5
Subject: Review of 19X6 cash budget

Introduction

The purpose of this paper is to highlight those areas arising out of the recent cash budgeting exercise which need to be addressed by the Board, in particular the short-term financing requirements for 19X6. Some possible courses of action to address these areas will also be discussed.

Funding requirements

The cashflow forecast for 19X6 shows that the current cash surplus will disappear during the first quarter of the year and be replaced by a rapidly growing deficit that peaks in September. Although the projections suggest that the situation should improve thereafter, a cash deficit of £75,000 is still forecast for the end of the year. At its worst, the deficit is likely to be nearly twice the size of the existing overdraft limit, and therefore urgent action needs to be taken to address this issue.

Over the course of the year, the total **net outflow of funds** is £138,000 (reduction in cash balance, plus estimated interest). This movement comes about as follows.

	£
Profit generated from operations	450,000
Increase in stocks	(170,000)
Increase in debtors	(235,000)
Increase in creditors	102,000
Dividends	(100,000)
Taxation	(65,000)
Capital expenditure	(120,000)
	(138,000)

Possible strategies for addressing the funding need

(i) **Improve control of working capital**. The net increase in working capital for the year is forecast at £303,000 which is significant in terms of the amounts involved. The item showing the largest increase is debtors, and there should be scope for improvement in this area since customers are currently taking on average 30 days more than their normal terms of trade. The normal terms of trade of 60 days does not seem to be an unreasonable target to aim at, and if the collection period could be reduced by only 15 days during the year, the closing debtors would fall by £110,000. Stock is also forecast to increase by the end of the year, and this increase should be fully justified in terms of additional sales before it is accepted as a budget figure.

(ii) **Change production scheduling**. The major increase in sales is not forecast to take place until the second half of the year, with increased receipts from debtors not being seen until the final quarter. However, production is scheduled evenly throughout the year. If production could be planned to mirror demand more closely, then the cash flow situation would be improved since the average stock level would be reduced, and payments to suppliers would not increase until the second half of the year.

(iii) **Defer capital expenditure**. If the investment in new plant and machinery is required in order to increase the level of production to meet increases in demand then it may be difficult to put off this item. However, it may be possible to delay the purchase of new motor vehicles and the building renovations, or alternatively to acquire the vehicles on a lease or hire basis and thus spread the cost of these assets more evenly over their useful lives.

(iv) **Defer the dividend**. Depending on the views of the shareholders it may be possible to defer or stage the payment of the dividend, or perhaps to offer a scrip alternative.

(The options outlined so far may be sufficient to keep the overdraft within its limits in 19X6, perhaps with some assistance from other sources such as invoice discounting in the second half of the year. However, if further growth is planned in 19X7, then the cash resources are likely to come under continuing pressure and KL may need to consider seeking additional funds from other sources as well as those suggested above.)

(v) **Take on some medium-term debt**. KL appears to be 100% equity financed at present. It should therefore be able to negotiate some form of medium-term loan given that the company is both growing and currently shows a good level of profits (26% before depreciation and tax). Although this would probably need to be secured on the assets, it is likely to be less risky than the overdraft which is both expensive and repayable on demand.

(vi) **Asset refinancing**. Although rental income is currently generated from some of the premises, KL might consider raising additional cash by selling part of the premises assuming that this is practicable and that they are not required for future expansion plans. Alternatively the company could consider some form of sale and leaseback of the property and/or some of the other fixed assets.

(vii) **Venture capital**. Although the company might be a little small for this source of development funds, KL may be able to attract a venture capital investment. However, it would have to be able to get the agreement of the shareholders to this and the directors would have to relinquish some degree of control to the venture capital organisation. Alternatively, some of the other shareholders may be able to make a further investment in the company.

Conclusions

The directors need to put a plan in place now to meet the forecast mid-year financing problems. Any changes to the credit and stockholding policies or to the production scheduling must be evaluated in terms of their effect on sales, and the budget reworked to take account of the revised figures.

It is suggested that the directors should also consider two more fundamental questions in the course of their review.

(i) Is the proposed expansion justified in terms of the amount of value added to the business? If the NPV of the incremental cashflow is low then slowing down the expansion programme would benefit the cashflow.

(ii) The directors could consider selling all or part of the business to a larger company with the desire and the resources to fund the expansion plans.

Signed: Management Accountant

39 MILLER-ORR MODEL

Pass marks. This question covers two important areas of cash management: electronic funds transfer systems and cash models for optimising cash balances. No detailed knowledge was expected of any of these areas but you were expected to provide a reasoned discussion of the advantages and disadvantages of the systems.

Examiner's comments. Part (a) was generally well answered, although few candidates gave examples of EFT systems such as SWIFT, BACS or CHAPS. In part (b) candidates tended to be either completely right or completely wrong in their calculations. Some candidates attempted to calculate the spread in the Miller-Orr model, even though it was given in the question.

(a) **Electronic funds transfer systems** (EFTS) enable funds to be transferred between bank accounts on the same day. Examples in the UK include BACS (Bankers Automated Clearing System) and CHAPS (Clearing House Automated Payment System). International transfers can be made via SWIFT (Society for Worldwide Interbank Financial Telecommunications).

The usual alternative is payment by cheque or bankers draft, which results in delays as the documentation passes through the postal, banking and clearing systems.

From the payer's point of view, the advantages of EFTS are savings in processing time and paperwork and hence in administration costs.

The disadvantages to payers are as follows.

(i) The prompt processing means here is no excuse for delayed payment (eg the postal system cannot be blamed) and hence there will possibly be an effective reduction in the free credit period and an increase in interest costs.

(ii) If processing is carried out in batches, an urgent request for payment by one customer may cause a whole batch of payments to be made early, again resulting in an increased interest cost.

(b) To: The Treasurer
From: A N Recruit, Accounts Date: 15 May 19X2
Subject: Cash management models

(i) **Cash management models** take into account the trade-off between the rate of return which can be earned on surplus funds and the need to maintain liquidity. For example, a company will need to keep a certain amount of cash in a non-interest or low-interest current account in order to meet known and expected liabilities. If, however, the balance in this account becomes unnecessarily high, the company is losing the interest which could be earned by transferring the funds to a higher interest deposit account or other form of investment.

For our department, this is particularly important as the more we can earn in additional interest the more we have to spend on the local community. Local authorities are increasingly being asked to demonstrate efficiency and effective use of resources and one of our largest resources is cash.

Cash management models effectively regard surplus cash as a form of stock. Stock management models attempt to minimise the sum of stock-holding costs, stock ordering costs and stock-out costs. Equivalent costs can be identified for cash balances. The cash model which is closest to the 'Economic Order Quantity' stock model is the Baumol model, but this is unrealistic in that it assumes that cash is used up at an even rate.

(ii) The **Miller-Orr model**, illustrated below, is more useful because it deals with receipts and payments of cash and provides trigger points for transferring cash to and from investment accounts when the current account balance becomes too high or low respectively. It does, however, make an unrealistic assumption that cash flows are entirely unpredictable.

We have already agreed with our bank that the minimum balance on our current account will be £15,000. This is referred to as the 'lower limit'. Thus when the balance falls to that level we will need to transfer money out of the investment account into the current account. To compute the 'upper limit' the Miller-Orr model uses three data items:

- the transaction cost for each cash transfer in or out of the account: £25;
- the variance of daily cash flows: $(£3{,}000)^2 =$ £9,000,000;
- the daily interest rate on invested cash: 0.0236%.

Using these items of data it can be shown that the 'spread' between the upper and lower limits is £26,820. This means that the upper limit is £15,000 + £26,820 = £41,820. When the current account reaches this high level, money will be transferred out into the investment account.

The final question is how much needs to be transferred in and out when the lower and upper limits are reached. The Miller-Orr model sets the 'return point' at a figure one third of the way between the upper and lower limits.

The return point is £15,000 + $\frac{1}{3} \times$ £26,820 = £15,000 + £8,940 = £23,940.

In summary, then, when the balance falls to £15,000, £8,940 is transferred into the account to bring it up to £23,940. When the balance rises to £41,820, £17,880 is transferred out of the account to return the balance to £23,940.

Signed: AN Recruit

> *Tutorial note.* You do not need to compute the spread in this question because it is given to you. However, future questions might not be so generous! Using the formula for the Miller-Orr model, the spread is $3\left(\frac{\frac{3}{4}\ TV}{R}\right)^{1/3}$ where T is the transaction cost, V is the variance of daily cash flows and R is daily interest rate.
>
> Hence the spread is $3\left(\frac{\frac{3}{4}\times 25\times 9{,}000{,}000}{0.000236\%}\right)^{1/3}$ = £26,827.
>
> This is approximately the same as the spread given in the question.

40 RP PLC

> **Pass marks**. You should state clearly your assumptions, in the timing of the various cash flows, the effects of inflation, and the treatment of the sale proceeds. Part (b) of the question encourages you to focus on the strengths and weaknesses of the evaluation technique, rather than on the quality of the cash flow estimates provided.

(a)

Time	*0*	*1*	2	3	4	5	6
	£'000	£'000	£'000	£'000	£'000	£'000	£'000
Profit (nominal values)		390.0	405.6	421.8	438.7	456.2	
Tax thereon (33%)			(128.7)	(133.8)	(139.2)	(144.8)	(150.6)
Capital outlay	(1,200.0)						
Machinery sale (W1)						284.8	
Capital allowances (W1)			99.0	74.3	55.7	41.8	31.3
Working capital (W2)	(104.0)	(112.3)	(121.2)	(130.4)	(140.4)	608.3	-
Net cashflow	(1,304.0)	277.7	254.7	231.9	214.8	1,246.3	(119.3)
16% factor	1.000	0.862	0.743	0.641	0.552	0.476	0.410
Present value	(1,304.0)	239.4	189.2	148.6	118.6	593.2	(48.9)
PV cumulative	(1,304.0)	(1,064.6)	(875.4)	(726.8)	(608.2)	(15.0)	(63.9)

NPV is therefore negative (£63,900).

Workings

1 **Capital allowances and resale value.** (*Note:* the question does not indicate whether the first allowance is claimed immediately or at the end of the first year. This answer assumes that latter. Either way, the final allowance will be at time 6.)

		£'000	*Time*
1st allowance	1,200 × 25% × 33%	99.0	2
2nd allowance	75% of previous	74.3	3
3rd allowance	75% of previous	55.7	4
4th allowance	75% of previous	41.8	5
5th allowance	75% of previous	31.3	6

There is no balancing allowance since the machinery is sold at its written down value.

Written down value = £1,200,000 × 0.75^5 = £284,400.

2 **Working capital requirements**

Note that the first year's capital requirement is inflated by a full 4%, despite becoming a time 0 cashflow. This is consistent with the inflation of profit figures by the same amount.

Time	*1*	*2*	*3*	*4*	*5*
	£'000	£'000	£'000	£'000	£'000
Real terms amount	100.0	200.0	300.0	400.0	500.0
Compound inflation	104.0	216.3	337.5	467.9	608.3

Time	*0*	*1*	*2*	*3*	*4*	*5*
	£'000	£'000	£'000	£'000	£'000	£'000
Increment	(104.0)	(112.3)	(121.2)	(130.4)	(140.4)	608.3

(b)

To: Financial Manager
From: Deputy Financial Manager
Date: 12 May 19X8
Subject: Evaluation of proposed new product investment

The financial evaluation of the proposed investment on the original basis suggests that the project will not be viable since the NPV at the end of five years is negative. However, the size of the shortfall is relatively small in relation to the size of the project, and it is worth considering the assumptions underlying the evaluation to ensure that these are appropriate. Otherwise, we run the risk of foregoing a potentially useful business opportunity. Areas that merit further work include the following.

Use of the WACC as the discount rate

The WACC approximates to the overall cost of capital to the business. However, this investment amounts to £1.7m (including working capital), and is therefore a relatively large investment. We should therefore consider whether undertaking the project would in itself affect the cost of capital to the business. If it does, then the WACC should be adjusted to take account of this. Further, it is assumed that the project carries the same level of risk as the existing operations. If the risk profile is different, then the cost of capital should be adjusted to reflect this.

The timescale of the project

The project is evaluated over a six-year time frame, taking into account the tax effects, which is a long time in forecasting terms. In practice it is unlikely that the same discount rate will be appropriate to the whole of this period, and it would be helpful to adjust the current WACC for the expected movements in the general economic situation, and in particular the level of interest rates during that period.

The nature of the cash flows

Single values have been used for each element of the cash flow projections. In practice, each of the different elements is likely to be subject to different levels of risk. For example, the projected level of sales could be affected by the speed of technological change within the industry as well as by more general economic influences. We should therefore attempt to estimate the levels of uncertainty in the forecast cash flows. The most likely cash flows can then be reduced in line with our perceived risk aversion before being discounted at a rate appropriate to each year.

The sensitivities inherent in the project

It is likely that certain elements within the cash flow projections are more important than others in determining the eventual outcome of the project. It would therefore be useful to undertake some form of sensitivity analysis to identify both the key variables and the likely impact of their deviating from forecasts on the financial outcome of the project.

I would be happy to discuss any of these areas further with you, and look forward to receiving your comments.

41 ALTERNATIVE SITES

(a) The **probability tree** for the project on site A is as follows.

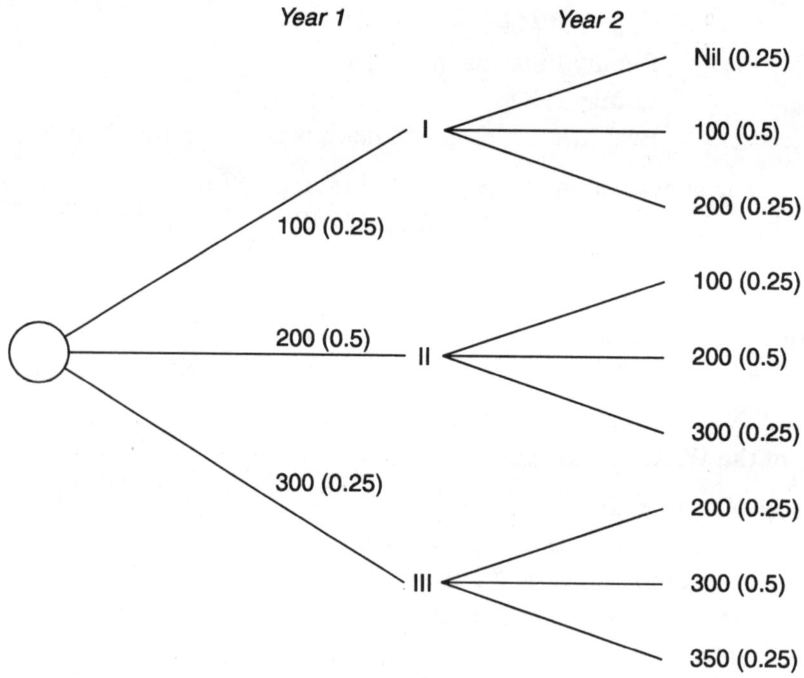

Cash inflows are shown in thousand of pounds and probabilities are stated in brackets.

	£'000
Expected cash flow at point I	
$100 \times 0.5 + 200 \times 0.25$	100
Expected cash flow at point II	
$100 \times 0.25 + 200 \times 0.5 + 300 \times 0.25$	200
Expected cash flow at point III	
$200 \times 0.25 + 300 \times 0.5 + 350 \times 0.25$	287.5

Expected net present value of site A =

$$
\begin{aligned}
& \quad 0.25\,(100 \times 0.909 + 100 \times 0.826) \\
+ & \quad 0.5\,(200 \times 0.909 + 200 \times 0.826) \\
+ & \quad 0.25\,(300 \times 0.909 + 287.5 \times 0.826) \\
- & \quad 300 \\
= & \quad 44.419
\end{aligned}
$$

The NPV on site A is about £44,000.

(b) (i) The **expected cash flows** on site B are identical to those on site A. Thus if the year 1 cash flow is £100,000, the expected year 2 cash flow is £100,000 occurring at end of year 2.

The value of this cash flow as at beginning of year 2 is therefore £100,000 × 0.909 and as this is clearly less than the disposal proceeds, the company would choose to abandon the project.

If the year 1 cash flow is £200,000, the expected year 2 cash flow is
£200,000 at the end of year 2
= £200,000 × 0.909 at the beginning of year 2
which is more than the disposal proceeds of £150,000.

Therefore the company would only choose abandonment if the year 1 cash flow is £100,000.

(ii) In view of (b)(i) above, the cash flows only differ from those for site A if the year 1 cash flow is £100,000.

	£
NPV for site A	44,419
Less ENPV at point I (0.826 × 100 × 0.25)	(20,650)
Add PV of disposal proceeds (0.909 × 150 × 0.25)	34,088
NPV of site B	57,857

(c) Both site A and site B have positive expected net present values and site B is better by about £13,000, the positive effect of the abandonment option.

42 CBA LTD

(a)

> **Pass marks**. This question can be well answered provided that you understand the advantage and disadvantage of each investment appraisal method and can adapt your answer to the questions as set. It is common for text books to show why the IRR method is inferior to the NPV method. More difficult is the discussion of why IRR remains as popular as it does.
>
> **Examiner's comment**. The most common failing in this question was for candidates simply to comment on NPV, IRR and other investment appraisal methods without directly answering the question. There was some confusion between IRR and ARR.

To: Managing Director
From: Financial Manager   Date: 15 May 19X7
Subject: Methods for evaluating capital investment appraisal

(i) **NPV and IRR**

The **net present value** (NPV) of an investment project is found by discounting the investment cash flows at a rate equal to the **cost of capital** (the **'hurdle rate'**) for the investment. This cost of capital depends on the time value of money, the risk of the investment and the company's gearing. The project is acceptable if it has a positive net present value, which represents the increase in investor wealth if the project is accepted. When choosing between investments, they would be ranked in order of NPV.

The **internal rate of return** (IRR) is simply the discount rate which produces a **zero NPV** when applied to the project cash flows. As such, it is a balancing figure which relates project outlay to cash inflows. A project is acceptable if its IRR is higher than the project's cost of capital.

For accept/reject decisions relating to a single investment there will be no conflict between the NPV and IRR decision criteria. However, when ranking projects in order of acceptability, the IRR method is frequently incorrect. This is because it takes no account of different sizes of projects or of different levels of project risk. For example, a return of 50% on £1 is worth less than a return of 10% on £10; an expected return of 12% from a highly speculative foreign investment is probably worth less than an expected return of 10% from an expansion of the company's existing business.

In addition, the IRR suffers from problems when the sequence of cash flows is unusual: there might be more than one IRR for a project, or no IRR at all.

However, many decision makers prefer IRR to NPV. CBA's past preference for IRR may be explained by the following.

(1) Ease of understanding and presentation of data to non-financial managers: most people understand the concept of rate of return, whereas NPV needs more explanation.

(2) The need to separate the mechanics of the discounting exercise from the discussion of the project's hurdle rate: the discounting exercise can be performed at a lower managerial level than the discussion of the project's minimum return. Once the project's IRR is known, the board of directors can judge whether this is good enough to cover its perceived level of risk, taking into account other qualitative factors. If the NPV method is used, the judgement on project risk has to made *before* the discounting can take place in order to compute the hurdle rate.

(ii) *The use of multiple methods of appraisal*

As well as the discounting methods of NPV and IRR, some companies use non-discounting methods such as **payback** or **accounting rate of return** (ARR). For example, a company may use the decision criteria 'accept the project if it has a positive net present value and pays back its initial outlay within four years'.

This is acceptable provided the relative strengths and weaknesses of each method are appreciated.

The payback method has the advantage that it can be used to screen out any proposals which simply take too long to produce cash returns. However, it should not be regarded as a reliable method of investment appraisal because it ignores the time value of money (unless **discounted payback** is used) and also ignores cash flows beyond the payback period. As such, it fails to provide information on the effect of the project on investor wealth.

The ARR also ignores the time value of money, suffers the same problems as IRR when ranking investments and, being based on accounting profit, is open to manipulation. However, it does provide valuable additional information, showing the effect on reported profits and return on capital employed.

In summary, these non-discounting methods are too unreliable to be used as major decision criteria but they do provide useful additional information when used in conjunction with discounting methods.

Signed: Financial Manager

(b)

Pass marks. This question is concerned specifically with the price and profit regulation of former nationalised industries which hold absolute or near monopoly positions, such as gas, electricity and telecommunicaions. The question is purely factual and easy to answer for those who have read the appropriate notes.

Examiner's comment. This discussion was generally better done by overseas candidates than by UK candidates. Some candidates appeared to be confused between the work of a regulatory body and that of the Competition Commission. There was not enough discussion on an appropriate formula for determining price increases.

Pricing policy in a regulated industry

Where there is competition in the supply of a service, efficient producers will be able to undercut the prices of less efficient competitors, ensuring that customers get the best possible price and that the industry remains competitive and efficient.

Where the provision of a service is in the hands of a monopoly, the firm can maximise its profits at a higher price level than where there is competition, despite the fact that its unit cost should be lower than if it had a lower share of the market. The result is that either the shareholders gain super-profits or that the organisation can operate inefficiently with above-average returns going to its managers and employees. These gains are all at the expense of the consumer.

The objective of the **regulatory body** is to intervene on behalf of the consumer, forcing the monopoly provider to lower its prices and hence to operate more efficiently. Often the regulatory body is only a first step, preceding genuine deregulation of the industry and the opening of the service to competition.

The two main methods used to regulate such industries are as follows.

(i) **Price control:** the regulator agrees the output prices with the industry. Usually the price is progressively reduced in real terms each year by setting price increases at a rate below that of inflation as measured by the Retail Prices Index (RPI). This has been used with success by regulators in the UK but can be confrontational.

(ii) **Profit control:** the regulator agrees the maximum profit which the industry can make. A typical method is to fix maximum profit at x% of capital employed, but this does not provide any incentive to making more efficient use of assets: the higher the capital employed, the higher the profit.

In addition the regulator will be concerned with:

(i) actively promoting competition by encouraging new firms in the industry and preventing unreasonable barriers to entry;

(ii) addressing quality and safety issues and considering the social implications of service provision and pricing.

Even when **competition** enters an industry (for example the UK telecommunications industry), the regulator (Oftel) is still needed because the original monopolist (BT) will still command enough market power to main high prices in the absence of such regulation until the market is completely open to international competition. In addition the regulator is needed to supervise industry-wide matters such as the policy on identification and issue of telephone numbers.

43 THREE OPPORTUNITIES

> **Pass marks**. In part (a)(i) you should be careful to define your method of calculation of the profitability index since different approaches are possible. In part (b) your discussion should include factors external to the firm such as the level of interest rates, and also the nature of the projects themselves. It is insufficient to concentrate solely on the effect of borrowing on the capital gearing.
>
> **Examiner's comment**. Part (a) should have been a straightforward investment decision in a situation of capital rationing. An astonishingly high percentage of candidates could not calculate profitability indexes (PIs). Many candidates did not inflate the cash flows, or did not compound the inflation rate. As a result, many answers provided negative NPVs.

(a) (i) The cash flows arising from each of the projects will be discounted at 15% to arrive at the expected net present value (NPV). The present value of the cash flows will then be used to calculate the **profitability index**, which is defined as the present value of all cash inflows divided by the present value of all cash outflows.

	Year 0	*Year 1*	*Year 2*	*Years 3*	*Total*
15% discount factors	1.000	0.870	0.756	0.658	
Project A	£	£	£	£	£
Uninflated cashflow	(350,000)	95,000	110,000	200,000	
Undiscounted cashflow	(350,000)	104,500	133,100	266,200	
PV (Total = NPV)	(350,000)	90,915	100,624	175,160	16,699
PV cash inflows					366,699
PV cash outflows					(350,000)
Profitability index					1.05
Project B					
Uninflated cashflow	(105,000)	45,000	45,000	45,000	
Undiscounted cashflow	(105,000)	49,500	54,450	59,895	
PV (Total = NPV)	(105,000)	43,065	41,164	39,411	18,640
PV cash inflows					123,640
PV cash outflows					(105,000)
Profitability index					1.18
Project C					
Uninflated cashflow	(35,000)	(40,000)	(25,000)	125,000	
Undiscounted cashflow	(35,000)	(44,000)	(30,250)	166,375	
PV (Total = NPV)	(35,000)	(38,280)	(22,869)	109,475	13,326
PV cash inflows					109,475
PV cash outflows					(96,149)
Profitability index					1.14

(ii) Since there is a £400,000 expenditure limit in place, the choice is restricted to either Project A and Project C, or Project B and Project C. The combination that yields the highest NPV should be selected.

Projects A and C: NPV = £30,025

Projects B and C: NPV = £31,966

On this basis, Projects B and C should be selected. Since the money market return is below the cost of capital, the return on the surplus funds can be ignored.

(b) The reasons underlying the directors' decision not to borrow are not given, and there is no information on the existing financial gearing of the company, or on the stability of earnings performance, and this makes it impossible to comment on the position of the shareholders in this particular case. All that can be said is that by not borrowing an additional £90,000, the company is foregoing an additional £16,699 of

NPV. However, the factors that would need to be considered in arriving at such a decision include the following.

(i) **The existing level of financial gearing.** The company must consider its existing interest commitments and its level of interest cover when deciding whether or not further borrowings are appropriate. It should also take into account the level of additional borrowings that would be required to undertake the projects, and the effect of undertaking the projects on the earnings stream out of which existing and additional interest charges must be paid.

(ii) **The absolute level and volatility of earnings.** Both these factors will influence the borrowing decision. The company must have sufficient earnings to take advantage of the tax relief available on interest payments, and the earnings stream must be sufficiently stable to avoid putting the shareholders' position at risk in the event of the company being unable to meet its interest commitments in a particular year.

(iii) **The cost of borrowing.** The anticipated level of interest rates over the life of the projects must be taken into account in evaluating the company's ability to borrow.

(iv) **The effect of not undertaking the investments.** It is not clear whether any of these projects are of strategic importance to the future of the company. It can be argued that a higher level of financial risk should be accepted if the project to be undertaken is of crucial strategic importance to the long-term development and performance of the company.

(v) **The risk profile of the projects.** It has been assumed that the projects carry similar levels of risk to that of the existing businesses. However, if they are large relative to the size of the company, and if their operational risk level is low, this could have the effect of reducing the beta factor for the company and thereby reducing the cost of capital. This should be considered when deciding whether additional borrowings are appropriate.

44 CP LTD

Pass marks. There is usually more than one interpretation of some items in this type of question, for example, exactly what is meant by a one year tax delay, and the method of calculating capital allowances. The examiner's comments show that credit was given for all sensible methods, so the key to passing is to ensure that you make sensible assumptions and keep pressing ahead. Use all the information in the question (including the target accounting rate of return). Make sure your conclusions are summarised in a narrative recommendation and that you mention other non-financial factors affecting the decision.

Examiner's comments. The question was popular and the computations were quite well answered. Common errors included not compounding the inflation rate, and not realising that the figure for working capital returned at the end of 5 years is already in nominal terms. Credit was given for all reasonable calculations and adjustments for capital allowances. The discussion section was less well answered.

To: The Board of CP Ltd
From: Financial Manager

Recommendations on investment alternatives

As you know, our company must choose one of two investment projects, because we do not have the physical capacity or the funds to undertake both. The calculations in the appendix show evaluation of the two projects by a number of standard investment appraisal techniques.

On the basis of the calculations, investment 2 should be accepted. It has a higher net present value, both in absolute terms and relative to the initial investment (profitability index). Discounted cash flow is the preferred method of evaluating projects which cover a number of years, because it allows for the time value of money. Of the various DCF methods, the net present value is the most reliable, and profitability index can give additional help when there is a scarcity of capital, as in this case. Internal rate of return may produce misleading results in this situation, and has not been calculated.

Although both projects achieve the target accounting rate of return on average investment, Project 2 shows a slightly higher figure. This method is not as reliable as NPV, as it ignores the time value of money.

Payback period (time taken to repay the initial investment) is sometimes relevant in screening projects for initial feasibility. However, there is no significant difference between the payback periods of the two investments.

Other non-financial factors which might be relevant to the decision include:

- the company's strategy for expansion and direction;
- effect on the company's values (ethics, environmental factors, etc).
- effect on other stakeholders (eg employees, customers, suppliers).
- positive or negative effects on other parts of the business.

Appendix

Investment 1

Year	*0*	*1*	*2*	*3*	*4*	*5*	*6*
	£'000	£'000	£'000	£'000	£'000	£'000	£'000
Fixed assets	(500)						
Tax saved by CAs (W1)		41	31	23	17	13	40
Working capital	(50)					50	
Forecast sales (total 2,762)		389	551	590	626	606	
Forecast costs (total 1,877)		(315)	(358)	(388)	(401)	(415)	
Tax at 33%			(24)	(64)	(67)	(74)	(63)
Net cash	(550)	115	200	161	175	180	(23)
12% discount factors	1.000	0.893	0.797	0.712	0.636	0.567	0.507
PV	(550)	103	159	115	111	102	(12)
NPV	28						

- The net present value is **£28,000**.
- Profitability index (NPV/outlay) = 28/550 = 0.051.
- Total profit before depreciation = 2,762 – 1,877 = 885. Total depreciation = 500. Profit before tax = 885 – 500 = 385. Average profit per year after tax = 385/5 = 77. Average investment is approximately 500/2 + 50 = 300. Accounting rate of return = 77/300 = 25.7%.
- The project pays back during its 4th year.

Workings

Capital allowances

Year	*0*	*1*	*2*	*3*	*4*	*5*	*6*
	£'000	£'000	£'000	£'000	£'000	£'000	£'000
Asset written down value	500	375	281	211	158	118	
25% WDA (reduc. balance)		125	94	70	53	40	
Tax saved at 33%		41	31	23	17	13	40

Investment 2

Year	*0*	*1*	*2*	*3*	*4*	*5*	*6*
	£'000	£'000	£'000	£'000	£'000	£'000	£'000
Fixed assets	(450)						
Tax saved by CAs (W2)		37	28	21	16	12	36
Working capital	(50)					50	
Forecast sales (total 2,989)		441	562	666	669	651	
Forecast costs (total 2,169)		(326)	(424)	(486)	(486)	(447)	
Tax at 33%			(38)	(46)	(59)	(60)	(67)
Net cash (total 250)	(500)	152	128	155	140	206	(31)
12% discount factors	1.000	0.893	0.797	0.712	0.636	0.567	0.507
PV	(500)	136	102	110	89	117	(16)
NPV	38						

- The net present value is **£38,000.**
- Profitability index (NPV/outlay) = 0.076.
- Total profit before depreciation = 2,989 – 2,169 = 820. Total depreciation = 450. Profit before tax = 820 – 450 = 370. Average profit per year after tax = 370/5 = 74. Average investment is approximately 450/2 + 50 = 275. Accounting rate of return = 74/275 = 26.9%.
- The project pays back during its 4th year.

W2: Capital allowances

Year	*0*	*1*	*2*	*3*	*4*	*5*	*6*
	£'000	£'000	£'000	£'000	£'000	£'000	£'000
Asset written down value	450	337	253	190	142	106	
25% WDA (reduc. balance)		113	84	63	48	36	
Tax saved at 33%		37	28	21	16	12	36

45 ADJUSTED PRESENT VALUE

> **Pass marks**. The first part of the question requires the calculation of an APV where the method of financing is changed from 100% equity to 100% debt. You should take care in your treatment of the issue costs. In part (b) it is not particularly obvious as to which interest rate should be used to evaluate the lease. You should therefore make it clear what your assumptions are in this respect.

(a) We need to make an assumption whether the £300,000 p.a. is before or after tax. This answer assumes it is **after** tax.

(i) **Basic value of the project appraised at 'r', the ungeared cost of equity**

	£
300,000 ÷ 0.16	1,875,000
Less: cost of machinery	1,900,000
Basic value	(25,000)

(ii) **The present value of tax shield**

Irredeemable debt makes it a short calculation: DT =£2,00,000 × 33% = £660,000.

Gross proceeds	100%
Issue costs are	5%
Capital expenditure is	95%

Debt raised is then £1,900,000 × 100/95 = £2,000,000.

(iii) **PV of issue costs**

Issue costs are payable at time 0: £100,000.

APV is then: (£25,000) + £660,000 + (£100,000) = £535,000.

This represents a gain to the shareholders and is therefore an **equity** value.

Adjusted rate, r* = (1 – T*L)

Where:		
	r	= 16% (used)
	T	= 33%
	L	= D/(D+E)
	D	= £2,000,000 (the amount borrowed)
	E	= £535,000 (the APV)

r* = 16(1 – 0.33 × 2,000/2,535) = **11.83%**

Note. This can be checked by discounting the £300,000 p.a. at 11.83% which should give the same PV result:

£300,000 ÷ 0.1183 =	£2,535,000
Initial costs	£2,000,000

This gives the NPV of **£535,000.**

This 'adjusted' rate could in theory be used in the case of future investments with the same specific certainty. In practice this is unlikely.

The benefits flowing from borrowing should be seen as applying to the enterprise as a whole, not just the project. A better approach is to look at the company's borrowing capacity in terms of its impact on the cost of capital for the entity.

(b) (i) Lease payments should be discounted at the **post-tax cost of borrowing** to allow an appropriate comparison:

ie 9% (1 – 0.33) = **6.03%** (use 6% factors in the tables as an approximation)

Time			*6% factor*	*PV*
		£'000		£'000
0 to 4	Payments made at the start of year	425	4.465	1,898

PV of **lease** is **£1,898,000**; PV of borrowing is £2m less tax capital allowances on £1.9m invested. No details are given of allowances available but at the 33% tax rate, they are bound to be higher than £200,000. **Leasing is therefore more costly.**

(ii) Consider the nature of the project, in particular:

- Cashflows arise indefinitely
- Cashflows are constant each year
- Estimated cost savings are £300,000 while the lease would cost £425,000

Also consider:

- Existing providers of finance - company is all equity-financed
- Costs of raising finance - debt costs £100,000, lease costs incorporated in £425,000

Leasing might be seen to have the following advantages over long-term debt.

- The company will remain all equity financed - this might suit investors' preferences
- Leasing does not incur initial 'issue costs', although similar costs are likely to be incorporated into the lease payments
- Leasing is more flexible in the case of needing to update equipment

The disadvantages of leasing compared to long-term debt might include the following.

- The additional cost might be seen as undesirable, especially since it outweighs the benefits for the first five years
- The company would be using short-term finance for a long-term project. It is more common so compare leasing to medium-term debt.

In theory, a project should have a certain value regardless of how it is financed. However, the **investment decision** might be affected by the choice of method of finance in that the **tax shield** if debt brings a **benefit to the shareholders** that leasing does not. In some more marginal cases, this might make the difference between a project being accepted or rejected.

46 MEGAPOWER PLC

> **Pass marks**. Part (a) of this question required a reconciliation of what appeared to be two different points of view. Part (b) required an answer in report format. Note that you should have reached a conclusion as to whether the project should be completed or abandoned. Part (c) gave no indication as to whether you should or should not have agreed with the statement. You should therefore have ensured that you presented a particularly well rounded argument and reached a logical conclusion.

(a) Most projects have cash flows that consist of an initial negative cash flow followed by positive cash inflows in later years. In this situation, the net cash flow is negative at the start of the project and positive in all future periods. If the net cash flow changes from positive to negative in successive periods, a **second internal rate of return** (IRR) occurs. It is possible for there to be as many IRRs as there are sign changes in the net cash flow.

The nuclear power station project appears to have two IRRs. This is possible because the cash flows associated with the project are not conventional due to the heavy expenditure which occurs at the end of the project's life and that 27% and 12% are both rates at which the NPV of the future cash flows is zero. This can be checked using the suggested IRRs as discount rates as follows.

Year		*Cash flow* £m	*Discount factor* 27%	*Net present value* £m	*Discount factor* 12%	*Net present value* £m
1	Work to complete in 19X3	(45)	0.787	(35)	0.893	(40)
2 - 13	Revenue per year 19X4-19Y5	18	2.751	50	5.531	100
6 - 13	Storage costs per year 19X8-19Y5	(5)	(0. 955)	(5)	2.819	(14)
13	Decommissioning costs 19Y5	(200)	0.045	(9)	0.229	(46)
				0		0

Similar calculations can be made at 0%, 10%, 20% and 30% with the result that a curve showing the net present value of the project, discounted at different rates, can be drawn. (The curve crosses the zero NPV line at 12% and 27%).

The graph shows that when the cost of capital of Mega Power plc is between 12% and 27% the NPV is positive and, if the NPV rule is followed, the project should be accepted. If it were believed that the only IRR was 12% then the project may have been abandoned. The graph has shown that the project is actually viable between rates of 12% and 27%. See the diagram below.

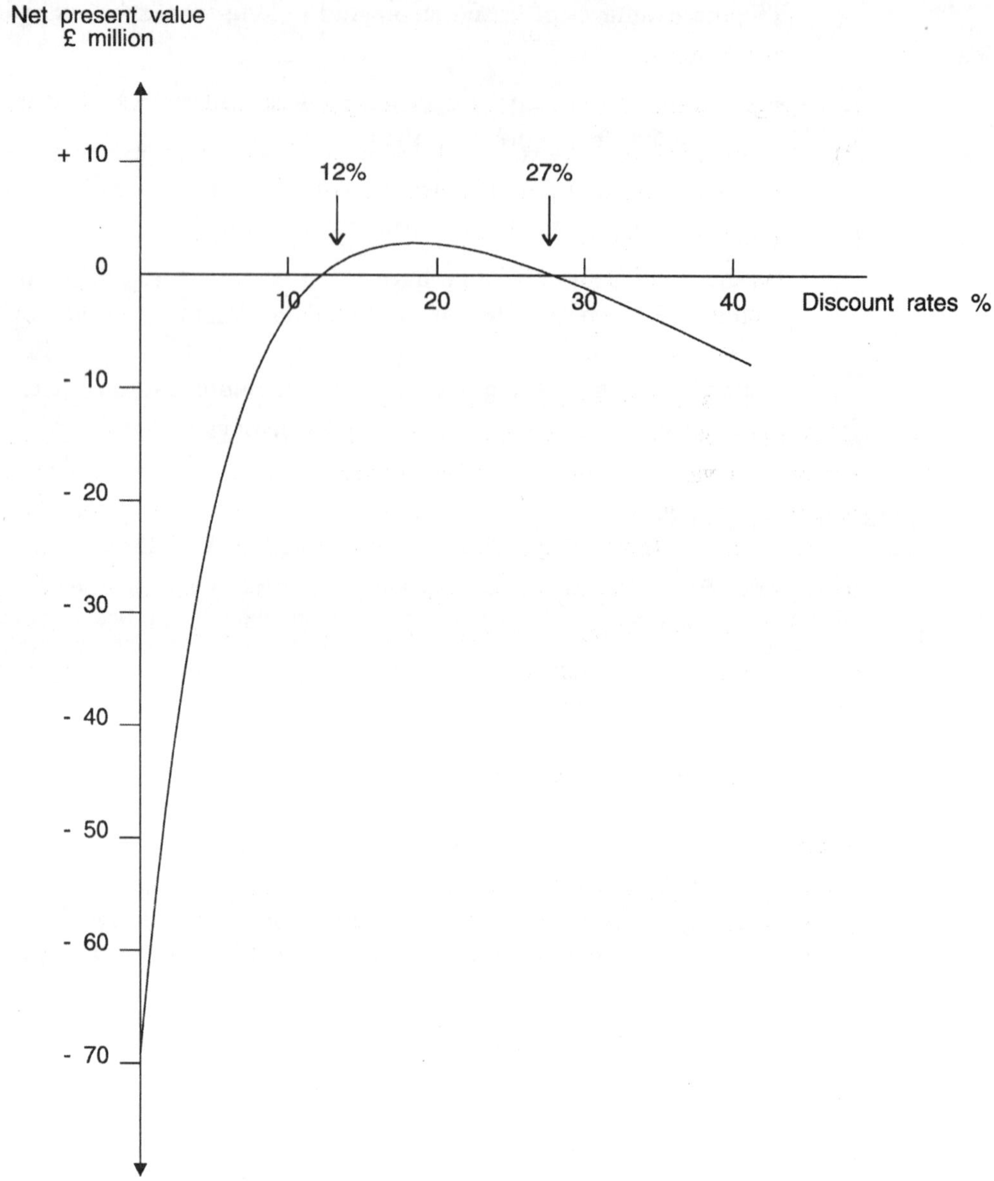

(b)

REPORT

To: The Board of Mega Power plc
From: Management Accountant Date: 1 December 19X2
Subject: Rules for capital investment appraisal and the action to be taken on MAGNAPHALL

The present rules for capital investment appraisal require the project's IRR to be in excess of the pre-tax hurdle rate of 15%. This approach is flawed in a number of ways.

(i) The cash flows of most projects are conventional in that they consist of one initial payment followed by a number of inflows. The project therefore has only one IRR. MAGNAPHALL has, however, **two IRRs** and it is not possible to say which IRR is the most appropriate.

(ii) The viability of a capital investment project is clearly affected by **taxation,** in some cases to a significant degree. Consequently, taxation should not be ignored in the appraisal of capital projects.

(iii) By using the **IRR as the key performance measure,** the implication is that if a project does not exceed the stipulated hurdle of 15%, the money saved should be banked. This ignores the fact that investment situations are very complex and alternatives to a proposal must be identified and appraised to allow comparisons to be made.

It is suggested that the capital investment appraisal rules be amended as follows.

(i) A **net present value** should be calculated using an appropriate post-tax cost of money and incorporating all tax related cash flows.

(ii) The **'cut off point' for the inclusion of tax related cash flows** should be the tax paid and saved by MegaPower plc. One can make a theoretical case for including the tax position of the company's owners but the appraisal then becomes too complex.

On this basis, the project should be appraised using a 10% post-tax cost of money (15% less 33% tax) and continuation of the MAGNAPHALL project would yield a net present value of £34 million by investing a further £45 million next year (see Appendix). However, if the project were to be abandoned the tax relief at 33% on the £180 million (amounting to £59 million) would be available.

With the present environmental movement away from nuclear energy production, the likelihood of tighter and more expensive control of uranium, and the advantage of recovering £59 million against expenditure of £45 million, it is recommended that the project be abandoned.

Signed: Management Accountant

Appendix

After tax results to the end of the project's life assuming no lag in tax payments and a 10% DCF rate are as follows.

	A	*B*	*C*	*D*	*E= A+B+D*	*F*	*G*
Year	*Income/ (expenditure)*	*Tax (paid)/ saved*	*Writing down allowance*	*Tax saved on capital allowance*	*Net cash flow*	*Discount factor*	*Net present value*
	£m	£m	£m	£m	£m	10%	£m
1	(45)				(45)	0.909	(41)
2	18	(6)	56	18	30	0.826	25
3	18	(6)	42	14	26	0.751	20
4	18	(6)	32	11	23	0.683	16
5	18	(6)	24	8	20	0.621	12
6	13	(4)	18	6	15	0.564	8
7	13	(4)	13	4	13	0.513	7
8	13	(4)	10	3	12	0.467	6
9	13	(4)	8	3	12	0.424	5
10	13	(4)	6	2	11	0.386	4
11	13	(4)	4	1	10	0.350	4
12	13	(4)	3	1	10	0.319	3
13	(187)	62	9	3	(122)	0.290	(35)
						NPV =	34

(c) It is possible, with hindsight, to see that the decision to build a privately owned nuclear power station was wrong. A lack of information on the circumstances in 19W7 precludes any conclusion that either more could have been done at that time or whether all the problems have arisen since then. The original project should be abandoned, £59 million recovered and £121 million written off. Management should review their decision-making process to ensure that the same mistakes are not made again.

Abandonment of the project means that MegaPower plc is faced with the option of efficiently converting MAGNAPHALL into a gas-fired power station.

(i) The power station will have the advantage of new technology developed since 19W7.

(ii) A prime site with road approaches and utilities supplies has already been procured. This can be transferred at a cost which is lower than current cost.

(iii) Many of the buildings will be suitable once adapted and have been constructed at a cost lower than current cost.

(iv) Environmental regulations have become stricter in recent years. Planning permission is therefore more difficult and costly to obtain for new projects.

(v) Legislation now enables power producers to buy natural gas directly from the oil company producers. Previously, supplies could only have been obtained through British Gas plc who was a monopoly supplier, with the result that competition has increased and the cost of gas decreased.

It would seem that the comment that the conversion will be 'the most inefficient gas-fired power station ever built' is based on the combined cost of the nuclear and gas-fired power station. The gas-fired power station on its own is, in fact, likely to be very efficient, if not the most efficient gas-fired power station ever built.

The conversion option would also have two other advantages.

(i) Abandonment may involve a loss of reputation for MegaPower plc. Conversion should avoid this.

(ii) MegaPower plc may not have the capacity to absorb all of the tax losses which would result from abandonment. This problem would not arise if the installation were converted.

47 TUTORIAL QUESTION: BASES OF VALUATION

(a) (i) Balance sheet value = £454,100.

(ii) Replacement cost value =

£454,100 + £(725,000 – 651,600) + £(550,000 – 515,900) = £561,600.

(iii) Realisable value =

£454,100 + £(450,000 – 651,600) + £(570,000 – 515,900) – £14,900 = £291,700.

Bad debts are 2% × £745,000 = £14,900. Bad debts are assumed not to be relevant to balance sheet and replacement cost values.

(iv) The Gordon dividend growth model value depends on an estimate of growth, which is far from clear given the wide variations in earnings over the five years.

(1) The lowest possible value, assuming zero growth, is as follows.

$$\text{Value ex div} = \frac{£25{,}000}{0.12} = £208{,}333.$$

It is not likely that this will be the basis taken.

(2) Looking at dividend growth over the past five years we have:

19X4 dividend = £25,000
19X0 dividend = £20,500

If the annual growth rate in dividends is g:

$$(1+g)^4 = \frac{(25{,}000)}{20{,}500} = 1.2195$$

$$1 + g = 1.0508$$

$$g = 0.0508, \text{ say } 5\%$$

Then, market value ex div

$$= \frac{\text{Dividend in 1 year}}{(0.12 - g)}$$

$$= \frac{25{,}000(1.05)}{0.07} = £375{,}000$$

(3) Looking at average proportion retained:

$$\frac{12{,}800 + 44{,}200 + 18{,}300 + 13{,}400 + 27{,}200}{33{,}300 + 66{,}800 + 43{,}300 + 38{,}400 + 52{,}200} = 0.495 \text{ (say b = 0.5)}$$

$$\text{Return on investment this year} = \frac{53{,}200}{\text{average investment}}$$

$$= \frac{53{,}200}{(454{,}100 - 27{,}200/2)}$$

$$= 0.1208 \text{ (say r = 12\%)}$$

Then $g = 0.5 \times 12\% = 6\%$

$$\text{so market value ex div} = \frac{£25{,}000(1.06)}{0.06} = £441{,}667$$

(v) **P/E ratio model**

Comparable quoted companies to Manon Ltd have P/E ratios of about 10. Manon is much smaller and being unquoted its P/E ratio would be less than 10, but how much less?

If we take a P/E ratio of 5, we have market value = £53,200 × 5 = £266,000.

If we take a P/E ratio of 10 × 2/3, we have market value = £53,200 × 10 × 2/3 = £354,667.

If we take a P/E ratio of 10, we have market value = £532,000.

(b) (i) **The balance sheet value**

The balance sheet value should not play a part in the negotiation process. Historical costs are not relevant to a decision on the future value of the company.

(ii) **The replacement cost**

This gives the cost of setting up a similar business. Since this gives a higher figure than any other valuation in this case, it could show the maximum price for Carmen to offer. There is clearly no goodwill to value.

(iii) **The realisable value**

This shows the cash which the shareholders in Manon could get by liquidating the business. It is therefore the minimum price which they would accept.

All the methods (i) to (iii) suffer from the limitation that they do not look at the going concern value of the business as a whole. Methods (iv) and (v) do consider this value. However, the realisable value is of use in assessing the risk attached to the business as a going concern, as it gives the base value if things go wrong and the business has to be abandoned.

(iv) **The dividend model**

The figures have been calculated using Manon's cost of equity (12%). If (2) or (3) were followed, the value would be the minimum that Manon's shareholders would accept, as the value in use exceeds scrap value in (iii). The relevance of a dividend valuation to Carmen will depend on whether the current retention and reinvestment policies would be continued. Certainly the value to Carmen should be based on 9% rather than 12%. Both companies are ungeared and in the same risk class so the different required returns must be due to their relative sizes and the fact that Carmen's shares are more marketable.

One of the main limitations on the dividend growth model is the problem of estimating the future value of g.

(v) **The P/E ratio model**

The P/E ratio model is an attempt to get at the value which the market would put on a company like Manon. It does provide an external yardstick, but is a very crude measure. As already stated, the P/E ratio which applies to larger quoted companies must be lowered to allow for the size of Manon and the non-marketability of its shares. Another limitation of P/E ratios is that the ratio is very dependent on the expected future growth of the firm. It is therefore not easy to find a P/E ratio of a 'similar firm'. However, in practice the P/E model may well feature in the negotiations over price simply because it is an easily understood yardstick.

(c) The range within which the purchase price is likely to be agreed will be the minimum price which the shareholder of Manon will accept and the maximum price which the directors of Carmen will pay.

Examining the figures in part (a), the range is £291,700 (realisable value) to £561,600 (replacement cost).

48 MR JONES

Pass marks. This involves calculation of the theoretical post-acquisition share price and the effect of the deal on the shareholders in the two companies. When calculating the effect of the asset sale on the value of LO in part (b) do not forget to discount this to take into account the fact that the funds will not be received until the end of year 1. Similarly you should make clear whether the administrative savings are assumed to be a one-off benefit or an on-going improvement.

Examiner's comment. This question used a textbook approach to valuing shares in a proposed takeover. The aim was to test not only candidates' knowledge of this approach but also their ability to evaluate the method. The question also examined for an understanding of the effect on the target company's bargaining position once synergy values become known. In part (b), many candidates failed to discount the savings given in the question, and many others performed the discounting incorrectly.

(a) (i) Mr Jones' estimate of the post acquisition share price of £8.33 is based on a total of 15m shares in issue at a market capitalisation of £125m. If this market capitalisation estimate was based on earnings, then it can only be assumed that he has applied RD's current P/E ratio of 12.5 to the group's combined earnings of £10m (£2.5m + £7.5m).

The estimated EPS is arrived at by dividing this combined earnings figure by the 15m total number of shares in issue post-acquisition.

The estimated equivalent value of one old LO share is then found by taking the estimated post-acquisition share price and multiplying by 10/15 - the basis of the offer for the shares.

(ii) REPORT

To: A N Other
From: Management Accountant 23 May 19X5
Subject: Pricing of RD plc's offer for LO plc

Calculation of likely post-acquisition share price

The probable post-acquisition share price can be estimated by finding the total market capitalisation of the new group and dividing this by the number of shares in issue following the acquisition. This method assumes that the existing market capitalisations are a fair reflection of the value of the two companies, and ignores any **synergistic effects** arising from the acquisition:

	RD	*LO*	*Group*
Earnings available to equity	£2.5m	£7.5m	
P/E ratio	12.5	7.5	
Market capitalisation	£31.25m	£56.25m	£87.5m
Number of shares in issue			15m
Theoretical share price			£5.83

Effect on shareholders in RD plc

The shareholders in RD plc will retain the same number of shares after the acquisition, but their price will have fallen from £6.25 to £5.83 per share. This represents a loss in value of £2.1m (5m × (£6.25 – £5.83)) to the shareholders. In addition RD will have to issue a further 10m shares to the shareholders of LO. This means that the shareholders in RD will have lost control of the group, owning only one third of the total number of shares in issue post-acquisition. Thus on the basis of the information provided, this bid does not appear to be in the best interests of the shareholders in RD. However, these calculations do not take into account any earnings improvement in LO after the change of ownership. If Mr Jones is indeed able to bring about a significant improvement in performance then the bid could hold some long term benefits for the shareholders, in financial terms at least.

Effect on shareholders in LO plc

As calculated above, the bid will result in a transfer of value of some £2m to the shareholders in LO. In addition the LO shareholders will hold the majority of shares in the new group. The bid is therefore in their interests and should be accepted unless the directors of LO believe they can produce substantial improvements in earnings performance in the near future.

Signed: Management Accountant

(b) The new information will affect the value of the combined group as follows. The improvement in net income of £7.5m will be capitalised at 15% (RD's cost of capital) to give a value of £50m.

	£m
Market capitalisation as calculated above	87.5
Add: One-off administrative savings	5.0
Sale of assets at end of year 1 £10m × 0.87 (discounted at 15%)	8.7
Improvement in net income	50.0
Revised market capitalisation	151.2
Number of shares in issue	15m
Theoretical share price	£10.08

The shareholders in LO therefore own an additional potential value of £63.7m (£151.2m – £87.5m). Whether they are able to use this knowledge to gain an improvement in the offer depends on their bargaining position. If a takeover of LO is an attractive proposition to other companies as well as RD this may mean that the shareholders are able to push the price up to what another bidder would be prepared to pay. The precise amount will depend on the size of the increase in value that the other bidders believe they could realise. If however there are no other potential offers then the shareholders may not be able to obtain much improvement on RD's initial offer.

49 PROVINCIAL PLC

> **Pass marks**. The first part of the question requires the calculation of the theoretical market capitalisation of the new group after merger. This can be derived by calculating the new level of equity earnings in National plc and applying the P/E ratio to find the new value of the earnings. The capital inflows and outflows arising from acquisition can then be included to arrive at the total post merger capitalisation. Since the number of shares in the new group is known, this can then be used to find the theoretical share prices.
>
> *Other points.* Parts (b) and (c) require an understanding of the way in which the market reacts to bids in practice, and of factors influencing the way in which investors will react to cash and paper offers.

(a) The first step is to calculate the theoretical **market capitalisation** of the two companies once the reorganisation has taken place.

National plc	£'000
Existing market capitalisation (45m × 166p)	74,700.0
P/E ratio: 74,700 ÷ 9,337.5 = 8.0	
Existing equity earnings	9,337.5
Less earnings lost on sale of division	(1,500.0)
	7,837.5
Add 20% efficiency savings	1,567.5
New annual equity earnings	9,405.0
Theoretical new capitalisation assuming P/E of 8.0 (9,405 × 8)	75,240.0
Add proceeds from sale of division	10,200.0
Total capitalisation	85,440.0

Provincial plc	
Existing market capitalisation (14m × 840p)	117,600.0
Add: proceeds from property sale	16,000.0
Less: reorganisation costs	(4,500.0)
Total capitalisation	129,100.0

The total combined market capitalisation after reorganisation is £85,440,000 + 129,100,000 = £214,540,000.

The total number of shares in issue in National plc is 45 million. A two for nine offer means that Provincial plc will need to issue a further 10 million shares, bringing the total number of Provincial shares in issue to 24 million.

The theoretical price of a Provincial share is therefore 214,540,000 ÷ 24,000,000 = 894 pence.

The theoretical price of a National share is 2/9 times the Provincial share price = 198.7 pence.

(b) The shares in National plc will not only be valued on the basis of market estimates of the potential merger synergy. In practice, the price will depend on the expectations of buyers and sellers of the likely success and ultimate format of the bid, as well as the amount of competition for the company from other bidders. If competition for the acquisition is strong, then it is likely that the shares in National plc will rise to a higher level as the market anticipates a premium having to be paid by the final buyer in order to secure the company. On the other hand, if there is little interest in the company from other bidders, Provincial may not need to offer much above the current market price of the shares in order to secure the acquisition, and National's shares will therefore be valued at a lower figure.

(c) Since investors are **risk averse,** a cash alternative will normally be more attractive than a share offer. This is supported by the fact that many mergers fail to achieve the forecast synergies as quickly as expected, and therefore earnings in the early years post-merger are often lower than anticipated. Thus a cash alternative is likely to be lower than the current value of the share exchange.

However, Provincial plc must also take into account the tax situation of the National shareholders and the reason why they are holding National shares. Thus although a cash offer will avoid the investors incurring transaction costs when they wish to sell their new shares, they will immediately become liable to capital gains tax and this may make a cash offer less attractive. Provincial should ascertain the ownership structure of the National equity, for example the proportion of institutional investors, and seek to ascertain the preferences of the major shareholders.

(d) The existing price of a National share is 166p. For the shareholders in National to achieve a 10% gain in the value of their shares, the price would have to be 166 × 1.1 = 182.6p.

A share price of 182.6 pence implies a market capitalisation for National of 45m × 182.6p = £82,170,000. The total market capitalisation of the new group is £214,540,000 (as calculated above). With a share price of 182.6 pence, the National shareholders would therefore hold 38.3% of the group.

The number of new shares to be issued by Provincial plc to achieve this can be calculated as follows.

Let n = additional number of shares to be issued

$$\frac{n}{14m+n} = \frac{38.3}{100}$$

$$100n = 38.3n + 536.2m$$

$$61.7n = 536.2m$$

$$n = 8.69m$$

Thus Provincial plc will have to offer 8.69million shares in exchange for the 45million existing National plc shares. This represents an offer of one for 5.18.

50 WT PLC AND SZ PLC

> **Pass marks**. Part (a) requires the calculation of the share price on the basis of P/E ratio and the dividend valuation model adjusted for earnings growth. Parts (b) and (c) required some understanding of the practicalities involved in making and defending takeover bids.
>
> The approach in part (d) is less obvious, and two methods could be used. The simplest approach is to weight the costs of capital in the two firms on the basis of market capitalisation to arrive at the cost of equity in the ungeared scenario. Assumptions about correlation of returns and about the basis used for the weighting should be stated clearly. Calculation of the costs of capital and equity in the geared situation can be based on the ungeared figures adjusted for taxation using the Modigliani and Miller equations.
>
> *Other points.* This question is testing two main areas of knowledge, namely share valuation techniques and the calculation of cost capital using the hypothesis developed by Modigliani and Miller.
>
> **Examiner's comment**. In part (b), relatively few candidates recognised the importance of the current share price in any bidding negotiations. Many suggested that the maximum bid price should be the current share price or (unforgivable) the nominal value of the shares. Part (c) was generally well answered although many candidates listed a large number of defence tactics, legal and illegal.

(a) (i) The **maximum price** that the directors of WT could pay given that their assumptions are correct can be found by applying WT's P/E ratio to SZ's earnings, plus the proceeds of the asset sale that will be made at the end of year 1.

The first step is to calculate WT's **P/E ratio**:

Earnings per share	= £40m/100m	= 40p
Share price	= 440p	
P/E ratio	= 11	

This can now be applied to SZ's current earnings (14m) to give a price of £154m. To this must be added the present value of the £25m asset sale at the end of year 1 - discounted at WT's cost of capital (14%) this amounts to a further £22m. The maximum price is therefore £176m of £1.76 per share.

The principal **weakness** of this approach is that no account is taken of the future earnings performance of the group or of wider market factors. The price is derived purely on the basis of current share prices and earnings, and share prices can vary widely from day to day due to factors over which the company has no control. This implies that the intrinsic value of the business also changes with the share price which is clearly not always the case.

(ii) The financial advisers are suggesting that SZ should be valued on its own merits, and that any future interrelationship of earnings and share price with WT should be ignored. The maximum price can be calculated using the dividend valuation model, plus the proceeds of the asset sale at the end of year 1 (this is assumed to be at the end of 19X4).

The first step is to calculate the average rate of growth in dividends over the period:

Year	*Earnings*	*Dividend*	*Growth*
19X0	12.1	6.05	
19X1	12.5	6.25	3.31%
19X2	13.5	6.75	8.00%
19X3	14.0	7.00	3.70%

The average rate of growth is 5.00%. SZ's cost of capital of 12% is used to reflect the correct level of risk. Dividend in year 0 will be £7.00m. These figures can be used in the dividend valuation model.

$$r = \frac{d_1}{p_o} + g$$

where

p_o = Market value

d_1 = Dividend in year 1

g = Annual rate of growth in dividends

r = Cost of capital

$$0.12 = \frac{7 \times 1.05}{p_o} + 0.05$$

$$0.07 = \frac{7 \times 1.05}{p_o}$$

$$p_o = \frac{7 \times 1.05}{0.07}$$

= £105 million

To this must be added the present value of the proceeds of the asset sale at the end of year 1 (£22m). This gives a maximum price of £127m or £1.27 per share.

This approach is more realistic than the P/E valuation because it is based on the income generation potential of the target firm. However, it is risky to assume a constant annual rate of earnings growth on the basis of past performance with no business projections to back this up.

(b) An initial bid is normally made at a premium (of say 10%) to the current market price of the target company's shares. In this case this would mean that WT would have to offer around 139 pence per share. The problem with this is that the maximum price as calculated by the advisers is only 127 pence per share (approximately the current market price).

If WT is to go ahead with the bid, it must therefore proceed on the basis of its own valuation of SZ and ignore the views of its financial advisers. In this case the maximum price which it could pay is £176m (or slightly less if it hopes to benefit financially from the deal).

(c) The **defence tactics** open to the management of SZ include the following.

(i) To issue a **defence document** containing a forecast of future profits and dividends. The aim of this is to convince shareholders that the offer price is too low and that their interests would be best served by retaining their shares and benefiting from future dividends and capital growth under the existing management.

(ii) To lobby the **Office of Fair Trading** with the aim of having the offer referred to the Monopolies and Mergers Commission.

(iii) To find a '**white knight**' - a company that will make an alternative welcome takeover bid.

(iv) To arrange a **management buyout**.

(d) (i) If a share exchange is made, the group would still be 100% equity financed. The new WACC will therefore be the same as the cost of equity.

It is not known what degree of correlation, if any, exists between the risk/return profiles of the two companies. It is assumed that there is no correlation. The WACC will therefore lie between 12% and 14%, and can be estimated by weighting on the basis of the market capitalisations of the two companies. The market capitalisation of SZ will be based on the price paid by WT. The WACC can be estimated as follows.

$$\text{WACC} = \frac{(14\% \times 440)}{(440+176)} + \frac{(12\% \times 176)}{(440+176)} = 13.43\%$$

(ii) The value of the company will change when debt is introduced.

$$V_g = V_u + DT$$
$$= (440 + 176) + 176 \times 0.33$$
$$= 674$$

The adjusted **average cost of capital** can be found using the following formula:

$$r^* = r(1 - T^*L)$$

$$r^* = 0.1343(1 - 0.33 \times \frac{176}{674})$$

$$= 12.27\%$$

51 FINANCIAL ANALYST

Pass marks. Part (a) is an enormous question for 5 marks! It is best to be content with a few relevant statements on determinants of share prices. Keep it simple, because almost anything relevant will score you the marks, whereas a few unfounded guesses will lose them.

For part (b) the figures work out reasonably if existing market values are used to predict the effect on share prices. The detailed information given about earnings growth is not of much use in answering the mainstream part of the question, but can be appended as additional information.

Examiner's comments. The examiner was surprised that this was not a more popular question. Part (a) was answered reasonably, but part (b) was not, with few candidates attempting many calculations beyond the pre-bid share price. The calculations required to answer this sort of question are not difficult.

(a) For large listed companies, the **share price** is the latest price at which small parcels of shares have changed hands on the stock market. The investors buying and selling are, in the main, financial institutions, are likely to have researched all available information before making their decision and will have no objective other than financial gain. The share price is therefore likely to be related to a logical estimate of the company's future ability to generate cash (ie its **going concern value,** or **economic value**).

This future cash will normally be paid out as **dividends,** but could also come from **share buy-backs** or the **break-up of the business**. Furthermore, if the company is taken over, the dividends will be paid out by the new parent company, rather than the original company.

The theory that a share is worth the discounted value of its expected future cash flows is therefore sensible but impossible to prove or disprove, because expected future cash flows are based on investors' beliefs about the company's future in relation to markets, development opportunities and merger/takeover possibilities. Looked at in this way, the **theoretical value** of a share is best found by examining its actual market price (a consequence of the **efficient market hypothesis**).

Share prices are, however, often very different from those calculated by the simplistic version of the **dividend valuation model,** in which the current dividend is adjusted by a simple expected growth rate and discounted to perpetuity. This 'theoretical value' is of limited use because (i) the model is too simple; and (ii) there is no reliable way of forecasting the growth factor. Share valuations by **P/E ratios** are subject to the same criticisms, but suffer additionally from the problem that no distinction is made for companies with different growth opportunities, resulting in high-growth companies being potentially undervalued.

The net realisable values of assets give an indication of company break-up value. As such, this shows the 'worst-case scenario', which is useful when assessing the risk of an investment. **Options pricing theory** shows that a company's value will always be higher than the higher of its break-up value and its going concern value.

Other methods of calculating asset values (eg **historical cost, replacement cost**) are of limited use in valuing businesses and shares.

(b) **Evaluation of the bid, based on current share prices**

From the data given, the following calculations can be made.

	ML plc	*CO plc*
	£'000	£'000
Profit before tax	4,600	5,200
Tax at 33%	1,518	1,716
Profit after tax	3,082	3,484

	ML plc	*CO plc*
No. of shares (m)	20	33
EPS pre-bid (pence)	15.41	10.56
P/E before bid	15	13
Share price pre-bid (pence)	231	137
Total market value of shares (£m)	46.23	45.29

Assuming:

(i) that the share prices of the two companies are a fair reflection of their true value (efficient market hypothesis); and

(ii) that any business synergy generated by the merger is already reflected in the share prices because the market has already guessed that a merger will take place;

then the value of the combined organisation will be £46.23m + £45.29m = £91.52m.

The number of new shares issued in ML plc = 2/3 × 33 million = 22 million, giving a total of 42 million shares, and a theoretical share price for ML after the merger announcement of £91.52/42 = **218 pence.**

The theoretical price of CO's shares after the merger announcement will be 2/3 × 218 = **145 pence.**

Based on these figures, ML shares lose value from 231p to 218p (6%) and CO shares increase from 137p to 145p (6%), as described in the question. The cash alternative of 135 pence is, as is normal, lower than the equivalent share offer, because cash is a less risky form of purchase consideration. However, it is unlikely to be attractive because it is below CO's current market price of 137 pence.

Based on these assumptions, a 'fairer' offer for the shareholders of ML would have been one where neither set of shareholders gained or lost. For the share price of ML plc to remain at 231p, the total number of shares in issue would have to be £91.52m/£2.31 = 39.6 million, say 40 million. This implies that only 20 million new shares in ML are offered in return for the 33 million in CO plc. However, it is then difficult to see why the shareholders of CO would be tempted to accept the offer.

As a fund manager with equivalent investments in both companies, no gain will result (a gain on CO offsets a loss on ML) unless the merger can produce synergetic gains which the market is so far unaware of. In general, however, you are likely to accept the merger if it makes clear economic sense, because otherwise the value of both companies is likely to fall, on the basis that expectations cannot be realised. If your investment is predominantly in CO, you should clearly accept the offer. If mainly in ML, you may care to object on the grounds that the offer to CO is too generous.

Valuation of shares by dividend valuation model

It is possible to apply the data given in the question to calculate the value of each company's shares, based on the dividend growth model.

	ML plc	*CO plc*
Cost of capital	12%	11%
Share pre-bid market price (pence)	231	137
Dividend yield	3.4%	3.6%
Dividend per share (pence)		
= share price × div yield (ignoring income tax)	7.85	4.93
Next year's dividend, D_1 : (growth = 5% and zero)	8.24	4.93
Future growth to perpetuity, g	5%	6%
Cost of capital, k	12%	11%
Share value from dividend growth model (pence)		
$V = D_1/(k - g)$	**118**	**99**

From these calculations, it is clear that the value computed by the dividend valuation model is well below the market price, probably indicating that the price of both companies has been bid up by expectations of synergetic gains from a takeover/merger.

Further useful information would include the following.

(i) Estimates of cost savings, asset sales, income enhancement and other potential synergetic gains arising from the merger. An attempt should be made to distinguish those effects which have already been factored into share prices (because of both hard information and rumour) from those which might surprise the market and cause further increases in share price.

(ii) Details of alternative bidders for either of the companies.

(iii) Details of alternative strategic plans for both companies.

Note: *Alternative calculations*

The examiner's comments indicated that sensible **alternative calculations** were accepted. One such suggestion is that the P/E ratio of ML plc (15) is applied to CO plc (previously 13) on the grounds that management efficiencies can be effected. The value of CO then becomes 15 × £3.484m = £52.26m, giving a total value of the combination of £46.23 + £52.26m = £98.49m. Theoretical value per share of ML after the merger announcement will be £98.49/42m = 235 pence (a 1.5% gain), and CO's price will move to 157 pence (a 14.6% gain).

52 EXPO PLC

Pass marks. The computational element of this question is very small and not particularly testing. It would have been more normal when using the money markets to hedge by borrowing an amount which grew to DM750,000 when three months interest was added. However the question is specific in its requirements that DM750,000 should be borrowed.

Other points. This question is predominantly about the overall strategic approach that the company should take towards foreign currency risk (should we eliminate risk or just partly reduce it?) and the principles of matching assets and liabilities in the same currency. In the last part of the question, the currency risk problems of selling to developing countries are examined.

(a) To: The Treasurer
From: Assistant
Date: 12 November 19X7

(i) **Comparison of two methods of hedging exchange risk**

Method 1

Expo borrows DM750,000.

Three months interest is DM750,000 × 3% × 3/12 = DM5,625.

The customer pays DM750,000, which repays the loan principal but not the interest. The interest must be paid by converting pounds. Since the interest is known in advance, this can be covered on the forward market at a cost of 5625/2.3688 = £2,375.

Meanwhile, the DM750,000 is converted to sterling at the original spot rate 2.3834 to give £314,677. Assume that this is used to repay the company's short-term borrowings. Interest saved will be £314,677 × 6% × 3/12 = £4,720.

So, at the end of three months, the net sterling cash from the transaction is:

£314,677 + £4,720 – £2,375 = £317,022.

Method 1: alternative working

(1) Asset of DM750,000 can be **matched** with a liability of DM750,000, in three months' time.

(2) To create a liability of DM750,000 in three months' time, borrow an amount which, with added interest, will be DM750,000. Note that annual interest of 3% for over 3 months is (3/4) = 0.75%. The discount factor is then **1.0075. 750,000/1.0075 = DM744,417.**

(3) Convert the borrowed currency to sterling at spot rate: **744,417/2.3834 = £312,344.**

(4) Earn UK interest (6%/4 = 1.5%) on the sterling value of the loan to establish how much sterling is received at the time the debtor pays. **£312,344 × 1.015 = £317,019.**

Method 2

The exchange rate is agreed in advance. Cash received in three months is converted to produce £750,000/2.3688 = £316,616.

Conclusion

On the basis of the above calculations, Method 1 gives a slightly better receipt. Banker's commission has been omitted from the figures.

(ii) **Factors to consider before deciding whether to hedge foreign exchange risk using the foreign currency markets**

The company should have a clear strategy concerning how much foreign exchange risk it is prepared to bear. A highly risk-averse or 'defensive' strategy of hedging all transactions is expensive in terms of commission costs but recognises that floating exchange rates are very unpredictable and can cause losses high enough to bankrupt the company.

An alternative 'predictive' strategy recognises that if all transactions are hedged, then the chance of currency gains is lost. The company could therefore attempt to forecast foreign exchange movements and only hedge those transactions where currency losses are predicted. The fact is that some currencies are relatively predictable (for example, if inflation is high, the currency will devalue and there is little to be gained by hedging payments in that currency).

This is, of course, a much more risky strategy but in the long run, if predictions are made sensibly, the strategy should lead to a higher expected value than that of hedging everything and will incur lower commission costs as well. The risk remains, though, that a single large uncovered transaction could cause severe problems if the currency moves in the opposite direction to that predicted.

A sensible strategy for our company could be to set a cash size for a foreign currency exposure above which all amounts must be hedged, but below this limit a predictive approach is taken or even, possibly, all amounts are left unhedged.

Before using any technique to hedge foreign currency transactions, receipts and payments in the same currency at the same date should be offset. This technique is known as 'matching'. For example, if the company is expecting to receive DM750,000 on 31 March and to pay DM600,000 on the same day, only the net amount of DM150,000 needs to be considered.

Matching can be extended to receipts and payments which do not take place on exactly the same day by simply hedging the period and amount of the difference between the receipt and payment. A company like ours which has many receipts and payments in European currencies should consider matching assets with liabilities in the same currency. For example if we have total German debtors of DM2million, we should borrow DM2million on overdraft to match the debtor.

(b) If the foreign subsidiary is selling predominantly in its own country, the principle of **matching assets and liabilities** says that the subsidiary should be financed as far as possible in the currency of that country. Ideally the subsidiary will be highly geared with loans and overdrafts in the developing country's currency. If local finance has not been used and the sales invoice which is about to be sent is large, then an overdraft in the same currency should be taken out and the receipt converted to sterling immediately.

If it is impossible to borrow in the local currency, Expo plc should attempt to find a hard currency which is highly positively correlated with the local currency. For example, some countries have a policy of pegging their currency to the US dollar. The receipt can then be hedged by selling the US dollar forward.

This technique is, however, open to the risk that the local currency suddenly devalues against the dollar, as happened in 1997 with a number of Asian currencies. The likelihood of this happening is high if there is high inflation in the country and it has low reserves.

If Expo plc is fairly certain that the local currency is going to devalue and that it cannot borrow in that currency, the **remaining alternatives** are:

- to increase the sales price by the amount of the expected devaluation and bear the risk;
- to invoice in a hard currency, for example US dollars, which can then be sold forward;
- to arrange a 'counter-trade' agreement (ie barter) in which the sale of Expo's textiles is paid for by the purchase of local raw materials or other products.

53 EASTASIA

> **Pass marks**. In part (a)(ii), the discount rate must be adjusted to take account of the different rates of interest in the two countries.
>
> In part (b) you should consider the effect of exchange rate movements and possible exchange controls as well as the relative levels of interest rates in the different countries.
>
> **Examiner's comment**. Very few candidates managed to produce correct calculations for part (a). However, those who realised that the NPV under both alternatives should be the same were given credit even if their calculations were incorrect.
>
> Some candidates discussed interest rate parity in part (b) despite having failed to apply in to part (a), where they had not realised that if UK rates were higher than Eastasia's, sterling could be expected to weaken. For part (b) many candidates discussed methods of raising finance in general rather than specifically in relation to overseas operations.

(a) **Calculating expected exchange rates**

Since the real rates of interest in the two countries are expected to remain the same (the **international Fisher Effect**), **interest rate parity** and **purchasing power parity** will give the same result.

The question gives both countries' interest rates and only on inflation rate. It is therefore quicker to use **interest rate parity.**

	UK	*Eastasia*
Now	£10,000	$20,000
Interest	× 1.09	× 1.07
+ 1 year	£10,900	$21,400

Predicted rate (21,400/10,900)	1.9633
Annual change in rate (1.9633/2)	0.9817
Year 2 rate (1.9633 × 0.9817)	1.9273
Year 3 rate (1.9273 × 0.9817)	1.8919
Year 4 rate (1.8919 × 0.9817)	1.8572

(i) **DCF of sterling receipts**

Year	$'000	$/£	£'000	*16% factor*	£'000
0	(2,500)	2	(1,250)	1	(1,250.0)
1	750	1.9633	382.0	0.862	329.3
2	950	1.9273	492.9	0.743	366.2
3	1,250	1.8919	660.7	0.641	423.5
4	1,350	1.8572	726.9	0.552	401.2
Total NPV (£'000)					270.2

(ii) **Discounting annual cash flows in Eastasian $**

In this case the discount rate must be adjusted to take into account the lower rate of interest in Eastasia.

The adjusted rate will be given by x in the following equation.

$$\frac{1+x}{1+0.16} = \frac{1+0.07}{1+0.09}$$

x = 13.87%, say 14% approximately.

Year	*Cashflow* EA$'000	*Discount factor*	*PV* EA$000
0	(2,500)	1.000	(2,500)
1	750	0.877	658
2	950	0.769	731
3	1,250	0.675	844
4	1,350	0.592	799
Total NPV (EA$'000)			532

This converts to sterling at the spot rate of 2.0000 to give £266,000 which differs slightly from the answer in (i) due to roundings.

(b) There are three principal **sources of funds** available for the financing of overseas operations.

(i) **Funds generated by the subsidiary** itself, ie retained earnings and depreciation. These are unlikely to be of much use in this situation since it appears from the cashflows that the project requires a single large investment at the outset. However, retained earnings may be a significant source of working capital as the levels of activity increase in later years.

(ii) **Funds transferred from within the group**. These include:

(1) equity provided by the parent company;
(2) loans provided by the parent company;
(3) loans from other subsidiaries;
(4) timing and pricing of inter-company transactions.

This is an attractive method since no new capital is introduced and the capital structure of the group as a whole remains unaltered. In addition it may be possible to move funds so as to take advantage of the different tax regimes in the various countries in which the group operates.

(iii) **Funds from outside the group**:

(1) borrowing or new equity raised in the home country;
(2) borrowing or new equity raised in the local country;
(3) funds raised on the international financial markets.

Borrowing in the local country is often attractive because it provides a means of matching revenues with payments and thereby minimising the level of exchange rate exposure. However, the relative costs of finance from alternative sources must be compared with the likely effect on the overall costs of the project arising from movements in the exchange rates.

Before deciding to borrow in the Scandinavian currency, the institute should attempt to evaluate the **likely relative movements in sterling**, the Eastasia $ and the Scandinavian currency over the life of the project. If the value of the EA$ falls, then both the interest costs and the cost of repayment will become relatively more expensive, and this must be evaluated against the savings in interest costs. The institute should also consider the ease with which currency can be remitted out of Eastasia. If there are **exchange control restrictions**, then local borrowing may become relatively more attractive since the size of remittances to the UK and/or to Scandinavia will be reduced.

A further consideration is the likely future movements in Scandinavian interest rates relative to those in the UK and the other capital markets.

54 OVERSEAS INVESTMENT

Pass marks. Parts (b) and (c) are fairly complex since a number of different cash flows are involved. It is helpful to isolate the main types (import to Hungary, local transactions, and exports to other countries).

Other points. Bear in mind that if the subsidiary is profitable, then one of the major transactions will be remittances of profit back to the UK.

(a) (i) Since the forward rate for the Em against the $W is lower than the spot rate, the implication is that the Eastland interest rate is lower than that in Westland. This is based on the **interest rate parity theory**, which states that in equilibrium the difference in interest rates between two countries is equal to the difference between the forward and the spot rates. The Eastland interest rate can be estimated as follows.

Day 1	1.0000 Em buys	0.4825 $W
Day 90	interest at 9.5%	0.0113 $W
	Total value	0.4938 $W

This is now worth 1.0215 Em (at 0.4834). The annualised Eastland interest rate is therefore 8.7% (0.0215 × 365/90).

(ii) If the forward rate was 0.4795 $W/Em, then the total value in the above calculations would become 1.0298 Em (0.4938/0.4795). The annualised Eastland interest rate is therefore 12.09%.

(iii) If the interest rate in Eastland is 8%, then the total value of the money in $W is 0.4938, and in Em is 1.0197. This implies a forward rate of 0.4843 $W/Em.

(b) (i) The new subsidiary will be incurring costs for raw materials and management denominated in sterling. It will be receiving income from sales denominated in HUF and other eastern European currencies. If the HUF weakens against the pound, this will make its raw material and management costs relatively more expensive. At the same time, if the HUF weakens against other eastern European countries, this will make its exports to these areas relatively cheaper. The weakening HUF will also mean that remittances to the UK will be subject to exchange losses.

One of the most effective ways to **hedge** is to ensure that receipts and payments in different currencies are, so far as is possible, in balanced amounts. By transferring production to Hungary, the company is improving the extent to which matching is achieved since a significant proportion of the labour costs as well as other expenses are now denominated in local currency. However, there is still likely to be some imbalance.

In terms of **financing the venture**, relatively few assets need to be acquired locally. The decision on whether to lease or buy the buildings will depend on the relative costs of the different options, the availability of funds, and the relative costs of borrowing in the UK and in Hungary. However, it is likely that some form of lease will be appropriate since this will allow the company to retain flexibility as well as providing another opportunity for the matching of receipts and payments denominated in HUF.

(ii) The company has a number of options available to it in detailed terms when it comes to hedging its foreign exchange risk. In the event of the HUF weakening, these will all involve some method of borrowing HUF and depositing sterling. Specific techniques include the use of **forward exchange contracts** if the size of the transactions are known in advance with reasonable certainty, or the use of **options** or **futures contracts**.

(c) The cash flows which arise locally (sales revenues, labour and overhead costs excluding management) would have been unaffected by the devaluation. Those costs which arose in the UK (management and raw materials) would have become cheaper. The value of remittances to the UK would also have increased on the devaluation.

The effect of these movements means that the group would have been in the best position had it not entered into any hedging transactions but simply taken advantage of favourable exchange rate movements. If it wished to continue to have some protection against a weakening of the HUF, then the best solution would have been to take out option contracts. These allow advantage to be taken of favourable exchange rate movements at the same time as hedging against unfavourable movements. However the cost of this approach would need to be taken into account since options are one of the most expensive forms of hedge on the market.

55 CANADA

> **Pass marks**. Both the calculations and the discussion are straightforward, and are well established questions in this paper. The adjusted discount rate is computed in the same manner as converting a real discount rate to a nominal one.
>
> **Examiner's comments.** The question was well answered by those who attempted it. The most common fault was the inability to compute the adjusted discount rate.

(a) **Method (i)**

Year	*0*	*1*	*2*	*3*	*4*
Investment C$'000	(150)				50
After tax cash flows C$'000		60	60	60	45
Net cash C$'000	(150)	60	60	60	95
Exchange rate	1.700	1.785	1.874	1.968	2.066
Net cash £'000	(88.24)	33.61	32.02	30.49	45.98
14% discount factors	1.000	0.877	0.769	0.675	0.592
PV in £'000	(88.24)	29.48	24.62	20.58	27.22
NPV in £'000	**13.66**				

Method (ii)

Adjusted discount rate: equivalent discount rate in C$, allowing for 5% appreciation of the pound, is given by 1 + r = 1.14, × 1.05 = 1.197. Discount rate = 19.7%.

Year	*0*	*1*	*2*	*3*	*4*
Net cash C$'000	(150)	60	60	60	95
19.7% discount factors	1.000	0.835	0.698	0.583	0.487
PV C$'000	(150)	50.10	41.88	34.98	46.27
NPV C$'000	23.23				
Exchange rate	1.700				
NPV £'000	**13.66**				

The adjusted discount rate is computed in the same way as a nominal discount rate is computed from a real discount rate and an inflation rate.

To provide a 14% rate on return in UK and to cope with a 5% annual strengthening of the pound, a dollar invested in Canada would have to grow by 14% to $1.14 and by a further 5% to $1.14 × 1.05 = $1.197. In other words it would have to show a rate of return of 19.7%. The company's cost of capital, translated into Canadian dollars is therefore 19.7%.

In a system of free floating exchange rates, if the C$ depreciates by 5% per year against sterling, the cost of borrowing in C$ is likely to be about 5% more expensive than borrowing in sterling.

(b) The decision to finance a foreign investment by borrowing in the foreign country's currency is influenced by a number of factors, including:

(i) the ability of the foreign borrowings to act as a currency hedge against currency risk;

(ii) the cost of the foreign borrowings compared with borrowing in the home currency;

(iii) other factors, including political risk.

For any income-generating foreign investment there is a risk that the foreign currency depreciates, resulting in a reduced value of income when converted to the home currency. If, however, borrowings are taken out in the same currency as that in which the income is generated, then the reduced income is at least partially offset by reduced loan interest costs. It should be noted, however, that this hedging effect also reduces the chances of currency gains: if the foreign currency appreciates, then the increased value of income is offset by an increased loan interest cost when converted to the home currency.

In the example, the Canadian dollar steadily devalues against the pound. Borrowing in Canadian dollars would therefore enable currency risk to be managed better than if borrowing is arranged in sterling. However, in a system of free floating exchange rates, if the C$ depreciates by 5% per year against sterling, the cost of borrowing in C$ is likely to be about 5% more expensive than borrowing in sterling. This increased interest cost will take away the advantage of the devaluation of the C$ loan. If currencies always moved in predictable ways, there would be little advantage in financing the Canadian investment with a Canadian loan. However, currency devaluations can sometimes be unexpected and much larger than predicted. It is to prevent these *unexpected* losses that hedging using a foreign loan is recommended.

The cost of foreign loans may be higher than the theoretical equivalent cost of a domestic loan because the company does not have such a good credit standing in the foreign country. Better rates may be obtained from the euromarkets or by arranging a currency loan swap. Care should be taken to match the duration of the loan with the expected duration of the project (4 years in this question), unless further foreign investments are anticipated. A further consideration is the availability of tax savings on the loan interest. The effect on the company's overall tax charge needs to be included in the decision process.

For countries with high political risk, which may impose exchange controls, or even expropriate assets, borrowing in the local currency is recommended to offset investment losses which might result from political action.

56 SWISS MULTINATIONAL

Pass marks. The first part of the question requires an understanding of the difference between transaction risk and translation risk in foreign currency accounting. It is helpful to think in terms of the overall restrictions that are applied to a company's ability to borrow, rather than the size of individual loans.

Part (a)(ii) requires a discussion of internal hedging techniques. You should take into account the fact that the company is operating in a specifically European context when setting out your suggestions.

Part (b) involves some straightforward calculations of the effects of currency investments. The subsequent discussion requires an outline knowledge of the purchasing power parity theory as applied to exchange rates.

(a) (i) **Translation risk** arises from differences in the currencies in which assets and liabilities are denominated. If a company has different proportions of its assets and liabilities denominated in particular currencies, then exchange rate movements are likely to have varying effects on the value of these assets and liabilities. However, although the value of these different elements within the balance sheet may vary, no cash flow effects arise from translation, and thus the MD is correct in identifying this as an accounting issue that should not normally require hedging.

The MD further suggests that hedging may become necessary if the company is close to its foreign currency borrowing limits. If the company has foreign currency borrowings, the absolute amount of such loans will be unaffected by translation, since both loan and interest will be denominated in the foreign currency. However, a problem could arise if the company has a high level of overall borrowings. If the sterling value of the borrowings exceeds a certain proportion of the sterling value of its assets, then the directors could be in breach of the Articles of Association and also in breach of any covenants on its borrowings. If such covenants are breached, then it is likely that a higher rate of interest will become payable.

(ii) The MD is correct in identifying the use of the forward market as a potential hedging tool for transaction risk. There are also a number of arguments that can be used to support a strategy of not hedging as follows.

- A certain level of risk is acceptable.
- The costs of hedging may outweigh the benefits.
- Currency gains and losses balance out in the long run.
- Hedging could mean that the opportunity to take advantage of currency gains is foregone.

Internal hedging strategies that could be used include the following.

- Negotiating with customers and suppliers to improve the opportunities for **matching** currency receipts and payments. This involves attempting to balance receipts and payments in a given currency so as to minimise transaction risk. In practice, this could mean that the currencies in which some supplier and customer invoices are denominated may have to change.
- Changing the timing of receipts and payments so as to optimise the level of matching achieved.
- The company currently trades throughout Europe. If there is a particular country which takes the majority of the sales, then the company could consider setting up a manufacturing plant in that country, thus increasing the proportion of the manufacturing costs denominated in the currency in which the goods are sold.

A further hedging approach after 1 January 19X9 could be to denominate all sales and purchases as far as possible in Euros, and to denominate loans in Euros as well so as to reduce the level of currency exposure.

(b) **Option 1: invest in US$**

This involves keeping the receipt in US$ and investing it in a one-year US$ bond at 7.625%. At the end of the year the interest receivable would be $76,250, giving a total value for the investment of $1,076,250. Since it is known that this amount will be receivable at the end of the year, the currency risk can be hedged by selling that amount of US$ forward at the 12-month forward rate of SFr 1.275 to US$1. The total value of the investment at the end of the year in Swiss francs would therefore be **SFr 1,372,219**.

Option 2: invest in Swiss francs

The first stage in this option is to convert the receipt from US$ to SFr at the current spot rate of SFr 1.3125 to US$1, giving a sum of SFr 1,312,500. This will then be invested in a one-year Swiss Franc bond with a yield of 4.5625%. The total value of the investment at the end of the year will therefore be **SFr 1,372,383** (SFr 1,312,500 × 1.045625).

The reason that there is so little difference between the expected yields on the two options can be attributed to the link that exists between exchange rates and interest rates. The forward rate equates to the spot rate adjusted for the difference between interest rates in the two countries, and can be estimated using the **purchasing power parity theory**. Therefore, there is little advantage to be gained in denominating the deposit in a different currency if the sum is required in the base currency at the end of the term.

57 SWAPS

> **Pass marks**. The first part of the question requires a clear definition of the nature and uses of swaps, as well as their relevance to a company in the specific situation described.
>
> In the second part of the question you should remember that you are writing for the benefit of a non-accountant, and you should therefore express yourself in a way that is accessible to such a reader, avoiding the excessive use of technical language.
>
> **Examiner's comment**. Credit was given to those candidates who managed to relate their answer for part (a) to the short scenario in the question, ie to a company just beginning to trade internationally. A detailed discussion of the three main types of exchange risk (economic, translation and transaction) was not required for part (b), although credit was given if the candidate linked the answer to the scenario.

(a) **Interest rate swaps** are transactions that exploit different interest rates in different markets for borrowing, to reduce interest costs for either fixed or floating rate loans. Such a swap is an arrangement whereby two parties, either two companies or a company and a bank, exchange their interest rate commitments. However each party retains its obligations to the original lenders which means that the parties must accept counterparty risk.

One of the principal benefits to an international company is that it may be able to take advantage of the differences between interest rates in the countries in which it trades. It may also mean that it can gain access to cheaper funds in a different capital market, even though it is little known and would normally have to pay a higher rate of interest if it tried to raise funds directly in that market.

In a **currency swap**, the parties agree to swap equivalent amounts of currency for a given period. This effectively involves the exchange of debt from one currency to another. As with interest rate swaps, liability on the principal is not transferred and the parties are liable to counterparty risk.

Both types of swap are easy to arrange and are flexible since they can be arranged in any size and are reversible. The only transaction costs incurred are legal fees and there is no commission or premium to be paid.

The main benefit to a fast growing company is that it gains **access to debt finance in another country and currency** where it is little known and consequently has a poorer credit rating than in its home country. Where a company is trading overseas, a swap will allow it to restructure the currency base of its liabilities so as to reduce its exchange rate exposure. It may also allow the company to match its liquidity in different currencies more closely to its operating requirements, thus reducing its needs to make additional borrowings in certain currencies.

It should be noted that both types of swap can alternatively be used as a means of **financial speculation,** and that if companies choose to act in this way they will expose themselves to a much higher degree of financial risk. It is therefore recommended that, particularly for a company that is only just beginning to trade internationally, any activity in the financial futures markets is very closely controlled and used only for specific hedging purposes. If staff in the company have little experience of international finance, then it may be more appropriate for them to begin by using some of the simpler hedging instruments such as forward exchange contracts, before moving on to more complex procedures such as swaps.

(b) REPORT

To: Managing Director
From: Treasurer Date: 19 November 19X6
Subject: Foreign exchange rate management for German imports

The purpose of this report is to discuss the points raised in your recent memo concerning the minimisation of our **exchange rate risk** in respect of our German imports. The points you raise can be addressed as follows.

(i) Our present policy of taking out **forward contracts** gives us the advantage of fixing our future liabilities and eliminating the risk of a large movement in exchange rates before payments become due. We therefore know exactly what our future commitments are going to be. Although it is possible that on some occasions we might save money by waiting and buying at spot when the funds are required, we also run the risk that rates could move against us and increase our costs.

(ii) The financial effect of buying Deutschmarks now and placing them on deposit for twelve months would be similar to our existing policy of using forward contracts. Although we might gain on the exchange rate, we would lose on the interest rates since the rate we would receive on the deposit in Deutschmarks would be less than that which we would forego on the Sterling deposits.

(iii) Although borrowing Deutschmarks to pay off our Sterling loans would reduce our interest rate liabilities, if Sterling depreciates against the Deutschmark as expected, then our capital commitment on the Deutschmark loan would increase. Thus the two effects would tend to cancel each other out.

All of these points demonstrate the fact that there is, in the medium to long term, a relationship between the relative rates of interest in different countries and their exchange rates. This is sometimes referred to as the **purchasing power parity theory**. If one country has a higher interest rate than another, then market pressures will mean that the currency of the former is likely to depreciate against that of the latter. This effect can be seen in its more extreme form in the case of some Latin American countries where there are very high rates of interest and inflation, and where the currency is depreciating relatively fast against the more stable European currencies.

Although our current policy is to use forward contracts to hedge our exchange rate exposure on the German contracts, there are in fact a number of alternative instruments that we could consider, such as the use of currency futures, and I would be delighted to discuss these with you further should you feel this to be helpful.

Signed: Treasurer

58 FREIMARKS

> **Examiner's comment**. Some pre-planning of the answer to part (a) is desirable. You are not told enough about the group to recommend a specific method, so you must write in more general terms, making clear what further information would be needed in order to select the best method.

(a) Likely future exchange rates should be considered. If it could be predicted that changes in the rate were very likely to be favourable, there would be little point in protecting the group against risk. However, as the rate has been very volatile, it is very unlikely that such a prediction can be made. Some protection against future adverse fluctuations is almost certainly desirable.

Likely future cash flows, beyond the next six months, should be considered. It may be that there will be a clear trend in net receipts or payments, which can be taken account of in devising a strategy.

The position of any other companies in the group may give opportunities for protection. If other companies have business denominated in the Freimark or in any other currencies which move in line with the Freimark, receipts by one company might be netted off against payments by another.

The group's own resources may limit the options available. Temporary funding is needed for several methods of protection, and specialised skills are needed for some methods. Such skills can of course be obtained by relying on a bank's services, but at a price.

Finally, the group's approach to **risk** should be considered. It may be that potential losses are not large enough to be of real concern, or that the directors prefer to take risks to obtain the chance of high rewards. On the other hand, the directors may prefer to take every opportunity to minimise risk.

(b) **Three techniques of exposure management**

(i) The company could **open a Freimark bank account**, possibly making an initial deposit so as to avoid having an overdraft in months 2 and 3. All transactions would be conducted through this account. Any planned withdrawals for conversion into sterling could be protected by forward exchange contracts.

(ii) **Forward exchange contracts** could be entered into for each of the next six months. For example, the company could contract with a bank now for the conversion of Fm 2,400,000 into sterling at the end of month 1, at a pre-arranged rate. As the cash flow forecasts may prove to be inaccurate, forward option contracts may be appropriate. These are binding contracts, but with some flexibility as to the completion date.

(iii) The company could use **leading and lagging**. This involves timing receipts and payments so as to take advantage of exchange rate movements. For example, if a payment in Freimarks is required, the currency should be bought and the payment made when sterling is strong against the Freimark.

(c) **Economic exposure** is the risk that a business's value and competitiveness will suffer through the impact of exchange rate movements on its future cash flows.

Transaction exposure arises on individual transactions, whereas economic exposure may affect the prosperity of a business for several years into the future.

A company may be affected by exchange rate movements in several ways. The domestic currency value of its receipts will clearly be affected directly. The company's competitive position in foreign markets will suffer if the domestic currency strengthens, though on the other hand imports will be cheaper, as will future capital investment overseas.

Economic exposure should be assessed using any available information, but long-term forecasts are unreliable. Simulation techniques may be needed to assess the level of risk.

59 X AND Y

> **Examiner's comment**. Few candidates attempted this question and those who did wasted time in explaining the advantages of the co-operation that the two companies were considering. Part (a) asked candidates to consider two different organisation structures. There was no mention as to whether XY (International) Limited was to be a holding or a trading company as it was hoped that candidates would bring this into their answers.

(a) Establishing a new company XY (International) is likely to involve more **set-up costs** such as legal expenses than the alternative of an exchange of shares. Furthermore, there could be complications regarding the **domicile** of a new company. Different domiciles will have different taxation implications and may also affect the ability of the company to remit dividends to its shareholders. Such implications will need to be considered in coming to a decision on the most advantageous arrangement.

The transfer option could be preferred under UK tax legislation because individual shareholders' translation gains would not be subject to tax liability at the time of exchange if no disposal of interest were involved.

XY (International) might be operated as a holding company or as a trading company. In either case, existing managements would continue to operate in the respective countries. There would need to be a single board of directors, presenting the possibility of difficulties in all parties reaching agreement, including on such matters as the level of distribution of profits and dividends. If XY (International) operated as a holding company this might offer the best prospect of dismantling the merger if that proved to be necessary.

Under either type of arrangement, there would need to be some **sacrifice of control** by each management team in the operations in their own country as they will need to take note of the views of the other management team.

Under the proposal to transfer shares on a 50/50 basis, neither side would have a voting majority. This could lead to difficulties if it did not prove to be possible to agree on operational issues (for example, on a capital expenditure project), and the businesses could each develop in very different ways.

(b) The arrangement involved here is effectively an **exchange of debt,** and will only be possible if covenants or other requirements are not breached. The exchange of risk will introduce currency exchange implications. The loan stock held by the UK company would bear a smaller return if the rand were to weaken in value and vice versa. The loan stock exchange would, however, help to demonstrate mutual confidence between the two companies.

There would be certain effects on the balance sheet of X Limited. The loan stock held in Y would be reflected in fixed assets, while the loan stock repayable to Y would be shown as other long term liabilities. In the profit and loss account, interest receivable from Y would appear as other income, while interest charges payable to Y would also be shown. There would be an increase in the apparent gearing of the company because of the higher level of debt.

(c) **Control of remittances** by a government is a form of exchange control which stops the currency being fully convertible. Such measures imposed by government as a form of protection in order to rectify, or avoid, a balance of payments deficit and to prevent a depreciation in the nation's currency. Such controls were imposed in 1939 in the UK as a wartime measure and the last controls were finally abolished in 1979. Exchange controls are discouraged by the OECD but are still imposed by many developing countries.

The foreign investor will suffer from the problem that it will be difficult to **'repatriate' dividends** from the investment. Faced with this difficulty, the investor may respond in different ways. If the investor is less concerned about the flow of dividends, he may not see the controls as a major impediment, but ultimately the value of the investment must depend upon the ability to receive distributions of profits. One response of the foreign investor is to avoid investments in countries in which controls over remittances exist. This could hamper investment in the local economy but on the other hand it may allow local entrepreneurs to operate more easily. However, this may mean that enterprises in the country are less efficient than they would be if there was foreign competition, to the possible detriment of consumers in the country.

Another possible response of the foreign investor is to find ways of avoiding the exchange controls, for example by seeking returns through **royalties** or by setting **transfer prices** for part-processed goods at non-market levels. The government exerting the controls will have to close such 'loopholes' through further control and regulation if it wants the controls to have an effect.

60 OJ LTD

Pass marks. The first part of this question is a straightforward computation illustrating how exchange controls can delay the repatriation of cash from foreign investments. Part (b) requires knowledge of the relationship between forward rates and spot rates and the workings of currency swaps as well as posing an interesting discussion on whether exchange control risk should affect the discount rate used in investment appraisal. All three statements in part (b) merit at least 6 marks to do justice to the discussion, so a knowledgeable student would have been hard-pressed to finish this question in time.

Examiner's comments. Most candidates did well on part (a) and reasonably well on part (b) although many failed to link their discussion to the specific circumstances of OJ Limited. The second statement in part (b) (about the discount rate) was the least well answered.

(a) (i) **OJ Limited: Joint venture NPV**

Assumption 1: exchange controls in operation

Year	*Project cash*	*OJ's 50% share*	*Cash repatriated*	*Exchange rate*		*Discount factor*	*PV*
	SA$'000	SA$'000	SA$'000	SA$/£	£'000	*16%*	£'000
0					(450.00)	1.000	(450.0)
1	4,250	2,125	1,062.5	10	106.25	0.862	91.6
2	6,500	3,250	1,625.0	15	108.33	0.743	80.5
3	8,350	4,175	6,862.5	21	326.79	0.641	209.5
		9,550	9,550.0				(68.4)

Assumption 2: removal of exchange controls

Year	*Project cash* SA$ '000	*OJ's 50% share* SA$ '000	*Cash repatriated* SA$ '000	*Exchange rate* SA$/£	£'000	*Discount factor 16%*	*PV* £'000
0					(450.00)	1.000	(450.0)
1	4,250	2,125	2,125	10	212.50	0.862	183.2
2	6,500	3,250	3,250	15	216.67	0.743	161.0
3	8,350	4,175	4,175	21	198.81	0.641	127.4
							21.6

(ii) Based solely on these calculations, the joint venture should only proceed if restrictions on repatriation of profits are lifted.

(b) **Reliability of forward rates as predictors of spot rates in the future**

A **forward rate** is a rate agreed today at which currency will be exchanged on an agreed future date. Forward rates offered by banks are calculated from today's spot exchange rate and the fixed interest rate in each currency for the period in question. Because these rates are known with certainty, the forward rate can be fixed with accuracy: any variation from the computed rate would allow speculators to engage in risk-free arbitrage between the money markets and currency markets.

In a **floating exchange rate system**, the spot rate in the future is dependent on many economic factors affecting supply and demand for the currency, not just current factors but new events that arise between now and the future date. Factors include balance of payments, capital investment cash flows, interest rates, inflation rates and actions by speculators. The future spot rate is therefore subject to enormous uncertainty, higher in some currencies than others.

Nevertheless, if the forward rate was consistently different from the **future spot rate** in one direction (eg consistently higher) the actions of arbitrageurs would tend to remove the difference. Hence **expectations theory** says that the forward rate will be an **unbiased predictor** of the expected value of the future spot rate. In other words, the future spot rate is just as likely to be above the forward rate as below it.

This is, however, completely different from saying that the forward rate is a reliable or accurate predictor of the spot rate. It clearly is *not a reliable predictor* because of the uncertainty in events which might arise between now and the future date. This is particularly likely to be true in a volatile currency such as the South American one in this question.

Should a higher discount rate be used when there are exchange controls?

The discount rate of 16% is assumed to allow for the time value of money and the normal business risk of the investment but not for the risk of exchange controls being retained. Since the company is not a public limited company and shareholders are probably undiversified, they are assumed to be concerned with total risk, not just systematic risk, and exchange controls are therefore a relevant risk which must be accounted for.

To allow for the uncertainty of exchange controls, consider **two contrasting techniques**, as follows.

(i) The cash flows are evaluated assuming there are no exchange controls (Assumption 2) and the discount rate is increased to allow for the uncertainty in the timing of the cash flows because of exchange controls. This would be a valid, but crude, way of tackling the problem.

(ii) Two scenarios are postulated, one with exchange controls and one without, as in the question. Both are discounted at 16% to allow for business risk, but the discount rate does not need to be increased to allow for exchange control risk, which is already being allowed for by the delayed cash flows in Assumption 1. (When delayed cash flows are discounted, there will automatically be a lower NPV). This method, used in the question, is valid and more detailed than the alternative method.

What is *not* valid is to postulate the scenario with delayed cash flows and in addition to increase its discount rate. This would be double-counting the exchange control risk. We conclude that the method used in the question is valid.

Can a currency swap help to minimise the exchange rate risk?

In a currency swap two parties lend each other agreed amounts of different currencies for a given time, the loans being repaid at the end of this period. This has the effect of fixing the exchange rate in advance for the repayment date and therefore reduces currency risk.

For example, OJ Limited could lend £450,000 sterling to a swap partner and at, say, 10 SA$ = £1, the swap partner lends SA$ 4.5 million to OJ which is used to invest in the project. Both parties charge interest on the loans. OJ pays the interest on its SA$ loan out of the earnings from its share of the project. At the end of the project both parties repay the loans. OJ receives its £450,000 and repays SA$ 4.5 million, which is cheap compared with the expected exchange rate of SA$21 = £1.

Of course there are no 'free gifts' in foreign exchange and the interest paid on OJ's loan in SA$ will probably be significantly higher than the interest it receives on its sterling loan. In addition, the swap exchange rate may well be higher than 10. These factors are subject to negotiation between the parties.

OJ must also consider the risk that its swap partner defaults on repayment or that exchange controls prevent the receipt of interest on its sterling loan. There will also be commission to pay to the intermediary which arranged the swap.

Given that there is a forward market for the SA$ then currency risk can be hedged sufficiently without using a swap. As this is OJ's first venture into South America, forward contracts may be easier to manage.

61 DOBSON LTD

Pass marks. The question covers working capital management, sources of finance and foreign currency risk management. In part (a) it is necessary to see the quickest way of generating the figures in order to complete them in time. Part (b) is a report which is best answered using as headings the three bullet points given in the question by the examiner. Part (c) is a standard discussion on foreign exchange risk.

Examiner's comments. Parts (a) and (b) were not done well. Figures in part (a) were presented poorly. The report in part (b) was often unstructured, without subheadings. Sources of funds suggested were often only applicable to much larger companies. Part (c) was much better answered, though sometimes candidates spent too long on this part, at the expense of the rest of the question.

(a) 31 March 19X9

Sales for the year:	£2,100,000
Debtors:	£163,400

Debtor days: 163,400/2,100,000 × 365 = 28.4 days.

Pass marks. March 19X9 debtors can also be calculated from the detailed data given. However, that approach would take too much time for the marks available. In your own time, you may care to check that the figures reconcile.

31 March 20X0

Alternative 1: continue existing policies

Sales rise to £2,400,000. If there is no change in policy, debtors will rise in proportion, and debtor days will remain at 28.4 days.

> **Pass marks.** Again you could calculate this from the detailed data given, but there is no point, under exam conditions.

Alternative 2: factoring

Sales = £2,500,000: home (70%) £1,750,000, overseas (30%) £750,000

It is assumed that 85% of home debtors are paid immediately by the factor. Outstanding home debtors are 15% × £1,750,000 × 30 days/365 = £21,575.

Overseas debtors: 80% is owing for 60 days after the deposit of 20% is paid.
80% × £750,000 × 60/365 = £98,630.

Total debtors = £21,575 + £98,630 = £120,205.

Debtor days = 120,205/2,500,000 = 17.5 days.

Alternative 3: Invoice discounting

There is no change in credit management policy. Debtor days remains at 28.4 days.

(i) *Forecast overdraft balance at 31 March 19Y0*

	£
Sales (home £1.75m, overseas £0.75m)	2,500,000
Prompt payment discounts: 50% × 1.5% × £1.75m)	(13,125)
Cost of sales: 40% × £2.5m	(1,000,000)
Other cash expense payments	(750,000)
Tax, dividends, etc	(700,000)
Bad debts: 1% × £1.75m	(17,500)
Debtor increase (W1)	(31,124)
Creditor reduction (W2)	(21,712)
Operational cash flow	(33,461)
Balance at 31.3.X9	(135,000)
Balance at 31.3.Y0, before interest	(168,461)

The above calculation does not include interest on the overdraft, which will be at 5% over base rate (ie 11%) up to a limit of £150,000, and at 2% more (ie 13%) above that. Since the £150,000 limit will be passed approximately halfway through the year, a rough estimate of interest is 11% × £150,000 × 6/12 + 13% × £168,461 × 6/12 = £19,200.

The closing overdraft balance is approximately £168,461 + £19,200 = £187,661.

> **Examiner's comment.** Any simple approximation for interest calculation would be acceptable.

Workings

1

	£
Debtors 31.3.X9	163,400
Debtors at 31.3.Y0: 163,400 × 2.5m/2.1m	194,524
Increase	31,124

2

	£
Creditors 31.3.X9	145,000
Creditors 31.3.Y0: 1m × 45/365	123,288
Reduction	21,712

(iii) **Alternative 2 (factoring) compared with alternative 1**

	£
Saving in discounts	13,125
Factor's commission: 2% × 85% × £1.75m	(29,750)
Elimination of bad debts (non-recourse factoring): 85% × £17,500	14,875
Administration saving	25,000
Redundancy cost	(35,000)
Reduction in debtors at 31.3.Y0: 194,524 – 120,205	74,319
Improved cash flow, before interest saving	62,569
Interest saved (approx.) 12% × 62,659	7,519
Incremental improvement in cash flow	70,088

Alternative 3 (invoice discounting) compared with alternative 1

	£
Loan raised on security of debtors: 90% × 194,524	175,072
Interest saving: approx. 12% – 10% = 2% × 175,072	3,501
Incremental improvement in cash flow	178,573

(b) To: Board of Directors, Dobson Ltd
From: Accountant
Date: 25 May 19X9

Report on working capital policy

The company is predicting an increase in sales for the period to 31 March 19Y0, which will increase the requirement for financing debtors. At the same time we are planning to pay our creditors more promptly than at present (45 days, compared with the current 63 days – see Appendix). Although no stock increases have been budgeted for, this may be unrealistic in the light of the sales increases. The budget may need to be reworked taking into account increased stock levels. Overall, the result will be a significant increase in working capital financing requirement.

In general, our management of debtors is sound, with an average payment period of 28 days, compared with the 45 days we are intending to take as credit from suppliers. The main point of discussion is the best way of financing the increased working capital requirement.

Advantages and disadvantages of the three financing methods

(i) **Continue existing policy**

The bank overdraft is a simple, transparent, flexible financing arrangement, which allows borrowings to increase in seasonal periods of high sales, and decrease in periods where sales are lower. Its main disadvantage is that it will become expensive if we exceed our agreed limit. This results in a continual need to renegotiate in a period when sales are expanding rapidly. Because of our increased sales projections and sound debtors management policy, we are unlikely to encounter difficulties in raising the overdraft limit, and should immediately start negotiations with the bank. There is no reason why the interest rate should be increased if we can demonstrate that the bank will not suffer increased default risk, but we may be asked to accept gearing or current ratio restrictions.

(ii) **Factoring**

Factoring has several advantages:

- reduces administration time and costs
- removes the risk of bad debts
- speeds up cash from debtors

- automatically provides finance varying with the size of sales, thus financing peaks and troughs of sales
- avoids the overdraft limit problem

Against this it has a number of drawbacks:

- the factor's fee needs careful negotiation: a fee based on level of services provided is more transparent than a percentage of turnover
- some customers object to debt factors
- our contact with customers may be reduced

(iii) **Invoice discounting**

This is a way of raising short-term loan finance on the security of debtors. In our case, the bank has agreed to lend us funds based on our average total debtors, rather than on the security of specific invoices. The advantage is that the interest rate is cheap. The disadvantage is that, unlike the overdraft or factoring arrangement, the loan is effectively fixed in amount, and interest will be charged even in seasonal periods when sales are low.

Effect on the company's debt capacity

The company's debt capacity is the amount which it is able to borrow. This will be based on a number of factors, including:

- assets available for security
- cash flow projections: size and stability
- underlying profitability and track record
- level of existing borrowings

In theory, the company's debt capacity is reduced by arrangement 2 (factoring) because the asset of debtors is reduced. However, the financial markets are sophisticated enough to see through the legal format of agreements such as factoring and invoice discounting and will view such arrangements as effectively part of existing borrowings. Any arguments for or against these methods presented on the basis of ratios such as liquidity or gearing are therefore usually invalid.

It is likely that there will be no significant differences between three methods when the company's debt capacity is concerned. The invoice discounting method will use up slightly more debt capacity in off-peak periods, because the suggested arrangement implies a loan of fixed amount.

Alternative financing methods

Expansion of sales and neglect of the effect on cash flow can cause the company to rely too much on short term finance. The three suggestions are all examples of this. Ideally the company's growth should be underpinned with longer term finance, which could be medium term bank loans or equity funds, depending in part on the company's existing gearing level.

Alternatives to bank loans would include leasing or hire purchase arrangements. Equity funds will normally be found by restricting dividend payouts and reinvesting the funds in the business. A rights issue is highly unlikely to be necessary. Alternatively, equity funds can be raised from outside investors who wish to take minority interests, possibly gaining tax advantages by doing this.

There is the possibility that funds can be released by reducing stock holdings, for example by introducing 'just in time' systems or operational improvements designed to reduce work in progress. However, such changes usually involve a significant initial investment, which would need to be financed by longer term funds.

Appendix: Creditor days in 19X9

Cost of sales = 40% × £2.1m = £840,000
Creditor days = 145,000/840,000 × 365 = 63 days

(c) **Implications of invoicing overseas customers in their own currency**

Sales invoicing in foreign currencies shifts exchange rate risk from the customer to the supplier. The advantages and disadvantages for Dobson Ltd are as follows.

Advantages

Demand for the company's products will increase for the following reasons.

- The number of potential customers increases.
- Pricing is more stable: currency fluctuations do not immediately cause price changes for customers.
- Customers avoid making transaction losses if the exchange rate moves between the date of purchase and the date of settlement of the debt.

Disadvantages

Dobson will have to accept the risks of exchange rate movement.

- Exchange losses can be made if the foreign currency weakens between the date of sale and the date of cash receipt (transaction exposure).
- It may be impossible to adjust prices upwards if the foreign currency weakens. This results in eroded profit margins (economic exposure).

Usefulness of foreign currency markets in managing overseas debtors

Foreign currency markets enable the company to hedge (that is, reduce) exchange rate transaction exposure and therefore to manage its cash flows more effectively. For example, a forward contract with a bank fixes the exchange rate in advance. If a debtor is expected to pay in a foreign currency in three months' time, the rate at which the cash can be exchanged at the bank can be agreed today, thus removing the uncertainty of exchange rate movements. Similarly, a currency option gives the holder the right to buy or sell currency at a given rate if it is to their advantage.

Before using these markets, however, the company must consider the following.

(i) Whether it wants to remove the risk. Hedging currency risk eliminates not only losses but potential currency gains.

(ii) The cost of using the currency instrument. Commission on forward contracts is likely to be too high to be worthwhile for small one-off transactions. Currency options have a non-refundable cost, even if they are not exercised. Such costs may have to be borne by the exported, or may be covered by increased sales prices.

(iii) The availability of the markets. The instruments are not available or many currencies.

Alternative methods not involving foreign currency markets

If the company imports and exports in the same foreign currency, it should open a bank account in that currency (if possible) so that receipts and payments are automatically netted off before conversion to the home currency.

A strategic decision may be made to source supplies from a country in which high sales are made, in order to reduce the currency exposure. It may also be worthwhile opening up a production facility in that country.

It is also possible to pass the exchange risk to other stakeholders such as employees or suppliers. For example, if a British company's major source of income is in euros, suppliers may be asked to invoice in euros and employees may be paid at least part of their remuneration at a rate based on the euro value.

62 SPEARHEAD

Pass marks. In part (b)(ii) the exchange rates could be calculated using either relative interest rates or inflation rates. Since inflation rates are available, this is the preferred method. In part (b)(iii) there are a variety of methods that could be used to calculate the return on assets. It is therefore most important that you state clearly the method that you have chosen, and that you calculate an annual rate as required, and not just an average rate for the contract.

When doing the calculations for Contract 2, there are no instructions as to how the penalty clause should be treated, and you should therefore explain your approach to this issue. If time permits, you could adjust the calculations to show the figures for the contract both including and excluding this item.

The report in the final section of the question accounts for 30 marks and you should therefore not neglect this at the expense of the calculation. You could structure your answer around the four sub-sections of the question, but if doing this, you must remember to discuss the non-financial factors and objectives as well as the financial areas.

Examiner's comment. In answer to part (a) of the question, a majority of candidates managed to comment on transaction, economic and political risk and make some reference to the problems of obtaining market data and betas for overseas investments. The cost of equity, exchange rate and NPV calculations for part (b) were generally done well, but there were also some very poor attempts.

Part (c) of the question could have been answered in general terms, if candidates had failed to answer part (b) or had arrived at figures they thought incorrect. However, very few candidates gained more than barely satisfactory marks for this section of the question.

(a) **International investment decisions** are based on exactly the same theory as domestic investment decisions, with cash flows being forecast and then discounted at an appropriate rate. However, there are a number of complicating factors:

- The expected movements in exchange rates over the life of the project.
- The relative tax positions in the different countries.
- The way in which funds will be transmitted to the home country.

The foreign investment decision involves two stages. The first stage is to determine whether the cash flows in the foreign country justify the project being undertaken. The second stage is to determine whether the cash flow remitted to the parent country justifies the cash invested from that country.

In terms of discount rates, although the company may be a multinational, it is effectively viewing itself as a UK company. It is judging its performance in terms of its group accounts denominated in sterling, and on the impact of these results on shareholders. Therefore the company will want a return on its investment that is at least equal to its opportunity cost of capital. For a multi-national, this will be based on the risk-free rate of return in its home country or on the world markets, plus a premium to cover risk. The CAPM is often used as a basis for these calculations.

The CAPM is based on three elements:

- **The beta factor,** which measures the systematic risk of the company, that is, the risk attaching to the company's operations that cannot be eliminated through diversification.
- **The risk-free rate of return** in the country in which the company operates.
- **The market rate of return** in the country in which the company operates.

Problems in using the model for international investment appraisal arise from the fact that where the company is raising funds and operating in a number of countries, it may be difficult to establish exactly what the risk-free and market rates of return are. Even within a country, the return on government securities (which is used to estimate the risk-free rate) varies according to their term to maturity, and the problems of estimation increase when the economic situation in more than one country has to be taken into account. Similarly it can be hard to estimate an equity beta for the operations of the firm as a whole. In practice, an international company will normally base its calculations on conditions in its home country, even though it may raise capital and operate in many different countries.

(b) (i) The cost of capital will be estimated using the CAPM. UK interest rates will be used in the calculations:

$$K_e = R_f + \beta(R_m - R_f)$$

where K_e = cost of equity capital
R_f = risk free rate of return (6%)
R_m = market rate of return (12%)
β = equity beta (1.5)

$$K_e = 6\% + 1.5(12\% - 6\%)$$
$$K_e = \mathbf{15\%}$$

(ii) The exchange rates can be estimated using purchasing power parity theory. This states that an exchange rate varies according to relative price changes, so that:

$$\text{'Old' exchange rate} \times \frac{\text{Price level in country A}}{\text{Price level in country B}} = \text{'New' exchange rate}$$

Deutschmarks/Sterling

Year 0 'spot' rate = 3.0 DM/£

	Opening rate	$\times \frac{1.02}{1.03}$	*Closing rate*
Year 1	3.0000		2.9709
Year 2	2.9709		2.9421
Year 3	2.9421		2.9135
Year 4	2.9135		2.8852

US dollars/Sterling

Year 0 'spot' rate = 1.6 $/£

	Opening rate	$\times \frac{1.04}{1.03}$	*Closing rate*
Year 1	1.6000		1.6155
Year 2	1.6155		1.6312
Year 3	1.6312		1.6470
Year 4	1.6470		1.6630

(iii) It is assumed that all cash flows arise at the end of the year.

Contract 1 cash flows

This contract will be discounted at the cost of equity of 15% since it is low risk.

	Year 0	*Year 1*	*Year 2*	*Year 3*	*Year 4*
Sales (DM million)		500	500	500	500
Exchange rate DM/£		2.9709	2.9421	2.9135	2.8852
Sales (£m)		168	170	172	173
Contract costs (£m)		(75)	(75)	(75)	(75)
Capital expenditure (£m)	(300)				
Residual value (£m)					50
Annual cash flow	(300)	93	95	97	148
15% discount factors	1.000	0.870	0.756	0.658	0.572
PV cash flow (£m)	(300)	81	72	64	85
Cumulative PV cash flow (£m)	(300)	(219)	(147)	(83)	2

The net present value of this contract at the end of four years is **£2m.**

The annual return on assets can be calculated using the annual accounting return after depreciation, and the average book value of assets for the year.

The annual depreciation charge will be £62.5m ((£300m – £50m)/4).

	Year 1	*Year 2*	*Year 3*	*Year 4*
	£m	£m	£m	£m
Opening asset value	300	238	175	113
Closing asset value	238	175	113	50
Average asset value	269	206	144	81
Sales	168	170	172	173
Contract costs	(75)	(75)	(75)	(75)
Depreciation	(63)	(63)	(63)	(63)
Accounting return	30	32	34	35
Annual return on assets	11.2%	15.5%	23.6%	43.2%

The average annual return on assets is **23.4%.**

Contract 2 cash flows

The first stage of this contract will be evaluated at the cost of capital plus a premium of 5% since this is a high risk project - effective discount rate 20%. The 10% penalty will also be included in this part of the calculations to give the worst case scenario.

The second stage of the contract will be evaluated at the low risk rate of 15%.

	Year 0	Year 1	Year 2	Year 3	Year 4	Year 5
Sales ($m) net of penalty	1,000		800			
Exchange rate $/£	1.6000		1.6312			
	£m	£m	£m	£m	£m	£m
Sales	625		490	200	200	200
Contract costs		(350)	(150)	(100)	(100)	(100)
Cost of lost business		(175)	(150)			
Contribution	625	(525)	190	100	100	100
Capital expenditure	(500)					
Net cash flow	125	(525)	190	100	100	100
20% discount factors	1.000	0.833	0.694			
15% discount factors				0.658	0.572	0.497
PV cash flow (£m)	125	(437)	132	66	57	50
Cumulative PV cash flow (£m)	125	(312)	(180)	(114)	(57)	(7)

The net present value of this contract at the end of five years is **£7m negative.**

If the penalty clause is excluded, the PV will rise by $200m × 0.694 ÷ 1.6312, = £85m, to **£78m positive.**

The annual return on assets can be calculated using the annual accounting return after depreciation, and the average book value of assets for the year.

For the purposes of calculation, the contribution in year 0 will be included with year 1.

The annual depreciation charge will be £100m ((£500m – £0m)/5))

	Year 1	Year 2	Year 3	Year 4	Year 5
	£m	£m	£m	£m	£m
Opening asset value	500	400	300	200	100
Closing asset value	400	300	200	100	0
Average asset value	450	350	250	150	50
Contribution	100	190	100	100	100
Depreciation	(100)	(100)	(100)	(100)	(100)
Accounting return	0	90	0	0	0
Annual return on assets	0.0%	25.7%	0.0%	0.0%	0.0%

The average annual return on assets is **5.1%**

If the penalty clause is excluded, the accounting return in Year 2 increases by £200 million to £290 million. £290m/350m = 82.9% annual return and the average annual return on assets is **16.6%.**

(c) To: Board of directors, Spearhead plc

From: Financial Manager

Date: 15 November 1998

Subject: Evaluation of potential contracts

This report deals with the financial evaluation of Contract 1 and Contract 2. In addition, it addresses the wider issue of the way in which risk has been incorporated into the evaluation, the problem of choosing between mutually exclusive projects, and methods available for hedging the risks that arise in the course of international trade.

Contract 1

This contract is classified as low risk and has therefore been evaluated at the cost of equity with no additional premium. It is a large project, with a four-year timespan, and requiring an initial investment of £300m. However, at the end of the four-year period it will only just exceed breakeven in NPV terms. Since all the sales income is denominated in deutschmarks, this means that the contract will be very sensitive to fluctuations in the exchange rate of the pound against the mark. Although it is forecast on the basis of relative inflation rates that the pound will weaken against the mark throughout the life of the contract, if sterling performs better than projected on the foreign exchanges, the contract is likely to show a negative NPV.

The other financial objective of Spearhead plc is to maintain an annual return on assets of 25%. While the absolute level of accounting returns remains relatively stable throughout the contract, the depreciating asset base means that the percentage return increases each year from 11.2% in year 1 to 43% in year 4. The rate of return only exceeds the target rate in the final year of the project, and the average return for the contract is 23.4%, which is a little below the target return on assets.

The main risk entailed in this contract is foreign exchange risk. Since the contract will be with a Western European government, political risk should be negligible. A further sensitivity arises in relation to the residual value of the capital equipment. If it proves impossible to realise £50m at the end of year 4, then this too could mean that the contract shows a negative NPV.

Contract 2

This contract carries a higher level of risk than Contract 1, with a level of political risk arising from the fact that the deal is with a government in a part of the world that is politically unstable. In addition, 50% of the payment does not fall due until the end of the second year of the contract. The contract has therefore been classified as carrying high levels of risk in the early stages, which have been evaluated at a discount rate with a premium of 5% to the cost of equity. The later, low risk stage has been evaluated at the cost of equity with no additional premium.

In financial terms, provided that Spearhead can deliver on time, the contract shows a positive NPV at the end of five years of £132m. However, the question of delivery is a major sensitivity, and if the penalty clause is invoked, then the NPV of the contract becomes £7m negative. The foreign exchange exposure is less than for contract 1, since all $ payments will be complete by the end of year 2, and 50% of the payments will be received at the start of the contract. However, there is still some risk that if the pound strengthens more than expected against the dollar, the value of the second instalment of the payment will be less than expected. Since the second stage of the contract is denominated entirely in sterling, there is no foreign exchange risk in years three to five.

Due to the high level of depreciation, and the unevenly phased nature of the payments, the contract only shows a positive return on assets in year 2. However, the average return over the life of the contract is only 16.6%, which is well below Spearhead's target rate of return.

Other factors

There are a number of **non-financial factors** that need to be considered, including the following.

(i) Both projects are large government contracts, and it is likely that there will be a good deal of prestige attaching to them. Spearhead should therefore consider whether it is worth accepting financial returns that are lower than the targets set in order to enhance the reputation and status of the company.

(ii) The second contract involves the use of state-of-the-art technology. If Spearhead needs to develop this technology in any case so as to maintain competitiveness, it may not be reasonable to allocate the full cost of development to this contract.

(iii) The allocation of design staff to Contract 2 will result in the loss of other business. Although the incremental cash flows have been taken into account, the company should also look in more detail at the financial performance of the alternative projects that will be foregone, both in NPV and ROI terms.

(iv) The company should consider which of these contracts contributes the most to the Spearhead's objective of becoming the UK's leading supplier of airport control equipment within the next ten years.

The treatment of risk

In this evaluation, the problem of differing levels of risk has been dealt with by adding a pre-determined premium to the cost of equity for each project, depending on its risk classification. This method recognises that risky investments ought to earn a higher return as reward for the risks that are taken, but the size of the risk premium is chosen arbitrarily. Other techniques that could be applied include the following.

(i) **Applying a time limit to the payback period.** Estimates of future cash flows are difficult to make at the best of times, and estimates of cash flows several years ahead are quite likely to be inaccurate. A method of limiting the risk on a project is to apply a payback time limit, so that a project should bot be undertaken unless it pays back within a given period. There are two ways of applying a payback time limit:

- A project might be expected to pay back within a certain time limit, and in addition show a positive NPV from its net cash flows.
- Alternatively, a project might be expected to pay back in DCF terms within a certain time period.

(ii) **Sensitivity analysis.** One method of applying sensitivity analysis tests to a project is to recalculate the NPV in a number of different situations. If the NPV is negative when costs are increased a little, or benefits are reduced a little, the project would be rejected on the grounds that it is too sensitive to variations in one or more key cost or revenue items.

(iii) **Certainty equivalent approach.** In this method, the expected cash flows of the project are converted to equivalent riskless amounts. The greater the risk of an expected cash flow, the smaller the certainty equivalent value (for receipts) or the larger the certainty equivalent value (for payments). One disadvantage of this approach is that the amount of the adjustment made to each cash flow is a subjective decision.

(iv) **Probability estimates of cash flows.** It may be possible to estimate a probability distribution of expected cash flows, and this may be used to calculate an expected value of the NPV. It can also be used to measure risk by calculating the worst possible outcome and its probability, and by calculating the probability that the project will fail to achieve a positive NPV.

(v) **Simulation models.** When project cash flows are given probability estimates, it might be more suitable to use simulation models to establish a probability distribution of the project's expected NPV, instead of simply calculating an expected value.

The problem of mutually exclusive projects

Both the NPV and the ROI approaches can be used as a basis for the comparison of mutually exclusive projects. However, the ROI approach runs into problems where the projects have unequal risk and unequal lives. In this situation, it is better to look at the risk-adjusted NPVs of the projects, and to choose the one with the greater NPV since this will add the most value to the company. In the situation under consideration, this would lead to Contract 2 being selected, given the provisos concerning risk and non-financial factors, already discussed.

Hedging the risks of international trade

The risks of international trade fall into three main categories.

(i) **Political risk.** This is the risk of political action by governments, which limit a company's freedom of action, for instance the introduction of exchange controls. There is little that can be done to hedge this risk – the company can only make a subjective judgement as to the safety or otherwise of entering into the contract.

(ii) **Economic risk.** This refers to the effect of exchange rate movements on the international competitiveness of a company. This arises in both of the contracts under consideration, since the contract costs are denominated in sterling, while the receipts are in foreign currency. Spearhead could look at the way in which it sources its raw materials to determine whether there is any scope for some level of matching of receipts and payments.

(iii) **Transaction risk.** This is the risk of adverse exchange rate movements occurring in the course of international trading transactions. Since the payments schedule is fixed for both of the contracts under consideration, Spearhead could look at the possibility of using currency hedges to reduce the level of exposure. Possibilities include the following.

- The use of forward exchange contracts to effectively fix the exchange rate at which the contract will be delivered.
- The use of option forward exchange contracts to limit the downside risk, but to allow the company to take advantage of any favourable movement in rates. This would be more expensive than a fixed contract.
- A money market hedge, borrowing an amount in the foreign currency at the start of the contract to be paid out of the receipts from the contract.

Conclusions

Neither of the two contracts meets all Spearhead's financial targets, although both can be justified in NPV terms. Contract 1 provides the safest option, and comes close to meeting the ROI target, and is therefore probably the preferred choice in financial terms. However, the final decision must take into account the non-financial factors discussed above, and a more detailed analysis of the various risks involved.

63 IBSEN

> **Pass marks**. In part (a) there are effectively three alternatives to discuss. You should take into account the particular situation faced by Ibsen plc when making your recommendations.
>
> In your report in part (b) you may find it helpful to structure your discussion of the issues in section (1) by considering the point of view of the shareholders separately from the point of view of the company.
>
> When calculating a possible issue price, you should remember that no new shares are being issued and that only a minority of the shares are being offered to the public. A number of approaches are possible to the question of an appropriate growth rate for use in the dividend valuation model, and your should make it clear how you have arrived at your estimate.
>
> The calculations in part (c) of the question are relatively straightforward, but you must remember the need to price in such a way as to make an issue, be it of debt or equity, attractive to potential investors. Once again, you will need to make assumptions about future performance, and you should therefore be careful to explain the reasons underlying your forecasts.
>
> Items to focus on in the discussion in the final section include the tax treatment of different types of capital, the attitude to risk of the company and the quality of the forecasts used. You should be able to make calculations to illustrate some of these issues.

(a) The main characteristics of the methods under consideration are as follows:

Private placing

This is an arrangement whereby the sponsoring market maker arranges for most of the issue to be bought at a fixed price by a small number of investors, usually (though not necessarily) institutional investors such as pension funds and insurance companies. This is a relatively cheap method of achieving a flotation, but is not suitable where a large number of shares are involved.

Offer for sale by fixed price

An offer for sale is a means of selling the shares of a company to the public at large. In a fixed price offer, a given number of shares are offered for sale at a price specified in advance by the company, this being the maximum price at which it is expected that the majority of the shares will be taken up. Since there is a risk that a proportion of the shares will remain unsold, such an offer is normally underwritten by institutions who undertake to purchase any unsold shares in return for a commission.

Offer for sale by tender

It is often difficult to decide upon the price at which the shares should be offered, and the use of an offer for sale by tender attempts to ensure that the issue price reflects the value of the shares as perceived by the market. A minimum price will be fixed and subscribers will be invited to tender for shares at prices equal to or above the minimum. The shares will then be allotted at the highest price at which they will all be taken up (the striking price). Issues of this type are generally larger issues in which there is competition between institutional investors for the purchase of the shares.

Since Ibsen plc is a small company, it is unlikely that an offer for sale by tender will be appropriate. An offer for sale by fixed price is likely to be the best method in this case, since it should allow the shareholders to realise a large part of their investment without transferring a significant amount of control to a small number of institutional investors, as could happen if a private placing were to be made.

(b) To: Board of directors of Ibsen plc
From: Financial adviser
Date: 20 January 19X8
Subject: Proposed stock exchange flotation

Advantages and disadvantages of public flotation

It is helpful to separate the position of the company from that of its existing shareholders when considering the merits of flotation.

The **effects on the existing shareholders** include the following.

- They are able to sell all or part of their holdings. In the case of Ibsen, each shareholder owns 4m shares. This is a sizeable holding which it would be difficult to sell privately. Since some of the shareholders wish to realise their investment, a public flotation would be in their interests.
- A wider market will be created for the remaining shares. Even if some of the shareholders in Ibsen do not wish to sell at the moment, a flotation will make it easier for them to do so in the future if their personal position changes.
- A quotation provides a ready share price, which lessens the uncertainties of inheritance tax by avoiding the problems of valuing unquoted shares.
- They will experience a dilution of control, which could mean that the company develops in ways that they would not have wished. Although it is currently proposed that only 49% of the shares should be released, dilution will still occur. The shareholders should consider releasing a higher percentage of their holdings since this would improve the price that could be expected on flotation.

The **effects on the company** will include the following.

- Flotation may lead to the shares being perceived as a less risky investment. This will mean that a better credit standing is obtained, which should make it easier to borrow money. The extra prominence and status given to public companies might also help the Ibsen to generate new business by attracting new customers.
- Additional shares can be issued more easily at a later date. It is difficult for companies to expand beyond a certain size without getting a quotation because of the difficulty of raising enough funds.
- Flotation will be an expensive process and will mean that the company has to comply with the stringent Stock Exchange regulations. It will put extra administrative burdens on the management.
- The profits and performance of the company will be much more in the public eye and the company cannot afford to show poor results without attracting considerable criticism. This can lead to the development of short-term pressures leading to decisions that are not in the best long-term interests of the business.
- The company will be able to offer share option schemes to its employees which should assist in the recruitment and retention of good staff.

The issue price

Possible approaches that can be used to arrive at an issue price include the following.

Dividend valuation model

This can be expressed as: $MV = \frac{d(1+g)}{(r-g)}$

where MV (ex div) is the current market price
d is the current net dividend = £17.5m/60m = 29.2 pence per share
r is the shareholders' cost of capital = 14%
g is the expected annual growth of dividend payments

Although the company has had a policy up to now of stable dividends, it is unlikely that this will be appropriate following flotation since investors will expect to see some level of growth in their income from the investment. There are a number of approaches that could be taken to estimate a suitable dividend growth rate, but one method is to base it on the rate of growth in distributable profits for the period 19X3 to 19X7. The 19X8 figures will be excluded since these are only an estimate, and forecast an unusually sharp increase in profits for the year, which may or may not be realistic.

Year	*Profit*	*Profit increase*	*% increase*
19X3	14.0		
19X4	15.4	1.4	10.0
19X5	17.4	2.0	13.0
19X6	18.1	0.7	4.0
19X7	16.8	–1.3	–7.2
Average rate of increase			**5.0%**

This can now be used in the dividend valuation model:

$$MV = \frac{29.2(1+0.05)}{(0.14-0.05)} = £3.41$$

Net asset value

At the end of 19X7 the net assets amounted to £120m, and the number of shares in issue was 60m. This gives a theoretical share price of **£2.00.**

P/E basis

The average P/E ratio for companies in Ibsen's industry is currently 11. However, Ibsen is unlikely to achieve this P/E ratio on the initial flotation since the company is not well established and known on the market, and only a minority of the shares are being made available. For the purposes of arriving at an offer price therefore, a discount will be applied to the P/E ratio of 10%, giving a ratio of 10. Earnings per share at the end of 19X7 amounted to £16.8m/60m = 28 pence per share. The theoretical share price on this basis is therefore **£2.80** (£0.28 × 10).

The methods of calculation show a significant variation in the theoretical share price. This is because they view the company from different perspectives. The net asset value basis provides what is effectively a break-up valuation, which is not appropriate for valuing the shares on flotation. While the P/E method is based on comparison with other firms in the industry, it is still backward looking, is over-influenced by the 19X7 dip in profits, and takes no account of future growth projections. The dividend valuation model is therefore the preferred method since it is based on projections of the earnings that are likely to accrue to shareholders in the future. However, the shares may need to be offered at a discount to the calculated price to make them attractive to potential investors.

Further pricing issues

Although calculations based on the fundamental value of the company are useful in establishing an appropriate level for pricing the issue, the actual price to be used must also take into account other factors. Possibly the most important of these is the current mood of the market – whether there is an optimistic view of equity performance – and the level of demand for equity investment. Current and projected economic conditions will also play a part in determining the likely success of the issue. For example, if it is widely expected that the manufacturing sector is heading for recession, this will make the shares less attractive, regardless of the company's track record. If the company has a significant level of exports, or is reliant on imported raw materials, then global economic conditions will also assume more importance.

In view of the positive projections for 19X8, it might be worth waiting until these results are confirmed before floating the company. If these projections are realised, this would have a significant impact on the level of price that the shares might be expected to achieve.

(c) To: Board of directors of Ibsen plc
From: Financial adviser
Date: 20 May 19Y2
Subject: Proposed new capital issue

Rights issue pricing

The first step in establishing the rights issue price is to calculate the current share price. There are still 60m shares in issue, and the most recent earnings figure is £45m, giving an earnings per share of 75 pence. At the current P/E ratio of 18, this implies a share price of £13.50 (18 × 75p). It is proposed to price the rights issue at a discount of 15% to the current share price, thus giving an issue price of **£11.48.** Since the company needs to raise £250m, this means that the number of shares to be issued must be **21,777,000**. The theoretical ex-rights price can be calculated as follows:

Existing shares 60m × £13.50 = £810m

New shares 21.777m × £11.48 = £250m

Total market capitalisation £1,060m

Total number of shares in issue = 60m + 21.777m = 81.777m

Theoretical ex-rights price = £1,060m ÷ 81.777m = **£12.96**

Conversion terms

The primary factor influencing the pricing of convertibles is the **forecast level of the share price at the date of conversion**. These forecasts must focus on the expected level of earnings growth during the period up to the exercise date, and any anticipated changes to the cost of capital. The average rate of earnings growth since flotation has been slightly in excess of 20%, and if this level of growth continues, earnings in 19Y7 would be around £112m (or £1.86 per share). The P/E ratio over the last year has averaged 15.75, which is slightly above the industry average. If it is assumed that there is no significant change in P/E ratios over the five-year period, this would give an expected share price of £29.30. Conversion terms would therefore be 3.4 shares per £100 of loan stock. However, it must be realised that this is the minimum number of shares that could be promised in order to make conversion attractive. In practice, a larger number should be offered to compensate for the risk of returns being lower than anticipated, and to make the issue attractive to investors. It is therefore suggested that between four and five shares per £100 loan stock should be offered.

The exact terms of the conversion will also be related to the **coupon rate of the debt** – although the coupon rate on convertibles is generally below the market rate, there is a trade-off between the size of the discount and the generosity of the conversion terms. To summarise, the total package of interest and conversion rights must be sufficiently attractive to ensure the success of the issue, and also appropriate to the company in terms of the timing and level of servicing costs, and the effect on the dividend requirements after conversion.

The relative merits of a rights issue as compared with convertible debt

The immediate question is effectively a choice between issuing equity or debt. The current market capitalisation of the company is £810m (£45m × 18), and it has long term debt of only £45m. The gearing level is therefore currently extremely low at only 5.5%. The effect of the convertible issue would be to increase gearing in the short term to 36.4% ((£250m + £45m) ÷ £810m). Although this is a significant increase, 36.4% would still be a perfectly reasonable level of gearing for the majority of companies. The key factor in determining whether or not this would be reasonable for Ibsen is the ease with which it would be able to service the debt. If it is assumed that the coupon rate is 9% (a small discount to the market rate) the annual interest charge would be £22.5m, giving an interest cover on the current earnings level of 2 times (in fact the real level of cover would be higher, but it is not known what the tax charge for the year is). Provided that Ibsen can continue to achieve the assumed rate of earnings growth, and that the volatility of earnings is not too great, the debt option is attractive because it allows the company to take advantage of the tax relief on debt interest.

However, the company must also consider the implications of failing to achieve the forecast level of performance. If the new project fails to deliver as anticipated and earnings performance is poor, the cost of servicing the debt could become a problem, and in this situation it is also unlikely that the share price would reach the anticipated level. The effect of this would be that holders of the debt might choose to opt for redemption rather than conversion, and this in turn will place a further financial burden on the company. Thus the safest option would be to make a rights issue, but although this would reduce downside risk, it would also limit the level of profits that are available to shareholders by earnings dilution and by foregoing the tax relief on the debt interest. The directors must therefore determine exactly what their position is in relation to financial risk, and they must also make careful, detailed and realistic forecasts of business performance over the next few years before making their decision.

64 PREMOCO PLC

Pass marks. This is a wide-ranging case study concerning a company which wishes to diversify by acquisition. It is a good question because it is not unnecessarily complex but it requires a good all-round grasp of the factors involved in the acquisition decision and requires you to explain in words the valuation methods and problems involved.

In part (d) there is, as the question says, no one right or wrong answer. A large amount of financial information could have been generated. We have concentrated on the most significant figures from the point of valuing the businesses. The best format for the report is to follow the question requirements directly, that is to use the headings 'price', 'terms of offer' and 'business implications' in a separate commentary on each company.

(a) **Services provided by merchant bank and stockbroker during an acquisition**

During the acquisition process, Premoco plc may be assisted in the following ways.

The merchant bank

- may provide the initial lead in identifying suitable acquisition targets; provides information on such target companies
- provides advice on and checks compliance with the City Code on Mergers and Takeovers, which is important from the very start of negotiations
- engages other advisors (for example lawyers and reporting accountants)
- provides some advice on the valuation of target companies; however, the valuation can only be properly decided by the Premoco plc board and the advice given by the banker will tend to avoid legal liability
- advises on the best method of financing the issue: normally cash (raised by borrowing) or a share issue or loan stock issue or a combination of these methods
- arranges the issue of finance
- handles a lot of the publicity surrounding the acquisition

The stockbroker

- sounds out the opinions of major institutional investors on the possible bids which could be made by Premoco plc
- provides background stock market information, such as share prices, P/E ratios, equity beta factors
- deals with the detailed documentation for share issues, share exchanges and so on

(b) (i) **Current market values and P/E ratios**

The market value of the company's shares (market capitalisation) is the share price multiplied by the number of shares in issue.

The P/E ratio (price/earnings ratio) is the share price divided by the latest earnings per share.

No figures are available for Carsals Ltd, which is a private company.

	Premoco plc	*Nafco plc*	*Oiltrans plc*
Share price (pence)	1,648	675	1,530
Number of issued shares (million)	20	10	12
Total market value of shares (£ million)	329.6	67.5	183.6
Earnings per share (pence)	103	75	85
P/E ratio	16	9	18

(ii) **Cost of equity (K_e) using the CAPM (capital asset pricing model)**

This is given by: $K_e = R_f + (R_m - R_f)\beta_e$

The market return, R_m, is 12% and the risk free rate, R_f, is 6%. The equity beta factor (β_e) for the first three companies is given directly, but for Carsals Ltd it is estimated by de-gearing the equity beta of a similar quoted company to get the asset beta or ungeared beta, β_a. This is because Carsals has no debt in its capital structure.

The formula is $\beta_a = \beta_e \frac{E}{E+D} + \beta_d \frac{D}{E+D}$ which is $\beta_a = \beta_e \frac{E}{E+D}$ when the debt beta is assumed to be zero.

Thus for Carsals $\beta_a = 1.25 \times \frac{80}{80 + 20} = 1.0$

	Premoco plc	Nafco plc	Oiltrans plc	Carsals Ltd
Beta factor	1.2	0.9	1.3	1.0
Cost of equity = 6% + (12% – 6%)β	13.2%	11.4%	13.8%	12.0%

(iii) **Prospective market value using the constant growth dividend valuation model**

The formula is $V_0 = \frac{D_1}{K_e - g}$ where D_1 (next year's dividend) = D_0 (1 + g).

	Premoco plc	Nafco plc	Oiltrans plc	Carsals Ltd
Latest dividend per share (D_0) (pence)	31	55	42	112
Expected growth, g	11%	5%	14%	9%
Next year's dividend, D_1 (pence)	34.41	57.75	47.88	122.08
Estimated value per share $D_1/(K_e\text{–}g)$ (£)	15.64	9.02	N/A	40.69
Number of issued shares (million)	20	10		0.5
Total prospective market capitalisation (£m)	312.8	90.2		20.3

Pass marks. The dividend growth formula does not work when g is greater than K_e. In practice g, which is supposed to be a growth rate to perpetuity, can never be higher than K_e. In fact, when g is expected to be very close to K_e, as for Premoco, the formula becomes very unreliable.

(c) **Usefulness of the three types of valuation in the acquisition decision**

The following values can be summarised for the four companies in £ million.

	Premoco plc £m	Nafco plc £m	Oiltrans plc £m	Carsals Ltd £m
Current market value	329.6	67.5	183.6	N/A
Prospective market value	312.8	90.2	N/A	20.3
Net asset value	250	60	65	6

The **current market value** shows the value of each of the listed companies to its existing shareholders. The efficient market hypothesis (semi-strong form) implies that the market value of each company is the best estimate of its fundamental value, based on public information. Despite criticisms of the EMH, there is a large body of evidence which shows that the semi-strong form is substantially correct. However, when making an acquisition decision, Premoco is concerned with the value of each target company to itself, not to that company's existing shareholders. Adjustments may therefore be needed

During the negotiations, information which is not known to the public may emerge. This will cause Premoco to adjust its valuations.

Premoco may also have plans for generating synergy when it combines a new business with its own (eg by elimination of duplicated assets and costs). This will affect the value of the new business to Premoco. However, extreme caution must be exercised when using estimates of synergy to adjust market values, because the market may already have anticipated the merger taking place and may have increased the price of the target company to allow for possible synergy. This effect can make the market values of companies unreliable if takeover rumours start.

Premoco will probably find it necessary to offer a price higher than the existing market value in order to induce target company shareholders to sell.

There is, of course, no market value for the private company, which cannot be valued by this method.

The **prospective value based on the constant growth dividend valuation model** is one method of attempting to compute the fundamental going concern value of the business from basic data concerning the company. The model itself is, however, very crude, assuming that dividend growth will be at a constant rate to perpetuity. More complex versions of this model exist where varying growth rates can be postulated. In particular, the model becomes meaningless if g exceeds the cost of equity and very unreliable when the two figures are close together, as for Premoco itself.

The **capital asset pricing model**, despite the fact that it is over-simple, is probably the best method of computing a company's cost of equity, so the main practical problem in using this method is not in estimating K_e but in estimating g. As with the other valuation methods, consideration must be given to adjusting the figures for previously unknown information and for expected synergetic effects.

The **net asset values** of the companies are probably based on historical cost, although some oil companies do use a current cost basis for reporting. In terms of relevance for an acquisition, historical cost is irrelevant except as an approximation to either net realisable value or current cost.

Current cost, or **replacement cost**, is useful in showing the cost of setting up a similar business from scratch but it is *not* a valuation of the business concerned. It ignores goodwill and intangible assets and, if Premoco did decide to set up a competing business from scratch, the original target company would still exist as a competitor.

Net realisable values of the business assets are probably the most useful asset figures which can be provided. This is obviously true if the business is acquired to be broken up but NRV asset values are also useful when viewing the business as a going concern: the break-up value of the business shows the worst-case scenario if the business is acquired as a going concern but fails. In other words, it is NRV which should be used as the basis of the 'asset backing' calculation, not historical cost.

In practice the businesses cannot be valued separately if they are going to be joined together, and a valuation method may well involve a combination of computing the present value of future improved operating cash flows together with the net realisable value of assets which are to be sold. The company will find the '**estimated NPV of the combined organisation**' more useful than any of the stand-alone valuations of the businesses.

(d)

> **Pass marks.** This answer assumes that the 'estimated NPV of the combined organisation' represents the NPV of shareholders' wealth when the organisations are combined. An alternative interpretation is that the NPV represents equity plus debt and must therefore be adjusted for the value of debt in the combined company.
>
> *Other points.* Our answer goes into more detail than would be expected of you under examination conditions.

To: David Wong
From: Financial Adviser
Date: 12 November 19X7

Report on three possible acquisitions available to Premoco plc

I have examined the information which you have supplied to me on the three potential acquisitions and set out my views on the strategic implications of each, bearing in mind your wish to diversify away from petroleum. Relevant calculations are shown in the Appendix. I have assumed that the existing market value of Premoco, £329.6 million, is a fair estimate of its true value.

Nafco plc

Price to be offered. On the basis of the financial advisers' figures (see Appendix), the combination will increase equity earnings by £3.9 million and creates added value (synergy) of £114.9 million (29%). The absolute *maximum* price which can be paid for Nafco plc is £182.4 million, which is £18.24 per share. The minimum that can be offered is the existing market price of £6.75 per share. There is of course no way that you should offer the maximum price. If the shareholders of Premoco are to get their fair share of value added from the merger, they should not pay more than 29% more than the current market price per share of Nafco. This gives a price of £8.71 per share (£87.1 million in total).

A suggested range for negotiation is therefore £7 to £9 per share. If your intelligence is correct, Nafco's institutional shareholders would be pleased to accept a reasonable offer from a more up-market firm like yours and there should be no reason to go above the figure of £8.71 unless a competing bid emerges.

Suggested terms of the offer. A price of £87.1 million could be financed substantially by cash in the bank but this would leave no investment funds for improving Nafco's operations. If you wish to pursue the cash route, you will need to borrow over the medium or long term. The gearing of Premoco is not high and borrowing will not be a problem, but you must recognise that group gearing will increase if this acquisition is made, because Nafco's debt ratio is much higher than your own.

If you intend to borrow, one option is to take up the supplier's offer of cheap loan finance in return for a long-term supply agreement. However, the decision on this source of finance should not be regarded as part of the acquisition decision. It is something which needs to be investigated in its own right as it would involve a major change in strategy from the existing policy of buying petrol in the open market.

The alternative to increasing borrowing is to issue shares in Premoco to the shareholders of Nafco (a share-for-share swap). The share price of Premoco (£16.48) is roughly twice the offer price for Nafco, so the terms of the offer would be approximately 1 for 2. This would have the advantage of keeping gearing low and would probably be very acceptable to the disaffected institutional shareholders of Nafco, who would be able to retain their investment in the petroleum industry and maintain the balance of their portfolios. However, the transactions costs of share issues are much higher than for borrowing. Share issues become more obviously advantageous for larger acquisitions.

Note. Actually, if the terms of the offer are pitched so that both groups of shareholders gain by 29%, Premoco's share price will rise from £16.48 to £21.26, which is 2.44 times the offer price for Nafco of £8.71. On this basis, the terms of the offer would be approximately 2.44 shares in Nafco for 1 in Premoco, say 5 for 2.

Business implications. The acquisition of Nafco would expand the company's operations in retailing of petroleum. Large economies of scale could be generated, which accounts for the very high synergy expected from the merger. A choice needs to be made as to whether Nafco's garages should be adapted to run in the same up-market way as Premoco's or whether they should concentrate on their existing low-price strategy. Whatever the strategy, substantial investment will be needed to improve the image with consumers and hence to improve on the company's existing growth prospects, which are low.

The acquisition of Nafco does not in itself represent a diversification away from petroleum products and is therefore not what you appear to be looking for at the moment. However, it appears to be a good buy if the price can be kept relatively low and there is much scope for developing convenience stores on the Nafco sites.

Oiltrans plc

Price to be offered. Using the same arguments as were put forward for Nafco plc, the absolute maximum value of Oiltrans (on the basis of NPV of the combined organisation) is £265.4 million or £22 per share, compared with the current price of £15.30. The added value generated by the merger is 16% which, when added to the current market price, gives £17.75. The suggested range of prices for negotiation is £16 to £18 per share but, because the bid is hostile, you might have to be prepared to go higher.

Terms of the offer. At £17.75 per share, the total cost of the acquisition is £213 million. This is too large to be financed entirely by cash, and borrowing would increase gearing significantly. A share issue is the most likely route for financing this acquisition. The share-for-share swap would be in the region of 1 for 1 (see tutorial note above) which would mean the issue of 12 million new shares. Since only 10 million shares are available for issue, this would mean that the authorised share capital would need to be increased, and this in turn would signal to the market that something major was about to happen. To avoid an increase in authorised share capital, the company could offer a choice of shares or a cash alternative. In cases like this, the cash alternative is usually less than the equivalent share value because it is less risky. A further problem of a large share issue is that existing share ownership of Premoco will become diluted and large shareholders in Oiltrans may become dominant in the combined company.

Business implications. The acquisition of Oiltrans plc would be a vertical integration of an existing supplier into the company's business. This represents more of a diversification than the acquisition of Nafco and is therefore more in line with your stated strategy but, judging from the figures, less synergy can be created because of the different nature of the two businesses. Oiltrans has significantly higher growth prospects than the existing business of Premoco.

Your problem with diversifying into a business of this type is that you cannot easily demonstrate expertise and experience at managing such companies. In the event of a contested takeover, shareholders will probably back the existing management unless you can demonstrate that they are inefficient in some way. Note that for most large shareholders there is no benefit if your company diversifies purely to reduce risk because these shareholders will already hold diversified portfolios. Indeed it is quite likely that they already own shares in Oiltrans plc as well as Premoco.

When two companies of similar size consider merging there is a real problem as to who will end up running the company. The directors of Oiltrans may turn the tables on you by arranging a counter-bid for the shares of Premoco. Alternatively, to agree bid terms, you will need to decide which directors from both sides should head the combined group.

Carsals Ltd

Price to be offered. The absolute maximum amount that could be paid for Carsals (on the basis of NPV of the combined organisation) is £38.4 million, which is £76.80 per share. Our dividend valuation model approach gave a figure of £40.69 per share. Synergy generated by the merger is 5%, so to give your own shareholders their fair share of this gain, the price paid should not be more than £42.72 per share, giving a total price of £21.36 million. The price paid would depend on how quickly the existing major shareholder needs to make the sale and on what other offers he is likely to receive. One major problem is that other car dealers can generate synergy from the acquisition and can therefore afford to pay more than Premoco. Before agreeing the price, you must be sure of the terms of the franchise, in particular the period for which it lasts and the renewal terms.

Terms of the issue. This company could be purchased using existing cash in the bank.

Business implications. Carsals Ltd represents a complete product diversification from the existing business but maintains the same up-market image in prestige locations. There will be no problems of control arising from the acquisition. The business is predicted to show reasonable growth but there will be no immediate synergy available from the business combination. The sort of longer term synergy available is in marketing the superior image for both cars, petroleum and other retail services.

You will need to appoint a suitable managing director from the car sales business if the owner has not groomed a suitable successor. The terms of the franchise must be investigated carefully and, finally, you must be aware that the success of this business depends to a large extent on the continued success of the motor manufacturer.

Conclusions

Despite your wish to diversify, I feel on balance that the opportunity of expanding the existing business by the acquisition of Nafco presents much higher wealth-producing opportunities than a contested bid for Oiltrans, which may well drain company resources and come to nothing. The acquisition of Carsals should also be followed up promptly, as a quick purchase may result in a bargain.

Signed: Financial Adviser

APPENDIX

	Premoco plc	*Nafco plc*	*Oiltrans plc*	*Carsals Ltd*
	£m	£m	£m	£m
Total equity earnings	20.6	7.5	10.2	0.8
Existing value of shares*	329.6	90.2	183.6	20.3
Company combination		P+N	P + O	P + C
Sum of existing earnings		28.1	30.8	21.4
Estimated post-merger earnings		32.0	35.0	23.0
Additional earnings predicted		3.9	4.2	1.6
Sum of existing valuations		397.1	513.2	349.9
Estimated NPV of combined organisation		512.0	595.0	368.0
Increase in value from the combination		114.9	81.8	18.1
% increase in value		29%	16%	5%
*Maximum price that can be paid for the acquisition***		182.4	265.4	38.4

*Dividend valuation model used for Carsals.

**NPV of combination minus value of Premoco £329.6 million.

65 LAVINIA PRODUCTS PLC

Pass marks. Part (a) of this question should be answered in terms of the principles involved. A small company often appears to be a higher risk investment than a larger one, resulting in a higher cost of capital. Your job is to identify the additional types of risk which investors and lenders perceive to be the problem with small companies.

Examiner's comments. The examiner's report said that most candidates made at least a satisfactory attempt at part (a) of the question. Those who did not misinterpreted the question. The question did not require a list of sources of finance with advantages and disadvantages.

(a) **Small and medium sized enterprises** (SMEs) usually find it more difficult to raise finance from external sources than large listed companies and their cost of capital is nearly always higher. The difficulties apply to both equity and debt finance but are more pronounced for equity.

Difficulties in raising equity finance

Demand for the shares of SMEs is much less than for shares in large listed companies. This is because shareholdings in large listed companies are liquid investments which can be disposed of quickly if the company does not perform satisfactorily. By contrast, minority shareholdings in small unlisted companies cannot easily be sold (there is often no easy 'exit route') and therefore carry more risk for the investor, regardless of the company's business risk.

The effect is that the price which outside investors will offer for shares in SMEs is often too low to be attractive to the existing shareholders. Even if an SME attempts to counter this problem by becoming quoted (for example on the **Alternative Investment Market**), the cost of capital is still likely to be high if there is a very thin market for the company's shares.

Other factors causing difficulty in raising equity funds include the following.

(i) Young growing companies may have too short a track record to convince investors of their potential.

(ii) The directors may not have the expertise to know where to raise funds or how to present their case. For example, the company's business plan may not be convincing.

(iii) SMEs often suffer more business risk than equivalent large companies. For example they may not have achieved the critical mass necessary for effective competition. This will raise their cost of capital.

Difficulties in raising debt finance

There are many ways in which SMEs can raise debt finance (for example overdraft, bank loans, factoring, invoice discounting). However, because the sums borrowed are less, SMEs inevitably pay higher interest rates than large organisations and suffer proportionately greater transaction costs when borrowing. For example, very large organisations can save costs by issuing securitised debt direct to lenders whereas SMEs must borrow through intermediaries like banks or finance houses.

SMEs are often less diversified businesses than large companies, which makes them riskier propositions to lenders because cash flow is less stable. As a result, SMEs are likely to have to advance more security for loans. It is common for the proprietors to have to borrow on the security of their personal assets.

A lack of expertise in knowing where to look or how to negotiate often causes unnecessarily high borrowing costs for SMEs.

Solutions

The problems of raising finance are best overcome by learning how to present the company's case effectively to the appropriate lenders or investors. This will mean developing a credible business plan. For example, venture capital companies report that the main reason for rejection of applications for funds is an inadequate marketing plan.

In the end the cost of funds depends on the number of competing investors who can be attracted. SMEs should work hard to attract equity and loan investors from as many sources as possible.

(b)

Pass marks. This is a standard question on medium-term financial planning, with the aim of identifying funding requirements during a period of cash deficit. The question is made easier because there is (unrealistically) no need to account for the changes in interest costs each year, but it does include the difference between accounting depreciation and capital allowances.

Examiner's comments. Many candidates made a good attempt at the calculations required for part (b). The main errors were:

- incorrect growth rate for operating expenses;
- incorrect treatment of depreciation and capital allowances;
- confusing profits with cash flow;
- wrong timing of dividend and tax payments;
- failure to calculate the cumulative cash balance;
- incorrect computation of return on shareholders' funds.

(i) *Lavinia Products plc profit and loss accounts*

	Actual		*Forecast*	
	19X6	*19X7*	*19X8*	*19X9*
	£'000	£'000	£'000	£'000
Turnover (increase 10% pa)	1,560	1,716	1,888	2,076
Cost of sales (increase 10% pa)	(950)	(1,045)	(1,150)	(1,264)
Gross profit	610	671	738	812
Operating expenses (increase 5% pa)	(325)	(341)	(358)	(376)
Depreciation (10% pa × £500,000)		(50)	(50)	(50)
Operating profit	285	280	330	386
Interest (assumed constant)	(30)	(30)	(30)	(30)
Profit before tax	255	250	300	356
Taxation (see working)	(84)	(58)	(85)	(111)
Net profit	171	192	215	245
Dividend (25% growth pa)	(68)	(85)	(106)	(133)
Retained profit	103	107	109	112
Reserves b/f	128	231	338	447
Reserves c/f	231	338	447	559
Share capital	500	500	500	500
Year end reserves	231	338	447	559
Year end shareholders' funds	731	838	947	1,059
Pre-tax return on shareholders funds	34.9%	29.8%	31.7%	33.6%

On the basis of these figures, the financial objective of a pre-tax return of 35% of year-end shareholders' funds is not achieved in any of the years.

Working: Tax payable

It is assumed that the company does not account for deferred taxation.

	Actual		Forecast	
	19X6	*19X7*	*19X8*	*19X9*
	£'000	£'000	£'000	£'000
Profit before tax	255	250	300	356
Add back depreciation		50	50	50
Less capital allowance (25% red./bal)		(125)	(94)	(70)
Taxable profit	255	175	256	336
Tax at 33%	84	58	84	111

(ii) *Cash flow forecasts*

> **Pass marks**. There are many ways of computing the cash flow forecasts. The examiner's comments state that these formats are equally acceptable. However, some ways are quicker than others! Our solution shows one of the quickest methods.

The 19X6 balance sheet figure for 'other creditors (including tax and dividends)' is in fact simply the sum of tax and dividends in the profit and loss account. It is assumed that this will continue to be the case in the following three years. The annual change in net current assets can be computed as follows.

Changes in net current assets

	Actual		Forecast	
	19X6	*19X7*	*19X8*	*19X9*
	£'000	£'000	£'000	£'000
Stock (scenario note (7))	326	361	361	361
Debtors (12.31% of sales) *	192	211	232	256
Trade creditors (14.21% of cost of sales) *	(135)	(148)	(163)	(180)
Tax and dividends payable (sum of P&L figures)	(152)	(143)	(191)	(244)
Net current assets	231	281	239	193
Increase/(decrease) net current assets		50	(42)	(46)

* Alternatively debtors and creditors can be computed as a 10% increase each year.

The cash flow forecasts can then be constructed.

Cash flow forecasts

	19X7	*19X8*	*19X9*
	£'000	£'000	£'000
Retained profit for the year	107	109	112
Add back depreciation	50	50	50
(Investment in working capital)/release of working capital (see working)	(50)	42	46
Expenditure on fixed assets	(500)		
Surplus/(deficit) for the year	(393)	201	208
Cash/(deficit) b/f	50	(343)	(142)
Cash/(deficit) c/f	(343)	(142)	66

The company will need to find finance of £343,000 in 19X7 but this can be completely repaid in the following two years. However, interest costs have been ignored in this computation.

> *Other points.* Alternative presentations include:
>
> - a detailed statement of cash receipts and payments; or
> - a cash flow statement in FRS1 format.
>
> Solutions by both of these methods are shown here, for comparison.

Appendices

1 *Cash receipts and payments*

	19X7	19X8	19X9
	£'000	£'000	£'000
Receipts			
Cash from sales			
(sales + opening debtors – closing debtors)	1,697	1,867	2,053
Payments			
For purchases (cost of sales + opening creditors – closing creditors)	1,032	1,135	1,248
Operating expenses	341	358	376
Additional stock purchase	35		
Machinery	500		
Interest (current year)	30	30	30
Tax (previous year)	84	58	85
Dividends (previous year)	68	85	106
	2,090	1,666	1,845
Net cash flow	(393)	201	208
Cash/(deficit) b/f	50	(343)	(142)
Cash/(deficit) c/f	(343)	(142)	66

2 *FRS 1 format*

	19X7	19X8	19X9
	£'000	£'000	£'000
Net cash inflow from operating activities (see working)	290	373	429
Interest paid	(30)	(30)	(30)
Dividends paid	(68)	(85)	(106)
Net cash inflow	192	258	293
Tax paid	(84)	(58)	(84)
Investing activities:			
Fixed assets	(500)		
Net cash outflow	(584)	(58)	(84)
Net cash flow before financing	(392)	200	209

Working: net cash inflow from operating activities

	19X6	19X7	19X8	19X9
	£'000	£'000	£'000	£'000
Stock	326	361	361	361
Debtors	192	211	232	256
Trade creditors	(135)	(149)	(163)	(180)
	383	423	430	437
Incremental working capital		(40)	(7)	(7)
Gross profit before depreciation		671	738	812
Less: operating expenses		(341)	(358)	(376)
Net cash inflow from operating activities		290	373	429

(c)

Pass marks. This report gives you an opportunity to show your knowledge of a wide range of different topics: interpretation and ratios, company objectives, shareholder value, dividend policy and forecasting techniques. The main problem for many candidates is knowing where to start. Questions like this are much easier to do when you have a general overview of how all the topics in the syllabus fit together.

> **Examiner's comments.** Part (c) was the worst answered part of this question, despite the fact that it gave candidates a chance to demonstrate their knowledge of a number of different areas of the syllabus. In (c) (i) marks were awarded for additional calculations in support of the discussion, but few candidates attempted this. Although part (c) (ii) was quite well attempted, many candidates continued to discuss the *achievability* of the objectives rather than their *suitability*. In (c) (iii) many candidates discussed investment appraisal instead of forecasting methods, despite the fact that financial analysis and forecasting is a separate distinct part of the syllabus.

REPORT

To: The directors of Lavinia Products plc
From: RT Consultants Date: 15 May 19X7
Subject: Report on the objectives and financial forecasts of Lavinia Products plc

As requested by the terms of reference, I have prepared forecast profit and loss accounts and cash flow forecasts for the years 19X7 to 19X9. These are shown as Appendix 1 to this report [part (b) of this solution]. In Appendix 2, I have added some additional calculations to assist with the interpretation of the forecasts.

(i) *Key aspects of the financial information and the likelihood of achieving the objectives*

The three key objectives given to me were concerned with **return on shareholders' funds, growth in dividends per share** and the **ability to gain a stock market quotation.**

Although the company is making good profits, the calculations show that the objective of continuing to earn a pre-tax return of 35% on the book value of shareholders funds is unlikely to be achieved over the next three years. The results for 19X7 show that the return will fall to 30%. In fact this figure will be further reduced by interest costs on the funding requirement of £343,000 if medium term capital is used. The figures for 19X8 to 19X9 show a slow improvement in the return.

Although the company will earn sufficient profits to enable it to increase dividend per share by 25% each year, this will result in a steadily increasing **pay-out ratio** (rising from 40% to 54% of equity earnings) because earnings per share will increase at a rate of only 12% to 14% per year. The large increase in dividend pay-out is one of the contributory factors to the high funding requirement in 19X7. A better alternative is probably to lower the targeted dividend growth.

The effect of the additional borrowing requirement in 19X7 will be to increase **gearing**. Measured as Total long-term/medium-term debt *to* Book value of shareholders' funds, this will reach a maximum of (300 + 343)/838 = 77% in 19X7, which may be too high for comfort. Although interest cover (operating profit/interest) is safe in 19X6 at 9.5 times, this figure will fall to less than half if borrowing more than doubles. These effects are not revealed by Appendix 1 [part (b) of the question] because of the assumptions made.

When evaluating the suitability of the company for a flotation, analysts will be more concerned with **sustainable growth in equity earnings** than with an artificially high growth rate in dividends. The projected growth in earnings per share is good but not exciting and the company will probably need a longer track record before it can achieve a quotation. Alternatively it should look for investments with faster growth opportunities. If, however, a flotation were obtained after three years, the likely valuation of the company's shares, at a P/E of 15, is £3.68 million.

In summary, the projections show that the company is profitable, with a reasonable growth rate, but that dividend growth should be held back in line with earnings growth in order to reduce the borrowing requirement in 19X7. A stock exchange quotation before the year 19Y0 is unlikely.

(ii) *Suitability of the objectives as stated*

The **target return on shareholders' funds** of 35% pre-tax seems to be based on results for 19X6. This figure is, however, too high to be used as a target. If used as the basis for investment decisions it is likely that the company will reject projects which are adequately profitable even though they earn less than 35%. This will slow down its growth, allowing competitors to gain from its rejected opportunities. In addition, replacement of fixed assets may be postponed because it would depress the rate of return. The directors may attempt to squeeze short-term profits at the expense of long-term sustainability.

What is needed is a fundamental objective based on the company's ability to generate wealth for its shareholders. Research shows that return on shareholders' funds is a very bad indicator of this ability. More effective measurements are based on the principles of **shareholder value analysis** (SVA) or related techniques such as **economic value added** (EVA) or **cash flow return on investment** (CFROI). We would be happy to explain the principles of these techniques to you in a further report.

The objective of a 25% growth in dividends is also over-ambitious since this is clearly not matched by the expected growth in earnings or available cash flow. If the company were to be floated on a stock market, the dividend policy needs to be reviewed in detail. It is generally considered that a steady growth in dividends is a good thing but that the rate of growth should signal the company's long-term growth prospects. Dividend policy is, however, a complex subject and we would be happy to explore this further with you.

Finally, the objective of seeking a stock exchange quotation should be carefully reviewed against other possibilities for the company's development. The advantages of a quotation are that it becomes much easier to raise share capital from outside investors and your own shareholdings will significantly increase in value. However you must seriously consider the proportion of shares which you wish to retain and the consequent effect on control of the company. **Alternatives to a flotation** include:

- continuing to grow using a combination of retained earnings and borrowings;
- identifying suitable individuals or organisations who wish to take a stake in your company;
- selling out to another company which wants to acquire your business.

The choice of a way forward will depend on your own personal goals, which may be different for each director and will need careful and honest discussion.

(iii) *Additional methods of financial forecasting*

The forecasts prepared for this report are prepared on the basis of the assumptions given to me, which are very generalised and over-simple. For example, the relationship between sales, costs, debtors and creditors remain the same over the period, no additional stockholdings have been budgeted after 19X7 and interest on additional borrowings (which is a significant figure) has been omitted.

A more detailed set of forecasts needs to be prepared, on a month-by-month basis, within the context of the company's strategic plans. A computerised planning model would be appropriate for assembling this information. Input to the forecasts will include:

- marketing, production and purchasing plans; estimates from line managers of sales, costs, stock levels and so on;
- statistical analysis of the relationship between the variables in the model and a cross-check against the managers' detailed estimates;
- estimates of general economic factors and their likely effect on the company and the industry as a whole;
- estimates of any likely changes in the behaviour and attitudes of competitors, customers and suppliers;
- the results of capital investment appraisal and other decisions.

There are many ways of handling **risk** and **uncertainty** in the estimates. Suitable techniques need to be chosen from:

- the preparation of best and worst case estimates;
- use of data tables to show ranges of possible results;
- sensitivity analysis and the identification of 'key' variables;
- assignment of probabilities to estimates;
- use of simulation for complex repetitive uncertain events;
- scenario planning and the development of contingency plans.

I would be happy to assist you with the use of these procedures to develop your company's plans.

Signed: RT Consultants

Appendix 1 – see part (b) of the solution

Appendix 2 – further calculations to assist with interpretation of the results

		19X6	*19X7*	*19X8*	*19X9*
Equity earnings (profit after tax)	(£'000)	171	192	215	245
Total dividend	(£'000)	68	85	106	133
Number of £1 shares	('000)	500	500	500	500
Earnings per share	(pence)	34.2	38.4	43.0	49.0
Dividend per share	(pence)	13.6	17.0	21.2	26.6
Annual growth in EPS	%		12.3%	12.5%	13.4%
Dividend payout ratio (dps/eps)	%	40%	44%	49%	54%
Market capitalisation of shares at a P/E of 15	(£ million)	2.57	2.88	3.23	3.68

66 DP PLC

Pass marks. In part (b) you should evaluate the position of the company and its supplier in the light of the forecasts made of the company's future prospects. The accuracy of these forecasts will affect the way in which the different parties reach a decision.

The calculations in part (c) are relatively simple. In answering the final section of this part, the key is to identify the fundamental differences in the assumptions underpinning the two methods of valuation used.

Examiner's comment. In part (b), there was widespread failure to appreciate that liquidation means the cessation of trading. In part (c) presentation in many cases was poor and many candidates made simple arithmetical errors which meant that they did not gain full marks.

Common errors were: omitting the opening cash balance; failing to remove the preference share dividend; double-counting the bank loan; revaluing incorrectly the fixed assets, stock and debtors; misunderstanding the meaning of net assets.

Part (d) was answered the least well (by far) and many answers were extremely brief. Many candidates appeared to be unable to structure their report or to provide any form of analysis.

(a) **Merchant banks** have historically been more associated than the clearing banks with the **provision of risk capital**. However, the amount of funds that they have available to invest is relatively small when compared with that of the clearing banks. Lending policies vary greatly from bank to bank and it is difficult to define what the typical investment might be. Although the larger banks are generally unwilling to invest amounts less than £250,000, some of the smaller banks may consider an investment as low as £50,000. Where much larger sums are required, a number of banks may combine together in a syndicate.

In terms of the type of investment made, the bank will not usually consider a permanent stake in the company, but is rather looking for a profitable equity investment from which it can secure a successful exit within 5-8 years' time. It will generally be looking to gain its return from capital appreciation rather than from dividend income during this period. When selecting companies in which to invest, the banks will be interested in the track record of the company and its management and the extent to which the owners have invested their own money in the enterprise. This means that medium sized companies seeking new capital for growth and development tend to be at an advantage to those in start-up situations.

Merchant banks can also offer **help and advice to companies seeking new capital** in a number of other areas.

(i) They can advise on the form, pricing and timing of new capital issues.

(ii) They can recommend alternative sources of finance in different capital markets.

(iii) They can advise on listing requirements and the associated administration.

(iv) They may assist with the underwriting of new issues.

(b) The relative **advantages and disadvantages of liquidation** to both parties will depend heavily on the forecast upturn in business being realised and the success of the reconstruction.

From the point of view of the shareholders, an early liquidation will only be advantageous if the upturn in business is not realised, the reconstruction is unsuccessful, and the company is forced into liquidation at a later date. If these situations arise then it is probable that the value of the equity attributable to the existing shareholders will have diminished and hence the amount that they receive under the later liquidation will be less than if the company was liquidated immediately. If the shareholders hold the same views as the directors on the future prospects for the company, then they would be unwise to opt for an early liquidation. The only circumstance in which such a liquidation might still be preferable is if they have an alternative project available in which they wish to invest, and which has prospects that are more secure and provide a better potential return than is expected from DP.

From the point of view of EF, a liquidation now would mean that at least a percentage of the debt owing would be repaid, although due to the time such a process would take there would still be a delay before the money was received. However, at least part of the uncertainty regarding the debt would be removed. The principal disadvantages of an early liquidation are that firstly, the reconstruction could mean that the debt is actually paid in full in the not too distant future and thus EF would do better to wait. Secondly, if DP continues to trade then EF should benefit from further business with the company. Early liquidation would mean that this opportunity would be foregone.

(c) (i) The market value of DP's equity can be estimated using projected earnings and P/E ratios for 19X7:

Projected 19X7 earnings	£320,000
Prospective P/E ratio	12
Projected 19X7 market capitalisation	£3,840,000

(ii)

	Original balance sheet	*Effect of reconstruction*	*Revised balance sheet*
	£'000	£'000	£'000
Total fixed assets (NBV)	4,350	(1,000)	3,350
Stock	825	(413)	412
Debtors	2,150	(215)	1,935
Cash (see *Note*)	5	285	290
Total current assets	2,980	(343)	2,637
Unsecured creditors	(750)	750	0
EF plc	(300)	300	0
Tax payable	(150)	150	0
Bank loan	(300)	300	0
Preference dividend	(100)	100	0
Total current liabilities	(1,600)	1,600	0
Total assets less current liabilities	5,730	257	5,730
Mortgage	(2,500)		(2,500)
Bank loan	(300)		(300)
Total long-term liabilities	(2,800)	0	(2,800)
Net assets	2,930	257	3,187
Ordinary share capital	2,500	687	3,187
Retained profit/(loss)	(820)	820	0
Preference shares	1,250	(1,250)	0
Total	2,930	257	3,187

Note. The merchant bank is to pay 140 pence per share for 51% of the ordinary shares. This represents a cash injection of £2,500,000 × 51% × 1.40 = £1,785,000. Of this figure, £1,500,000 will be absorbed in repaying the current liabilities, leaving a cash adjustment of £285,000.

(iii) The value attributable to equity calculated on the basis of the proposed reconstruction is £653,000 less than that calculated on the basis of projected cash flows. The main reasons for this are as follows.

(1) The reconstruction is made on the basis of figures as at today's date, whereas the cash flow valuation is based on 19X7 figures.

(2) The reconstruction is based on the current realisable value of the assets. Some of these assets, for instance stock, will have a higher value if the company continues to trade and thus the reconstruction value will tend to undervalue the company as a going concern.

(3) The reconstruction value is based on tangible assets only, whereas the earnings based valuation is based on the valuation of the projected future cash flows.

(d) REPORT

To: Board of Directors
From: Management Accountant Date: 19 November 19X6
Subject: Proposed rescue package and management for DP plc

The purpose of this report is to evaluate the proposed rescue package for DP plc, to recommend a system of financial controls to be implemented within the company, and to consider some possible methods of profit improvement for the organisation.

Evaluation of rescue package

The company is currently in a very poor financial position, and any investment carries a significant level of risk to the bank. It is therefore of paramount importance that the bank should gain overall control of the company if it is to make a significant financial investment so that it is able to have freedom of action to direct the decisions that are made within the company and to secure a successful exit at an appropriate time. Under the proposals, the bank would gain 51% of the equity, but at the same time it is most important that the preference shares are cancelled in order to eliminate the special rights conferred upon their owners.

The bank is proposing to make an immediate investment of £1.785m in the company, to hold the stock for between five and seven years and then to **exit via an AIM flotation**. For this strategy to be successful, it is imperative that an effective system of financial controls is introduced and that a coherent strategic plan for the business is developed and implemented at the earliest opportunity.

A further factor influencing the decision is the return that the bank is likely to receive during the period of the investment. The appraisal suggests that total earnings in 19X7 are likely to be £320,000, of which 51% or £163,200 would be attributable to the bank. Assuming a P/E ratio of 12, the market value of the shares at the end of 19X7 would be £1.9584m, a capital appreciation of £173,400. Thus the total return would be £336,600 which equates to a rate of 19.15%. This would be a satisfactory level of return, but it is important to appreciate that a significant level of risk is attached to this forecast.

The current exit proposal is via an AIM flotation. However, the bank should also consider **alternative exit routes** should this not prove to be feasible or if it is not possible to improve performance to the planned level. Other options that could be considered include the possible demerger and subsequent sale of the two divisions, a trade sale of the business as a whole, or a management buyout.

Proposed financial controls

An effective system of financial controls cannot be implemented in isolation from a coherent **strategic plan** for the business. The possibilities for this will be included in the final section of the report, but the first imperative will be to agree and define in a measurable way the principal financial objectives of the company.

Once the objectives have been defined, it will then be possible to define the levels of control required to achieve the desired strategy, and budgets prepared to meet these objectives. A **monthly reporting system** that is tied in directly to the budget must then be introduced, together with the regular monitoring of performance and the implementation of action plans to correct performance where necessary.

An investment appraisal system should be introduced that focuses attention on **maximising the NPV return of the company** and encourages medium to long-term investment aimed at maximising the advantage taken of strategic opportunities for the business. Such an approach should maximise the projected medium to long-term cash flows and hence the value of the business as a whole.

Techniques for profit improvement

Profit improvement has an obvious importance in that this should enhance the cash flows of the business and improve the financial security. However, it is most important to take into account the timescale over which the improvement is to be measured. The danger in this situation is to focus too closely on short-term profits, which carries the risk of harming the long-term potential of the business. For example, while development expenditure should be carefully controlled, as in all areas of expenditure, this should not be at the expense of jeopardising long-term performance.

Some of the areas to which attention could be directed include the following.

(i) Potential new contracts should be **evaluated** carefully to ensure that they deliver an acceptable level of contribution. The **costing system** used should be investigated to ensure that all relevant direct costs are fully accounted for. It is recommended that if a fully absorbed costing system is used it should be replaced with a system that directs more attention to marginal contributions.

(ii) The existing **relationships between revenues, volumes and costs** should be examined to ensure that an optimal level of volume an price is sought in order to maximise contributions.

(iii) The **fixed cost base** should be scrutinised to ensure that all departments are operating as efficiently as possible, and that the support departments are structured in such a way as to maximise efficiency while controlling costs.

(iv) **Working capital control** appears to have become slack judging from the increase in the levels of debtors and stocks. This is costing the company money in stockholding costs, sales ledger administration and interest charges, and measures should be implemented to improve the level of control.

(v) The failures to **restructure the bank facility** at an earlier date and to reschedule the order from EF suggest weaknesses in the treasury and purchasing areas which are costing the company money. Particular attention should be given to improving the performance of these departments.

(vi) Work should be undertaken to ensure that the company is providing the best possible level of **customer service** in order to foster and maintain good customer relationships. This will help to enhance the company's reputation and enable it to gain new business more easily while at the same time helping it to retain its existing customer base.

The principle underlying all these areas of activity should be the aim of maximising the amount of **value added** to the firm. Over-emphasis on cost reduction could be counter productive if it jeopardises the long term performance of the business.

Signed: Management Accountant

67 TUTWILER PLC

Pass marks. In calculating the NPV costs of the different alternatives, a relatively lengthy tabular approach has been used in the interests of clarity. A quicker approach would be to make more use of annuity values in calculating the NPV cost of the different elements of the cash flow. Other alternatives could be discussed in part (d), such as the use of expected values and sensitivity analysis.

Examiner's comment. Part (a) was answered very badly. The question was really about cost of capital and the applications of Modigliani and Miller's (MM) theories and demonstrated the link between CAPM and MM.

In part (b) there were many incorrect approaches to the application of writing down allowances or tax relief on expenses; many candidates omitted them completely. Inflation was sometime ignored or incorrectly calculated and annuity factors, when used, were often a year out. Many candidates simply did not know what equivalent annual costs were, although credit was given for reasonable attempts.

Some provided a well structured report for part (c), including a summary of the terms of reference as an introduction. A summary of the three alternative NPVs and equivalent annual costs was also a good starting point.

Few marks were available in part (d) for simply listing the limitations of the CAPM. Use of the dividend valuation model, suggested by many candidates, was not appropriate in answer to this question.

For section (ii) of part (e), candidates were rewarded for any sensible understanding of the differences between risk and uncertainty. The comment that 'in practice the words are used interchangeably' is quite correct and was given credit.

For part (f), many did not understand the term 'venture capital'. Some thought it meant joint venture. Many thought that venture capital finance was 'quick, cheap and easy to obtain'. Nothing could be further from the truth. It is reported that less than five per cent of applications to venture capitalists are considered further, and the required return on investment may be as high as 50%.

(a) **Using proxy company**:

(i) Equity beta of 1.2 gives r_e of 14%.

(ii) Debt beta of 0.2 gives r_e of 9%.

(iii) $r^* = r_e E/(E+D) + r_d D/(E+D)$ gives r* for proxy company of 12.75 (Note that (1 – t) adjustment is not made since figures are already after tax.)

(iv) $r^* = r(1 - T^*L)$ means that r is 13.9%.

(v) Putting Tutwiler's capital structure (£2m debt to £10m equity) in the same formula gives r* to be 13.1%.

(b) *Alternative 1*

It is assumed that the cost of the extension will be fixed in the contract with the builders and that it therefore need not be adjusted for inflation even though it is not paid until the end of 19X7.

Time	*1*	*2*	*3*	*4*	*5*
	£'000	£'000	£'000	£'000	£'000
Rental	525	551	579	608	638
Cost and resale	950				(950)
Total cost	1,475	551	579	608	(312)
Tax at 33%	(487)	(182)	(191)	(201)	103
Net of tax	988	369	388	407	(209)
13% factors	0.885	0.783	0.693	0.613	0.543
Present value	875	289	269	249	(113)
Cumulative	875	1,164	1,433	1,682	1,569

The NPV cost over five years is therefore £1.569m.

The equivalent annual cost can be found by dividing the NPV cost by the five year annuity value of 3.517, giving £446,000.

Alternative 2

Time		£'000	13% factors	PV (£'000)
0	Outlay	2,500.0	1.000	2,500.4
1	Renovation (750 × (1 – 0.33))	502.5	0.885	444.7
1 to 10	Rates (250 × 1 – 0.33))	167.5	5.426	908.9
1 to 10	Capital allowance	(33.0)	5.426	(179.0)
10	Resale	(5,000.0)	0.295	(1,475.0)
Total PV of costs				2,199.6

The NPV cost over five years is therefore £2.1996m.

The equivalent annual cost can be found by dividing the NPV cost by the ten year annuity value of 5.426, giving £405,000.

Alternative 3

Time		£'000	13% factors	PV (£'000)
0	Land	1,000.0	1.000	1,000.0
0	Rent (500 × (1 – 0.33))	335.0	1.000	335.0
1	Building (1,250 × (1 – 0.33))	837.5	0.885	714.2
1	Training etc (600 × (1 – 0.33))	402.0	0.885	355.8
4 to 15	Rates (150 × (1- 0.33))	100.5	4.101	545.3
Total PV of costs				2,977.3

The equivalent annual cost can be found by dividing the NPV cost of £2.9773 million by the fifteen year annuity value of 6.462, giving £440,000.

(c) REPORT

To: Finance Director
From: Management Accountant Date: 15 May 19X6
Subject: Expansion plans

The projects have been evaluated using a discount rate of 13% which is the current estimated weighted average cost of capital based on the beta of a similar firm in the industry. Since the alternatives are all based on the same expansion plan, the level of **business risk** associated with each alternative should not alter, and it is therefore appropriate to use the same discount rate in their evaluation.

I have put together calculations of the **net present value (NPV) cost** and the **equivalent annual cost** for each of the three options currently under consideration.

These can be summarised as follows.

Alternative	*NPV cost*	*Equivalent annual cost*	*Life*
	£'000		Yrs
1: Rent and extend	1,569	446	5
2: Buy larger, locally	2,203	406	10
3: Build new	2,844	440	15

On the face of it, the figures suggest that alternative 2 should be the preferred choice since this has the lowest equivalent annual cost at £406,000 per annum. However, in reality the costs for alternatives 1 and 2 should be adjusted using residual values to make them directly comparable with alternative 3. In other words, a view should be taken of the 15 year cost implications for each of the alternatives before a final decision is made.

In addition there are a number of **financial and non-financial risks and uncertainties** that should also be taken into consideration, as follows.

(1) There is a significant difference between the total NPV cost of the three options, alternatives 2 and 3 demanding a higher total NPV cost and also a higher initial investment than alternative 1. The implication of these two factors is that the cost of financing is higher for these two options thus increasing the level of financial risk. It will also be necessary to find a larger amount of finance for the second two alternatives.

(2) If Tutwiler experiences a reduction in the level of activity and no longer requires the amount of additional capacity originally envisaged, it will have to decide what to do with the excess space. This possibility increases the level of risk associated with the two longer term alternatives.

(3) Tutwiler should take a view on the options that will be available at the end of the appraisal period for each of the alternatives, and take the likely opportunities and costs into account when making the evaluation.

(4) Since the alternatives have been evaluated over different timescales, it is necessary to take into account the fact that the level of uncertainty associated with cost projections is likely to increase with the length of the timescale. Thus the cost projections for alternatives 2 and 3 will be subject to a higher degree of potential variability than those for alternative one.

Perhaps we should meet to discuss whether further calculations should be undertaken in the light of these comments.

Signed: Management Accountant

(d) The main advantage of **the CAPM when used for investment appraisal** is that it produces a discount rate which is based on the systematic risk of the individual investment. However, it was primarily developed with respect to securities and is therefore constructed from the point of view of investors external to the firm. By applying it to an investment within the firm, the company must assume that the shareholders wish the investment to be evaluated as if it were a security in the capital market and that the shareholders all hold fully diversified portfolios and do not wish the company to achieve diversification for them.

A further problem with the CAPM, and one which it shares with many other such models, is that it is essentially backward looking. The **cost of capital** thus arrived at is **based on historical information** and not on current or future conditions. It can therefore be dangerous to apply it without question for capital investment appraisal, particularly in cases such as this where the timeframe under consideration is so long.

This effect is magnified by the fact that the CAPM is really just a **single period model**, and to extend its application beyond this requires both project performance relative to the market and the economic environment to be reasonably stable. Although it is possible in theory to apply the CAPM for each time period under consideration, this greatly increases the problems both of estimation and of calculation.

An **alternative approach** is to attempt to isolate the margin of error in the projected cash flows that is specific to the investment itself, and to decrement the cash flows by this amount. The actual size of the adjustment will obviously also reflect the attitude to risk of the management. The decremented cash flows can then be discounted at the cost of capital excluding any element added to reflect the risk premium. This often provides a clearer way of assessing and comparing the outcome of different alternatives and can form the basis for subsequent monitoring of the NPV performance of different projects.

(e) (i) **Augmenting the discount rate by a premium** to reflect the additional risk of a given alternative is a simple and quite widely used approach to dealing with varying degrees of uncertainty in project evaluation. However, the amount by which the discount rate is augmented is usually quite a subjective decision and one which may in practice bear little relation to the possible variation in cash flows or the probability that such a variation might occur. The approach described in (d) above provides an analysis that can be more easily related to the specific uncertainties of the given project, and provides a clearer method for subsequent monitoring if the project is undertaken. A further alternative would be the use of expected values combined with the NPV calculation.

(ii) In practice, the terms 'risk' and 'uncertainty' are often used interchangeably, but one convenient way of distinguishing between them is as follows.

(1) **Risk** can be applied to a situation where there are several possible outcomes and, on the basis of past relevant experience, probabilities can be assigned to the various outcomes that could prevail.

(2) **Uncertainty** can be applied to a situation where there are several possible outcomes but there is little past relevant experience to enable the probability of the possible outcomes to be predicted.

(f) Although Tutwiler has a good growth record, it has only been quoted on the **AIM** for twelve months. In practice, such newer smaller firms find it harder to obtain funds from a rights issue to finance their expansion than well established bigger companies. The capital markets will normally have more confidence in older larger firms than in the relatively new entrants because they have more experience of their business performance. **Venture capital funds** are by their nature prepared to accept a higher level of risk than the market as a whole, and this is an advantage to a firm in Tutwiler's position. A further advantage is that since the venture capital company will have been through the process many times before, Tutwiler will be able to benefit from its experience and administrative procedures and this will be simpler than raising additional funds on the open market.

However, there are also a number of **potential drawbacks** to be considered.

(1) The venture capital fund is likely to demand a high level of performance from the company, and Tutwiler must be confident of its ability to continue to deliver growth in both turnover and earnings.

(2) The fund is likely to demand detailed information on Tutwiler's organisation, performance and business plans, as well as a seat on the board.

This will result in some loss of control by the existing management and shareholders.

(3) Venture capital funds traditionally seek to secure their exit route prior to making an investment. Tutwiler will have to give consideration to this.

Thus Tutwiler must consider both the advantages and the disadvantages before committing itself to the venture capital route. It may be that additional sources of debt finance could be attractive, given that the gearing level is not excessive at present. However Tutwiler must be confident of its ability to generate growth in earnings as well as turnover if it is to be able to service the additional interest charges and generate sufficient funds to repay the debt at the end of the term.

68 TS PRODUCTS PLC

Pass marks. In your calculations in part (b), it is necessary to make assumptions about the dividend policy of TS Products after the expansion. These should be stated clearly in your answer. This is important because the level of dividends impacts on the level of retained earnings, and hence on both the gearing level and the expected P/E ratios.

In your report in part (c) you should take account of the impact of the proposals on the control structure of the company. Although part (c) of the question just refers to the part (a) findings, it is also appropriate to bring in the part (b) calculations.

In part (d) you should take account of issues external to the firm in determining the P/E ratio and the share price, and of the effect of the release of information on the competitive position of TS Products.

Examiner's comment

Part (a). Many candidates clearly did not understand some fundamental aspects of accounting and finance. The vast majority were not able to calculate return on shareholders' funds.

Part (b) proved to be the most difficult part of the question for most candidates and many did not even attempt it. A difficulty often experienced by markers when marking this type of question is of finding the answer amongst a large jumble of figures which often spreads over many pages. More care should be taken over presentation.

Part (c). Most candidates attempted this part of the question even if they had incorrect, or no, answers to parts (a) and (b).

Part (d). The aim of this part of the question was to test for an understanding of market efficiency and the signalling mechanisms available to companies. Most candidates mentioned market efficiency but failed to develop their argument.

Part (e). Few candidates appeared to understand what share options are, despite the amount of media attention given to them recently.

(a) (i) **Earnings per share** is calculated as the earnings after profit and tax divided by the number of shares in issue and ranking for dividend.

	19X4	*19X5*
Earnings	£4,613,000	£5,936,000
Number of shares in issue	10,000	10,000
EPS	46.13p	59.36p

Return on closing shareholders' funds

	19X4	*19X5*
	£'000	£'000
Earnings	4,613	5,936
Equity	16,864	20,500
Return on equity	27.35%	28.96%

(ii) Today's share price can be found by multiplying the earnings per share calculated above by the P/E ratio:

$$59.36 \times 9 = 534.24 \text{ pence per share}$$

(iii) The probabilities provided can be used to calculate the expected sales volume.

	Sales (No of packs)	*Prob*	
	a	*b*	*a × b*
	5,000	0.1	500
	12,500	0.3	3,750
	20,000	0.4	8,000
	25,000	0.2	5,000
Expected sales volume (packs)	17,250		
Selling price per pack	£500.00		
Expected sales value	£8,625,000		

(b) *Option (1)*

(i) The shares will be issued **at a discount of 15%** to the current price of 534.24p ie an issue price of 454 pence per share. The total number of new shares to be issued is therefore £20m/£4.54 = 4,405,286 shares. This brings the total number of shares in issue to 14,405,286.

The next step is to calculate the **projected earnings for 19X6**. These are made up of two components - the **existing earnings stream,** up by 15% in 19X6, and the **earnings accruing from the new project.** It is assumed that interest on the existing debt will be unchanged at £1m, and that the tax rate is also unchanged at 33%. It is further assumed that the existing level of dividends per share (23p in 19X5) will be maintained.

Earnings from new project

	£'000
Sales	8,625
Variable costs (40%)	(3,450)
Fixed costs	(2,500)
Additional earnings	2,675
Earnings from existing operations (9,860 × 1.15)	11,339
Earnings before interest and tax	14,014
Interest	(1,000)
	13,014
Tax at 33%	(4,295)
Earnings attributable to equity	8,719
Dividends (23p per share - see above)	(3,313)
Retained profit	5,406

The financing side of the balance sheet at 30 September 19X6 will be as follows.

	£'000
Ordinary share capital	7,203
Share premium account	17,797
Retained profit (15,500 +5,406)	20,906
Long-term debt: 10%	10,000
Total financing	55,906

The debt to total asset ratio is therefore 10,000:55,906 = 17.9%. This is below 30% and therefore the estimated P/E ratio is 10.5. The estimated ordinary share price can now be found.

Earnings attributable to equity	£8,719,000
P/E ratio	10.5
Market capitalisation	£91,550,000
Number of shares in issue	14,405,286
Estimated price per share	£6.36

(ii) The market value of the equity is the market capitalisation calculated above, ie £91,550,000.

(iii) The combined market value of the £10m debt and the equity will be £101,550,000. It is assumed that the debt continues to be valued at par.

Option (2)

(i) The shares will be issued **at a discount of 15%** to the price of 534.24p ie an issue price of 454 pence per share. The total number of new shares to be issued is £10m/£4.54 = 2,202,644 shares, bringing the **total number of shares in issue** to 12,202,644.

The earnings for the year can now be calculated.

	£'000
Earnings before interest and tax	14,014
Interest on new loan at 12%	(1,200)
Interest on existing loan at 10%	(1,000)
	11,814
Tax at 33%	(3,899)
Earnings attributable to equity	7,915
Dividends	(2,807)
Retained profit	5,109

The financing side of the balance sheet at 30 September 19X6 will be as follows.

	£'000
Ordinary share capital	6,101
Share premium account	8,899
Retained profit (15,500 + 5,109)	20,609
Long-term debt: 12%	10,000
Long-term debt: 10%	10,000
Total financing	55,609

The debt to total asset ratio is 20,000:55,609 = 36.0%. This is between 30% and 40% and the expected P/E is 10.0. The estimated ordinary share price can be found as follows.

Earnings attributable to equity	£7,915,000
P/E ratio	10.0
Market capitalisation	£79,150,000
Number of shares in issue	12,202,644
Estimated price per share	£6.49

(ii) The market value of the equity is the market capitalisation of £79,150,000.

(iii) The combined market value of the £20m debt and the equity will be £99,150,000, assuming that the debt continues to be valued at par.

Option (3)

(i) No new shares will be issued and the total number in issue remains **constant** at 10,000,000.

The **earnings for the year** can now be calculated as above.

	£'000
Earnings before interest and tax	14,014
Interest on new loan at 14%	(2,800)
Interest on existing loan at 10%	(1,000)
	10,214
Tax at 33%	(3,371)
Earnings attributable to equity	6,843
Dividends	(2,300)
Retained profit	4,543

The financing side of the balance sheet at 30 September 19X6 will be as follows.

	£'000
Ordinary share capital	5,000
Retained profit (15,500 + 4,543)	20,043
Long-term debt: 14%	20,000
Long-term debt: 10%	10,000
Total financing	55,043

The debt to total asset ratio is 30,000:55,043 = 54.5%. This is above 50% and the expected P/E is 8.5. The estimated ordinary share price can now be found.

Earnings attributable to equity	£6,843,000
P/E ratio	8.5
Market capitalisation	£58,165,000
Number of shares in issue	10,000,000
Estimated price per share	£5.82

(ii) The market value of the equity is the market capitalisation of £58,165,000.

(iii) The combined market value of the £30m debt and the equity will be £88,165,000, assuming the debt to be valued at par.

Summary of the effect of the proposals on the market capitalisation:

	Option 1	*Option 2*	*Option 3*
Existing market capitalisation	53,424	53,424	53,424
New market capitalisation	91,550	79,150	58,165
Less sum subscribed	(20,000)	(10,000)	0
Net rise in market capitalisation	18,126	15,726	4,741

(c) REPORT

To: Terry and Susan
From: Management Accountant Date: 21 November 19X5
Subject: TS Products plc - capital structure proposals

Introduction

The purpose of this report is to evaluate the **alternative capital structure proposals** that have been put forward to allow the expansion of TS Products plc. This appraisal has been made on purely financial grounds, although some comments on the wider implications of the alternatives under discussion have been included.

Nature of the business

The current operations of the company have shown strong growth in turnover and earnings. Profitability is high at 29% (profit before interest and tax: turnover), and this should increase still further by the addition of the new production process which shows a projected return on sales of 31%. However, the new process is more at risk from the effect of sales being lower than expected since fixed costs are relatively high at £2.5m pa. The breakeven level for the new operation is 8,334 packs per year, and this should be achievable if the sales projections are reasonable.

However, sales would not need to fall far below projections for the level of earnings to fall significantly.

It is not known how the cost structure of the new process compares with that of the existing operations, but given that both sales and earnings from these areas are projected to increase by the same percentage next year it seems reasonable to suppose that the fixed cost element of the existing process is much lower.

Thus when evaluating the alternative financial structures, the directors should be aware of the fact that future earnings could show more volatility than has been the case in the past.

Evaluation of the financing alternatives

The summary of the effect of the proposals on the **market capitalisation** shows that although Option 2 results in the largest rise in the share price, Option 1 gives the greatest net increase in the market capitalisation and hence the greatest increase in the wealth of the ordinary shareholders.

The calculations do not support the view of the Finance Director that the expansion should be financed through debt since the increase in **financial risk** results in an increase in the cost of debt at higher levels, and a lower P/E value presumably on account of the perception of increased risk. Since general projections of inflation are that it is likely to remain constant and not to increase as she suggests, this adds further weight to the argument for including some form of additional equity in the new capital structure.

The data appear to support the views of the non-executive director in some respects in that the estimated share price does fall when the gearing level reaches a higher level. However, the calculations show that the share price is maximised by the inclusion of some degree of debt in the capital structure, the 50:50 option appearing to give the best results in these terms. It is difficult to comment on his view that interest rates are likely to fall since this conflicts with the view of the Finance Director that inflation is likely to increase. Since the general view is that inflation is likely to remain constant it seems reasonable to suppose that if rates do come down it is only likely to be by a very small amount which is probably not significant in the context of these discussions.

The directors should also consider some **further factors** before reaching their decision. These include the following.

(i) The **relative costs** of the three options. The issue costs of Option 2 are likely to be the highest, followed by Option 1, with Option 3 being the cheapest.

(ii) Expectations of movements in the **tax rate** and the **interest rate** would impact upon the calculations.

(iii) If equity is to be issued, the form which this would take is important since the number of shares is significant in relation to the number currently in issue. If the issue took the form of a placing with a small number of institutions this could have a significant effect on the balance of ownership and control. Terry and Susan currently own 52% of the shares and hence retain control of the company. Even Option 2 would mean that this level of control would be lost unless they were able to subscribe for a significant number of the new shares themselves.

(iv) The calculations are sensitive to the assumptions made about **dividend payout ratios**. This is an issue that needs to be addressed at the same time as the financing decision.

Conclusions

In purely financial terms and on the basis of the information provided, Option 1 provides the best alternative from the point of view of the shareholders. However, as has been discussed, a number of other factors must be taken into account before reaching a decision. In particular, it would be interesting to know more about how the financial advisers have arrived at their estimates of the **relationship between the P/E ratio and the gearing level,** and to have information on which to evaluate the **NPV of the projected cash flows to the shareholders.**

Signed: Management Accountant

(d) (i) It is presumed that the Finance Director is basing his comment on the movement in the **P/E ratio**. This can be summarised as follows.

		P/E
30 September 19X4	£40m/£4.613m	8.7
30 September 19X5	£56m/£5.936m	9.4
Current		9.0
Projected		10.5 - based on existing gearing

The projections made by the financial advisers suggest that the P/E ratio should increase to 10.5 as a result of the investment being undertaken and with the existing level of gearing (less than 30%). In fact, the P/E ratio has fallen since the end of the year, and it is this fall that has presumably led to the Finance Director's comment, since it might be assumed that if investors were aware of the project then the P/E ratio would have risen due to the expected increase in the level of earnings.

However, it is possible that the investing public is aware of the proposals but that the P/E ratio has still fallen, for one of the following reasons.

(1) The overall level of prices on the market has fallen for reasons outside the control of the company, for example due to expectations of a rise in interest rates. What is really important is the movement in the P/E ratio relative to the market as a whole and to the sector in which TS Products operates.

(2) It is possible that the investing public are aware of the proposed expansion, but that they believe that the company will have to make a significant increase in its gearing level in order to achieve it. If the increase in the gearing level is being factored into their evaluation then, given the projections of the financial advisers, it is not surprising that the P/E ratio should fall.

(ii) It will be in the interests of the company to inform investors if three conditions are fulfilled.

(1) The directors should be close to reaching a consensus on the both the detailed form of the project and the method by which it is to be financed. Once information is released about the project, they are likely to come under pressure to provide further information on these subjects and if clear decisions have not been reached they run the risk of appearing not to know what they are doing. Such an appearance of indecision could result in a drop in confidence in the company leading to a fall in the share price and making it harder to raise large amounts of debt capital from the potential lenders.

(2) The directors should be confident that an early release of the information will have a positive effect on the P/E ratio and the share price.

(3) The directors must be confident that the early release of the information will not have an adverse impact on the company's market position by providing sensitive information to competitors earlier than is necessary.

It will be to the advantage of the company if the P/E ratio and the share price can be increased prior to the date of the new capital being issued since this will help to make new shares more attractive to the investing public and hence help to maximise the price at which they can be issued. This will mean that less shares have to be issued and hence that the amount of dilution in earnings in the coming years is minimised, and that a good level of **dividend cover** is maintained.

There are various ways in which the market could be informed of the proposals. Probably the most effective method would be to prepare a **press release** for publication in the trade and the financial press. If the company has informal links with the institutional investors then it would be advisable to make use of these as well.

(e) The fact that the directors and some senior managers hold **share options** does not of itself change the nature of the decision making process. Knowledge of the options should be in the public domain since information on this area must be provided in the annual report of the company. The key factor is that the directors must be able to show that at all times they acted in the best interests of *all* the shareholders, and that for example they did not issue misleading information with a view to 'talking up' the share price in order to maximise their personal gains through transactions involving the share options. They should also be able to demonstrate that they did not trade in the shares on the basis of privileged insider information.

69 GLOBAL TELECOMMUNICATIONS INC

Pass marks. In part (a)(i) you should summarise the arguments for the use of the NPV approach to capital investment decisions. You should then evaluate the specific risks attaching to this project in relation to the other operations of the company in arriving at your recommendations relating to the discount rate.

In your calculations in part (a)(ii) you should take a five year timeframe for all the options, capitalising the terminal values at the cost of capital in year 5. When calculating the terminal value in Option 2 remember that GTI holds only an 80% stake in the subsidiary. Do not forget to work in US$, not sterling.

In part (b) you should take into account the political position of the IFC as well as the effect of the options upon the capital structure and the opportunity for additional profitable uses of the funds released in the event of a loan being raised.

In part (c) you can draw on your knowledge of the UK regulatory authorities and apply this to the Zenobia situation. Bear in mind that the activities of the regulators will be different in industries which still have effective monopolies from those where an element of true competition is being introduced.

Examiner's comment. The question aimed to test the candidate's ability to apply conventional investment appraisal techniques, including the determination of the discount rate, to an investment decision. The question also examined for knowledge and understanding of how social benefits and costs, as perceived by a government, can influence investment decisions. Also covered by this case study were the influence of external constraints on policy decisions, methods of financing the investment, knowledge of regulatory bodies and their ability to affect financial transactions. However, many candidates were clearly unprepared for a question carrying 60 marks.

(a) (i)

REPORT

To: Board of Directors
From: Management Accountant Date: 23 May 19X5
Subject: Evaluation of international investment decisions

Introduction

This paper is concerned with the selection of the appropriate method to be used in **evaluating international investment decisions** with particular regard to the Zenobia opportunity. Choice of an **appropriate discount rate** for NPV appraisal will be considered, together with the effect of risk on the evaluation method.

Choice of appraisal method

The decision on whether to invest in a particular project in a foreign country is based on exactly the same theory as home investment decisions. The principal aim is to **maximise the wealth of the ordinary shareholders** as measured by the **net present value (NPV)** of the projected cash flows. From the point of view of achieving this stated aim therefore, the appraisal should be based on an evaluation of the NPV of the project cashflows discounted at the cost of capital. This approach is superior to others available such as the payback period or the accounting rate of return.

Choice of discount rate

The current **cost of capital** to GTI is 15%. In situations where the project is small in relation to the size of the company and where the risk profile is similar to that of the existing operations, then the cost of capital provides an appropriate discount rate to use in investment appraisal since it requires each project to increase the net present worth of the organisation and hence to increase shareholder value. However, the Zenobia project does not fit into this category for two reasons.

(1) The investment required is large in relation to the estimated potential market capitalisation of GTI of £200m. It is as yet uncertain how the finance is to be raised, but if the cost of new capital is significantly more expensive than the present rate then this should be taken into account in the evaluation of the project.

(2) It is likely to carry more risk than existing operations due to the following.

    Exchange rate exposure. As the Managing Director points out, receipts and payments are not matched, most of the investment required being in dollars while the revenues are in local currency. Traditional hedging methods are not available since there is no forward market in the local currency, and therefore if the dollar strengthens as is likely, GTI will face a loss on exchange. Since such a depreciation is probable this negates any potential benefits of risk reduction through international diversification.

    Political risk. Although there is a new democratically elected government which has an expressed desire to attract foreign direct investment, there is a history of political instability in this part of the world. Any change in government represents a risk to GTI of a radical change in this policy which could result in the nationalisation of assets and restrictions on currency remittances out of the country. This would result in a discontinuity in the cash flows which as the Finance Director points out would otherwise show a strong correlation from one year to the next.

Diversification. This will be GTI's first experience of direct investment in a developing country. It is therefore likely that mistakes will be made while the management passes through the learning curve. This means that returns could be lower than projected.

There are various methods available to allow for the higher than normal level of risk associated with this project. Probably the simplest and most effective approach is to add a premium to the existing cost of capital. Since this is cumulative, it should provide sufficient allowance for the fact that the three options have different lifespans.

Conclusions

It is recommended that GTI should undertake an NPV comparison of the different options. A premium should be added to the cost of capital to allow for the significantly higher level of risk attaching to this project as compared with our other investments.

Signed: Management Accountant

(ii) REPORT

To: Board of Directors
From: Management Accountant Date: 23 May 19X5
Subject: Evaluation of proposed investment in Zenobia

Introduction

This report is concerned with the financial evaluation of the three options under consideration with regard to the proposed investment in Zenobia. Detailed numerical analysis is provided in the Appendix to this report.

Financial evaluation

The three options have been evaluated at a discount rate of 20% over a five year timescale. The calculations suggest that the GoZ Option 2 provides the best NPV and should therefore be the preferred option. However, it is apparent that the **terminal value** is of key importance in determining the outcome of the calculations. The estimates for all the options are subject to a high degree of uncertainty, and GTI must be very confident of obtaining the projected price for the subsidiary before making a final choice of this option. The terminal values are particularly subject to **political risk** as discussed in a previous paper, and the Board would be well advised to look further into this area before making any decisions as to the investment route.

Signed: Management Accountant

Appendix

Year	*0*	*1*	*2*	*3*	*4*	*5*
20% discount factor	1.000	0.833	0.694	0.579	0.482	0.402
	$m	$m	$m	$m	$m	$m
GTI proposal						
Initial investment	(25.0)					
Operating cashflow		3.5	4.8	5.6	6.8	7.2
Residual (6.0/20%)[1]						30.0
Net cashflow	(25.0)	3.5	4.8	5.6	6.8	37.2
DCF	(25.0)	2.9	3.3	3.2	3.3	15.0
Cumulative DCF	(25.0)	(22.1)	(18.8)	(15.5)	(12.2)	2.7
GoZ Option 1						
Initial investment	(30.0)					
Operating cashflow		3.0	4.3	5.1	6.3	6.7
Further investment[2]				(5.2)		
Extra operating cashflow					1.6	1.6
Residual (6.7 + 1.6)/20%)						41.5
Net cashflow	(30.0)	3.0	4.3	(0.1)	7.9	49.8
DCF	(30.0)	2.5	3.0	(0.1)	3.8	20.0
Cumulative DCF	(30.0)	(27.5)	(24.5)	(24.6)	(20.8)	(0.8)
GoZ Option 2						
Initial investment	(20.0)					
Operating cashflow		3.9	5.3	6.2	7.5	7.9
Residual (7.9 × 80%/20%)						31.6
Net cashflow	(20.0)	3.9	5.3	6.2	7.5	39.5
DCF	(20.0)	3.2	3.7	3.6	3.6	15.9
Cumulative DCF	(20.0)	(16.8)	(13.1)	(9.5)	(5.9)	10.0

Notes

1. Residual values have been capitalised at the cost of capital (20%) and added to the income in the fifth year.

2. The further investment required in year 3 under Option 1 is calculated as the expected number of additional lines (2,600) multiplied by the cost of connection ($2,000 per line).

(b) Since the size of the investment required is large in relation to the size of the company, the **choice of financing method** is likely to have a significant impact on GTI's **capital structure**. At present the company is 100% equity financed. This guarantees full control to the shareholders and minimises the amount of financial risk, but it also means that the cost of capital, currently estimated at 15% is high when one considers that the market rate of interest is 12.5% and this is tax deductible at 40%. If GTI chose to introduce debt into the capital structure it should be able to achieve a noticeable reduction in its weighted average cost of capital (WACC) due to the effect of the tax shield on the interest payments.

Given the above, GTI should consider taking on some form of debt provided that it has worthwhile alternative opportunities in which to invest the surplus internally generated funds. The benefit of the IFC loan in this situation is that it offers a fixed rate of interest which is below the current market level. If it is expected that market rates will remain stable or rise over the next five years then this loan becomes increasingly attractive. Alternatively, if rates were to fall then this weakens the case for the IFC loan.

A further benefit of obtaining IFC investment is that if **political problems** do arise during the course of the project, GTI would have an ally with superior political influence which could assist in obtaining a reasonable outcome.

(c) (i) In industries which have a fully competitive structure, the view is that the process of competition will ensure that, in the long term, resources are allocated reasonably fairly between the different stakeholders in the firm. Competition should result in improvements in the value delivered to customers which should in turn lead to growth, and this should provide the firm with the ability to offer good working conditions, fair trading terms and to generate cash for the shareholders and for the government through taxes.

However, the process of privatisation has resulted in industries where there is either a **local monopoly**, for example the water companies, or where there is only limited, albeit growing competition, for example telecommunications. In these situations, the lack of full competition means that there is a danger that the interests of customers will be subordinated to those of other stakeholders such as shareholders and employees. One solution to these problems is to create regulatory authorities whose main objectives are to ensure a reasonable equality of interest between the different stakeholder groups and to prevent the abuse of monopoly power.

The activities of the regulators will depend to some extent on whether there is a full or a partial monopoly. Examples include:

(1) setting pricing formulae, for example those in UK telecommunications that are linked to inflation;

(2) ensuring that funds for long-term investment are used appropriately, for example investment in the water industry to reduce the level of leakage, and to improve the quality of drinking water to given standards by given dates;

(3) in industries where there is a gradually increasing level of competition such as telecommunications, the regulator will monitor the levels of pricing within different market segments. The purpose of this is to prevent unfair competition through the use of cross-subsidisation whereby one sector where there is still a monopoly subsidises another where there is a higher degree of competition;

(4) in privatised industries where there is a level of inter-company trading between what were previously operating divisions the regulator will be concerned to establish a fair transfer pricing system. An example of this is the relationship between Railtrack and the regional railway companies.

(ii) Since Zoftel is only now being established it is not in a position to play a role in the current negotiations between GTI and the GoZ. Neither should it be able to alter the structure of the agreement once signed. Since all the options under consideration have an initial exclusivity period of varying length, followed by the introduction of competition, the role of Zoftel is likely to change over time.

During the initial period of exclusivity, its role is likely to be similar to that of Ofwat in the UK where there is an effective monopoly situation. It is likely to attempt to regulate price through some type of formula and to ensure that GTI complies with the detail of the agreement made with the GoZ, particularly if Option 1 is selected which provides for a subsidised rural service in addition to the main cellular service in the 'urban rectangle'.

Once other competitors enter the market, Zoftel's role is likely to become more similar to that of Oftel in the UK where the emphasis is on quality of service and the promotion of open competition within each of the market segments.

70 GARDEN WORLD PLC

Pass marks. In part (a) be careful to explain which discount rate you have used and the reasons for your choice, together with any other assumptions about taxation and the timing of payments.

In part (b) it is helpful to explain the effect of the terminal value on the calculations, and in part (d) to separate the use of the terminal value for investment appraisal from the actual intentions of the management with regard to the new business.

Other points. This is a wide ranging question which deals with the certainty equivalent method of adjusting for risk in investment appraisal, as well as other issues concerned with capital structure.

(a) **Garden World plc - retail investment - cash flow projections**

	Yr 0	*Yr 1*	*Yr 2*	*Yr 3*	*Yr 4*	*Yr 5*
	£'000	£'000	£'000	£'000	£'000	£'000
Contribution		(182)	406	1,828	2,837	
Taxation			143	(72)	(557)	(901)
Land and buildings	(4,750)				4,750	
Fittings and equipment	(1,000)				315	
Working capital	(500)	(100)	(150)	(50)	800	
W/cap inflation (W2)		(24)	(37)	(39)	100	
Disposal proceeds (W3)					5,487	
Disposal - tax						(1,811)
	(6,250)	(306)	361	1,667	13,732	(2,712)
Certainty equiv.	1.00	0.90	0.85	0.80	0.75	0.70
8% discount factor	1.000	0.926	0.857	0.794	0.735	0.681
Discounted certainty equivalent	(6,250)	(255)	263	1,059	7,570	(1,293)
Cumulative PV	(6,250)	(6,505)	(6,242)	(5,183)	2,387	1,094

Workings

1

	Yr 1	*Yr 2*	*Yr 3*	*Yr 4*	*Yr 5*
	£'000	£'000	£'000	£'000	£'000
Sales	1,750	3,250	5,250	6,250	
Direct costs	(1,500)	(2,300)	(3,100)	(3,300)	
Marketing	(300)	(450)	(400)	(400)	
Overhead	(125)	(125)	(125)	(125)	
Cont'n before inflation	(175)	375	1,625	2,425	
After inflation	(182)	406	1,828	2,837	
Capital allowances	(250)	(188)	(141)	(107)	
Taxable profit	(432)	218	1,687	2,730	
Taxation at 33%		143	(72)	(557)	(901)

2 Working capital inflation is calculated as follows.

$600\,(1.04 - 1) = 24$

$750\,(1.04^2 - 1) = 61 = 24 + 37$

$800\,(1.04^3 - 1) = 100 = 61 + 39$

3 Disposal proceeds will be as follows.

	£
Taxable profit in year 4*	2,730
Tax at 33%	(901)
Post-tax profit	1,829
Post-tax profit × 3	5,487
Tax on disposal proceeds - payable year 5	(1,811)

* This can be used since the depreciation is calculated on the same basis as the capital allowances.

Notes

1 Depreciation is excluded from the calculations since this does not have a cash component.

2 The allocation of head office operating costs is excluded since this will be incurred whether or not the project is undertaken.

3 Surveyors' fees of £250,000 are excluded since these are sunk costs.

4 Since certainty equivalents are being used, the project cash flows will be discounted at the risk free rate of 8%.

5 It is assumed that the tax loss in year 1 can be offset against other group income.

On the basis of the calculations above, the investment should produce a positive net present value of £1.096m. It therefore appears to be financially worthwhile.

(b) (i) In reality, the appraisal might differ from that shown above for the following reasons.

(1) A critical element in the calculations is the terminal value of the project. In reality there are likely to be a number of possible exit routes which would need to be evaluated. The company might also consider the possibility of continuing to operate the retail arm directly for longer than the projected four years.

(2) Reality is likely to be much more complex than the projections suggest. It is unlikely that all the factors in the cash flow will be subject to exactly 4% inflation and the rates are also likely to vary over time. It would therefore be helpful to carry out a more detailed sensitivity analysis in this area, and also to consider the effect of changes in the tax rate.

(3) It is unlikely that the risk free rate will remain constant over the period. It would therefore be helpful to consider the effect of changes in the cost of capital and perhaps to look at the internal rate of return of the project.

(4) There are likely to be more choices available than a simple 'go ahead or abandon' decision. For instance, the scale, degree of specialisation and location could all be varied.

(5) Assumptions about overall market growth and market share would need to be examined and the project evaluated in the light of different operating scenarios.

(6) The availability of capital and the projected contribution of other alternative investments will affect the final choice of projects.

(ii) Judgmental factors to be considered include the following.

(1) The likely effect of the investment on the company's other markets. Since Garden World is considering competing directly with some of its

customers, this may depress sales of other divisions and cause a deterioration in the relationships with its customers.

(2) The technical ability and managerial capacity of the company to achieve the target growth.

(3) Where this investment fits into the long-term strategic plan and aims of the company. If it is crucial to achieving the company's long-term objectives then it will not be looked at on the same basis as an opportunistic diversification.

(4) The interrelationships between volume, price, direct costs and fixed overheads, including price sensitivity and the effect of marketing and advertising.

(c) Two alternative methods which could be used to adjust for risk are as follows.

(i) **Restricting the payback period.** This approach recognises the fact that the level of uncertainty increases with the length of the time horizon. Therefore the company may decide to set a limit to the amount of time a project will be allowed to pay back. In practice this is often between three and five years. Even if a limit is not set it is helpful to compare the payback period of different projects since this provides some measure of their relative risk.

(ii) **Capital asset pricing model**. This can be used to quantify the effect on the cost of equity to the company due to the change in the level of risk arising from the new investment. This can then be used to calculate the new cost of capital which in turn is used to evaluate the project. Thus the CAPM provides a means of adjusting the discount rate to take into account the additional risk which the company will face as a result of undertaking the investment. The advantage of this method is that it allows the direct comparison of projects which fall into different risk classes. However the method is complex to use in practice and it must be remembered that estimates of returns and probabilities will be subjective. In addition, the CAPM is really a single period model and thus it should only be used when it is expected that conditions will be stable for the life of the project.

(d) The retail investment project will require a capital outlay in the region of £6.5m. The projected cash flows show that the capital outlay should be recouped quickly, with the cumulative net present value becoming positive in year 4. This implies that any loan could be repaid in year 4. However, this is very dependent on Garden World achieving a successful sale of the business at that time. The calculations are also sensitive to the accuracy of the certainty equivalents and the way in which they reflect the relationship between risk and return in the capital market.

The **type of debt to be selected** will depend on:

(i) whether the directors are actually intending to sell the subsidiary in year 4, or whether the sale price has only been calculated for the purpose of providing a terminal value to enable the investment to be evaluated over four years;

(ii) the way in which interest rates are expected to move in the medium term.

If the directors are intending to sell the subsidiary, then the **medium-term borrowing option** looks attractive. This offers the lowest rate and could be repaid at the end of year 4 from the proceeds of the sale. Thus the company is not left with debt which it no longer requires. On the face of it this is also the cheapest option, although it is not stated whether the rates quoted are fixed or floating. Assuming that the rates are fixed, and in the situation where a sale of the subsidiary is not being seriously considered, this option would also be attractive if the directors expect that interest rates are set to fall. The investment could then be refinanced at a lower rate within the next five years since the company would not be locked into long-term borrowings.

Long-term borrowing becomes attractive in the situation where interest rates are expected to rise. This would allow maximum advantage to be taken of the existing low level of rates. It is also a better option if the company is intending to continue to operate the subsidiary directly for the foreseeable future since the need to roll over debt at the end of a shorter term is avoided.

Convertibles will also be attractive if the company is not intending to sell the new business in year 4. They provide a means of taking advantage of the lower cost of debt and the tax advantages of debt in the medium term, and have the added benefit of being self-liquidating, provided that the share price increases in line with expectations at the date of issue. The long-term borrowing capacity of the company is therefore not impaired.

Preference shares are less attractive. Although they possess many of the features of loan stock, the preference dividend is not allowable for tax and therefore they are relatively expensive to service. Since the dividend can be passed in the event of the company having a poor year, and since they rank behind other debt for repayment, they are also relatively unattractive to investors.

(e) **Merchant banks** provide companies with a point of access to the capital markets. Companies can take advantage of their knowledge of and technical ability in the markets to achieve the most suitable and efficient form of financing. The services which they offer include the following.

(i) They can advise Garden World on the current view of interest rates and suggest to them particularly appropriate financing opportunities which are currently available.

(ii) They can advise on the procedure to be followed in making the issue and help the company to ensure that all legislative and regulatory requirements are complied with.

(iii) They can advise on the timing and pricing of any issue.

(iv) They may offer an underwriting service to ensure that the offer is adequately subscribed.

(f) (i) A key factor for an established company in deciding on the method of issue is the **effect of the choice on the existing shareholders**. Shareholders normally have **pre-emptive rights** which means that any new issue of shares must first be offered to them. However it is possible for the company to obtain a waiver of the pre-emptive rights in general meeting. This can be done up to a year in advance in the AGM.

In practice, the choice of issue method for an established company is generally between a **rights issue** and a **placing**. One of the main advantages of the rights issue is that the existing structure of ownership and control remains unchanged.

In a placing, the shares are sold in large blocks to a small number of large, usually institutional investors. As a result, no underwriting is needed since a purchaser for the shares is arranged as a part of the issue process. It may also be possible to obtain a higher price than could be obtained from a rights issue.

(ii) In setting the issue price, the directors will be aiming to obtain the required amount of capital for the minimum number of shares. Although in theory, any number of shares could be issued provided that the authorised capital is not breached, in practice the number will be kept to a minimum. The **new shares will have to be priced at a discount** to the current market price of the existing shares in order to make them attractive to investors. However if the discount is too large this could result in a significant dilution in earnings per share which could in turn impact on the share price.

Stage 4 **MOCK EXAM**

Paper 13 *November 1999*

Strategic Financial Management

SFM

INSTRUCTIONS TO CANDIDATES

You are allowed three hours to answer this question paper. *Tables, formulae and symbols for use in the examination are to be found on pages (xxx) to (xxxiv) of this Kit.*
Answer the ONE question in section A. *Answer TWO questions ONLY from section B.*

DO NOT OPEN THIS PAPER UNTIL YOU ARE READY TO START UNDER EXAMINATION CONDITIONS

SECTION A - 60 MARKS

THE QUESTION IS ON PAGE 266

This question relates to the scenario below.

VG PLC

Background

VG is a manufacturer of electrical equipment. It is based in the south of England. The company trades with a large number of customers, mainly in Europe and Asia. Less than 10% of the company's business is in the United Kingdom. Over the past 2 to 3 years, it has experienced difficulties in its chosen markets and has been forced to cut back some of its operations. Its turnover has fallen from £48 million in 1998 to £33 million in the year to 31 October 1999. Profits have also fallen steadily and in the year to 31 October 1999 the company sustained a loss, in part because of exchange rate losses. It is now in serious financial difficulties and may be forced into liquidation unless the Directors can negotiate a re-financing package.

Extracts from VG plc's balance sheet at	*31 October 1998*		*31 October 1999 (Draft)*	
	£'000	£'000	£'000	£'000
Fixed assets				
Freehold property		3,500		3,500
Plant, equipment and vehicles (NBV)		4,850		3,850
Current assets				
Stock	5,250		4,500	
Debtors	6,250		5,250	
Total current assets		11,500		9,750
Less current liabilities				
Overdraft (Note 1)	(1,900)		(2,475)	
Trade creditors (Note 2)	(9,100)		(9,500)	
Tax payable (Note 3)	(650)		-	
Dividends payable	-		-	
10% debenture 2000 (Note 4)	(3,000)		(3,000)	
Total current liabilities		(14,650)		(14,975)
Net assets		5,200		2,125
Financed by				
Ordinary shares (50 pence par value)		4,000		4,000
Reserves		1,200		(1,875)
		5,200		2,125

Notes

1 The overdraft at 31 October 1999 is the maximum agreed facility and is unsecured. Interest is payable at 6% above base rates, which are currently 6%. No change in rates is expected for the foreseeable future.

2 80% of trade creditors at 31 October 1999 are seriously overdue.

3 The company's marginal tax rate is 30%.

4 The debenture is secured on the company's fixed assets. It is due to be repaid at the end of June 2000.

Asset valuation

The company's fixed assets are old and, in many cases, obsolete because of the fast changing technology required in the industry. The realisable value of plant, equipment and vehicles is estimated at £2.25 million. The value of its property has also fallen and the current expected realisable value is £2.5 million. The valuation of current assets is also likely to be less than shown in the balance sheet. 25% of stock is considered unsaleable. The balance could probably be sold at an average of 80% of its book value. An estimated 10% of debtors are expected to default.

Market information

The company is listed on the Alternative Investment Market (AIM). It was floated in 1992 at a price of 325 pence per share. The original owners of the firm retained, and still own, 60% of the issued shares. One institutional investor owns 20% of the shares and around a thousand private investors own the remainder.

The current share price (at 23 November 1999) is 28 pence compared with 68 pence at the same time last year. No dividend has been paid for the past two years. The debentures are trading at £95 per £100 nominal, ex interest.

The return on the market is forecast at 12% and the risk-free rate at 6%. The company's quoted equity beta is currently 1.4. However, the restructuring is likely to result in a fall in beta to 1.2.

Profit improvement proposals

The company has the opportunity to bid for a number of new contracts but would need to upgrade much of its plant and equipment. This would require £2.5 million of capital expenditure and £0.5 million of working capital Some of its old equipment could be sold to raise an estimated £1 million. If won, these contracts would improve the company's pre-tax profits by an estimated £1,200,000 per annum.

Restructuring proposal

The board of VG plc has been approached by a venture capital organisation which is willing to provide £4 million in new equity and £2 million in new 12% unsecured debt, repayable in 2005, if the company agrees to restructure its capital base. The conditions are as follows.

(i) All existing shares are effectively cancelled and 8.6 million new £1 shares are issued at par. The venture capitalise will take 4 million of the shares. The existing shareholders will be given one new share for every five old ones currently held.

(ii) The debenture is cancelled and the existing debenture holders are given 100 new ordinary shares in exchange for every £100 debenture.

(iii) Warrants will be attached to the new shares issued to the debenture holders in exchange for their debt. These warrants will give the option to purchase in three years' time, at par, one share for every two shares issued to them at the time of the reconstruction. The holders of the old ordinary shares and the venture capitalist will not be given these warrants.

(iv) No dividends will be paid for the next three years. Shareholders will be given annually a scrip dividend of 1 share for every 10 held. This policy will be reviewed in three years' time.

(v) The venture capitalist company will take two seats on the board of directors, including the position of Chairman.

(vi) The company's bank will be asked to agreed to convert the outstanding overdraft facility into a medium-term loan at 10% interest secured on the company's fixed assets. The bank will also be asked to provide an overdraft facility of £1 million secured by a floating charge on the company's current assets.

(vii) The trade creditors will be paid 40 pence in the pound immediately the reconstruction is approved, and the remainder six months later.

Finish reading the scenario above before attempting this question.

Parts (b), (c) and (d) of this question relate specifically to the scenario.

Answers to part (a) of the question should be in general terms, although the scenario details may be used for illustration purposes.

1 **(a)** During a period of financial difficulties, the liquidation value of a company may appear to be higher than its value as a going concern.

Discuss reasons why, in such a situation, liquidation might not be in the best interest of the shareholders. **8 Marks**

(b) Calculate and comment briefly on:

(i) VG plc's expected value if liquidated
(ii) the cash disbursements to the various creditors on liquidation
(iii) the effect on VG plc's cash position if the venture capitalist provides re-financing. **10 Marks**

(c) Assume you are a financial adviser to VG plc.

Write a report to the Directors of the company that assessed whether the proposals are likely to be acceptable to shareholders and other providers of finance. Your report should have two main sections.

Section 1: the immediate effect on all providers of finance. **15 Marks**

Section 2 should include, but not necessarily be limited to, a discussion of the following matters:

- the effects the revised capital structure and dividend policy might have on the company's share price and value of the company
- the medium-term effects of the proposals
- possible exit routes for the venture capitalist
- alternative actions in respect of financial or organisational issues that the company could consider to relieve the current financial difficulties **17 Marks**

Note. You are not expected to restate the balance sheet or prepare an investment appraisal.

(d) Many of VG plc's problems have arisen as a result of difficulties in overseas markets, including poor management of debtors.

(i) Explain the risks faced by an exporting company with a large number of overseas customers

(ii) Discuss ways in which VG plc could have managed these risks better than it appears to have done. **10 Marks**

Total Marks = 60

SECTION B - 40 MARKS

ANSWER ***TWO*** QUESTIONS ONLY - 20 MARKS EACH

2 RP plc is a medium-sized importer and exporter of textile and other heavy machinery. It sells its products worldwide and has a policy of hedging all its overseas transactions in excess of a sterling equivalent of £100,000. Typically the company uses money market hedges or forward contracts. Below £100,000, the company bears the exchange risk itself.

The company's profits after interest for the past two years were as follows:

Year to	*30 September 1998*	*30 September 1999*
	£ million	£ million
Profit after interest	2.919	2.026

If the company had *not* hedged its currency risks, the profits would have been £2.141 million in 1998 and 2.373 million in 1999.

The Chief Executive is concerned about the effect hedging costs have had on the bottom line, especially as a hedging operation for a large contract is currently being arranged. He has asked for a report with a view to considering changing the company's policy on hedging.

The details of the proposed hedge are as follows.

The company is due to pay a French supplier FFr 2.5 million in three months' time for machinery for which RP plc has already found a buyer within the UK for £300,000. Today's exchange rate is FFr 8.9321 to the £1. On the advice of the Treasurer, the company is proposing to take out a contract to purchase FFr 2.5 million in three months' time at the forward rate of FFr 8.8820

REQUIREMENT:

As Financial Manager with RP plc, write a report to the Chief Executive explaining:

- the purpose of hedging and the advantages and disadvantages of the company's current policy;
- the financial implications of the hedging contract currently being considered. For the purposes of illustration and comparison, assume the FFr:
  - (a) weakens against the £ sterling in three months' time to 8.9975; and
  - (b) strengthens against the £ to 8.6500;
- the factors the company should consider before changing its policy, in particular taking a decision not to hedge future foreign currency transactions;
- alternative methods of managing currency risks which might be available to the company.

Total Marks = 20

3 ABC Limited is considering the purchase of a fleet of small delivery vehicles. The usage of the vehicles would be very heavy as they would be operated round the clock by teams of drivers working on shifts. The estimated maximum life of the vehicles is therefore only three years, after which they would be virtually worthless and scrapped. However, if they were taken out of service before the end of three years, they would have a positive 'abandonment' cash flow. The estimated post-tax cash flows for each vehicle are as follows.

Year	*Initial investment and operating cash flow*	*End of year 'abandonment' cash flow*
	£	£
0	(10,000)	(10,000)
1	4,200	6,200
2	4,000	4,000
3	3,500	0

The company uses a cost of capital of 12% to evaluate investment of this type.

REQUIREMENTS:

(a) (i) Calculate

- the NPV for each vehicle if it is operated for the full three years
- the NPV for each vehicle if it is abandoned at the end of year 2 or year 1.

(ii) Comment on the economic life of this project and discuss, briefly, the advantages of including an abandonment option in the investment appraisal exercise. **7 Marks**

(b) Assume the company decides to run the vehicles for three years. The cost of each vehicle is as above, ie £10,000 with zero scrap value. The company is considering the most appropriate method of financing the vehicles. Two alternatives are being considered.

Alternative 1 A three-year loan from the bank with equal repayments at the end of each year that would comprise principal and interest at 10% per annum gross.

Alternative 2 A three-year finance lease. The costs would be £4,000 per vehicle per year, payable at the beginning of each year. Assume tax relief is available on the full lease payments.

Notes

- ABC Limited would be responsible for all maintenance, insurance etc with either alternative
- The company pays tax at the rate of 33%
- Writing down allowances are available on the vehicles at 25% reducing balance
- Loan payments are made gross at the end of each year. Tax is paid and allowances are received with a one-year time lag

Work to the nearest whole number throughout.

REQUIREMENT:

Recommend, with reasons, which alternative ABC Limited should choose.

13 Marks

Total Marks = 20

---

4 Public sector organisations do not have the requirement to produce 'profit' in the same sense as the private sector. However, they are expected to work within budgets and recognise aspects of financial management familiar to the private sector.

The following are four examples of differences between the public and private sector.

1. A company which operates a chain of private hospitals uses a discount rate of 16% to evaluate its investment decisions and generally expects an accounting rate of return of 25%. A government-funded hospital trust is required to achieve a return of only 6% on assets.
2. Private sector companies are moving towards a more flexible approach to budgeting. Organisations in the public sector are moving in the opposite direction, ie towards a more rigid approach to budgeting, enforced by the Treasury (up to three years).
3. Public sector pay is subject to government controls and has for many years failed to keep pace with inflation. Market forces determine wages and salaries in the private sector.
4. Private sector companies can borrow in the market to finance their operations, subject only to normal business cautions such as gearing ratios, investor preferences and current economic conditions. The public sector is either not allowed or severely discounted from borrowing to fund operations.

REQUIREMENT:

Discuss the causes and consequences of THREE of the four scenarios outlined above, using examples to illustrate your answer where appropriate.

Note. Overseas candidates may use examples of organisations in their own country.

20 Marks

---

5 **(a)** Official statistics show that over the past four to five years, overdraft usage has been falling by around 5% per annum and is being replaced by other forms of asset-based lending.

REQUIREMENT:

Explain the main uses of overdraft facilities as part of a company's working capital management policy and discuss the alternative sources of finance which are available.

10 Marks

(b) The following comments were overheard at a recent conference of financial managers and directors:

1 'All our company's borrowings are at fixed rates of interest, so we do not have any interest rate risk.'

2 'A consultant's recent report has suggested we should investigate the use of derivatives to manage our interest rate risk. My view is that derivatives are too risky.'

REQUIREMENT:

Discuss the management of interest rate risk. Include in your answer an explanation of why the comments quoted above might not necessarily be correct. **10 Marks**

Total Marks = 20

MOCK EXAM: ANSWERS

DO NOT TURN THIS PAGE UNTIL YOU HAVE COMPLETED THE MOCK EXAM

Examiner's notes

Question 1 is a scenario case which concerns a manufacturer of electrical equipment in serious financial difficulties. The company may face liquidation unless the directors can negotiate a refinancing package, possibly with a venture capital company. The question meets three of the syllabus Aims – to evaluate the impact of different financial strategies on organisations; to evaluate investment decisions; and to identify and assess risk.

Areas of the syllabus covered are:

- Illiquidity and corporate collapse [section (a)];
- Cost of capital and capital structure [section (b)];
- Dividend policy [section (b)];
- Working capital management [section (b)];
- Corporate restructuring [section (c)];
- Risks and methods of reducing risks related to foreign operations [section (d)].

Question 2 involves an importing and exporting company which selectively uses hedging methods to manage currency risk. In particular it examines the argument for *not* hedging and the effect on profit of forgone 'windfalls'. The syllabus topics tested are *theoretical foreign exchange relationships* and *the use of hedging techniques* in section (d). The question meets the fourth Aim of the syllabus.

Question 3 concerns a company's investment decision to purchase a fleet of delivery vehicles either with a medium-term loan from its bankers or by a financial lease. It also examines the advantages of including an abandonment option in its investment appraisal procedures. The areas of the syllabus tested are *sources of capital and their advantages and disadvantages* in section (b) and *evaluating and reporting on investment decisions* in section (c). The question meets the second and third Aims of the syllabus.

Question 4 concerns the similarities and differences between public and private sector organisations in various situations. The area of the syllabus tested is *Identifying, quantifying and achieving the financial objectives of the organisations* [section (a)]. The question meets the first syllabus Aim.

Question 5 examines methods of financing working capital and the management of interest rate risk. The areas of the syllabus tested are *working capital management* and *interest risk rate management* – both in section (b). The question meets the second and fourth Aims of the syllabus.

Section A

1

> **Pass marks.** This case study is centred round a reconstruction scheme. Before writing any report on such a scheme, it is best to compute the effect of liquidation and the total cash raised by the scheme. This question emphasises that approach by asking specifically for these calculations in part (b). Note that only 10 marks are given for the calculations, however, whereas 15 are given for discussing the effects of the scheme on the various participants. This discussion is straightforward provided you remember that it involves a comparison with the liquidation position. Parts (a), (c) 2 and (d) involve a number of standard discussions on a range of topics (company valuation, venture capital, dividend policy, gearing, export risks and foreign exchange risks). Although you should tailor your answer to the details of the case, most of the marks can be gained by stating basic financial management principles.

(a) It is always difficult to estimate the **going concern value** of a company, and this is particularly so when it is in financial difficulties. At such times shareholders may sell out to avoid risk, and the value of the company's shares may fall below the net realisable value of its assets. This is particularly true if there is a dominant group of shareholders (as in the case of VG plc) who have not made the most of the company's potential and are able to oppose reforms to management structure or block a potential takeover and thus limit the choices open to the company. In such a situation the share price may not reflect the company's true potential earning ability.

Although **liquidation** is often the route favoured by **creditors**, it is unlikely to benefit **shareholders,** who rank last in the distribution of proceeds and have to bear all the administration costs. Shareholders should therefore consider all alternatives, including the following.

- **Takeover offers from competitors or other companies,** allowing gains from 'synergy' (eg cost savings, complementary businesses).
- **Sale of parts of the business, or product lines**. Often there are parts of diversified companies which are more valuable to others than to their current owners.
- **Restructuring of management,** if existing management is responsible for the current crisis and the business can be 'turned round', for example by a new chief executive.
- **Complete financial restructuring schemes,** such as is proposed for VG plc.
- **Management buy-outs, or buy-ins.**

Some of these alternatives are discussed in part (d).

(b) (i) **VG asset value if liquidated**

	£'000	£'000
Fixed assets		
Freehold property	2,500	
Plant, equipment and vehicles	2,250	
		4,750
Current assets		
Stock: 75% × 80% × 4,500	2,700	
Debtors: 90% × 5,250	4,725	
		7,425
		12,175

(ii) **Disbursements to creditors**

	£'000	
Secured creditors:		
10% debenture (secured on fixed assets)	3,000	paid in full
Available for unsecured creditors	9,175	
	12,175	
Book value of unsecured creditors:		
Overdraft	2,475	
Trade creditors	9,500	
	11,975	
Percentage disbursement to unsecured creditors:		
9,175/11,975	76.62%	

In summary, the cash disbursement to creditors would be:

	£'000
10% debenture (secured)	3,000
Overdraft (unsecured – 76.62%)	1,896
Trade creditors (unsecured – 76.62%)	7,279
	12,175

Shareholders receive no payment in the event of a liquidation.

(iii) **VG's cash position if the venture capitalist provides financing**

	£'000	£'000
Opening overdraft balance:		(2,475)
Conversion to medium term loan		2,475
Venture capital: New equity shares		4,000
New debt		2,000
		6,000
New capital expenditure	(2,500)	
New working capital	(500)	
Sale of old equipment	1,000	
First payment to trade creditors (40%)	(3,800)	
		(5,800)
Cash balance after refinancing		200

The cash balance will be £200,000 in credit. The agreed overdraft limit of £1 million will allow further investment.

Working: Reconciliation of new share capital issued

	£'000
Issued to venture capital company at £1 per share	4,000
Given to original shareholders: 8 million × 1/5	1,600
Given to debenture holders: 100 × £3m/£100	3,000
Total shares issued	8,600

This confirms that the only shares issued for cash are to the venture capital company.

(c) To: Directors of VG plc
From: Financial advisor
Date: 15 November 1999

Report on the acceptability of the new financing proposals for VG plc

This report assesses whether the proposed plans for refinancing the company, upgrading equipment and bidding for new contracts are acceptable to shareholders and other providers of finance. For the scheme to proceed, the agreement of 75% by value of each class of participant is needed, together with the approval of the Court.

Section 1: The immediate effect on providers of finance

Original shareholders

The original shareholders receive 1.6 million shares of £1, in return for cancelling 8 million shares with a current market value of 28 pence, total theoretical value £2.24 million. Although this appears to be a loss of value, the restructuring must be compared with the realistic alternatives available to shareholders. If liquidation is the only alternative, shareholders will receive nothing, but if there is an offer from another company to buy VG for 28 pence per share then clearly this would be the better option. If shareholders all attempted to sell their shares on the open market, the price would slump to well below 28 pence.

Assuming no takeover bid is likely, the shareholders should be pleased with the restructuring plans. They will receive no dividends for three years, however, and should note that if the company is successful, their shareholding is likely to be diluted in three years time, when previous debenture holders exercise their warrants.

The required approval of 75% of shareholders by value would be obtained if the original owners and the institutional shareholder voted in favour. However, the Court would look carefully to ensure that the minority were not being unfairly oppressed.

Venture capital company

It is difficult to assess the likely returns that the venture capital company will receive from the proposals because of the uncertainties involved. Assuming that the first year's pre-tax profits are £1.2 million (and that this figure is *after* interest charges, the after tax profit will be approximately £840,000 giving earnings per share of nearly 10 pence. This represents a 10% rate of return on the £1 investment per share, against a cost of equity capital of 13.2%*. The venture capital company is unlikely to be pressed by these projections.

* Cost of equity capital (CAPM) = 6% + (12% – 6%) × 1.2 = 13.2%.

Bank

The company's bankers will probably be pleased with the proposals because, if the company were to liquidate they would lose £579,000 on the unsecured overdraft. The plans convert this overdraft to a secured loan, which would almost certainly be repaid in the event of any subsequent liquidation. There is, however, a fall in interest rate from 12% to 10% to compensate for the security offered. Although there is no requirement for any further overdraft at the outset, subsequent losses would put the new overdraft at risk, with potential losses of up to £1 million.

Debenture holders

The debenture holders would have the whole £3 million of their debt repaid if the company were to go into liquidation. They could also sell on the market for a price of £95 ex interest. This would leave them with them the entitlement to the next six month instalment of interest (£5), giving total proceeds of £100 (£3 million) exactly the same as on a liquidation.

Under the refinancing scheme, they receive 3 million shares, value £3 million, together with warrants giving the option of purchasing 1.5 million more shares at the fixed price of £1 in three years. If the company performs well, they will make gains both from thc 3 million original shares and from the additional shares available with the warrants. If the company performs badly, their shares will lose value and the warrants will be valueless and will not be exercised.

The proposals represent a shift to a much higher risk level than the 10% debentures. It may be possible to reduce this risk somewhat by selling the warrants at market price (no details of this possibility have been given). Although some debenture holders are likely to accept the proposals, the majority will probably not wish to exchange the relative security of fixed interest investment for shares in a high risk speculative venture, because this would upset the balance of their portfolios. The debenture holders are likely to reject the proposals.

Trade creditors

The trade creditors are being asked to accept an immediate payment of 40 pence in the pound and to wait six months for the balance, with no interest on the delayed payment. There is a risk that, if the restructured company fails, the balance of 60 pence will not be paid. The alternative is to receive 77 pence in the pound if there is a liquidation, accepting a loss of 33 pence.

The creditors are likely to have varying attitudes to these proposals. Large creditors whose business depends on VG being a customer will probably accept the proposals, whereas many other creditors may prefer the certainty of 77 pence to the uncertainty of the 60 pence balance. All creditors would welcome some compensation offered for the delayed payment of the balance, in the form of interest or, possibly, warrants.

On balance it is likely that the trade creditors reject the scheme as it stands.

Summary: Section 1

Although acceptable to shareholders, the proposals will probably be rejected by the debenture holders and the trade creditors. Because the scheme must be accepted by all classes of participant, it is our opinion that it will need to be revised before presentation to the parties concerned. It is important in schemes of this type that creditors are at least as well off as they would be in a liquidation, and they are likely to demand quite high returns to compensate for additional risks suffered. The venture capital company will also be looking for higher rates of return than those implied by the first year's profits. Further information is needed about future growth potential.

Section 2: Other matters

Effects of revised capital structure and dividend policy on company value

The company's present capital structure by market values is:

Equity shares: 8m × 28p = £2.24m. Debt: £2.475m + £3.0m = £5.475m

Gearing ratio (debt/equity) = 244%.

This is extremely high gearing which has resulted in actual or near bankruptcy of the company with a resulting fall crash in the share price.

After restructuring, the equity will be £8.6m and the debt £2m + £2.475m = £4.475m, giving a gearing ratio of 52%. While still high, the gearing ratio will be much more acceptable to shareholders, allowing a higher share price and company value because of the reduction in bankruptcy risk.

In the absence of cash dividends, the reinvestment of equity earnings at above the cost of capital will create growth in company value. This growth in company value would be reflected by growth in share price, were it not for the issue of **scrip dividends (bonus issue of shares)**. The scrip dividends will have little effect on the total company value (in theory they should have no effect at all) but will reduce the value per share by dilution. Overall, these two opposing effects on share price will tend to offset each other, resulting in a stable share price. The purpose of the scrip dividend is to allow shareholders who need the cash the option of selling their scrip shares but, apart from tax considerations, the wealth of individual shareholders will not be affected by the scrip issue.

The medium-term effects of the proposals

As noted above, the restriction of cash dividends and reinvestment of cash will work towards an increase in share price, whereas the issue of scrip dividends will offset this effect by reducing the price. In three years' time, if the share price is above £1, the share capital will increase by 1.5m shares (17%) when warrants are exercised. This will further reduce the gearing ratio, but it will also reduce the share price and will give a gain to the warrant holders at the expense of existing shareholders. This will allow a progressive reduction in the gearing ratio. If the company cannot maintain a share price above £1, however, the warrants will not be exercised.

In approximately 5 years, assuming the company is still trading profitably, the £2 million loan from the venture capital company will be repaid, further reducing the gearing, unless debt is used for refinancing.

Possible exit routes for the venture capitalist

The purpose of most venture capital is to assist the company through a period of rapid change and growth. After a period of five to seven years, the company should have reached a more stable position and the venture capital company will probably wish to withdraw its investment. For this reason, venture capital companies always look for exit routes when appraising investments. The exit route for the £2 million loan is repayment after five years. For the equity investment there are a number of alternatives, all of which depend on the overall success of the company. If the company is highly successful, the shares may be refloated on the **Alternative Investment Market (AIM)**, giving the venture capital company the chance to sell out. Alternatively, a private sale may be arranged to another institution 'over the counter'. It is also possible that the original owners and other shareholders may wish to buy the shares from the venture capital company, or that employees are interested in taking an equity stake.

Alternatives to the restructuring scheme

The proposed restructuring scheme must be compared with alternative courses of action, which include the following.

- **Takeover by a competitor or other organisation.** This is often the most convenient route for shareholders when faced with financial difficulties. It cannot be assumed that VG's best opportunities lie in continued independence. The company may be worth more if it is added to an existing organisation, allowing synergies through factors such as cost savings, complementary activities or enhanced market share.

- **Management buy-out.** If the management team is opposed to the existing proposals, they may offer their own alternative for purchasing control from existing shareholders. Such a scheme is likely to be similar to existing proposals but involve a different power structure amongst shareholders.

- **Management buy-in.** A team of entrepreneurs may wish to purchase the company, on the basis that they could manage it better and that they have access to the funds to pay creditors.

(d) (i) An exporting company with a large number of overseas customers faces risks not present in domestic trading, as follows.

Foreign exchange risks:

(1) **transaction exposure**: risk of an adverse movement in exchange rates between the date of the contract and the date of payment.

(2) **economic exposure**: for example, the risk that foreign currencies devalue, or the home currency appreciates, leaving foreign customers unable to afford the company's goods

Political (or country) risk: for example, the imposition of exchange control regulations, or discrimination imposed by foreign governments.

Cultural risk: for example, misunderstandings concerning contracts can arise from differences in laws, language or customs.

In addition, the normal **trade risks** of bad debts, delayed payments by customers, and physical security of goods in transit are higher for export than for domestic sales.

(ii) Most of the company's losses are caused by **foreign exchange risk,** because of the increased strength of the pound against both European and Asian currencies. The effect of **transaction exposure** can be seen from foreign exchange losses in the profit and loss account. However a larger proportion of the losses are caused by the reduction in export sales, which is due to **economic exposure**.

The foreign exchange losses from transaction exposure could have been reduced by **hedging techniques**, especially by selling currencies on the **forward market**, and also by using **futures** or **options**. **Alternative techniques** would include sourcing raw materials and components from countries to which export sales are made, in order to offset losses on sales against gains from purchases.

The loss of export custom would have been difficult to predict in advance because the pound rose on foreign exchange markets almost as swiftly as the Asian currencies fell, resulting in reduced European exports and a double blow to Asian export sales. The company should have taken speedy action to rectify the problem, however. With the benefit of hindsight, the most appropriate action would have been to relocate production facilities into those regions where sales were the highest, thus taking advantage of reduced costs and the ability to lower selling prices. A production facility in South East Asia, for example, in a country where the required skills at electrical manufacture are high, would have enabled sales prices to be reduced, thus maintaining demand in Europe and Asia, and may even have increased UK demand.

The disadvantage of this approach is the almost certain reduction in the size of UK operations, with redundancies and possible effects on reputation. However, because of the company's low market share in the UK, this 'goodwill' factor would not be particularly significant. The company should learn from its past mistakes and avoid currency risk by diversifying its production facilities to match its diversity of export locations.

2

> **Pass marks.** Although there are few easy marks for computation in this question, the key marks are earned by describing clearly (i) why hedging, despite its costs, is necessary in some circumstances; and (ii) why transactions cannot be looked at individually when deciding whether to hedge.

To: Chief Executive
From: Financial Manager

Report on the company's foreign exchange risk management policy

This report compares the company's existing foreign exchange risk management policy with alternative approaches.

1. **Purposes of hedging foreign exchange risk**

Our company sells world-wide, invoicing for most transactions in the currency of the foreign country (the 'local currency') rather than in pounds sterling (the 'home currency'). Some of our foreign suppliers also invoice in their local currencies. Sales transactions may suffer from exchange losses, if the local currency weakens between the date of the contract and the date of cash settlement. Likewise, exchange losses on **purchases** can be made when foreign currencies strengthen.

The purpose of hedging is to limit or eliminate these exchange losses on transactions. The main hedging technique we use is the **forward foreign exchange contract**, in which the exchange rate is agreed in advance for future receipts or payments in foreign currencies. The hedge is applied to individual transactions over £100,000.

The **advantages** of this policy are that the cash flows for all material foreign transactions are predictable, exchange losses are eliminated and cash planning is made easier because of this.

The **disadvantages** are that:

(i) the bank commission payable and exchange rates obtainable on forward transactions significantly erode our profits; and

(ii) potential exchange gains are eliminated along with the losses. In the year to 30 September 1998, hedging eliminated £778,000 of foreign exchange losses, but in 1999 potential exchange gains of £347,000 were forgone.

2. **Financial implications of hedging the purchase of French machinery**

Whereas the UK sales price for this machinery is fixed at £300,000, the purchase price depends on how the French franc moves against the pound sterling over the next three months. At today's spot rate of 8,9321, FFr 2.5 million is £279,889, giving a trading profit of £20,111.

For the purpose of illustration, assume (a) that the FFr weakens in three months time to 8.9975. The supplier's invoice would be settled by a payment of £277,855, giving an exchange gain of £2,034 and a total profit on the transaction of £22,145.

However, if we assume (b) that the FFr strengthens to 8.6500, the payment is £289,017, resulting in an exchange loss of £9,128 and a net profit of only £10,983.

If the transaction is hedged using a forward contract, the payment is known in advance to be 2,500,000 / 8.8820 = £281,468, giving a profit of £18,532 which is not affected by any future exchange rate movements. A small amount of the target profit is sacrificed in order to reduce risk.

3. **Factors to consider before changing foreign exchange risk management policy**

Factors in favour of reducing hedging include the following:

(i) Because we import and export, there will be instances where receipts and payments in the same currency can be matched, reducing the requirement for hedging, because any losses on the imports will be offset by gains on the exports, or vice versa. Even if the transaction amounts and dates do not match exactly, the amount, duration and cost of hedging can be significantly reduced by planning along these lines. For those European countries which have adopted the euro, the currencies can now be regarded as identical, which greatly increases the chances of matching foreign imports and exports.

(ii) Because we trade in many countries world-wide, the **portfolio effect** will automatically reduce some of our currency risk: gains from some currencies will be offset by losses from others.

(iii) Although many short-term currency movements are unpredictable, there are various factors which cause longer term movements. For example, if there is high inflation in a country from which we are purchasing, the currency is likely to devalue, and there will be little sense in always hedging against purchase transactions for that country.

Against these arguments are the following points.

(i) Although currency losses may be offset by gains in the longer run, the 'embarrassment factor' of a significant loss in any one year might cause customers to lose confidence in our management ability.

(ii) In extreme cases, currency losses may threaten the company's continued operations. Sudden dramatic realignments of currency are not uncommon and, although predictable with hindsight, can take firms by surprise and cause huge losses.

(iii) For very large transactions, even small currency movements can create significant losses. It is wiser to hedge these transactions (assuming that matching cannot help) even if losses are not predicted.

The company's **attitude to risk** for foreign transactions therefore needs to be evaluated. The consequences of making currency losses, compared with the advantages of gains, need to be debated from the viewpoint of both the company as a whole and the individual managers involved. For transactions that cannot be matched, the alternative to our existing policy is not necessarily to abandon hedging altogether, but to develop a policy which takes into account both predicted currency movement and the size of the transactions involved. It is likely that the threshold figure of £100,000 needs to be increased.

4. **Alternative methods of managing currency risks**

As indicated above, one of the most powerful techniques for managing currency risk is to **match receipts and payments in the same currency**. This is conveniently done by opening a bank account in that currency. The company should consider opening open bank accounts in several major currencies (eg euros, US dollars and Japanese yen).

Progressing this argument, we should also think more about trying to match both sides of our import-export transactions in the same currency. For example we may be able to pay a German supplier in US dollars and sell the product to the USA, invoicing in dollars. We should also consider sourcing more products from those countries for which our sales are highest.

When financing our working capital, we should not necessarily be limited to loans in pounds sterling. For example, if our main assets (debtors) are mainly designated in US dollars, we should consider borrowing in dollars to offset the currency risk.

There are many alternatives to the forward contract for managing currency risks. I will be pleased to write a paper on the alternatives, which include money market hedges, futures markets and option contracts. These instruments can be used to reduce risk to whatever level the company deems appropriate.

3

> **Pass marks.** Note that different assumptions about capital allowances in part (b) would lead to a different answer. Indicate your assumptions clearly.

(a) (i) **NPV if vehicle is operated for full three years**

Year	*Cash flow* £	*12% factors*	*PV* £
0	(10,000)	1.000	(10,000)
1	4,200	0.893	3,751
2	4,000	0.797	3,188
3	3,500	0.712	2,492
		NPV	(569)

The NPV is negative, indicating that the return earned over the vehicle's whole life is unsatisfactory, being less than the cost of capital.

Abandonment at end of year 2

Year	*Cash flow* £	*12% factors*	*PV* £
0	(10,000)	1.000	(10,000)
1	4,200	0.893	3,751
2	8,000	0.797	6,376
		NPV	127

The NPV is positive, indicating a satisfactory return if the vehicle is 'abandoned' (ie sold or transferred) after two years.

Abandonment at end of year 1

Year	*Cash flow* £	*12% factors*	*PV* £
0	(10,000)	1.000	(10,000)
1	10,400	0.893	9,287
		NPV	(713)

If the vehicle is abandoned after one year, the NPV is again negative.

(ii) On the basis of the figures given, the vehicles are only worthwhile if they are kept for two years and then abandoned.

Where assets have resale values which are relatively easy to estimate, it is useful to build abandonment values into the investment appraisal process, in order to ensure that all alternative courses of action are considered. This is a particularly useful exercise when considering motor vehicles or other items of equipment which have market-determined resale values. The technique is clearly less easy to implement when considering specialist assets or construction projects which gain most of their value in the final stages, but the principle is still applicable. The idea that 'we've got to finish because we've started' is not always logical.

(b) The cash flows of the loan can be compared with those of the lease, by discounting at the company's cost of debt, assumed to be 10% per year. The cost of debt is used because the lease is an alternative to debt finance and carries the same types of risk.

Alternative 1 - Loan

The 3-year 10% cumulative discount factor is 2.487. The loan is repaid by three annual instalments of £10,000/2.487 = £4,021. There will be tax savings on the interest element only.

Year	*Loan at start of year*	*10% interest*	*Repayment*
	£	£	£
1	10,000	1,000	(4,021)
2	6,979	698	(4,021)
3	3,656	366	(4,022)

Balance at the end of year 3 is zero. The loan cash flows are reduced by 33% tax savings on the interest, one year in arrears: Year 2: £330; Year 3: £230; Year 4: £121.

Tax savings from the capital allowances on the equipment are as follows.

Year	*Asset value*	*25% WDA*	*Tax saved*
	£	£	£
1	10,000	2,500	
2	7,500	1,875	825
3	5,625	1,406	619
4			464

An alternative assumption is that there is a balancing allowance at the end of year 3, to bring the written down value to zero.

DCF evaluation of Alternative 1

Year	*1*	*2*	*3*	*4*
	£	£	£	£
Loan repayments	(4,021)	(4,021)	(4,022)	
Tax saving at 33%:				
Capital allowances		825	619	464
Interest		330	230	121
	(4,021)	(2,866)	(3,173)	585
10%	0.909	0.826	0.751	0.683
PV	(3,655)	(2,367)	(2,383)	400

The net present value of loan repayments and tax savings is a cost of £8,005.

Note. If a balancing allowance had been included at end of year 3, the resulting cost of this alternative would have been significantly lower, £7,055.

Alternative 2 – Lease

Year	*0*	*1*	*2*	*3*	*4*
	£	£	£	£	£
Lease payments	(4,000)	(4,000)	(4,000)		
Tax saving			1,320	1,320	1,320
	(4,000)	(4,000)	(2,680)	1,320	1,320
10%	1.000	0.909	0.826	0.751	0.683
PV	(4,000)	(3,636)	(2,214)	991	902

The net present value of lease payments and tax savings is a cost of £7,957.

On the basis of these figures, ABC Limited should choose the lease payment, because it is slightly cheaper in NPV terms. However, an alternative assumption about capital allowances would have changed the decision. **Specific factors in the loan or lease contracts** (eg restrictive covenants, flexibility of payments or early termination) may also influence the choice of financing used.

4

> **Pass marks.** These questions are not at all easy to answer, even for those who work in the public sector! Each question is the subject of much debate and it is difficult to summarise the main points adequately in the time available. In general, you are advised to avoid questions like this in the exam, unless you have written answers to very similar questions during your studies.
>
> You were asked to comment on three scenarios. Our answer covers four.

Scenario 1

Like most private sector organisations, a company running private hospitals will be financed by a **mix of equity and debt** funds and will need to pay market rates of return on these funds to its investors. For investors, the hospital is compared with profitable alternative uses of the funds, not just in the health sector but in the whole economy. The 16% cost of capital is the average DCF return payable on the equity and debt finance in use. There is no easy relationship between this and the accounting rate of return, which may be higher because it is based on the depreciated historical cost of ageing assets.

The rate of return required on government funded projects has been much debated. One suggestion is that funds used for government projects displace private sector funds and that government projects should therefore be evaluated at market rates of return. The alternative view is that government funded health projects are a social necessity, and the only cost of capital is the low cost of government borrowing. The 6% real terms charge made on public sector organisations is a very rough compromise between these two views.

In recent years there has been an emphasis on proper **asset accounting in public sector organisations,** and the charge of 6% on assets has been imposed in order to make the organisations aware of the cost of using their assets, in particular land and buildings, which had previously been regarded as 'free'. The consequences of this charge are numerous but one effect is the pressure on government funded hospitals in high cost locations to make more efficient use of space.

In theory, private hospitals, which attract risk capital, should be better placed to pioneer innovation than state hospitals, which should concentrate on delivering efficient services using known technology. However, the rapid pace of change and the extremely complex structure of the UK health service means that the boundary between the work carried out by private and public sector hospitals is very blurred, with private hospitals often simply being used to enable wealthier patients to obtain quicker treatment.

Scenario 2

Historically, budgeting in the private sector has been concerned with a financial quantification of the organisation's plans for the coming year. Although there were many ways of approaching budgeting, it is fair to say that (i) the main concern was with short term budgeted profit, directly linked to the end of year financial statements, and (ii) non-financial measures of performance were less common than today.

The development of cheap computing power has enabled many new techniques to be developed. Not only can budgets be produced under different assumptions and scenarios and updated quickly in the light of changing information, but a whole range of quantitative performance measures, financial and non-financial, can be maintained for control purposes. This has stimulated much debate on the most effective methods of planning and control, and ideas such as the **balanced scorecard** emphasise the necessity of a range of strategic objectives and performance measures related to them. In many cases the financial budget is now more of a summary document, with details and targets being recorded as non-financial measures. Because private sector budgets are not public documents, firms are free to choose those techniques which are most useful for their individual circumstances, resulting in a wide range of different budget approaches. This is in contrast, however, to their annual financial statements, produced for public inspection, which have become increasingly regulated and standardised.

In the public sector, the budget has always had a legal status which is absent in the private sector. In many cases it acts mainly as the expenditure authorisation for the coming year. Much of the increased standardisation of public sector budgets is therefore more fairly compared with the regulation of private sector annual financial statements than with private sector budgets. Standardisation has also resulted from the progressive centralisation of the public sector, and central government's need to prepare consolidated budget statements and to report to international bodies. For example, the requirement to budget in a three year cycle (the **Public Expenditure Survey**) is in line with international practice recommended by the **IMF**.

Traditionally, public sector budgets contained no measures of output, performance or efficiency, little detailed cost analysis, and were produced on an annual incremental basis. Although cheap computing power has provided the same performance measurement opportunities to the public as to the private sector, only some forward-looking public sector organisations took pro-active advantage of new techniques. The driving force behind improvement has come from the Treasury, though initiatives such as resource accounting and budgeting, including the requirement for measures of output performance. Because these initiatives are centrally driven, with the objective of taking the best ideas and applying them across the whole public sector, the budgeting approach may appear to be increasingly rigid. However, more flexibility will develop as public sector organisations attempt to emphasise those measures which are key to their particular activities.

Scenario 3

Although **private sector pay** is determined by market forces, it is a major concern of government because it is a key component of inflation. Attempts to control inflation no longer involve private sector pay ceilings but focus instead on controlling **interest rates** and **public sector expenditure**, and maintaining public confidence in price stability. Private sector companies need to control the wage demands of their employees, or face pricing themselves out of the market. Supply side reforms, including trade union legislation and flexibility of labour markets, were key elements in achieving this position of stability. The main controversy that seems to be emerging is an increasing gap between the remuneration of top company directors and their employees. These pay differences may be an inevitable result of the economic reforms of the past two decades though, in some cases, the salaries of 'fat cats' are possible because their companies have positions of near monopoly and shareholders are unwilling to bargain for higher rates of return.

Public sector pay is subject to national **negotiations between employees and government**. The government has been able to exercise a restraining influence over public sector pay for nearly two decades, principally by reducing the number of public sector jobs. Efficiencies have been introduced and many parts of the public sector have been privatised or threatened with privatisation. Opinions differ sharply as to whether this process should be further continued or whether it should be halted or reversed.

The fact that public sector pay has drifted downwards compared with the private sector may indicate that in the 1970s public sector pay rates were abnormally high. At that time pay scales were set by comparison with the private sector and ignored the higher employment risks borne by private sector employees and the superior pension rights of public sector employees. Lower public sector pay may be, on average, a more realistic position.

However, within the public sector pay scales there are clearly anomalies resulting from **lack of flexibility**. Employees doing very different types of jobs are placed on the same pay scales. Similarly, employees doing the same job in different parts of the country, are placed on the same pay scale, subject to small regional allowances which do not properly reflect differences in living costs or difficulty of working conditions. This rigidity in the system means that the labour market does not operate efficiently. For example, it is more difficult to recruit teachers in inner London than in some rural areas and some hospitals find it much more difficult to attract nurses than others. In many cases, competent employees leave to join the private sector. The government's current approach is therefore to begin to increase rewards for those employees where market forces indicate severe shortages and for employees who exhibit special skills, while resisting general increases in public sector remuneration.

Scenario 4

Private sector companies are financed by a **mix of equity capital and debt**. Debt is a convenient source of capital that does not dilute the ownership of the company and which is cheap because of the tax relief available on interest payments. Overuse of debt will, however, increase the risk of bankruptcy and, as a safeguard, lenders will often impose restrictions on the total amount borrowed, for example by stating a maximum allowable gearing ratio.

The public sector is financed by a mix of taxation and borrowing. There is debate as to how much borrowing a country should use, but a 'common sense' view would allow borrowing to finance capital expenditure, but not current expenditure. In practice borrowing is used to smooth out peaks and troughs in taxation revenues.

Borrowing in the public sector is arranged mainly by central governments and large local governments, on the basis that if individual organisations borrowed, the rates obtainable would not be so favourable, and aggregate government borrowing would be more difficult to predict and control. The money raised by these central bodies is then allocated to individual public sector organisations. The advantage of this for individual organisations is that the cost of funds is cheap. The disadvantage is that funds are subject to absolute capital rationing and under the control of central bodies. New funds can only be obtained by making reasoned requests in the budgets for future years. Not only does this create time delays, but the requests may be turned down on a 'broad brush' basis by the central authorities. One consequence of this sort of approach is that annual investments which create efficiencies and save future costs are continually postponed, resulting in cumulative long-term inefficiencies.

Privatisation is a way out of this problem for some agencies. For others, the best route forward is a tightening up of the management accounting system, enabling a clearer analysis of costs and the ability to make a forceful case for capital investment.

5

> **Pass marks.** Part (a), on alternatives to overdraft financing, is very common in this paper. Ensure that your answer does more than simply listing the alternatives.
>
> For part (b) it is essential to be able to describe in a concise way what interest rate risk is, what derivatives are and what they do. Do not fall into the trap of describing the details of futures, options or swaps

(a) An **overdraft** is a negative balance on a current account at a bank. This constitutes borrowing and, because the balance will vary daily, the interest on the borrowing is normally computed on a daily basis at an agreed rate. A maximum limit to the overdraft is agreed with the bank and above this limit penalty charges will apply. In theory, the overdraft can be cancelled immediately if the bank is not happy with the company's **credit worthiness**. An overdraft can be **unsecured,** or **secured** on company assets or the personal assets of the proprietors.

The overdraft is a key source of finance for working capital because of its flexibility: the finance varies automatically up to the agreed limit, enabling the company to handle peaks and troughs in cash flows without incurring excess interest charges with the company's cash flow. The potential disadvantage for an expanding company is that the overdraft limit may have to be frequently renegotiated. There is also a tendency for expanding companies to ignore the need to underpin their growth with longer term finance.

When considering alternatives to the bank overdraft, it is essential to consider the need for longer term funds (loans or equity funds) to finance the permanent element of working capital. Although such funds may be more expensive than short term finance, they provide a longer term stability for planning.

Alternative short-term sources of finance include the following.

Short-term bank loans. A short-term bank loan (eg six months) can be arranged to cover a forecast cash deficit. The disadvantage compared with the overdraft is that the interest is chargeable on the full amount of the loan even if the finance is not required for part of the period.

Commercial paper. Large companies can issue certificates promising to pay the bearer a given amount on the maturity date in, say, one year's time. These certificates can be sold at a discount to provide immediate cash.

Debt factoring. A specialist organisation will collect the company's debts and advance cash, effectively on the security of the company's debtors. The effective cost of the finance is sometimes difficult to compute but, for an expanding company, an advantage over overdrafts is that the source of finance effectively grows with the sales ledger.

Discounting of invoices and bills of exchange. The company presents invoices or bills of exchange to the bank in return for immediate cash, slightly less than the face value (ie discounted). When the debtors pay, the cash goes direct to the bank. The discount represents the effective interest on the funds advanced. An extension of this process is the **acceptance credit**, whereby the company draws a bill of exchange on a bank, on the security of debts owed by customers. This banker's bill can then be discounted for immediate cash.

Supplier finance. Some suppliers will provide extended credit periods on stock, or alternatively finance can be raised from finance houses on the security of stock.

The key to evaluating these different sources of finance is to compute the true annual percentage interest rate implicit in each arrangement and to quantify other relevant cash flows, such as administration costs, variations to selling prices and the likely effect on bad debts. Other issues which are less easy to quantify include the effect on customer, supplier and lender loyalty.

(b) Interest rates vary over time, because of **supply and demand for money**, and the policies of home and foreign governments. Though some of these variations are predictable, many are not, and result in significant risks to borrowers and lenders.

Interest rate risk takes a number of forms. For borrowers, the risk is that interest rates rise, resulting in higher interest charges, whereas for lenders the risk is that interest rates fall.

Statement 1 is incorrect for three main reasons.

(i) Even if all existing borrowing is fixed interest, the company will still have a need for future borrowing. Unless all existing borrowing is long term and no expansion is foreseen, there will be a continued need for refinancing and new finance, and interest rates may rise before the new loans are negotiated.

(ii) A fixed interest loan negotiated at a time when interest rates were higher than average results in an opportunity loss when interest rates fall. This is another way of saying that 'fixing' an interest rate prevents gains as well as losses.

(iii) The company may have cash surpluses invested in deposits at variable rates. If interest rates fall, income from these deposits will suffer, but the payments on fixed interest loans will not reduce correspondingly.

To prevent unforeseen losses, a company can 'hedge' interest rates using a variety of methods. This means taking action to ensure that future interest rates paid or received by the company are not far different from today's rate. Methods used include **derivatives**, that is financial instruments which derive from the main loan markets. These include **futures** and **options**, both of which effectively involve an agreed rate of interest being used for loans or deposits starting on a future date. Futures carry the obligation to accept the agreed rate, whereas options can be abandoned if the agreed rate becomes unsatisfactory. **Swaps**, another rapidly growing derivative market, involve two organisations swapping interest payments over time, for example swapping fixed for floating rate.

Referring to statement 2, the derivative markets are safe to use for hedging purposes, provided they are used properly. A company wishing to avoid the risk of rising interest rates on borrowings can do this perfectly safely by selling futures contracts, purchasing options, or swapping from floating to fixed interest. No unforeseen risks will be incurred provided that the derivatives are matched by the company's underlying borrowings.

Derivatives can become very risky, however, when they are used with no underlying financial instruments, that is when they are used for speculation rather than for hedging. In particular, the **margin system** which operates on the futures markets means that losses many times the size of the original investment can be made. It is therefore essential, before allowing a treasury department to use derivatives markets, that all staff are properly trained and experienced and that key control rules are established and agreed at the highest management level.

REVIEW FORM & FREE PRIZE DRAW

All original review forms from the entire BPP range, completed with genuine comments, will be entered into one of two draws on 31 July 2000 and 31 January 2001. The names on the first four forms picked out on each occasion will be sent a cheque for £50.

Name: ______________________ **Address**: ______________________

____

____

How have you used this Kit?
(Tick one box only)

- ☐ Home study (book only)
- ☐ On a course: college ______________
- ☐ With 'correspondence' package
- ☐ Other ______________

Why did you decide to purchase this Kit?
(Tick one box only)

- ☐ Have used complementary Study Text
- ☐ Have used BPP Kits in the past
- ☐ Recommendation by friend/colleague
- ☐ Recommendation by a lecturer at college
- ☐ Saw advertising
- ☐ Other ______________

During the past six months do you recall seeing/receiving any of the following?
(Tick as many boxes as are relevant)

- ☐ Our advertisement in *CIMA Student*
- ☐ Our advertisement in *Management Accounting*
- ☐ Our advertisement in *Pass*
- ☐ Our brochure with a letter through the post

Which (if any) aspects of our advertising do you find useful?
(Tick as many boxes as are relevant)

- ☐ Prices and publication dates of new editions
- ☐ Information on Kit content
- ☐ Facility to order books off-the-page
- ☐ None of the above

Have you used the companion Study Text for this subject? ☐ Yes ☐ No

Your ratings, comments and suggestions would be appreciated on the following areas

	Very useful	*Useful*	*Not useful*
Introductory section (Advice on revision, question practice and exam technique, question and answer checklist, etc)	☐	☐	☐
'Do you know?/Did you know?' checklists	☐	☐	☐
Tutorial questions	☐	☐	☐
Examination-standard questions	☐	☐	☐
Pass marks	☐	☐	☐
Content of answers	☐	☐	☐
Mock exam	☐	☐	☐
Structure and presentation	☐	☐	☐

	Excellent	*Good*	*Adequate*	*Poor*
Overall opinion of this Kit	☐	☐	☐	☐

Do you intend to continue using BPP Study Texts/Kits? ☐ Yes ☐ No

Please note any further comments and suggestions/errors on the reverse of this page or write by email to alisonmchugh@bpp.co.uk

Please return to: Alison McHugh, BPP Publishing Ltd, FREEPOST, London, W12 8BR

REVIEW FORM & FREE PRIZE DRAW (continued)

Please note any further comments and suggestions/errors below

FREE PRIZE DRAW RULES

1. Closing date for 31 July 2000 draw is 30 June 2000. Closing date for 31 January 2001 draw is 31 December 2000.
2. Restricted to entries with UK and Eire addresses only. BPP employees, their families and business associates are excluded.
3. No purchase necessary. Entry forms are available upon request from BPP Publishing. No more than one entry per title, per person. Draw restricted to persons aged 16 and over.
4. Winners will be notified by post and receive their cheques not later than 6 weeks after the relevant draw date. Lists of winners will be published in BPP's *focus* newsletter following the relevant draw.
5. The decision of the promoter in all matters is final and binding. No correspondence will be entered into.

See overleaf for information on other
BPP products and how to order

CIMA Order

To BPP Publishing Ltd, Aldine Place, London W12 8AA

Tel: 020 8740 2211. Fax: 020 8740 1184

Mr/Mrs/Ms (Full name)

Daytime delivery address

Postcode

Daytime Tel

Date of exam (month/year)

	7/99 Texts	1/2000 Kits	1/2000 Psscrds	1999 Tapes	1999 Videos	1999 CDs
STAGE 1						
1 Financial Accounting Fundamentals	£18.95 ☐	£9.95 ☐	£5.95 ☐	£12.95 ☐	£25.00 ☐	£34.95 ☐
2 Cost Accounting and Quantitative Methods	£18.95 ☐	£9.95 ☐	£5.95 ☐	£12.95 ☐	£25.00 ☐	£34.95 ☐
3 Economic Environment	£18.95 ☐	£9.95 ☐	£5.95 ☐	£12.95 ☐	£25.00 ☐	£34.95 ☐
4 Business Environment & Information Technology	£18.95 ☐	£9.95 ☐	£5.95 ☐	£12.95 ☐	£25.00 ☐	£34.95 ☐
STAGE 2						
5 Financial Accounting	£18.95 ☐	£9.95 ☐	£5.95 ☐	£12.95 ☐	£25.00 ☐	£34.95 ☐
6 Operational Cost Accounting	£18.95 ☐	£9.95 ☐	£5.95 ☐	£12.95 ☐	£25.00 ☐	£34.95 ☐
7 Management Science Applications	£18.95 ☐	£9.95 ☐	£5.95 ☐	£12.95 ☐	£25.00 ☐	£34.95 ☐
8 Business and Company Law	£18.95 ☐	£9.95 ☐	£5.95 ☐	£12.95 ☐	£25.00 ☐	£34.95 ☐
STAGE 3						
9 Financial Reporting	£19.95 ☐	£10.95 ☐	£5.95 ☐	£12.95 ☐	£25.00 ☐	£34.95 ☐
10 Management Accounting Applications	£19.95 ☐	£10.95 ☐	£5.95 ☐	£12.95 ☐	£25.00 ☐	
11 Organisational Management & Development	£19.95 ☐	£10.95 ☐	£5.95 ☐	£12.95 ☐	£25.00 ☐	
12 Business Taxation (FA 99)	£19.95 ☐	£10.95 ☐	£5.95 ☐	£12.95 ☐	£25.00 ☐	
STAGE 4						
13 Strategic Financial Management	£20.95 ☐	£10.95 ☐	£5.95 ☐	£12.95 ☐	£25.00 ☐	
14 Strategic Management Accountancy & Mktg	£20.95 ☐	£10.95 ☐	£5.95 ☐	£12.95 ☐	£25.00 ☐	
15 Information Management	£20.95 ☐	£10.95 ☐	£5.95 ☐	£12.95 ☐	£25.00 ☐	
16 Management Accounting Control Systems	£20.95 ☐	£10.95 ☐	£5.95 ☐	£12.95 ☐	£25.00 ☐	

£

POSTAGE & PACKING

Study Texts

	First	Each extra	
UK	£3.00	£2.00	£
Europe*	£5.00	£4.00	£
Rest of world	£20.00	£10.00	£

Kits/Passcards/Success Tapes

	First	Each extra	
UK	£2.00	£1.00	£
Europe*	£2.50	£1.00	£
Rest of world	£15.00	£8.00	£

Master CDs/Breakthrough Videos

	First	Each extra	
UK	£2.00	£2.00	£
Europe*	£2.00	£2.00	£
Rest of world	£20.00	£10.00	£

Grand Total (Cheques to *BPP Publishing*) I enclose a cheque for (incl. Postage) **£**

Or charge to Access/Visa/Switch

Card Number

Expiry date Start Date

Issue Number (Switch Only)

Signature

We aim to deliver to all UK addresses inside 5 working days. Orders to all EU addresses should be delivered within 6 working days. All other orders to overseas addresses should be delivered within 8 working days.

* Europe includes the Republic of Ireland and the Channel Islands.